The Political Economy of War and Peace

The Political Economy of War and Peace

The Sino-Soviet-American Triangle and the
Modern Security Problematique

Richard K. Ashley

School of International Relations
University of Southern California

Frances Pinter (Publishers) Ltd., London
Nichols Publishing Company, New York

First published in Great Britain in 1980 by
Frances Pinter (Publishers) Limited
5 Dryden Street, London WC2E 9NW

ISBN 0 903804 69 7

Published in the U.S.A. in 1980 by
Nichols Publishing Company
P.O. Box 96, New York, N.Y. 10024

Library of Congress Catalog Card Number 80-17298
ISBN 0-89397-087-5

Typeset by Anne Joshua Associates, Oxford
Printed in Great Britain by A. Wheaton & Co. Ltd., Exeter

CONTENTS

List of Tables   vi
List of Figures   vii
Preface   ix
Introduction   1

PART I
Chapter 1   Conceptual Framework   9
Chapter 2   Method of Analysis: The General Model   50

PART II
Chapter 3   Traces of Conflict: Twenty-Three Years of Systemic
             Interaction   83
Chapter 4   Expansion: The Extension of Interests
             and Commitments   100
Chapter 5   Intersections: Collisions of External Activities   111
Chapter 6   Provocations: Local Wars at Points of Intersection   121
Chapter 7   Military Capability: The Capacity
             for Force and Violence   132
Chapter 8   Normal Conflict Behavior   144
Chapter 9   Thresholds of Violence   159

PART III
Chapter 10   Elements of the Modern Security Problematique   174
Chapter 11   Implications for Theory   231

APPENDICES   290
Appendix A An Interpretational Supplement   290
Appendix B Analysis of a System in Change   330
Appendix C Data, Measures, and Persistent Problems   341
Appendix D Some Technical Issues in Econometric Analysis   357
Appendix E The System of Equations   367

INDEX

LIST OF TABLES

1.1	Schematic Overview of Three Classes of Dynamics	18
1.2	Four Purpose-Specific Balance of Power Models	40
2.1	The Concept-to-Measure Links	56
4.1	Expansion (Trade Dispersion), 1951–1972: Results of Estimation from a Simultaneous Equation System	106
5.1	Bilateral Intersections, 1950–1972: Results of Estimation from a Simultaneous Equation System	117
6.1	Bilateral Provocations, 1951–1972: Results of Estimation from a Simultaneous Equation System	126
7.1	Military Capability (Defense Expenditure), 1952–1972: Results of Estimation from a Simultaneous Equation System	138
8.1	Normal Conflict Behavior (Mean Conflict Levels), 1951–1972: Results of Estimation from a Simultaneous Equation System	148
9.1	Thresholds of Violence (Peak Conflict Levels), 1951–1972: Results of Estimation from a Simultaneous Equation System	164
B.1	Chow F Statistics for Unilateral 'Military Capability' Equations: Uncontrolled for Extrnal Factors	333
B.2	Subperiod Regression Results for Bilateral Provocations, 1951–1965 and 1961–1972 (Measured as Provocations #2)	334
C.1	Data Sources	352
C.2	Data Source List	353
D.1	Four Time-Dependence Process Models	363
D.2	Steps in a Combined IV–GLS Estimating Procedure	365
E.1	Illustration of Notation	368
E.2	The Six Heuristic Equations	370
E.3	The System of Equations	372

LIST OF FIGURES

2.1	The general model: main causal flows among four blocks, with relationships to systemic-environmental factors	63
2.2A	Block A: expansion, intersections, and military capabilities	66
2.2B	Block B: provocations	67
2.2C	Block C: normal conflict and cooperation behavior	68
2.2D	Block D: thresholds of violence	69
2.2E	Notation: symbols used in the model	70
3.1	Annual systemic mean and peak conflict levels 1950–1972	84
3.2A	The Sino-Soviet dyad: CPR → USSR — crises and selected representative peak events — 1950–1972	86
3.2B	The Sino-Soviet dyad: USSR → CPR — crises and selected representative peak events — 1950–1972	87
3.3A	The Sino-American dyad: CPR → US — crises and selected representative peak events — 1950–1972	89
3.3B	The Sino-American dyad: US → CPR — crises and selected representative peak events — 1950–1972	90
3.4A	The Soviet-American dyad: US → USSR — crises and selected representative peak events — 1950–1972	93
3.4B	The Soviet-American dyad: USSR → US — crises and selected representative peak events — 1950–1972	94
4.1	US expansion (Trade Dispersion #2) 1950–1972	101
4.2	USSR expansion (Trade Dispersion #2) 1950–1972	101
4.3	CPR expansion (Trade Dispersion #2) 1950–1972	102
4.4	The hypothesized dynamics of expansion	103
5.1	The hypothesized dynamics of bilateral intersections	111
5.2	Soviet-American intersections (Intersection #2) 1950–1972	114
5.3	Sino-American intersections (Intersection #2) 1950–1972	115
5.4	Sino-Soviet intersections (Intersection #2) 1950–1972	115

6.1	Soviet-American provocations (Provocation #2) 1950–1972	122
6.2	Sino-American provocations (Provocation #2) 1950–1972	122
6.3	Sino-Soviet provocations (Provocation #2) 1950–1972	123
6.4	The hypothesized dynamics of bilateral provocations	123
7.1	The hypothesized dynamics of Military Capability (Defense Expenditure)	134
7.2	US Defense Expenditure 1950–1973	136
7.3	USSR Defense Expenditure 1950–1973	136
7.4	CPR Defense Expenditure 1950–1973	137
8.1	The hypothesized dynamics of Normal Conflict Behavior	146
9.1	The hypothesized dynamics of Thresholds of Violence	161
10.1A	Block A: expansion, intersections, and military capabilities	177
10.1B	Block B: provocations	178
10.1C	Block C: Normal Conflict and cooperation	179
10.1D	Block D: Thresholds of Violence	180
10.1E	Notation: symbols used in the model	181
10.2	Significant links illustrating Proposition B.1	192
10.3	Significant links illustrating Proposition B.2	192
10.4	Significant links illustrating Proposition B.3	192
10.5	Significant links illustrating Proposition B.5	194
10.6	Significant links illustrating Proposition B.6	194
10.7	Significant causal paths from Growth to Conflict: the Sino-Soviet dyad	196
A.1	A unilateral model	325
A.2	A unilateral/bilateral model	328

PREFACE

This book is about the sources of conflict and violence among today's major military powers: the Chinese People's Republic, the Soviet Union, and the United States. It focuses upon the long-term processes entangling these three major powers in a common, nearly ineluctable problematique: what I call the modern security problematique. In large measure, this problematique involves the dynamics and dilemmas of military rivalry and balance of power upon which theorists of international politics have long focused. Inescapably, the search for a lasting peaceful order must contend with these dynamics.

This book is a study in international political economy. Like all international political economy studies, it is concerned with processes of growth — differential technological, economic, and population growth in a world of finite resources and unevenly distributed capabilities. It is concerned with the long-term transnational flows of resources and activities among groups and states and with the politically salient patterns of dependence and interdependence to which these flows give rise. Like all international political economy studies, too, this book is interested in values of welfare, equity, national autonomy, and the environment. How these values are 'shaped and shared' internationally is a principal concern.

This book is an example of what has come to be called world modeling research. It uses sophisticated modeling techniques — in this case, the structural modeling approach of econometrics — in order to represent and empirically examine long-term aggregate social processes on a global scale. Like so many other world modeling studies, it may be read as a contribution to the still burgeoning 'limits to growth' literature, although in many respects it is much more concerned with political limits than with socio-economic limits. As a study in the world modeling genre, this book also seeks to explore some of the methodological possibilities and limitations of empirically grounded econometric modeling.

This book contributes to and further develops a theory of international relations. Specifically, it builds upon and elaborates the 'proto-theory' developed by Nazli Choucri and Robert C. North and presented in their book, *Nations in Conflict: National Growth and International Violence*.[1] In it, Choucri and North developed a framework whose key concept is lateral pressure. Drawing upon their framework, they then constructed a model of the long-term processes leading to conflict and violence among six major European powers in the period, 1870–1914. Their empirical analysis lent corroboration to their proto-theory. As they put it, 'growth can be a lethal process.' The present study builds upon the Choucri–North perspective, and along the way it explicitly confronts and criticizes contending theories of international relations: balance of power theory, integration theory, imperialism theory, and liberal and neomercantilist theories of international political economy. As in the Choucri–North work, this study also seeks empirical corroboration for its theoretical assertions. It finds that corroboration in an empirical analysis of the same European system studies by Choucri and North, albeit at a later stage of its development.

Is this one book or four? How is it possible for me to claim that this book is so many obviously different things? Is it not exceedingly ambitious, even audacious, to claim so much? Is it not likely that a book claiming to be so many different things will in fact be a patchwork assemblage of disparate ideas? I suspect that at least some readers will be inclined to ask such questions. In my opinion, though, the questions ought to be turned around. Why is it that the things I have claimed this book to be appear so manifestly different, perhaps even mutually exclusive? What is it about the ways in which we have come to think about international relations that leads us to see the preceding four paragraphs as candidate opening paragraphs for four different books? Why is it difficult for our grammars of thought to contain the idea that a study in international political economy might focus on rivalry and balance of power among China, the Soviet Union, and the United States? Why is it difficult to imagine a world modeling study that would both focus upon contemporary limits to growth and build upon a study of the forty-five years preceding the outbreak of World War I? Why is it hard to attach meaning to the claim that a book concentrating upon Sino-Soviet-American

[1] Nazli Choucri and Robert C. North, *Nations in Conflict: National Growth and International Violence* (San Francisco: W.H. Freeman, 1975).

relations is a study of the same system, the European system, studied by Choucri and North? Why is it difficult to come to terms with a study that would at once criticize balance of power theory and declare that balance of power dynamics must be contended with in Sino-Soviet-American relations?

I think that there is an answer to these questions, although it is an answer that is not easily grasped. Most thought about international relations is framed by what might be called a technical-rational grammar. This is a grammar of thought whose most distinguishing feature is that it denies the possibility that people and social organizations might to a large extent become what they do. This shows up in several ways. A technical-rational grammar

Orients all contemplation and all social action upon the dual premise that (*a*) all people and all groups are no more than what they now appear to be — i.e., what they have become — and (*b*) must behave rationally to survive and grow as whatever they have become;

Rules out of active discourse any notion of rational action wherein a person or group would strive to deny its existence as whatever it has become;

Rules out of active discourse consideration of how a social unit's rational attempts to survive and grow as what it now is might transform it into something else that it does not now want to be;

Celebrates and denies criticism of whatever social structurations, patternings, and partitions people and groups might have created through their interactive rational attempts to survive and grow;

Identifies boundaries in reality in terms of the spatial-temporal spans of effective control of certain classes of instruments that participants might rationally employ;

Finds no merit in contemplating cross-sectoral effects except insofar as such contemplation might inform either the closing of sectoral boundaries or the creation of more far-reaching instrumentalities of rational control;

Sees history episodically, as a sequence of distinct but possibly analogous systems, because it disallows the possibility that the interests and constraints of rationally acting people and groups during any 'episode' might be deeply rooted in the rational actions and inter-actions of the same and other people and groups during earlier 'episodes.'

In short, a technical-rational grammar is a 'generative grammar' to the extent that it guides action and creates new relationships, but it is also a very limited grammar. It is limited because, in awe of its creations, it disallows criticism of how the rational things it creates were created, and it disallows consideration of what its creations deny.

As I say, these aspects of a technical-rational grammar are hard to grasp, but that is precisely the point. Most thinking about international relations is framed by a grammar of thought that cannot even contemplate its own very serious limitations. And when such a grammar confronts a set of statements that it cannot contain — such as the assertion that the first four paragraphs of this preface refer to one book — its only response can be to reject them as irrational or unwarranted.

I spend time on these points because, most of all, this book is about the ultimate failure of technical-rationality. The theoretical perspective advanced in this book is, in effect, a story. It is a story of human beings behaving quite rationally to gain and extend mastery over nature and creating an irrational global state of nature that masters humans and threatens their destruction. It is the story of the emergence of a security problematique in which the dynamics of growth, rivalry, and balance of power are at once 'rational' and poised in violence-prone tension. It is the story of the modern security problematique, first experienced in Europe and since carried by differential growth and expansion to global proportions. It is a story that is telescoped and registered in a global model of contemporary relations among China, the Soviet Union, and the United States.

Today various theoretical traditions contemplate aspects of the modern security problematique. The proponents of these traditions all seek peace. All seek to find technical-rational solutions to the problems they see. Yet, in portraying the modern security problematique, this book points to a complex, far-reaching set of dilemmas that transcend divisions of theoretical labor, defy piecemeal solution, and, taken as a whole, are beyond the effective reaches of even the most powerful leaders of the most powerful countries on earth. The book says that humankind is caught in the most tragic of traps, that the trap is made through a long, cumulative history of false technical-rational solutions, and that the search for technical-rational solutions can never set us free.

If this argument smacks of despair, however, it must be said that the writing of this book is, for me, an act of optimism. My optimism resides in the idea, the hope really, that I might be able to effectively communicate what I have tried to do and mean to say. If I can, then I will have begun to show that transnational social science, social scientists, and their tools need not entirely be captives of the violence-prone grammar of thought that dominates all other aspects of life on this planet. And I will have to some extent strengthened my argument that people need not necessarily await the ultimate demonstration of the limits to technical-rational growth — war and technological self-destruction — before being motivated to struggle out of a trap that is both around them and within them.

In a sense, then, this book is an experiment in social scientific communicative praxis. The act of communication is an experiment between me and the reader, and I take the results of the experiment very seriously. I hope that my limited research accomplishments and my ability to communicate give the experiment a fair chance to succeed.

My intellectual debts are many and great. Hayward Alker's thought and writings have been particularly stimulating. Often I have been troubled by my inability to grasp the thrust of one of his comments or methodological contributions, only to return to it months later, after progressing in my own research and thinking, to discover that he had anticipated many of the ideas and controversies that I would encounter along the way. My debts to Douglas Hibbs' methodological developments are shared by many in the discipline. Lincoln Bloomfield has provided thoughtful criticism — helping me to identify theoretical oversights, questionable interpretations of history, and moments of literary pretension — as well as needed encouragement.

At the University of Southern California, Jonathan Aronson, Ross N. Berkes, Lisa Boswell, Elizabeth Bowen, Robert Boydston, Laurie Brand, Craig Etchison, Robert L. Friedheim, Felicia Harmer, W. Ladd Hollist, Thomas Johnson, Margaret Leahy, James Lebovic, Constance Lynch, Edwin McClain, Charles McClelland, Kevin McDonough, Patrick McGowan, Gunnar Nielsson, James Rosenau, and David Winters have provided important stimuli and valued criticism. Students of International Relations 200, 400, 408, 500, 508, and 608 have graciously suffered my attempts to 'try out' various ideas reflected here. Beyond USC, various aspects of my work have benefited from the generous comments, criticisms, and encouragement of Davis Bobrow, Harold Guetzkow, Urs Luterbacher, Warren Phillips, J. David Singer, Susan Strange, and Michael Ward.

My greatest intellectual debt, though, is obvious from a glance through the text. Nazli Choucri and Robert North have broken the theoretical and methodological path that I have pursued. As they extend that path still further, they offer the field an exemplar — a model combination of insight, persistence, care, skill, and criticism consciousness in international relations research. No contribution that I have made could have been possible in the absence of their prior work. Indeed, I think that this will be a sentiment echoed by many international relations scholars for years to come.

All systematic research reported in this study has been undertaken on TROLL, an interactive computer system developed by the MIT Department of Economics under the auspices of the National Bureau of Economic Research. I owe personal thanks to Walter Mailing, formerly of NBER, who, at critical junctures, corrected my misunderstandings about the TROLL system and rescued my overdrawn account number from premature oblivion.

Funding for this work has been extended by the University Consortium for World Order Studies, the MIT Department of Political Science, the School of International Relations at USC, and USC's Program for International Political Economy Research. Preparation of drafts of this book was made possible by a timely summer grant from the Haynes Foundation.

It is conventional to acknowledge one's debt to one's family members for their help, tolerance, support, and the productive atmosphere that they have provided. I must heed this convention by at least mentioning Janet Hanson Ashley's enormous, even indispensable, contribution as critic, editor, research associate, and data manager. But beyond this, neither of my sons, Geoffrey and Jonathan, is yet able to read what I write here (I cannot express on paper what I feel, anyway). Janet Ashley has asked not to be publicly embarrassed by overly personal references. And a sentence or two here could not adequately relate my sense of good fortune in having John and Dorothy Ashley as parents. I will try to express my gratitude to my family at other times in other ways.

All of these people and institutions have had an influence upon this book, knowingly or unknowingly. If there are errors of omission or commission in this study, however, there should be no mystery as to the perpetrator. I absolve all others and confess to total responsibility.

As I scan once more across the pages of the completed manuscript, I sense that I have another debt: a debt to the reader. This book places harsh demands upon the reader. It quite literally asks the reader to struggle. It does so for two reasons.

First, this study is itself a product of a long, often halting, and still continuing struggle to come to terms with and to some degree integrate competing sets of ideas and ways of thinking. As such, it asks the reader to wage the same struggle in condensed and therefore more intense form.

Second, as the earlier remarks suggest, this study can be said to represent what Hayward Alker once called a 'calculated insult' to technical rationality, the very grammar of thought in which most social scientific communications are framed. This grammar of thought does not constitute a necessary approach to life. Nevertheless, it has come over several centuries to infuse all aspects of life on a global scale — including social science. As Ellul, Habermas, and others have pointed out, it is a dominant ideology, masked as the end of ideology, and succeeding in the masking because of its dominance.[2] Indeed, so thoroughly is this grammar of thought reflected in the language and practice of systematic social science that every attempt to critically employ scientific techniques and communicate scientifically tends to be bent into a celebration and reaffirmation of the dominant grammar itself. Yet, as will become evident soon enough, this study struggles against this tendency, and it asks the reader to struggle as well.

I think that the struggle is worth the effort. For while I am no doubt dead wrong on very many things, on this much I think I am correct: the modern security problematique owes its form and tragic dynamism, not to natural law and not to historical accident, but to the cumulations of choices and the interactions of processes framed by a technical-rational grammar of thought. We may find in technical-rationality the roots of what we have come to call progress. But we cannot even begin to meaningfully contemplate peace within a grammar of thought that frames choices in a way producing the absence of peace.

[2] Jacques Ellul, *The Technological Society* (New York: Knopf, 1964); Jürgen Habermas, 'Technology and Science as "Ideology," ' in *Toward a Rational Society* (Boston: Beacon Press, 1971), pp. 81–122; Herbert Marcuse, 'Industrialization and Capitalism in the Work of Max Weber,' in *Negations: Essays in Critical Theory* (Boston: Beacon Press, 1968).

INTRODUCTION

Some of the more important sources of international conflict and violence are to be found in the dynamics of national *growth*, bilateral *rivalry*, and multilateral *balance of power*. The three are tightly intertwined. Through a complex network of relationships, differential technological, economic, and population growth can spur expansion, collisions of activities and interests, competition, military rivalry, confrontations, and crises. In so doing, growth and differential growth can disturb the international distribution of military capabilities, affect systemic patterns of conflict and alignment, and both occasion and constrain the several powers' reactive, potentially violent efforts to restore balance. What is more, as they are propelled toward global scope by differential growth and expansion, the violence-prone dynamics of rivalry and balance of power tend to reproduce and extend the local political conditions of their own existence. Even among preindustrial societies that would resist prevailing patterns of growth and expansion, the widening circle of insecurity generates tendencies to politically adapt to the requisites of participation in military rivalry and balance of power. In turn, once carried to global proportions, these political conditions present serious obstacles to the collective management of growth itself.

These propositions are reminiscent of Nazli Choucri and Robert C. North's analysis of the long-term processes underlying conflict and violence among capitalist and pre-capitalist European powers in the 1870–1914 period. As reported in *Nations in Conflict: National Growth and International Violence*,[1] Choucri and North synthesized a conceptual

---

[1] Nazli Choucri and Robert C. North, *Nations in Conflict: National Growth and International Violence* (San Francisco: W. H. Freeman, 1975). See also Nazli Choucri and Robert C. North, 'Dynamics of International Conflict: Some Policy Implications of Population, Resources, and Technology,' *World Politics*, Vol. xxix, special

framework from a wide array of theoretical traditions, assembled a large data base, and constructed a causal model specifying interdependencies among domestic growth factors, colonial expansion, clashes of colonial interests, military expenditures, total alliances, and violence behavior for each of six powers. The results of that analysis lend empirical corroboration to the hypothesized relationships among dynamics of growth and expansion, competition, and conflict. In the words of Choucri and North, patterns uncovered in the forty-four years preceding World War I clearly show that 'growth can be a lethal process.'[2]

Despite profound changes in world politics and economics since 1914, the thesis of this book is that the same propositions retain equally serious implications for *contemporary* international politics. In the future, as in the past, preserving long-term security and peace will require more than benign intentions, cautious political restraint, or carefully calculated responses to security problems. It will require more than the deliberate creation of multilateral high political regimes. The long-term preservation of peace will require persistent efforts to come to terms with a complex, far-reaching 'problematique' — a web of reproducing dilemmas in which the dynamics of growth have critical roles. *This book amplifies and qualifies these propositions, explores their implications, and inquires into the sources of their enduring relevance. Drawing upon the results of a systematic analysis of Sino-Soviet-American relations since 1950, this book seeks to shed light on some of the broad proportions of the modern security problematique.*

This book draws from an ongoing research enterprise whose aim is to uncover the longer-term processes underlying conflict among major military powers of today. Focusing upon contemporary states, the enterprise necessarily embraces socialist as well as capitalist economies, large underdeveloped societies as well as advanced industrial states. Specifically, this continuing enterprise has so far concentrated upon relations among China, the Soviet Union, and the United States — three societies having quite different economic and demographic profiles, evidencing contrasting modes of production, exhibiting quite different world views, but, nonetheless, representing the three major military powers of today.

Sharing the premises of the Choucri–North analysis, inquiry into relations among these powers began from the assumption that individuals, groups, and nations are profoundly dependent upon the earth and its

---

supplement (1974); and Nazli Choucri and Robert C. North, 'In Search of Peace Systems: Scandinavia and the Netherlands,' in Bruce Russett (ed.), *Peace, War, and Numbers.* (Beverly Hills: Sage Publishers, 1972).

[2] Choucri and North, *Nations in Conflict*, p. 1.

resources. They are dependent even in their most intensely political relations. In line with this premise, a principal objective has been the identification of some of the international political implications of growth and differential growth in a world of scarce, unevenly distributed resources and capabilities.

At the same time, efforts to investigate these patterns in the Sino-Soviet-American context have reflected a second premise. International political behavior can be attributed to no one factor, no single level of explanation, and no one kind of process. Uncovering the dynamics of international conflict and violence requires a conceptual framework and a mode of analysis that permit the systematic synthesis of a constellation of factors and the empirical weighting of persistent relationships among them.

Thus, the research reported here has built upon and extended the Choucri–North framework, revising it to reflect historical changes and to express more adequately the complex cross-actor, cross-level interdependencies of international relations. A large data base to represent the changing attributes of China, the Soviet Union, and the United States, their external activities, and their patterns of interaction has been assembled.[3] Using these data, guided by the revised framework, and applying econometric research techniques, the project then involved a multiple-stage research progression.[4] The main product of this progression is a general model. Like the Choucri–North model presented in *Nations in Conflict*, the general model presented here specifies interdependencies linking growth factors to international conflict and violence. Unlike the Choucri–North model, this general model joins the dynamics affecting all relevant actors in a single representation of a multi-state system — in this case, the Sino-Soviet-American 'triangle.' Systematic empirical analysis of the model corroborates propositions of the framework and suggests how tightly intertwined are the dynamics of growth, rivalry, and balance of power. Unfinished as such an enterprise must always be, its results so far do illuminate some of the extended elements of the modern security problematique.

The results and the present expression of the problematique are likely to be controversial, if only because they come at a time when conventional images of the international system, of major power rivalries, and of growth

---

[3] Characteristics of these data — including data sources and problems — are discussed in Appendix C.

[4] The methodological underpinnings of this progression are discussed in Chapter 2. Although a complete description of every step in the progression would require literally hundreds of pages, an understanding of key aspects of this progression is essential to a critical interpretation of the general model deriving from it. Accordingly, Appendix A provides some of these details.

and its consequences are being questioned. With the apparent dissolution of political bipolarity, with the detente-accelerated but largely economic tensions surfacing within cold war blocs, and with the emergence of new centers and instruments of international influence, time-honored models of a balance of power system seem inadequate in their depictions of complex problems of leadership and policy coordination.[5] Similarly, doubt is cast on prevailing images of superpower rivalry, and ways to manage it, as fragmented detente-related efforts are overshadowed by events in Africa and the Middle East, as military technologies rapidly advance, and as arms expenditures continue to mount.[6]

Even positive images of technological and economic growth — images that stress growth as a basis for welfare, domestic equity, internal stability, and international power — have been subjected to new challenges. Some observers emphasize international cooperative imperatives rising out of growth's potentially damaging impacts upon a finite, easily despoiled biosphere.[7] Others aver that transnational interchanges partially born of sustained growth will weave a web of cooperative bonds among peoples.[8] And still others assert that differential growth, differential access to scarce resources, and differential experiencing and evaluation of growth's consequences can generate new issues, instruments, and alignments of international politics.[9] In part, the celebrity of the word 'interdependence'

[5] See, e.g., Stanley Hoffmann, 'Notes on the Elusiveness of Modern Power,' *International Journal*, Vol. XXX (Spring 1975); Stanley Hoffmann, 'Choices,' *Foreign Policy*, No. 12 (Fall 1973), Zbigniew Brzezinski, 'The Balance of Power Delusion,' *Foreign Policy*, No. 7 (Summer 1972).

[6] See, for example, Alexander George and Richard Smoke, *Deterrence in American Foreign Policy* (New York: Columbia University Press, 1974); John Steinbrunner, 'Beyond Rational Deterrence: The Struggle for New Conceptions,' *World Politics*, Vol. XXVIII, No. 2 (January 1976); Paul H. Nitze, 'Assuring Strategic Stability in an Era of Detente,' *Foreign Affairs*, Vol. LIV, No. 2 (January 1976); Jan Lodal, 'Assuring Strategic Stability: An Alternative View,' *Foreign Affairs*, Vol. LIV, No. 3 (April 1976); Adam Ulam, 'Detente Under Soviet Eyes,' *Foreign Policy*, No. 24 (Fall 1976); and Alton Frye, 'Strategic Restraint, Mutual and Assured,' *Foreign Policy*, No. 27 (Summer 1977).

[7] The existence (or possibility) of emergent cooperative imperatives is often asserted by, for instance, participants in the World Order Models Project headed by Saul Mendlovitz and Richard Falk. Claims to this effect also appear in both the first and second reports to the Club of Rome; see Donella H. Meadows *et al.*, *The Limits to Growth* (New York: Universe Books, 1972) and M. Mesarovic and E. Pestel, *Mankind at the Turning Point* (New York: Dutton, 1974).

[8] See, for example, Lester R. Brown, *World Without Borders: The Interdependence of Nations* (New York: Foreign Policy Association, 1972); and Robert Angell, *Peace on the March: Transnational Participation* (New York: Van Nostrand, 1969).

[9] Of relevance here, for instance, are the literatures on economic interdependence, with its emphasis on asymmetrical vulnerabilities and sensitivities, and on dependence. See Richard Cooper, *The Economics of Interdependence* (New York: McGraw-Hill, 1968); Susan Strange, 'What is Economic Power and Who Has It?'

can be attributed to a vague but widely shared feeling that, in each of these areas, the world has changed and the models inherited from the past no longer seem to fit.[10]

Against this background, this book takes a controversial stance. It is not change but continuity in the deeply structured interdependencies among all three classes of dynamics that largely accounts for the confounding aspects of today's global predicaments. Today, as in the period preceding World War I, these interdependencies transcend the usual divisions of academic labor between security politics and political-economics. In systematic ways, they override prevailing means of social control, constrain the successes of well-meant solutions, transmit reverberations across domains and levels of human activity, and potentially subvert the most deliberate designs for the establishment of a lasting peaceful order.

More specifically, this analysis suggests that efforts to manage major power security by concentrating upon the high political dynamics of rivalry and balance of power alone are very likely to fail over the longer term. The dynamics of differential technological, economic and population growth are also important elements of the security problematique. They, too, must be monitored and managed. Indeed, every effort to manage growth — whether to accelerate, limit, stabilize, or redistribute — has potential security ramifications. In its linkages to growth, the security problematique is thus on the 'hidden' global agenda even when dilemmas of welfare, equity, ecology, and national autonomy are given topical priority. It does more than join these dilemmas, however. Carried by differential growth and expansion beyond Europe and outward to global scope, the political conditions of the security problematique also confound the collective resolution of these dilemmas.

To elucidate these relationships and describe the dimensions of the

International Journal, Vol. XXX (Spring 1975); Robert O. Keohane and Joseph S. Nye, Jr., 'Transgovernmental Relations and International Organizations,' *World Politics*, Vol. XVII, No. 1 (October 1974); Robert O. Keohane and Joseph S. Nye, Jr., *Power and Interdependence* (Boston: Little, Brown, 1977); Theotonio Dos Santos, 'The Structure of Dependence,' *American Economic Review*, Vol. LX, No. 2 (May 1970); Fernando H. Cardoso, 'Imperialism and Dependency in Latin America,' in Frank H. Bonilla and Robert Girling (eds.) *Structures of Dependency* (Palo Alto: Stanford University Press, 1973); Raymond Duvall, 'Dependence and Dependencia Theory: Notes Toward Precision of Concept and Argument,' *International Organization*, Vol. XXXII, No. 1 (Winter 1978); Osvaldo Sunkel, 'Big Business and "Dependencia," ' *Foreign Affairs*, Vol. L, No. 3 (1972); Andre Gunder Frank, 'The Development of Underdevelopment,' in James D. Cockcroft, Andre Gunder Frank, Dale L. Johnson, *Dependence and Underdevelopment: Latin America's Political Economy* (New York: Anchor, 1972); Samir Amin, *Unequal Development: An Essay on the Social Formations of Peripheral Capitalism* (New York: Monthly Review Press, 1976).
[10] Keohane and Nye, *Power and Interdependence*, p. 222.

security problematique so far uncovered, this book follows a developmental presentation strategy. Part I presents the conceptual framework informing this analysis and describes the overall research methodology. As will be seen in Chapter 1's presentation of the conceptual framework, many of the individual propositions, taken in isolation, appear familiar, conventional, almost intuitive in character.[11] But assembled systematically, the several propositions suggest the existence of a system in which the extended consequences of immediate choices are far from intuitively obvious. The methodological discussion in Chapter 2 identifies some of the philosophical and technical issues encountered in systematically synthesizing and empirically examining verbal theoretical statements in the form of

[11] For example, the theoretical strains reflected in the conceptual framework can be traced to (among many others): Perry Anderson, *Lineages of the Absolutist State* (London: New Left Books, 1974); Raymond Aron, *Peace and War* (New York: Praeger, 1967); Hedley Bull, *The Anarchical Society* (New York: Columbia University Press, 1977); John W. Burton and others, *The Study of World Society: A London Perspective* (Pittsburgh: International Studies Association, 1974); Karl W. Deutsch, *Nationalism and Social Communication* (Cambridge, Mass.: MIT Press, 1966); Karl W. Deutsch, *The Nerves of Government* (New York: Free Press, second edition, 1966); Johan Galtung, 'A Structural Theory of Imperialism,' *Journal of Peace Research*, Vol. XIII, No. 2, (1971); A Gramsci, *The Modern Prince* (New York: International Publishers, 1968); Ernst Haas, *Beyond the Nation-State: Functionalism and International Organization* (Stanford, Calif.: Stanford University Press, 1968); J. A. Hobson, *Imperialism: A Study* (London: Allen and Unwin, 1938); Harold J. Lasswell, *World Politics and Personal Insecurity* (New York: Free Press, 1965); V. I. Lenin, *Imperialism: The Highest Stage of Capitalism* (Moscow: Foreign Languages Publishing House, 1955); Karl Marx and Frederick Engels, *The German Ideology*, trans. by R. Pascal (London: Lawrence and Wishart, 1942); Charles A. McClelland, *Theory and the International System* (New York: Macmillan, 1966); Hans Morgenthau, *Politics Among Nations: The Struggle for Power and Peace* (New York: Knopf, 1968); Lewis F. Richardson, *Arms and Insecurity* (Pittsburgh: Boxwood Press, 1960); Richard Rosecrance, *Action and Reaction in World Politics* (Boston: Little, Brown, 1963); James N. Rosenau, *The Adaptation of National Societies: A Theory of Political System Behavior and Transformation* (New York: McCaleb-Seiler, 1970); Rudolph J. Rummel, 'Dimensions of Dyadic War, 1820–1952,' *Journal of Conflict Resolution*, Vol. X (March 1966); Joseph A. Schumpeter, *Imperialism and Social Classes: Two Essays* (New York: World Publishing, 1951); Joseph A. Schumpeter, *Capitalism, Socialism, and Democracy* (London: Allen & Unwin, third edition, 1950); Herbert A. Simon, *The Sciences of the Artificial* (Cambridge: MIT Press, 1969); Harold and Margaret Sprout, *Foundations of International Politics* (Princeton, N.J.: Van Nostrand, 1962); Arnold Toynbee, *A Study of History* (London: Oxford University Press for the Royal Institute of International Affairs, 12 volumes, 1933–61); Immanuel Wallerstein, 'The Rise and Future Demise of the World Capitalist System,' *Comparative Studies in Society and History*, Vol. XVI, No. 4 (September, 1974); Immanuel Wallerstein, *The Modern World System: Capitalist Agriculture and the Origins of the European World-Economy* (New York: Academic Press, 1974); Kenneth Waltz, *Man, the State, and War* (New York: Columbia University Press, 1959); Max Weber, *The Theory of Social and Economic Organization* (New York: Free Press, 1964); and Quincy Wright, *A Study of War* (Chicago: University of Chicago Press, 1942).

a general structural model. It is here, in Chapter 2, that the general model is formally introduced. As a symbolic representation — one expressed both graphically and as a multi-equation system — this model has permitted the application of econometric techniques to empirically examine hypothesized relationships.

Part II presents the results of empirical analysis. It begins in Chapter 3 by setting the recent historical context. It briefly reviews trends and variation in normal conflict and thresholds of violence among China, the Soviet Union, and the United States from 1950 through 1972. Chapters 4 through 9 then analyze the dynamics underlying variation in the model's key system-determined variables: national expansion, intersections of activities and interests, provocations, military capability building, normal conflict behavior, and thresholds of violence.

Not until Part III, however, will the extended interconnections among the several aspects of the model become evident. To bring the modern security problematique sharply into focus, Chapter 10 offers an overview of empirical results and provides a synthesis. Tracing significant causal paths from domestic growth factors to conflict behavior variables, Chapter 10 enumerates some emergent propositions regarding the critical but often neglected effects of technological, economic, and population growth on major power politics. It begins to suggest how growth, whether in capitalist or socialist societies, can be a source of violence among major powers. It indicates, too, some of the many complicating factors that impede the management or transformation of growth processes in a world of pervasive insecurity and widely and unevenly dispersed resources and capabilities. The far-reaching implications of the present study are identified in Chapter 11, where the overall synthesis is viewed from several theoretical vantage points. In particular, as a synthesis, the present depiction of the modern security problematique invites a joining and possible revision of theories of balance of power, integration, classical imperialism, and international political economy. Indeed, it is in the mutual dependencies transcending these theoretical domains that some of the most fundamental dilemmas in the design of a lasting peaceful order are to be found.

While an important aim of the overall research enterprise is to provide improved linkages between research and participants' day-to-day concerns, the immediate practical relevance of this book is limited to an alerting function. It advances but one prescription. If peoples and leaders can acknowledge interdependence at this moment in history, then they must also come to terms with their dependence upon knowledge of historical processes. The problem of knowing and acting amidst mounting complexity does not wholly derive from the occurrence of sudden and dramatic breaks with the system's past, and the appearance of disorder and radical change does not necessarily require sharp departures from established theoretical foundations. On the contrary, the sense of change and disorder largely derives from the fact that conventional perspectives individually address just some of history's dynamics while today and the future are shaped by congruities and clashes within the whole. When a long view is taken, when competing perspectives are systematically joined and each is allowed to challenge the *ceteris paribus* clauses of all, the emerging controversies and incongruities help to identify the dilemmas whose resolutions have shaped the past and will shape the future.

To view the magnitude of these dilemmas is to be humbled before history. To view them is to see reaction and tragedy in even the most well-intended efforts to find guidance in partial theory, solve problems, manage conflict, and exert control. Yet it is within these compound dilemmas, and not within the confines of discrete traditions, that the critical choice points reside. Herein is the latitude for change that history affords.

PART I

CHAPTER 1
Conceptual Framework

I ORIENTATION

The purpose of this chapter is to develop some of the conceptual tools needed to give definition to the modern security problematique. More specifically, it is meant to do so in a way that (*a*) synthesizes insights and propositions from diverse literatures bearing on the causes of war and preconditions for peace and (*b*) embeds an understanding of the problematique's contemporary forms within concepts capable of interpreting its historic emergence and future passing.

Thus, the presentation to follow does not begin with a definition of the security problematique. Such a beginning might leave the quite mistaken impression that the security problematique and the patterns that give it form are somehow universal, eternal, almost natural lawful conditions. Instead, the argument begins with bald assertions. *In all its complexity, the modern security problematique is an emergent expression of an historical progression recurring among societies within an ever-widening geographic compass. It is, more precisely, an expression of the asynchronous, equifinal, cumulative, irreversible, and antagonistic joining of the dynamics of growth, rivalry, and balance of power.*[1] *It is a product of an historical progression that has gradually and unevenly entangled all societies of the globe in a web of relations that perpetuates differential growth, reproduces rivalry, disturbs violence-prone balances of power, and denies lasting peace.* The task of this presentation of a conceptual framework is to make these assertions meaningful and thereby shed light on the security problematique. It tries to do so, first, by synthesizing an interpretation of this historical progression from growth through rivalry to

---

[1] Each of these terms is defined in Section III below.

balance of power and, second, by considering the patternings of its recurrence. Before undertaking this task, though, it is important to briefly situate the effort in terms of its premises and some of the traditions to which it responds.

A   Premises

The conceptual framework developed here owes its origins, most immediately, to the 'proto-theory' developed by Choucri and North and, more distantly, to the wide array of theoretical traditions that they have sought to synthesize over several years.[2] Like the Choucri–North perspective, the present conceptualization views international relations from a particular vantage point: the vantage point of peace research, with its long-standing (albeit far from exclusive) concern for the causes of war. Not exploitation, not inequality, not environmental destruction, but the violence-proneness and pervasive insecurity of international relations is the aspect upon which attention centers. Initially such a vantage point surely limits the search for relevant insights, but only initially. For as in the work of Choucri and North, this vantage point does not impose final boundaries. It provides instead one among many possible research anchoring points of departure for the attempt to discern important interdependencies among the seemingly distinct aspects of human experience. If one is willing to search beyond appearances for the deeper, longer-term, 'submerged' relations that do or might intimately join the 'parts' of international reality, then viewing the system from the vantage point of its violence-proneness will lead inescapably to a concern for the interconnections between physical violence, on the one hand, and exploitation, inequality, and environmental destruction, on the other.

As in the Choucri–North perspective, then, the present conceptualization is formulated at a quite general level. The several propositions are meant to apply, not to discrete events or specific nations or leaders, but to the *long-range historical processes* underlying organized intersocietal conflict and violence in general. Three premises regarding these processes merit attention.

First, these long-term processes are conceived to consist in large part of

[2] Nazli Choucri and Robert C. North, *Nations in Conflict: National Growth and International Violence* (San Francisco: W. H. Freeman, 1975). See also Nazli Choucri and Robert C. North, 'Dynamics of International Conflict: Some Implications of Population, Resources, and Technology,' *World Politics*, Vol. XXIV, special supplement (1974); and Nazli Choucri and Robert C. North, 'In Search of Peace Systems: Scandinavia and the Netherlands,' in Bruce Russett (ed.), *Peace, War, and Numbers* (Beverly Hills: Sage, 1972).

human decisions and non-decisions at several levels. It is assumed that decision situations, though never identical across time and space, very often exhibit recurring close similarities. Given the perseverance of habit, conventional imagery, and human purposes, some situations make some kinds of decisions very likely. In turn, each decision cumulates with numerous others to form trends, generate other situations, influence still other decisions, and contribute to the shaping of historical experience in which habits, ways of thinking, and human purposes all assume form and content. Constrained human choices are at the core of the historical processes conceptualized here. The individual human being is the fundamental unit of analysis.[3]

Second, throughout all human history and prehistory, human choice and human development have been intimately interconnected with the natural environment. As basic biological necessities, Robert North argues, 'every person requires at the very minimum such resources as air, food, water, and some certain amount of territory. To stay alive, every human being must ingest energy in some form from the environment. And this requires sustained access to critical resources.' 'From these naive propositions,' North continues, 'we can infer that the larger a given population, the greater will be the amount of resources demanded.'[4] Moreover, while it sometimes appears that the story of human development has been one of man's growing technological mastery over an impersonal environment — while it sometimes seems that technology has permitted humankind to escape the determinism of natural constraints — just the reverse is the case. For if the alleged technological mastery of the environment is what has set man apart from nature, then man needs nature in order to assert his mastery and reproduce himself as what he has become. It is in this sense that North asserts that technology 'may . . . alter people's perceptions of what they "need" ' and 'generate demands of its own for resources.'[5] In the same sense, every advance in technology, just as much as the birth of a human being, at once expresses the reproductive powers of humankind and testifies to man's existence as part of the natural environment he would control.

Third, the assertion that the human being is the fundamental unit of analysis does not imply a neglect of aggregate social patterns and patterns of interaction among 'impersonal' institutions, such as corporations, bureaucracies, and states. Rather, that human beings are fundamental implies that aggregate social patterns — population size, national income,

---

[3] Choucri and North, *Nations in Conflict*, p. 2.
[4] Robert C. North, *The World That Could Be* (Stanford, Calif.: Stanford Alumni Association, 1976), p. 13.   [5] Ibid., p. 13.

volumes of trade, and so on — are to be viewed as the cumulative *traces* of countless constrained human decisions. It implies, too, that institutions are to be seen as social structurations given form and identity through (often complex) reproductive patterns of choice among individuals. And it implies that both aggregate social patterns and institutions might assume other forms and different identities were people somehow to choose and act differently. Put simply, the implication is this: all units of analysis above the human being are to be seen as social manifestations of historical processes. As for the systems of relations in which these units are said to be 'actors,' the emergence, actuality, and possible passing of these units should be part of any complete analysis.[6]

These premises all find expression in the concept of *lateral pressure*, the key concept developed by North and his associates, applied in the studies of Choucri and North, and orienting the present study. Unlike the majority of social scientific concepts, the concept of lateral pressure is not a singular, data-classifying term. It is relational. It is processual. Indeed, it contains within a term a whole theory of the processes contributing to conflict and organized social violence. The following eight paragraphs develop the concept of lateral pressure. One should study them very carefully. They constitute what might be called the 'theory kernel' — the hard core conceptual basis — of this study:

> *In what they are and become, individuals, humanity, and the natural environment are one and inseparable. Among the natural characteristics of the human being — characteristics that link humankind to nature in unyielding interdependence — are capacities to develop knowledge and skills and to communicate.* These capacities may be exercised to sustain manifest relations of oneness among human beings and between society and nature. That is, they may be exercised to interiorize within each social unit, from the individual to the social organization, a sense of identity between each unit's immediate fulfillment of itself and the realization of socio-environmental potentialities of the present and future. On the other hand, knowledge, skills, and capacities to communicate may also be used *technologically*. They may be used by human beings to objectify their 'environments,' including one another, as elements of life external to themselves — elements to be managed, manipulated, and controlled through the application of knowledge and skills. The technological exercise of these natural capacities does not

---

[6] See Hayward R. Alker, Jr., 'Can the End of Power Politics Be Part of the Concepts with which Its Story Is Told?' paper presented at the annual meeting of the American Political Science Association, Washington, D.C., September 1977.

finally separate humanity from nature or human being from human being, however. For in technologically 'subjugating' nature and other people, each technological act alters what both humanity and nature are and will become while also sustaining each social unit's dependence upon what is seen to be an 'external' environment.

The demands generated by any social unit are the requisites of its existence that must be satisfied if the unit is to survive as what it has become. To speak of 'basic biological necessities' is to refer to those demands that must be satisfied if the human organism is to survive and function as such. However, the demands generated by any social unit will also be directly and indirectly shaped by what people have become accustomed to having (and hence believe that they 'need'). A social unit's demands are not just a direct reflection of a summation of human felt-needs. They are also indirect reflections: they include the second-order requisites for the preservation of the social, political, and economic structures of life, as these shape human experiences, alter human purposes, and provide for human demands.

The technological exercise of knowledge, skills, and capacities for communication contributes to the generation of limitless demands, and presupposes the social unit's limitless ability to satisfy them, even as it contributes to the partitioning of social reality within limits. On the one hand, every substantial technological act entails distinctions between the means and the ends, the solution and the problem, the manager and the managed, the dominant society and the subordinate nature, the relevant and the irrelevant, and the isolated moment and the totality of time. It entails some specific mobilization of human energies, some specific commitment of resources, some specific symbolic rationalizations, and some specific adaptations of social organization and human expectations in the service of some specific purpose. On the other hand, every technological act presupposes limitlessness as it contributes to the generation of unlimited demands. It presupposes the limitless availability of resources and energies to sustain means applied to ends, support and manage the managers, substitute for depleted natural resources, solve problems born of prior solutions, innovatively make the irrelevant relevant, and satisfy the future demands of human beings who adapt to experiences shaped by cumulations of momentary choices. It presupposes the open-ended capacity of the social unit to answer demands through the continuing and expanding technological mastery of the unit's environment.

Lateral pressure is the tendency of a social unit to expand its geographic compass, to push outward the boundaries that partition reality between the 'external' environment and the unit itself, and to draw an ever greater expanse of reality within itself. Baldly put, lateral pressure is a manifestation of each unit's unceasing movement toward the realization of an expanded socio-environmental unity as an expression of its own growth and self-realization. Lateral pressure is generated by each social unit's growing population and technological demands as these combine with its previously developed specialized capabilities under environmental constraints. To the extent that social units differ across space and time in their technology, their population, their demands, and their environmental limits, they also generate differential rates of growth and exhibit lateral pressure unevenly and asynchronously.

Given sustained lateral pressure, it becomes likely that sooner or later the geographic compasses of two or more social units will intersect, at least on some dimensions of activity. In effect, then, each of two or more social units becomes a manifest part of others' environments. For low lateral pressure social units that acknowledge and interiorize the identity of humankind and the natural environment — that are not organized as units to master the environment — such mutual environing relations may be said to present no necessary implications for violence. Such a social unit may effectively accept and adapt to the presence of others as a part of nature and hence as a part of itself and its future. However, for high lateral pressure social units — social units that take their forms from an accelerated history of technological solutions to problems and further technological responses to the demands occasioned thereby — such mutual environing relations present circumstances that are likely to be perceived and responded to as problems of technological domination and control.

Owing to the asynchronous and differential growth among social units, intersections tend to involve greater or lesser disparities in the units' relative abilities and dispositions to affect or control their environments, including one another. Where the disparities are great, the relationship tends to be asymmetrically integrative, as the units less able and disposed to subjugate their environments are bent to conform to the demands and capabilities of the technologically more advanced units. By contrast, where the disparities are not so great, and where social units both exhibit high degrees of lateral pressure, *competition* is likely to result.

Competition and rivalry are likely to eventuate from each social unit's attempts to respond to a 'hostile' environment, including other social units, through a unilateral extension of technological logics of domination and control. In interaction, the social units shape a violence-prone environment to which they all adapt and which they jointly reproduce. Units starting from quite different historical conditions converge through their mutual adaptations to the commonality of their rivalry.

Crisis and the 'conflict spiral' represent an acceleration of the competition process and a deepening of each social unit's commitments to the domination of the 'environment,' including other social units. As a possible culmination, catastrophic war is a dynamic wherein the social units that are organized to technically-rationally manage and subjugate an alien natural environment at last manifest the identity of humankind and nature in technological self-destruction.

Several key features of this theory kernel should be underlined. It is evident that the kernel relates a kind of 'story' accounting for the emergence of the preconditions for violence. As told, this story of lateral pressure begins and is wholly contained in some historical act of technological 'subjugation' of an objectified environment and the consequent creation of new demands, new 'needs,' and new implications for further, more extensive mastery and control. It is also evident that this story fixes on no single level or unit of analysis. Individuals, families, clans, ethnic groups, social classes, societies, states, and empires — each of these words might be substituted for the term 'social units' without loss of meaning. The theory kernel thus allows for the possible co-occurrence of such processes of social development and interaction at several mutually contextualizing levels of analysis. Moreover, it should be clear that the theory kernel reflects a striving for a *non-ahistorical explanation* of the sources of a global problematic of pervasive insecurity and recurring, institutionalized force and violence. It reflects an attempt to concentrate on certain timeless regularities and to avoid the insinuation of concepts and ideas that are captive expressions of this or that historically emergent aspect of life.

Perhaps most importantly, *the kernel contains an implicit critique of Western metaphysical grammars of means–ends rational social action.* It implies that some of the most important processes leading to war are deeply embedded within long-dominant technical-rational ways of thinking about and 'solving' human problems, problems of war and peace among them. Until the limits of this way of thinking are exposed, until its 'promise' is discredited, and until social science is emancipated from its domination, researchers focusing on insecurity and war cannot escape complicity in the violence-prone processes they study.

These features of the theory kernel have profound implications for research, theory, and the tasks of social science. As a kind of 'interpretational supplement,' Appendix A elaborates upon these implications at some length. For now, it is necessary only to stress the status of this theory kernel within the present attempt to contribute to international relations theory.

The theory kernel represents the hard core conceptualization, the non-ahistorical starting point, from which proceeds the attempt to interpret critically and synthesize propositions and insights developed by a wide array of analytic traditions bearing on the causes of war and the preconditions for peace. This means that competing traditions addressing, say, imperialism, integration, inter-state competition, military rivalry, politico-military crisis, and balance of power are *not* dismissed, out of hand, as somehow wrong or once-and-for-all incompatible with a lateral pressure explanation of international conflict and war. The task of theory-building is not so easy as assigning the labels 'right' and 'wrong' to distinct propositions or whole traditions. All such traditions do contain *relative* truths as seen from particular vantage points on reality. The point, rather, is that these competing traditions are *ahistorical.* Although often mistaken for timeless universals, the patterns identified by such traditions are historically dependent relations. They are patterns whose existences depend upon contextualizing historical processes that individual traditions have relegated to their unspoken and unexamined *ceteris paribus* clauses. The assumption here is that the historically generalizable relationships articulated in the lateral pressure theory kernel represent some of the most important long-term processes in which historically dependent patterns find their contexts and assume their recognizable forms — the very forms that competing traditions have identified and isolated.

Thus, the task of synthesis can be stated. *It is to elaborate upon and refine the theory kernel by interpreting the patterns identified by competing theoretical traditions as historically emergent, mutually dependent, and always contingent expressions of long-term processes identified in the theory kernel itself.* This approach, and not an additive joining of distinct propositions, is reflected in the framework's attempt to synthesize competing theoretical traditions.

This fact imposes harsh demands upon the reader confronting Section II's presentation of the conceptual framework. Within the framework, many terms and propositions are familiar. Or at least they are strongly reminiscent of ideas contained in one or another familiar analytic tradition.

From time to time, therefore, the reader might be cued to lift a concept or proposition out of its place in Section II, to see it in isolation, or to mentally situate it in a more familiar tradition. Such tendencies must be resisted. For within Section II's presentation, each word, each phrase, each sentence, and each paragraph has its intended meaning only in the context of the overall historical progression described. The reader is challenged, as it were, to read *through* each statement — to see each statement as somehow connected to and therefore containing all others. Each statement must be understood to be prefigured by, and to implicate, all other arguments.

B   Competing Theoeretical Traditions

In building upon the premises and propositions of the Choucri-North 'proto-theory,' the present conceptual statement also makes some important revisions. Specifically, the present statement sharpens the original by systematically distinguishing three classes of dynamics: unilateral, bilateral, and multilateral dynamics. Unilateral processes are the processes with immediate roots internal to the individual society but finding their expression in the society's outward activities. These processes involve primarily the effects of technological, economic, and population *growth*. As described below, unilateral dynamics also include the effects of a society's decision-making processes and domestic political and economic structures upon its behaviors. Bilateral processes involve the interactions and interpenetrative activities of two societies. They embrace the effects of collisions of activities and interests; cross-national antagonistic comparison; competition for markets, resources, prestige, and military superiority; and crisis — in a word, *rivalry*. Multilateral processes, finally, are the emergent, largely rule-oriented processes tending to regularize the expectations and interactions among three or more powers. In the military security domain, multilateral processes are principally the dynamics of *balance of power* — the dynamics of alliance, alignment, and general adjustment to shifting configurations of conflict and capability. Table 1.1 presents a schematic overview of the three classes of dynamics. Section II, below, presents the specific propositions associated with the unilateral dynamics of growth, the bilateral dynamics of rivalry, and the multilateral dynamics of balance of power. As will be seen, these three classes of dynamics embrace most of the propositions contained in the Choucri–North 'proto-theory.'

As will become completely clear only near the concluding pages of this chapter, however, the propositions are reinterpreted to some extent. The

Table 1.1 *Schematic Overview of Three Classes of Dynamics*

	Unilateral dynamics	Bilateral dynamics	Multilateral dynamics
Definitive features	Actor A's external behaviors causally affected by factors wholly internal to actor A.	A's behaviors toward B causally affected by B's attributes, capabilities, behaviors, or A–B relationships in these factors — directly or indirectly. Not decomposable into strictly unilateral dynamics.	A's behaviors toward B causally affected by C's attributes, capabilities, behaviors, and/or relationships to A or B. Dynamics extend across bilateral relationships. Not decomposable into strictly unilateral or bilateral dynamics.
Source	Choucri–North proto-theory.	Choucri–North proto-theory.	Balance of power literatures.
Selected representative propositions	Rising population and technology generate demands. Technology combines resources to produce specialized capabilities. Demands combine with capabilities to generate 'lateral pressure' and external expansion of activities. Outwardly extended activities can become politicized, identified with national interests. Decisions of society are reached through cumbersome, complex processes often involving countless individual decisions. Centralized decisions tend to exhibit inertial, bureacratic patterns.	Any two societies' expansion accounts for their intersections, their regional collisions of activities, interests, and commitments. Bilateral intersections can generate suspicion, antagonism, and competition. Competition is multidimensional. Competition can assume military dimensions if war seems possible. Actor attempts to build capabilities sufficient to achieve ends, given changes in others' capabilities. Provocations become more likely with intensification of intersections and conflict. Provocations can occasion crises. In crisis, with heightened probability of war, options narrow to increasingly conflictual ones. Action–reaction conflict spiral becomes likely in mutual behaviors (thresholds of violence).	Actors individually apply cognitive balance of power models as means of 'knowing' and ordering their responses to the system. The models indicate appropriate conflictual or military capability building behaviors given the systemic configuration of conflict and overall military capability distribution. All models are highly idealized, unobservable constructs indicating 'rules' of behavior in objective circumstances. The four models are introduced in Table 1.2. Their operation is inferred from patterned relationships among observables. States regularly conforming to rules tend to interiorize requisites of participation in system within their institutions, purposes, *raisons d'être*, and definitions of interest.
Variables affected	Expansion, military capability building, normal conflict and cooperation behavior, thresholds of violence.	Bilateral intersections, bilateral provocations, military capability building, normal conflict and cooperation behavior, thresholds of violence.	Military capability building, normal conflict and cooperation behavior, thresholds of violence.

reinterpretation is subtle. It involves an explication of an idea that is not expressly articulated by Choucri and North but, nonetheless, is part of the grammar in which their assertions are framed. *The relationship between growth, rivalry, and balance of power is here seen as a three-phase historical progression through which different societies have moved, do move, and might move at different times, from different initial conditions, and in different ways.* This is the historical progression mentioned above. This much is thoroughly consistent with explicit statements of the Choucri–North perspective. The difference is that the present statement explicitly draws out the idea that *the societies, the units, transiting the progression are transformed by it.* That is, the progression involves more than changes in the dynamics external to the units — their behaviors and policies, for example. It involves changes in internal relations, in what the societies are and become. In transiting the progression, the individual society is becoming something different from what it was. Once having transited it, the society can never return to what it was before — and events much like those experienced in the society's past assume meanings that they did not have before. Only in light of this important difference is it possible to see how the asynchronous, equifinal, and irreversible recurrence of this historical progression has reproduced and widened the modern security problematique. Indeed, only in this light is it possible to discern the dimensions of the security problematique as it is.[7]

It is especially with respect to the third class of dynamics, the multilateral dynamics of balance of power, that the present statement extends the Choucri–North framework. The Choucri–North framework does attend to alliances, principally as augmentations of national capabilities,[8] but it gives little attention to the more specific logics or rules of balance of power. Accordingly, the analysis is limited by an inadequate conceptualization of the dominant regime (or quasi-regime) of security politics.[9] Unclear are the multilateral alignment and adjustment processes by which actors might seek to respond to — and might effectively compensate for — the disturbing and constraining influences of socio-economic–environmental change. Equally unclear are the ways in which these same balance of

[7] Although the Choucri–North proto-theory does not make this idea an explicit theme, the idea does find occasional expression in their work. Moreover, the book by North, op. cit., does represent an important attempt to amplify this aspect of their thinking.

[8] *Nations in Conflict*, pp. 21, 219–33.

[9] As discussed below, the treatment of balance of power as a regime — a widely observed multilateral regulative rule system 'in depth' — represents a departure from the main thrust of the balance of power literature. The discussion of the theoretical implications of this usage, which are surely controversial, is reserved for Chapter 11.

power dynamics might transmit the political impacts of growth and differential growth beyond immediate origins, perhaps amplifying them elsewhere in a complex system. In short, due to incomplete conceptualization, the capacities of power political regimes to absorb, adapt to, and transmit the impacts of environmental change cannot be sharply specified, cannot be directly subjected to empirical examination, and cannot be explicitly incorporated in the analysis of growth's implications for security and peace.[10]

In correcting for this omission, the present statement departs from the main thrust of the balance of power literature. It does not assume, *a priori*, the existence of a balance of power dynamic dominating state behavior at the systemic level. As seen below, it instead starts from the level of the individual society, and it assumes the existence of balance of power logics or rule systems that *might* find expression in individual societies' actions and military capability building in a multi-state system. To the extent that individual societies do adapt their state institutions, instruments, and behaviors so as to be regularly responsive to these rules, a *multilateral balance of power regime* may be said to exist at the systemic level. Such a regime may be examined for its stability, its tendencies to cue or elicit similar, predictable rule-following behaviors that reproduce the same regime through time.

As here conceptualized, though, the logics or rules of balance of power do not exhaust the possible influences upon state behavior. A number of other processes, including processes of growth and differential growth, are posited in the framework to potentially disturb and constrain the same political actions and capability building that a balance of power regime would regulate. Thus, within the revised framework, balance of power is neither natural law nor mechanical process. On the contrary, viewed at the systemic level, *balance of power is a possible regime whose emergence, actuality, and adequacy in the face of growth and differential growth remain important empirical questions.*

While this revision suggests a concern for socio-economic impacts and constraints upon the state as actor in high political regimes, it should be clear that it does not imply 'economism'[11] — the viewpoint wherein all

[10] As to the significance of this omission for 'interdependence research,' see Hayward R. Alker, Jr., 'A Methodology for Design Research on Interdependence Alternatives,' *International Organization*, Vol. XXXI, No. 1 (Winter 1977).

[11] With Ralph Miliband, 'economism' is here taken to mean 'the attribution of an exaggerated — almost an exclusive — importance to the economic sphere in the shaping of social and political relations, leading precisely to "economic determinism." ' It also involves an 'underestimation of the importance of the "superstructural" sphere.' See Ralph Miliband, *Marxism and Politics* (Oxford: Oxford University Press, 1977), p. 9.

state behaviors are seen as epiphenomenal reflections of an economic base. What it does imply is a concern for a puzzling question long reflected in other traditions joined in this analysis. The question centers on the basis of *state autonomy*. How, why, and to what extent are state agencies, instruments, and policies independent of domestic social and economic demands? The query is central to classic theories of imperialism, theories partly reflected in the framework's expression of growth and expansion processes. The query is central, too, to modern international political economic perspectives addressing the political management and transformation of technological and economic growth processes. And the query is raised yet again by analysts of military rivalry and balance of power, where arms race theorists tend to assume political autonomy and balance of power theorists since Machiavelli routinely elevate state autonomy to the level of an imperative.

Yet balance of power, as here conceived, does more than raise the state autonomy question. It also affords partial answers. The state's claims to autonomy do not necessarily derive solely from the state's role as mediator of pluralistic domestic demands, from the state's institutionalization of prior demands made upon it, or from the state's manipulations of historic symbols. As suggested below, the state's claim to autonomy may also derive from its historic adaptations to the requisites of participation in an international rule system, balance of power. In adapting to the dominant rule system of a threatening world, a state effectively interiorizes within itself — within its agencies, instruments, and *raison d'être* — the demanding logic of a systemic regime. It interiorizes a logic that may be strikingly at variance with domestic social and economic demands upon the state. And once adapted, each state — whether pre-capitalist, capitalist, or socialist — will tend to behave in ways contributing to the perpetuation of this regime by which all rationalize their partial autonomy through time.

This means that the revised framework allows for a cross-level 'double limiting'[12] relationship between the state as it relates to domestic socioeconomic demands and the state as it relates to the international political order. On the one hand, this formulation allows that states confronted by an expanding balance of power regime might tend to adapt their agencies and instruments — indeed, their identities — to its demanding logic, assuming a partial autonomy of domestic demands thereby. On the other hand, it allows that this autonomy is never complete, never final. For as here conceptualized, the political behaviors and military capability building of each state — and hence, the stability of a balance of power regime —

[12] The notion of 'double limiting' is due to Nicos Poulantzas. See his *Pouvoir Politique et Classes Sociales de l'Etat Capitaliste* (Paris: Maspero, 1968).

remain potentially sensitive to and constrained by the dynamics of differential growth and their consequences.

This view of balance of power is developed below and further amplified in Chapter 11. As will be seen, the revised framework represents an attempt to set balance of power, classically limited to 'the politics of appropriation,' squarely in the context of 'the politics of production, of cooperation, and of growth.'[13] Such a joining permits the critical analysis of balance of power without denying its reality. As will be stressed in Chapter 11, this view has salient implications for other bodies of theory that are concerned with the role of the state in world economics — integration theory, imperialism theory, and liberal and neomercantilist political economic theory, in particular.

II   THREE CLASSES OF DYNAMICS: GROWTH, RIVALRY, AND BALANCE OF POWER

The framework presented here is thus addressed to a complex system characterized by cross-societal, cross-sectoral, and cross-level interdependencies. As conceived, though, this complexity is largely emergent and artificial. It is created through the recurrence of a long-historical progression involving the growth, interactions, and recombinations of what were once relatively simple systems. The sequence of presentation — from the unilateral dynamics of growth, through the bilateral dynamics of rivalry, to the multilateral dynamics of balance — roughly retraces this progression. It starts simply. It starts by envisaging the single society neither caught in military rivalry nor responding to the global balance of power but experiencing growth-born pressures toward outward expansion.

A   Unilateral Processes: The Dynamics of Growth and Expansion

Following Choucri and North, the articulation of unilateral dynamics emphasizes the concept of *lateral pressure*, its roots in population, economic, and technological growth, and its manifestations in a growing society's outwardly expanding activities, commitments, and felt-interests. The general proposition is expressed:

> When [a society's growth-generated technological, economic, and population] demands are unmet and existing capabilities are insufficient to

[13] The phrases are those of Karl W. Deutsch in his *The Analysis of International Relations* (Englewood Cliffs, N.J.: Prentice-Hall, second edition, 1978), p. 174.

satisfy them, new capabilities may have to be developed. But a society can develop particular capabilities (including resources) only if it has the necessary existing capabilities to do so. Moreover, if necessary capabilities cannot be attained at a reasonable cost within national boundaries, they may be sought beyond. Any activity — selling wheat, buying oil, investing capital, increasing the labor force, or moving troops — takes on new meaning once it is extended into foreign territory. We use the term lateral pressure to refer to the process of foreign expansion of any activity.[14]

Choucri and North distinguish three aspects of the lateral pressure process: (1) the *disposition* of a society to extend activities beyond original boundaries, (2) the particular *activities* that result, and (3) the *impacts* that these activities have on the people of other territories and their environments.[15]

Although the present discussion of unilateral dynamics concentrates upon the 'dispositional' and 'activity' aspects of lateral pressure, attention to the third aspect, 'impacts,' is critical to an understanding of the processes contextualizing the expression of unilateral dynamics. As will be argued, at any moment a given society's matrix of technological and population demands and available capabilities, coupled with available local resources and environmental constraints, largely shape its predispositions to expand outward and the kinds and degrees of activity in which it in fact expresses this predisposition. Yet looking back in history beyond this moment, it can always be seen that the technology, specialized capabilities, population, and overall demands generated within a territory are not just spontaneous reflections of local conditions. Instead, they are in large measure attributable to the historically prior *impacts* of other societies' growth and expansion into the same territory.

Throughout history and prehistory, population levels and levels of technology within any territory reflect, at a minimum, the impacts of previous migration and technological diffusion into that territory, and both migration and technological diffusion are expressions of the historically prior predispositions of other societies to expand activities beyond their earlier geographic boundaries. Indeed, far from being a timeless given, the very existence, forms of social and economic organization, and geographic boundaries of any society bear and reflect the full weight of prior expressions, convergences, and re-expressions of lateral pressure touching a territory through history. The units expressing the unilateral dynamics of

---

[14] *Nations in Conflict*, p. 16, emphasis omitted.   [15] Ibid., p. 16.

lateral pressure at any moment thus owe much of what they are, what they are predisposed to do, and what they are capable of doing to the cumulative historical impacts of other societies that acted on their pre-dispositions to expand. In expressing their own predispositions in action, these same units will have impacts that help to determine what other societies become, can do, and will do in the future.

Put figuratively, for any period of time, the set of relationships between societies' *dispositional factors* and their expanding *activities* can be visualized as a cycle bearing some resemblances to cycles occurring among societies at earlier and later periods of time. To additionally acknowledge the *impacts* of lateral pressure is to acknowledge that each such cycle might somehow be joined in an unbroken, open-ended spiral to cycles that were and will be.

Growing societies can manifest lateral pressure in a number of different types of activity — including many activities not directly associated with the pursuit of raw materials, markets, or living space. In fact, many foreign activities reflect a desire for security, status, prestige, or military advantage. But in general, the kinds of foreign activity, and the overall extent of activity, are likely to reflect the *combination of demands and capabilities within a society.*

A growing population, of itself, generates new demands — demands for an ever greater 'irreducible minimum of food and other indispensable resources.'[16] This 'irreducible minimum' is determined in part by basic biological requirements, but also largely by historic experience and what individuals have come to expect. In this regard, every application of technology — insofar as it is seen to better citizens' material lot — generates new and higher thresholds of popular demands.

Moreover, while popular demands are often fueled by technological advancement, technological growth can create demands of its own. Technology (i.e., knowledge and skills) permits people to explore new vistas, harness energy, and exert some influence over their environment. Technology is instrumental, even definitive, in the development of new specialized capabilities, and these, in turn, are crucial to the quest for resources and energy. Yet, while having some obvious benefits, the practical application of technology requires new and/or greater resources. In the words of Choucri and North:

> *The more advanced the level of [a society's] technology — from the stone axe to the nuclear reactor — the greater the variety and quantity of resources needed by that society.* Applications of technology

---

[16] Choucri and North, 'Dynamics,' p. 86, emphasis omitted.

consume (or, more properly, 'degrade') certain amounts of energy even when technology is used for 'positive' purposes.[17]

Only as the demands of a growing population and advancing technology combine with a society's specialized capabilities, however, is lateral pressure produced. A society's specialized capabilities can include commerce, finance, mechanized agriculture, light industry, heavy industry, merchant marine, geological and marine exploitation capabilities, and so on. But a characteristic of all specialized capabilities is that they are costly and time-consuming to develop. On short-notice, the quantities and qualities of specialized capabilities cannot be significantly advanced except at extremely high costs. As a result, the specialized capabilities developed (or not developed) by a society at any one time introduce constraints and help to determine what a society can and cannot do at some future time.

So it is with lateral pressure and its manifestations. A kind of 'law of the instrument' appears to operate. A society experiencing urgent demands is very likely to express lateral pressure, if at all, via means made possible and economical by the particular specialized capabilities *previously* developed. Similarly, a society generating very high demands but lacking specialized capabilities as vehicles of outward expansion would tend to have its skills, energies, and resources absorbed by the urgent task of satisfying these demands, not in the time-consuming, resource-draining, and reward-postponing development of specialized capabilities.

Once demands and capabilities generate lateral pressure and expansion, the resulting extended activities can become politicized. 'Politicization' here refers to the process by which a society's political leaders (*a*) come to claim and believe that some of the society's outwardly extended activities constitute society-wide (or national or imperial) 'interests' that 'ought' to be fostered and protected and (*b*) can mobilize overall societal resources and energies at some costs toward the end of fostering and protecting them.

The politicization process is relatively simple where the society's economy is simple, class differences are not sharply articulated, the absence of surplus production has precluded the development of partially autonomous state apparatus, and rank or status is accorded only on the basis of age, sex, or birthright. Under these circumstances, whether or not a given extended activity is in some sense necessary to the preservation of a social order is, relatively speaking, a straightforward question. It is a question likely to be similarly answered by all participants in the society,

---

[17] Choucri and North, 'Dynamics,' p. 87, emphasis in original.

whatever their positions. And even where families or bands or clans within a society have their own particular extended interests and proceed to protect them by their own means, this is not problematical. For in the absence of a state claiming a monopoly over the legitimate use of force, such actions do not constitute threats to the established order.[18] Such circumstances have in fact characterized social organizations throughout the vast majority of humankind's nearly four million year existence. Comparatively recent has been the history of social development departing from these circumstances. The story of that development is also the story of increasing complexity in the politicization process.

Critical components of that story involve the emergence of the state as an agent claiming to monopolize the legitimate use of violence within the society *and* the development of complex forms of economic organization. Far from distinct, the two developments are mutually dependent and largely rooted in technological and population changes that make them possible. Despite differences, the many occurrences of these joined developments have several noteworthy features in common. In general, forms of economic organization emerging out of technological changes, population developments, and prior experiences (*a*) would occasion possibilities for a more complex division of labor, (*b*) would enable the generation and extraction of production surpluses above and beyond what people would immediately consume, (*c*) would open the way for increased competition among people and groups for resources and wealth, (*d*) would provide possibilities for the uneven accumulation of wealth, and (*e*) would enhance opportunities for experimentation, innovation, and further technological developments and associated demographic changes. It would thereby make possible (and, in the eyes of those who stand to benefit, 'necessary') the erection of state-like agencies to (*f*) maintain and administer the general social order, (*g*) defend the stratification of society, and (*h*) create, rationalize, and enforce norms and values assuring preferential access to social benefits among those who legally possess resources or otherwise control the flow and distribution of resources.

To be sure, the commonalities across such developments are often masked by differences in degrees of absolutism, pluralism, or democracy or by differences in domestic modes of production. They are masked, also, by differences in the degrees to which states are able to turn patternings of, say, religion or language to their advantage. And they are masked, still further, by differences in terms of states' capacities to maintain order through the manipulation of symbols, through the distribution of rewards, or through the crude exercise of naked force and terror upon the populace.

[18] North, op. cit., p. 38.

The differences in these and other significant details are many — as many and varied as are the historical and environmental conditions in which different states emerge and evolve.

Despite the differences across the long-historical sweep and many geographic locales of such occurrences, it is the commonalities that must be underscored. States can be said to emerge amidst the confluence of opportunities and demands generated by patterns of technological and population growth and the development of specialized capabilities — *the same processes that predispose societies to expand.* Insofar as these opportunities make competition among groups and classes for accumulations of surplus production and other resources possible and likely, the emergence of the state is necessary to discipline and perpetuate that competition, and the emergence of the state is possible because it is from some accumulated surplus that the state can extract the energy of its own existence. Owing its own existence to the society's growth and the portion of the surplus it can extract, the state is then inclined to sustain and amplify the processes out of which it was born.

If the state and the society are to endure, however, *the state must be partially autonomous.* It must be more than a vector off the forces that made it possible. For it is the partial autonomy of the state that permits it to intervene and make creative corrections in the social and economic order when the myopic and competitive choices of those who immediately stand to benefit would carry the system into crisis and disintegration. To the extent that the state succeeds in this partially autonomous capacity, it does so in part by enunciating, enforcing, and acting in accordance with general social values and norms that reproduce the overall social order and rationalize each person's place within it. It does so in part by claiming to embody the history, present, and possible futures of the society as a bounded, identifiable, final social unity. It does so in part by constructing and revising administrative arrangements to manage the consequences of technological changes and reconcile social manifestations within the pre-existing order. And it does so in part by claiming, enforcing, and exercising the exclusive right to the use of force and violence.

The state does not always succeed, though. Those who would seize upon opportunities to establish a state undertake what can only be seen as a formidable, almost insurmountable task. Nearly as formidable are the tasks of those whose participation gives the state its later form. And accordingly, many are the instances of abortive attempts to establish state apparatus and of established states disintegrating. In large part, the difficulties stem from the fact that the state cannot escape the demands, constraints, and pressures generated by technological and population growth.

Moreover, with each problem 'solved,' with each layer of bureaucratic growth in the state itself, with each new symbol of authority, and with each new function assumed, the state establishes commitments that are difficult to rescind, has social effects limiting choices of the future, imposes greater claims upon the resources of the society, and constrains the recombinatorial possibilities for creative adjustment.

In short, the state, like any agency of political leadership, must contend with dilemmas of mounting demands and diminishing resources. Only the dilemmas are more serious. *Born amidst opportunities and demands generated by processes of lateral pressure, and disciplining and contributing to the acceleration of these processes, the state claims and tries to impose a final social unity where none can exist.*

Complexity in the politicization of a society's outwardly extended activities reflects these historical processes and the complex social, economic, and political forms to which they give rise. Whether or not a given extended activity is in fact seen to represent a 'national interest' that 'ought' to be fostered and defended depends upon configurations and interplay among many factors. Some of these, the least yielding, are to be found in the degree to which a given kind, quantity, or locus of extended activity is critical to the answering of actual and likely technological and population demands of the present and future. The question, essentially, is this: what would be the overall costs to the society — in terms of its capacity to maintain normal structures, answer demands, and sustain growth (however unequal) — of not engaging in this or that activity? In principle, the more costly it would be to stop (or not undertake) a kind or level of expansionist activity, the more likely would be the politicization of the activity, and the more extensive would be the costs taken by the society in its defense.

Yet overlaying this and severely complicating the politicization process are patternings of competition and conflict among groups and classes, each seeking, with varying degrees of success, to equate its own interests with those of society at large; societal norms, values, symbols, and expectations built up under the weight of historical experience; the state itself, with its own cumbersome bureaucracy, its own need to rationalize its past practices, and its own need to justify its own burden upon society; and countless, highly subjective individual decisions, each taken under conditions of uncertainty. In the face of this complexity, it is small wonder that Choucri and North assert that 'it is often very difficult to predict which interests are likely to be defended . . .'[19] Small wonder, too, that

---

[19] Choucri and North, *Nations in Conflict* p. 19.

states sometimes politicize and undertake to foster and defend foreign 'interests' in ways that, in retrospect, appear unnecessary, even suicidal.

B   Bilateral Processes: The Dynamics of Rivalry

A society's continuing expansion increases the probability that its spheres of activities and politicized interests will collide with those of other societies. As these *intersections* intensify, the resulting possible outcomes are almost boundless. Indeed, much of the generative quality of history — the tendencies of enduring historical trends and structures to converge, recombine, and produce a rich new set of relationships seemingly marking the opening of a new epoch — can be attributed to the emergent combinatorial possibilities that such intersections afford. Intersections always bear implications for both conflict and integration: integration proceeds through the creative working through of conflicts occasioned by historically emergent intersections. Conflict occasioned by intersections always results in some degree of integration among as well as within the societies whose activities collide.

To simplify, three general patterns, each pointing to relationships between intersections and resulting political–economic outcomes and effects, can be identified: (1) where a 'stronger' society's lateral pressure generates expanding activities penetrating a 'weaker' society, (2) where a society predisposed to lateral pressure cannot express it due to obstacles posed by a 'stronger' society, and (3) where two expanding societies having roughly equivalent specialized capabilities collide. At any historical moment, a single society may find itself involved in two or more such relationships at once (e.g., a 'strong' society may be penetrating 'weaker' societies at the same moment it is colliding with others that are equally 'strong'). Over time, the fact of differential growth among societies means that a single society may pass through several such relationships with respect to others (e.g., a society whose disposition to lateral pressure is blocked by a 'stronger' society — even a 'weak' society that is one-sidedly penetrated by a 'stronger' society — may later emerge as equally 'strong,' and may later begin to penetrate other 'weaker' societies).

The labels 'strong' and 'weak' are highly relative. They refer, in particular, to the relative capacities of societies' specialized capabilities to express lateral pressure and to resist or limit other societies' expressions of lateral pressure. Specialized capabilities include not only military arms but also diplomatic skills, comparative production and trading advantages, foreign assistance resources, investment capital, administrative capabilities, communications and transportation technologies, means of cultural diffusion (such as missionaries and foreign advisors), colonists and homesteaders willing to secure and transform distant lands, and much more.

The first pattern occurs where an expanding society encounters a much weaker society, a society having insufficient specialized capabilities to resist. The emerging relationship tends to be integrative, but asymmetrically so. In general, and with the intensification of intersections over time, much of the social and economic structures of the weaker society will be bent to conform to the satisfaction of the demographic and technological demands of the expanding, high lateral pressure society. This may occur, as among feudal monarchs, as part of a conscious will to control more territory — thereby to enhance the resources to be extracted by the state; but it also tends to occur even where people of the stronger society initially *express* no intention to dominate or control. The stronger society may draw upon the population of the weaker to import slaves or to provide inexpensive local labor for the extraction of raw materials, or it may send forth its own colonists to drive the indigenous populations back from the coastline, away from the fertile plains, or into the confinement of reservations. Members of the stronger society may seek to create certain forms of industry in the weaker society, and may destroy indigenous industry at the same time. The stronger may construct transportation and communication systems so as to abet the economic integration of the weaker within the stronger's now expanded frontiers, and it may simultaneously distort the patterns of social movement and communication that had long preexisted. The stronger may send missionaries or educators or experts in agronomy to bring local peoples under the tutelage of 'superior' culture so that they too might 'master' their environments, and it may also wreck an existing culture that had sustained the local society through famine, flood, and centuries of long winters. The result, overall, is to transform the weaker into a 'reflection' of the stronger.

But the result involves the stronger society as well. Having wielded power beyond itself, the stronger society is likely to begin to order itself as *a power*. That is, widely shared norms, values, and expectations may come to include notions of 'manifest destiny,' 'white man's burden,' or the 'grandeur' of empire. The society's political structures may come to include large bureaucratic agencies of colonial administration or foreign assistance. Its military may begin to rationalize its domestic support by reference to the 'necessity' of conquest, and the military may alter patterns of bestowing rank and honor to correspond to experience in extending an empire. Large sectors of the economy — from agriculture to finance to light manufacturing to weapons industry — may come to be predicated on the expectation of sustained access to a widening field of raw materials, markets, inexpensive labor, and so on. *All such changes have profound influences upon the politicization process* — on what will and will not be defined as the 'national interest' of the future.

The second pattern occurs where a society with a disposition to expand encounters the extended sphere of influence of a society that is stronger in terms of its specialized capabilities — a society that is able to limit the expansion of the first. If the first society is simply overwhelmed by the stronger — whether by military force, competitive economic advantages, or other means — then this pattern is just the reverse of the first. But if the expansion of the first is resisted or turned back by the stronger, and if the stronger expresses its own lateral pressure, not toward the first, but in *other* directions, then the weaker represents the case of a society whose predisposition to express lateral pressure simply cannot be acted upon. The moment is not without its impacts. For being unable to exercise in activity the dynamics of its lateral pressure disposition, the society may internalize this moment within the shared beliefs comprising the society's collective memory. It may internalize it as a moment of frustrated rightful aims or perhaps as an episode in a long history of 'encirclement' or 'containment' by others.

Moreover, in the society somehow blocked from realizing its lateral pressure predisposition, the state may crumble if it is unable to creatively respond to sharpening dilemmas of demands and resources. The society as a whole may disintegrate in the absence of political means to effectively regulate and turn to productive ends the mounting competitive tensions of the overall economy. Alternatively, the society encountering obstacles in one geographic direction, or one kind of activity, may redirect its expansionist energies in other directions or in other ways. It may turn toward the consolidation of vast unsettled frontiers, for example.

Or, as a third alternative, there may emerge among some groups, classes, and political leaders an inclination to strengthen the state toward certain ends. That is, in a way reflecting the politicization process, the state may seek to turn shared frustrations to advantage, establish pretexts and rationales for extracting or redirecting increasing amounts of resources, mobilize social energies, limit foreign influence, and encourage the building of specialized capabilities intended to confront and overcome obstacles in the future. It may do so by purporting to embody the society's destiny beyond the obstacles of the present. Importantly, the qualities of such internal developments tend to reflect the obstacles the society confronts (as these refract through the politicization process shaped through the society's history). Whether these developments take the form of economic mercantilism, militaristic developments as expressed in such rationales as *Lebensraum*, are resource specific as in notions of 'energy independence' or are more general as in notions of 'self-reliance' — all are to some degree reflections of the society's external environment and the kinds of specialized capabilities poised against its growth and expansion. In the very process of withdrawal in the face of obstacles, the society tends to interiorize within its economy, social norms and values, and visions of its future the obstacles it has met and will prepare to meet in the future. *The external obstacles of the present may enter and become part of the politicization process bearing on the society's future.*

The third pattern, the pattern of principal concern here, occurs where the expanding activities of one society intersect with those of a second and the two societies' specialized capabilities are situated in very rough parity. The pattern bears both integrative and conflictual potential. Integrative possibilities exist to the extent that groups or sectors within each society can increase their wealth, status, and prestige under conditions of political cooperation *and* the political structures of each society can sustain or enhance their capacities to extract resources, maintain the existing social order, and sustain growth through encouraging or permitting interchange. Conflictual possibilities exist to the extent that the prestige, wealth, or status of groups or sectors within each society are threatened by prospects of interchange under conditions of political cooperation *and* the political structures of each society are unable to sustain growth through encouraging or permitting interchange.

Seldom, if ever, does an intersection entail only integrative possibilities or only conflictual possibilities. To the degree that the intersecting societies are complex, a mix of integrative and conflictual possibilities emerges. To the same degree, the societies' capacities to discern and act upon these possibilities are seriously confounded by complexities of the politicization process described earlier.

In principle, there can exist circumstances wherein two societies, neither clearly dominant, intersect on limited dimensions of activity such that the growth potential of each is enhanced for some time and ramifications within each society generate further mutually productive intersections. Under some circumstances, groups within each society or elements of each state (particular agencies with particular constituencies and tasks) might find it to their advantage to encourage or create cooperative political arrangements or institutions to manage or coordinate certain intersecting activities.

Yet to the extent that these cooperative endeavors foster growth of the societies involved — to the extent that other dimensions of activity are drawn into intersection — it becomes likely that sooner or later historically-wedded patterns of the two societies will come into conflict. It becomes likely that further cooperative momentum will entail what are widely perceived to be serious costs in terms of a society's norms, values, expectations, (relative) growth potentialities, and governmental systems — all of which reflect the partially unique history of each society. And these costs are likely to be perceived as greater to the extent that differential growth between the two societies yields the widening of socio-economic gaps in certain dimensions. Again, surely, when and over what dimensions of activity conflicts emerge depend upon the complexities of the two societies' respective politicization processes. But the generalization remains. *Unless each society is able to direct these conflict-prone aspects of its lateral pressure, not into intersection, but in another direction outside the bilateral relationship — and unless the two societies are able to do so in a way that sustains roughly equal growth between them — then integrative tendencies can be part of the process generating conflict among societies.* In many circumstances, protracted integrative movement between two high lateral pressure societies requires, at the same moment, their abilities to direct some aspects of their lateral pressure toward other societies having fewer specialized capabilities and therefore unable to resist. It may even require their *coordination* of their 'externalizations of costs.' Baldly put, *sustained integration among the 'strong' sometimes presupposes their protracted dominion over the 'weak'.*

Competition, then, is perhaps the more likely consequence of extended intersections between two societies having comparatively equal specialized capabilities. 'Competition' implies that two societies are increasingly attending to, and responding to, the activities, resources, and capabilities of one another. More specifically, it refers to

... rivalry between two or more individuals or groups for some prize. The prize may involve either a constant or expanding surplus within a society, a valuable but diminishing resource; a rank, status, or position of power ...; or some other social, economic, political, or cultural advantage. Competition may also be viewed as an effort on the part of each individual or group to keep ahead of the rival in some type of race. ... The prize may be fixed: a particular resource; an absolute level of industrial, military, or other capability; a constant rate of growth. ... Or, the prize may be relative and subject to change: achieving or maintaining 'first place' in terms of production, armament, wealth, power, prestige.[20]

[20] North, op. cit., p. 39.

Competition, furthermore, need not be antagonistic. But where the stakes include scarce resources or scarce positions that can be interpreted as vital to the societies, hostile attitudes are likely to emerge. Here, still again, the complexities of the politicization process are critical.

Against this background, a critical feature of competitive dynamics can be seen. *The moment that even one kind of intersecting activity between two high capability societies is politicized — and to the degree that the intersection is intense — at that moment a dynamic logic is likely to be set in motion. The intensification of competition between two societies is likely to involve strong tendencies to draw more and more dimensions of each society's activities into the vortex of competition and under the rubric of overall 'societal interests.'* The whole politicization process is likely to be skewed by virtue of the fact that each step toward identifying an extended activity as a 'societal interest,' and each taking of some societal costs toward its competitive protection, involves some form of social and economic commitment, some reallocation of scarce societal resources, some mobilization of human energies, and some set of symbolic rationalizations that together limit the choices of all who participate in determining what is and is not in the societal interest at some future time.

The process may be long protracted. And especially if it is, it becomes likely that every aspect of society — from the education of children to its highest level of industry — will partially reflect it. Bending more and more aspects of life to the race, the competing societies may each become more tightly integrated than before. But they may also come to assume norms, expectations, purposes, economic patterns, and governmental structures quite unlike what individual people, groups, or whole classes of either society might have earlier wanted. It is true that the two societies can become more clearly identifiable as unitary, single-minded 'actors' in international politics. But it is also true that, in so becoming, the societies can surrender much of what they were and might have become to the rivalry in which they are entangled. In short, *integration within each can come to reflect and express the interdependencies of rivalry between the two societies.*

Competition is thus *multidimensional.*[21] Each competing society can come to gauge its own level, advancement, or rate of advancement against others along several dimensions in the belief that a failure to match or exceed others along these dimensions somehow endangers important societal interests. Technology, industrialization, standard of living, culture, military capabilities, external areas of interest or influence, outer space,

---

[21] Choucri and North, *Nations in Conflict*, p. 19.

agriculture — these are among the dimensions along which competition can occur. Even among allies, gross and growing discrepancies along these dimensions can awaken actors to the proposition that theirs is not a partnership among equals.

Of these dimensions, military capabilities are often assumed to be the most salient. When two societies are mutual rivals and a military gap between them is wide or widening, the lagging actor can come to feel that its interests, perhaps its survival, are threatened. One possible response for the lagging but aspiring actor — the actor's preferred response if the necessary resources are available at acceptable opportunity costs — is to narrow or close the gap by building military capabilities. When tendencies to respond in this way are intense and reciprocated, the bilateral competitive processes interlock, yielding the reaction process usually called an arms race.[22] But competition *is* multidimensional, and an alternative response for the military lagging actor is to become more assertive, and hence more openly conflictful, in proclaiming its interests and commitments — as if to replace with expressed resolve what it lacks in firepower, hardware, or manpower. This last relationship might be called a 'compensatory dynamic.'[23]

While the more profound roots of major power confrontations are to be found in the mutual antagonism engendered, even institutionalized, by bilateral competition, the more proximate occasions for these confrontations include both (*a*) the states' issue-specific assertions of commitment and resolve and (*b*) the provocations that become more likely as the societies' intersections intensify. A *provocation* is an incident, event or situation occurring at a point of intersection in the extended activities of two societies. More specifically, it is an incident or situation that, by its nature, poses a significant threat of sudden change in a region's internal political character, external orientation and alignment, and/or external economic relationships. Though they are often beyond the two states' exact control, such happenings are frequently seen to pose significant threats (or exploitable opportunities) to one or both. And because such happenings occur at points of the societies' intersecting interests — indeed, to the degree that intersections are intense — the threats that result assume salience for the societies' mutual relations.

When they see threats to their societies' extended interests, state leaders may be disposed to directly intervene, to attempt to stabilize (or exploit) a situation, and to engage in demonstrations of strength and resolve. If two

[22] See Lewis Richardson, *Arms and Insecurity* (Pittsburgh: Boxwood Press, 1960), the seminal work in the area.
[23] The notion of a 'compensatory' dynamic is further elaborated in Chapter 10.

intersecting powers are on friendly terms, such activities might be co-operatively undertaken. But between rivals, such activities have explosive potential. One state's involvement, whether to stabilize or exploit, can heighten a rival's perception of threat and lead it to take counter-action: warnings, ultimata and counter-demonstrations of resolve. With the continuation of this process, the intensity of conflict can spiral upward.[24] Viewing the situation as a test of wills, each leadership is likely to assert its unwillingness to retreat and sacrifice interests in the face of force or threat of force. And in the meantime, each feels compelled to prepare for a contingency that it views as increasingly probable: war.

C   Multilateral Processes: The Dynamics of Balance

As states respond individually to their rivals, as they engage in conflicts, and as they are constrained by a variety of domestic factors, their acts and their failures to act can profoundly affect the systemic distribution of military capabilities and the overall configuration of conflict. A state simultaneously engaged in conflict with several others can become isolated. A state whose capability developments lag behind those of others can lose influence and become vulnerable. And a rapidly growing society — one whose mounting military preparations are commensurate with its outwardly expanding interests and commitments — can pose a threat of preponderance in the system.

State leaders tend to be sensitive to these changes. They tend to be sensitive, that is, to the degree that (*a*) they perceive a potentiality of physical violence in their conflicts and (*b*) they perceive an absence of supranational norms or authorities capable of limiting the use of violence.[25] Given these conditions, changes in the military capability distribution and conflict configuration are seen to profoundly alter the external contexts of their purposive acts, creating new opportunities, new constraints, and new perceived imperatives for their own performance. Acting under these new conditions, state leaders are inclined to point to 'anarchy' and take guidance from a variety of balance of power logics. They are inclined to appeal to images of balance of power amidst anarchy

[24] See e.g., Ole Holsti and Robert C. North, 'The History of Human Conflict,' in Elton B. McNeil (ed.), *The Nature of Human Conflict* (Englewood Cliffs, N.J.: Prentice-Hall, 1965); Eugenia V. Nomikos and Robert C. North, *International Crisis: The Outbreak of World War I* (Montreal: McGill–Queens University Press, 1972).

[25] Kenneth Waltz puts it this way: 'two or more states coexist in a self-help system, one with no superior agent to come to the aid of states that may be weakening or to deny any of them the use of whatever instruments they think will serve their purposes.' Kenneth Waltz, *Theory of International Politics* (Reading, Mass.: Addison-Wesley, 1979), p. 118.

to help them order information, and orient and rationalize their choices, in a complex system.

When a state's leaders point to anarchy and respond to the balance of power logic of any moment, it *seems* an almost primordial act. It is an act well rationalized with reference to Enlightenment philosophical metaphors regarding the human being in a pre-contractual state of nature. It is an act finding historical precedents in episodes in relations among, say, Henry VIII of England, Francis I of France, and Charles V, emperor. It is an act equally well explained in terms of a 'prisoner's dilemma' in which states have somehow found themselves entangled: the separate survival-seeking units, the states, exist in one another's presence, and there are no agents that can effectively guarantee each state's survival in the face of the military threats that others might present. As for the individual of a society whose once orderly fabric is suddenly torn apart in crisis, the individual state is stripped bare of all moral and legal restrictions, and self-help principles *necessarily* prevail. The apparent difference is that, at the international level, the crisis is eternal. It is eternal because, unlike the national society in collapse, an orderly international society seems never to have been constructed. This, at least, is the *appearance* of the isolated moment in time.[26]

Yet, when one lifts one's sights from the immediate instance, it can be seen that *the appearance of global anarchy among states, far from being an eternal condition, is a social structuration taking form and moment through long-historical processes that were rich in their possibilities.* In the long sweep of human experience, conditions resembling anarchy among multiplicities of interacting, mutually aware societies — conditions occasioning the exercise of balance of power logics — may have occurred many times. But up until quite recently within this long time frame, these conditions were rare and represented passing, localized instances resulting from improbable intersections among differentially expanding social groups. Up until quite recently, these conditions were so infrequent that, with the exception of occasional centers of growth and expansion, expectations of external anarchy and balance of power seldom if ever were so regularized as to become routine aspects of a society's political structures and practices. Only with growth, mounting lateral pressure, and the recurrence of intersections among multiplicities of societies did notions of anarchy and multilateral balance of power come to be of lasting relevance to the lives of the world's societies. And even then, importantly, the sustained relevance of these notions has always presupposed the

---

[26] See Waltz, *Theory*, as the best statement of this position.

intersecting societies' *prior* developments of state apparatus to monopolize the legitimate use of violence. It is only the superimposition of the state upon the society, a superimposition firehardened through the recurrence of its rivalries, that permits the society to act as a singular unit in a 'state of nature.'

Moreover, upon close inspection, the appearance of anarchy can be seen as an expression of an historically emergent regime of international society, and the balance of power logics of any moment can be seen as among the rules by which the regime is known and reproduced. The proposition is this: The leader's seeming primordial act of responding to the balance of power logic of any moment, while founded upon claims of 'necessity' with respect to state survival, is in fact *contingent* upon the long-historical processes by which each state and its possible competitors took form amidst differential growth and lateral pressure. It is contingent upon the historical process wherein a multiplicity of states emerged to enforce and extend social unities, discipline competition, maintain social stratifications, and accelerate growth. At the same time, the act of responding to a balance of power logic has its own consequences. In perceiving images of anarchy and conforming to balance of power logic at any moment, the leader can take actions reproducing the state as an agent capable of so conforming and can contribute to the perpetuation of violence-prone international political conditions wherein other leaders are likely to apply the same imagery, perceive similar 'imperatives,' and conform to the same logics. In this way, the balance of power logics of any moment can become routinized as the moments of their applicability are reproduced. The logics can become routinized as rules of an enduring regime. And through the routinization of their separate responses over time, the states can come to interiorize the regime and its rules within their own unquestioned identities — within their instruments, plans, policies, and relations to their respective societies. Indeed, so deeply can the regime become bound within the identities of the participant societies that their observations of the rules become acts, not of conscious obedience to something external, but of self-realization, of survival as what they have become.

Western European absolutist monarchs, being closer to the emergence of such relationships, often understood this. Consequently, they could speak of European society, on the one hand, and balance of power and anarchy, on the other, as two sides of the same system. It is a point often lost among modern leaders, however. It is seldom understood that the prisoner's dilemma of violence-prone anarchy is not just an external relationship in which pre-identified states have somehow become entrapped but an internal relationship deeply embedded in what the world's societies have come to be. In fact, among contemporary states, the regime is often unseen, often mistaken for a pre-contractual state of nature, because without this regime with the appearance of anarchy, the societies and states would be something other than what they have become.

A state leader's balance of power logics, then, are historically conditioned subjective behaviors. They are crucial links between a society's systemic environment and the state's objective behavior within it. Being subjective, cognitive behavior cannot be directly observed. One can only infer the operation of guiding logics, and the rule system they reflect, from the observation of patterned relationships between systemic characteristics, on the one hand, and a state's observable behavior, on the other. Four alternative balance of power logics are discussed here and outlined in Table 1.2. Each logic is specific to a particular purpose.

At a basic, sometimes subconscious 'psycho-logical' level, a national leader is often inclined to *maintain consistency* in the perceived configuration of conflict by altering the directions and intensities of his state's conflict and cooperation behaviors.[27] A 'consistency maintenance' logic is in fact a kind of psycho-logic involving balance, or congruence, in the relations among the components of a cognitive structure. In this regard, a leader's private cognitive structure and public policy rationalizations are each 'consistent' when, for every pair of other powers, a leader can observe in effect: 'a friend of my friend is my friend,' 'a friend of my enemy is my enemy,' and so on. In general, these logics dispose a leader to reshape his beliefs about relationships, and his own policies and actions, such that these will constitute a consistent structure. In general, also, to the degree that the leader publicly rationalizes policies and practices by reference to such a psycho-logic, and to the degree that such a psycho-logic is widely shared among participants in the politicization process — to that degree the leader's decisions and actions may be constrained by the limits of consistency in the future.

At the same time, a state leader must reconcile his efforts to maintain consistency with a felt-need to maintain balance of power in the more conventional sense of the term.[28] When confronted with a prospect of war

[27] The word 'psycho-logic' is used here to represent that class of models addressing balance or consistency in cognitive fields. The term was coined by Robert Abelson and Milton Rosenberg in 'Symbolic Psycho-logic: A Model of Attitudinal Cognition,' *Behavioral Sciences*, Vol. III (1958). As Abelson and Rosenberg describe it, such a logic might mortify a logician.

[28] See, for instance, Morton Kaplan, *System and Process in International Politics* (New York: Wiley, 1957); Richard Rosecrance, *Action and Reaction in World Politics* Boston: Little, Brown, 1963); Martin Wight, 'Balance of Power,' in Herbert Butterfield

Table 1.2 *Four Purpose-Specific Balance of Power Models*

Model	Purpose	External referents	'Rules': prescribed action	Observable multilateral dynamics
Consistency maintenance	A psychological predisposition to maintain consistency in the conflictual/cooperative relationships among actors, so that, of any pair of 'others', an actor can observe, in effect, 'a friend of my friend is my friend,' 'an enemy of my friend is my enemy,' etc.	Degrees and directions of conflict/cooperation exhibited by 'others.'	When 'others' are seen as mutual enemies, differentiate between them: friendly/unfriendly relations with one demands unfriendly/friendly relations with the other. When 'others' are seen as mutual friends, generalize across them: friendly/unfriendly relations with one requires friendly/unfriendly relations with the other.	Negative links across an actor's two directions of behavior can reflect this or an 'isolation avoidance' model. Positive links reflect an actor's tendency to psychologically generalize across 'mutually friendly others.'
Isolation avoidance	Avoid resource draining two-front confrontations, and gain allies in confronting immediate adversaries, so as to (a) deter adversaries from offensive action or (b) defeat adversaries in event of war.	An actor's recent and current peak levels of hostility with others.	Reduce conflict/increase co-operation/avoid crises with one actor when involved in high level hostilities with another.	Negative causal links from an actor's peaks of conflict (thresholds of violence) in one direction to its routine (normal) and peak (threshold of violence) levels of conflict in another.

Preponderance opposition	One nation's preponderance means others' decline to subordinate status, so 'defeat or constrain' actors that are most threatening to gain military preponderance.	The relative military capabilities of others in the system, especially as these relationships change.	Reduce conflict/increase co-operation/avoid war with the 'weaker' among others and join with them in opposing the proto-preponderant 'stronger.'	Where A is an actor, B and C are others, and B's capabilities are increasing relative to C's there is a positive link from the B-C gap to A's conflict toward B and a negative link from the B-C gap to A's conflict toward C.
Threat assessment	Build military capabilities in response to an external threat, and calculate threat in terms of both capabilities and intentions of others.	Others' military capabilities interacting with the directions and intensities of others' conflict in system.	Increase/decrease proportional response to others' capability advances as actor is increasingly/decreasingly the exclusive target of others' conflict.	Response coefficients of arms race processes mediated by (i.e, interact with) directions and intensities of others' conflict and cooperation in the system.

most leaders are inclined to *avoid isolation*. For a leader guided by what might be called an 'isolation avoidance' logic, the international system is less balanced or imbalanced to the extent that the actor is the prime focus, or target, of others' conflict and military capabilities. Thus, when one state is engaged in intense conflict with a second, the first will be inclined to reduce conflict and increase cooperation toward 'third powers' — perhaps to form alliances with third powers, possibly to free its own capabilities that were formerly committed against third powers, and almost certainly to deny the immediate adversary analogous opportunities. Isolation avoidance dynamics are particularly likely as conflict levels approach the brink of war.

A state's leaders also seek to *constrain other powers' aspirations to preponderance in the system*. A 'preponderance opposition' logic[29] takes as central the goals of national survival and independence. It assumes (*a*) that other states' military capabilities potentially threaten these goals and (*b*) that the minimal condition for the pursuit of these goals is that no other power is militarily preponderant. Thus, according to this logic, the closer another state advances to preponderance, the less balanced the system. A state will be inclined to increase its opposition to the other state that is most rapidly advancing militarily while increasing cooperative initiatives toward remaining states. The logic extends as well to the case of a leading military power reaching to extend its own dominion.

A power's military capability building reflects its leaders' efforts to accurately *assess the threats to its interests inherent in others' capability advances in the context of a multi-power system*. Within a two-power system, one actor is likely to view all military advances of a second as a threat to itself and respond accordingly.[30] But with three or more powers, a first power's competitive responses are likely to reflect the propositions that (*a*) a second power's capability building is directed in part at third powers, or (*b*) its own capability commitments can be reduced by virtue of its alliances. A 'threat assessment' logic directs attention to the international configuration of conflict for indications of the changing directions to which others' military capabilities are committed. It weighs in particular the relative concentrations of others'

and Martin Wight (eds.), *Diplomatic Investigations* (Cambridge, Mass.: Harvard University Press, 1966).

[29] My treatment of this logic reflects in part the sociological literature on coalitions in the triad. See Theodore Caplow, 'A Theory of Coalition Formation,' *American Sociological Review*, Vol. XXVI (1961); Jerome A. Chertkoff, 'A Revision of Caplow's Coalition Theory,' *Journal of Experimental Social Psychology*, Vol. II (1967). See also William H. Riker, *The Theory of Political Coalitions* (New Haven, Conn.: Yale University Press, 1962).

[30] Thus, one would have the pure case of the two-nation arms race. See Richardson, op. cit.

conflict behavior within the system.[31]

While this brief review of several balance of power logics suggests more or less immediate links between systemic characteristics and state behaviors, it also suggests why, as implied above, the logics potentially cut deeply into the identities of the states themselves. For if the logics of balance of power make certain choices 'imperative,' they also establish requisites for the political structures in which choices are made. They require the establishment, sustained support, and continual rationalization of political institutions that are capable of mobilizing the full resources and energies of a society in response to the perceived imperatives of balance on their own terms. They require agencies of state that can claim sovereignty *vis-à-vis* external demands, and a partial autonomy *vis-à-vis* immediate societal demands, while acting in the name of society to maintain consistency, avoid isolation, oppose others' aspirations to preponderance, and build military capabilities in response to changing threats. Reproduced in the dominant security regime, the logics of balance of power do more than orient and rationalize the state's high political choices. They also rationalize elements of the state itself.

Thus, for societies entering such a system — due to their own growth and expansion or to the growth and expansion of others — deep political adaptations to the requisites of participation become likely. Regardless of a society's mode of production, its central or peripheral place in the world economy, or its leaders' long-run worldly vision, the demanding logics of balance of power impact upon the state. This, for example, was the American experience, where American growth eventually thrust the US within the globally extending politics of Europe, led to a denial of the original sentiments of Washington's Farewell Address, and helped to rationalize the creation, sustained support, and political institutionalization of a large military establishment. Too, this process is echoed in the Soviet experience, where the Soviet Union's history amidst the politics and economics of Europe lent justification to the growth of the state and its devotion of scarce resources toward the building of an enormous military capabilitiy. And it is a process recurring in recent Chinese experience, where Mao's attempts to pursue a nativist socialist road were constrained by a 'need' to adapt to the logics of participation in a balance of power in which Western growth had engulfed China. In a process continuing today, the enduring regime of balance of power tends to fashion the political elements that participate in its reproduction.

[31] For a relevant treatment, see Karl W. Deutsch and J. David Singer, 'Multipolar Power Systems and International Stability,' *World Politics*, Vol. XVI, No. 3 (April 1964).

III   A RECURRING HISTORICAL PROGRESSION

This presentation of the three classes of dynamics began simply. It began by envisaging the single society responding to technological and population demands amidst environmental constraints. Following a progression toward greater complexity, it then traced how domestic growth might generate lateral pressure, expansion, intersections of interests, competition, military rivalry, confrontations, balance of power, and deep societal adaptations to the 'requisites' of participaton in a violence-prone order. This progression has unfolded repeatedly throughout history – sometimes partially and sometimes completely. In the patterns of its recurrence, it has left its imprint on all societies of the world.

The unfoldings of this progression among the peoples of the globe have not resembled 'symphonic' form. As experienced through time and among societies, the progression has not proceeded with the continuous and homogeneous temporality of an orchestral whole. One cannot envision the world's societies starting from some common point of departure, advancing in harmony within a uniform temporal medium through movements and passages, together reaching some stirring climax, and then settling into a satisfying and tranquil coda. Rather, over long-history and among societies, the progression has been experienced in a way resembling the musical form of the period in which the frequency of its recurrence most definitely began to quicken. If anything, the progression can be said to have recurred in a way resembling a fugue. And as in a fugue, it is the variations, dissonances, partial expressions, counterpoint, and welling tensions that give the overall form its texture and energy. Five concepts describe the patterns of recurrence in the progression from growth through rivalry to balance of power.

First, among societies throughout history, the progression from growth through rivalry to balance of power has occurred *asynchronously*. The asynchrony concept refers to the proposition that societies have neither initiated the progression at the same moment nor traversed it at the same pace. On the contrary, the progression has *at least partially* unfolded whenever and wherever environmental conditions, demographic patterns, knowledge and skills, forms of economic organization, and relative capabilities have combined to generate lateral pressure and collisions of peoples and cultures. Asynchrony thus implies that one should not expect to find the same dynamics at work among all societies at any moment in history. However, the asynchronous unfoldings of this progression are not necessarily independent, spontaneous events reflecting only conditions and experiences local to the individual societies themselves — as the next concept indicates.

Second, among any set of societies, the progression unfolds *equifinally*. Derived from general systems theory,[32] the equifinality concept indicates that among social groups, similar 'paths' of development and sequences of dynamics often lead to different outcomes, and similar outcomes are often reached by different 'paths' and sequences of dynamics. With respect to international relations, equifinality reflects the existence of an international system that differentially impacts upon and elicits uneven adaptations among various societies. To this one must add the notion that the international system itself involves and is unevenly shaped by the asynchronous, phase-related actions, interactions, and interchanges of societies through time. In these terms, insofar as rapidly growing, high lateral pressure societies differentially shape the system inhabited by themselves and others, their own expressions of the progression can help to determine when, where, and in what forms other societies will experience the progression from growth through balance of power. In these same terms, what is remarkable about the modern era is that these equifinal tendencies have come to join nearly all societies in the continuous reproduction of a common global system — a comon system whose most obvious characteristic is that it accelerates differential growth, turns the differentials to productive advantage, and further accelerates differential growth thereby.

Third, so long as patterns of differential growth are sustained among any set of societies, and so long as societies are more or less continuously propelled into interaction thereby, the progression described above tends to be *irreversible*. Irreversibility implies that societies, once adapted to the complexities of later phases, cannot return to what they were. They cannot, in general, because a society's adaptations to each phase involves the mounting of material constraints and demands, the establishment and rationalization of institutional responses, and the assembling and recombination of experiences in people's beliefs and values. They cannot, more specifically, because later phases tend to be self-reproducing given continuous interaction among a multiplicity of political units. As indicated above, societies that adapt to rivalry and balance of power in effect reshape their identities through their internalizations within states of a dominant rule system — ironically, a rule system whose appearance is of anarchy. Well justified by the ready argument that others might confirm the prophecy of violence contained in the image of anarchy, states are constrained to perform according to their justifications in order to sustain support. Well

[32] See Ludwig Von Bertalanffy, *General Systems Theory* (New York: Braziller, 1968), pp. 131–49.

supported, their performance contributes to the reproduction of the systemic conditions by which their imagery is validated, their support is justified, and their identities are reconfirmed. The termination of later phases thus becomes likely only when altered patterns of growth incapacitate state action conforming to later phases, when diminishing lateral pressure among the several no longer propels societies into interaction, or when, through violence, empire supersedes pluralism.

Fourth, the progression is *cumulative*. In traversing its phases, societies do not divest themselves of the influences of prior phases. Instead, complexity emerges as the demanding tasks and challenges of each subsequent phase mount atop the old. As societies respond to the threats born of emergent rivalry, they remain constrained to answer the demands of technological, economic, and population growth. As societies adapt their state institutions, instruments, and policies to the logics of balance of power, the dilemmas of rivalry continue to claim attention and resources, and the dynamics of differential growth continue to generate mounting demands, limit the mobilization of capabilities, and constrain the latitude of official choice.

Fifth, the several phases of dynamics are joined in *antagonistic* relation. Antagonism does not refer to interpersonal or interstate conflicts that are subjectively known among participants. It refers, rather, to the absence of indefinite harmony — and the likelihood of emergent contradictions — among the several phases and the purposes and processes associated with them. In ways that participants do not readily comprehend, the dynamics associated with each phase will tend to produce purposes, behaviors, and conditions that — given time, movement, and the aggregation of small changes — come into relations of mutual incompatibility. In particular, the long-recurrence of attempts to answer the demands of growth can contribute to the emergence of new purposes — the politicized felt-need to maintain or extend access to resources, for example. These, in turn, can motivate behaviors or limit choices in ways sharply at variance with the logics of balance of power. Likewise, a state's persistent efforts to answer the threats of rivals can give rise to institutional patterns, investments of resources, and external commitments amidst which prior patterns of growth cannot be sustained unchanged. These are just two very general examples. They suffice, though, to illustrate the significance of antagonism. The phases are joined — inextricably so — but they are not joined in additive, steady-state relation. They are joined by the long-term tensions among them.

The antagonism of phases makes it probable that the aggregation of fragmented attempts to respond to the demands of growth, or answer the threats of rivals, or sustain balance of power will prove to be mutually defeating at some future time. The antagonism of phases makes it likely that well-meant 'solutions' to any set of problems will contribute to the reproduction and sharpening of other, often more costly problems. And the antagonism of phases makes it certain that, for dilemmas of 'welfare' and 'warfare,' lasting solutions cannot be separately designed.

The progression from growth through rivalry to balance of power, then, is a creative progression, and what it creates and recreates is the modern security problematique. The problematique takes its form from the emergence of a complex network of relationships intertwining the concurrent dynamics of growth, rivalry, and balance of power among a multiplicity of interacting societies. It finds its definition in the fact that, due to the intertwining, the dilemmas associated with the three classes of dynamics are antagonistically poised: they are mutually confounding, mutually perpetuating, and insusceptible to piecemeal resolution. The problematique found its earliest crystalization as an irreversible phenomenon, enduring to this day, when the dawn of absolutism first signalled the antagonistic conjuncture of differential growth, rivalry, and balance of power in pre-capitalist Europe. It draws its vitality and persistence from its perseverance beyond feudalism and into the modern era — an era in which accelerating differential growth and expansion have sustained societies in interaction, denied their withdrawals from the network, and drawn still other societies within. And it takes its current global scope from the most recent cycles of a long-historical spiral — a spiral involving the asynchronous, equifinal, and cumulative unfoldings of the historical progression among a widening span of the world's societies. Here, in this complex, far-reaching network of relationships, are some of the most important sources of conflict and some of the most formidable obstacles to peace among modern societies.

Choucri and North's study of pre-World War I relations among European powers focused on one forty-five year cycle in the long-historical spiral just described. Their analysis and their model grasped important aspects of the network of relationships giving form to the modern security problematique in the period 1870–1914. As experienced in this period, the problematique reflected the very dynamics whose recurrence through history contributed to its emergence. Here, in Europe of 1870–1914, were the dynamics of differential growth, rivalry, and balance of power joined in violence-prone tension. Here, too, the several societies' experiences of these dynamics were asynchronous and equifinal, cumulative and irreversible. It was as if this long European moment leading to World War I telescoped within it the whole history of the spiral — and its possible future as well.

World War I did not afford a final resolution to the tensions it released. Nor have any of the wars to follow resolved them. Nor have any of today's 'new and unprecedented' issues of resource scarcity, or environmental deterioration, or economic instability, or nuclear terror, or global interdependence somehow supplanted the modern security problematique. On the contrary, it is of the very nature of the security problematique that it at once presents itself as a set of new and particular problems requiring particular solutions and takes its tragic dynamism from the fragmented attempts to resolve the problems it presents. It is of the very nature of the security problematique that it unevenly confronts groups of people with crises and conflicts requiring their rational responses and joins these responses in secret complicity with the reproduction of an irrationally destructive global system. It is of the nature of the security problematique that it seems susceptible to decomposition and analysis within disciplinary and traditional boundaries yet dominates thought by confining it therein. And it is of the nature of the security problematique that it invites people to mistake the leading edge of technological and social change for a new epoch and, in so doing, condemns people to refashion the dilemmas and crises of the past.

These are serious and no doubt controversial charges. They require elaboration. In fact, as will be argued later in this book, they bear critical implications for international relations theory, its practical responsibilities, and even for the very grammar of thought underlying scientific research on international security dilemmas.

For the moment, though, a more immediate task presents itself. So far, the charges just made remain bald assertions, and their relevance to contemporary international relations remains to be seen. Still in doubt at this point in the presentation is the capacity of the conceptual framework to orient operationally reproducible, empirically grounded inquiry bearing critically on contemporary international politics. Indeed, it remains to be seen whether or not the dynamics of growth, rivalry, and balance of power are today as tightly intertwined as Choucri and North found them to be in the period preceding World War I. The contemporary forms in which the security problematique finds expression have yet to be illuminated. Thus, the task before the chapters of Part II is to draw upon the framework and begin to sharpen the depiction of the modern security problematique as it has come to be manifested among today's major military powers: the Chinese People's Republic, the Soviet Union, and the United States. The charges advanced above, together with their theoretical implications, can be precisely articulated and adequately qualified only after this task is performed.

What has been said in this framework might be encapsulated in many ways. One approach is by way of a metaphor to natural phenomena: sometimes when ocean currents collide they generate an eddy. Sometimes small eddies, when they come into contact, form a violently swirling whirlpool. And sometimes a whirlpool, once set in motion, bends adjacent currents into its turbulent vortex, widening its arc and increasing its energy thereby. The story of the emergence and globalization of the modern security problematique bears a resemblance to such phenomena.

A second approach to summarization refers to the two contrary themata that have long oriented internationalist thinkers: the Kantian vision of an emergent global unity and the Hobbesian vision of persistent war among states.[33] In the modern security problematique, the two tendencies are joined as one. The story of the modern security problematique is the story of an emergent global unity manifested in the individuation of fragmented and violence-prone social and political forms.

But the third approach to encapsulation is perhaps the truest to the premises and arguments of the conceptual framework. It focuses neither on impersonal phenomena nor on abstract theoretical traditions. It focuses, instead, upon humankind — individuals and societies — in relationship with the environment. The concepts developed here, it might be said, address the historical processes of human and social alienation on a global scale. They address the historical processes by which there emerged a humankind that is at once arrogant in its mastery of nature and humbled before the violence-prone global 'state of nature' that it has created.

[33] These two themata are well articulated by Hedley Bull, *The Anarchical Society* (New York: Columbia University Press, 1977).

CHAPTER 2

Method of Analysis: The General Model

I OVERVIEW OF A MODELING PROGRESSION

As observed earlier, few of the conceptual framework's propositions, taken individually, are unfamiliar. The framework developed in Chapter 1 is synthetic. Most of its propositions regarding growth, rivalry, and balance of power are deeply rooted in one or more of the analytic traditions addressed to the causes of war and the preconditions for peace. Yet the framework differs from many of these traditions. It differs in that it deals with numerous interconnected hypotheses that cut across several levels of analysis and transcend the domains of security politics and political economy. Underlying the synthesized framework is the premise that the long-term sources of conflict and violence among societies are embedded, not in discrete causal factors, but in an historically emergent network of interdependencies among variables. It is only within the context of an overall system, the network of relations posed by the framework, that individual propositions can be examined and the extended implications of each proposed relationship can be seen. It is only within the context of the system that one can begin to discern the far-reaching proportions of the modern security problematique.

The extended interconnections and processes posed by the framework, though, are not readily apparent from Chapter 1's strictly verbal presentation. As the several hypothesized relationships are taken together — as they must be — the complexities are compounded. It becomes difficult to grasp how happenings in any one sector or at any one level are hypothesized to reverberate through time and across sectors to yield a variety of consequences. It becomes difficult to discern how the patterns of well-intended choice that give form to any one process reverberate through a network of relationships to constrain other choices, shape dilemmas, and contribute to unwelcome outcomes. What is more, given the inter-dependencies and return effects posed, it is especially difficult to maintain rigor and consistency in the empirical examination of hypothesized relationships as they apply to contemporary relations among China, the Soviet Union, and the United States.

For these reasons, the research reported in this book has necessarily advanced from the strictly verbal framework of Chapter 1 to the systematic symbolic representation of hypothesized relationships in the form of a probabilistic general model. Unlike the verbal representation, the explicit modeling of ordered relationships among China, the Soviet Union, and the United States permits the application of systematic quantitative techniques. In turn, these techniques lend discipline to the empirical analysis of complex relationships. They provide established, explicit, consistent, and operationally reproducible decision rules. Used in conjunction with a model's expression of prior theory, they provide useful guidelines for the interpretation of historical patterns and the complex processes they reflect.

The transition from verbal framework to general model has been neither direct nor automatic, however. Serious problems attend any reasonably large-scale model-building enterprise. The problems are all the more serious in this study for reasons discussed at length in Appendix A. As there elaborated, the conceptual framework reflects a dialectical conception of reality, and modeling is conceived of as an open-ended, criticism-conscious enterprise participating within this reality. These commitments raise profound challenges to the alleged scientific expectations, norms, and conventions that today dominate methodological discourse in the study of international relations: the expectations, norms, and conventions contained in positivist philosophers' reconstructions of natural scientific practice. Appendix A thus attempts to reconstruct a research logic that is more expressive of these commitments — and is more appropriate to model-building in international relations generally. It is a logic intended to orient the application of scientific research tools, and sustain the operational reproducibility and empirical grounding of modeling practice, as researchers participate in an international reality whose 'laws' are often historically emergent, susceptible to change, and deplorable. This is the rational logic approximated in this study.

This logic has oriented a three-stage econometric modeling progression from the conceptual framework to the development of the general model.[1] In effect, this modeling progression has emulated the historical

[1] This progression is outlined at greater length in Appendix A. All research has been conducted using TROLL (Time-shared Reactive On-Line Laboratory), an

progression presented in Chapter 1. At the first stage, model-building concentrated upon propositions regarding 'unilateral processes' – the dynamics of growth, expansion, and domestic decision-making, as these might impact upon patterns of conflict, cooperation, and thresholds of violence among China, the Soviet Union, and the United States. At this first stage, alternative measures, functional forms, equation formulations, and parameter estimation strategies were used; regressions were run over various subperiods as well as the full 1950–72 period; and the sensitivity of results to these alternatives was assessed. The main product of this first stage was a single structural model, a unilateral process model, that was uniformly specified for all three powers.

Next, in the second stage, the unilateral process model was treated as strong prior information for the specification of unilateral dynamics, and model-building concentrated upon the framework's propositions regarding 'bilateral processes.' Model-building here focused on the dynamics of inter-sections, competition, rivalry, and provocations. Again, alternative measures, functional forms, equation formulations, and estimation strategies were used and assessed over the full period and subperiods. A combined unilateral–bilateral process model was produced.

Finally, the third stage involved the repetition of this approach – this time incorporating propositions on the multilateral dynamics of balance of power. The main result was a combined unilateral–bilateral–multilateral process model: *the general model of the Sino-Soviet-American triangle.*

The purpose of this chapter is to introduce the general model resulting from this progression and thereby set the stage for the empirical analysis of Part II. The introduction begins with a discussion of the data base and measures developed for this study. Next it presents the model in both equation and graphic form. It concludes by considering some of the methodological and interpretational issues that frame Part II's empirical analysis.

II CONCEPTS, DATA, AND MEASURES

Throughout the research progression described above, one anchoring focus has been upon societal attributes – the three societies' technological,

interactive computer system for data analysis, modeling, regression analysis, simulation and forecasting. Developed by the Massachusetts Institute of Technology Department of Economics under the auspices of the National Bureau of Economic Research, TROLL is now administered by the NBER and is accessible internationally through NBERNET, the NBER's computer network. See *TROLL Reference Manual* (Cambridge, Mass.: National Bureau of Economic Research, 1977).

economic, demographic, and resource matrices. Change in these attributes among societies reflects processes of differential growth. For purposes of analysis, these slow-changing, difficult-to-manipulate variables have been treated as *exogenous* or predetermined with respect to Sino-Soviet-American relations.

Reflecting the conceptual framework, six classes of *endogenous* or system-determined variables have been identified. It is variation in these variables that the analysis is intended to explain. The six classes of endogenous variables are:

Expansion: Each society's outwardly extending activities. Its manifestations of extended felt interests, commitments, and 'psycho-political borders.'

Military Capabilities: Each society's specialized capabilities with the capacities to physically take, punish, and destroy.

Bilateral Intersections: Overall regional collisions in the outwardly expanding activities, felt interests, and commitments of each *pair* of major powers.

Bilateral Provocations: Overall destabilizing events and situations occurring at points of intersections for a *pair* of major powers that (*a*) can threaten (or pose exploitative opportunities for) the powers and their extended interests and, hence, (*b*) are likely to be proximate occasions for confrontations and intense conflicts.

Normal Conflict and Cooperation: The level of conflict and cooperation that best represents each actor's routine, day-to-day activities toward each target over a period of time. Normal levels are sensitive to the full cooperative-conflictual range of activities. Consequently, they reflect the overall degree of amity/enmity, trust/suspicion, and perceived interest complementarity/incompatibility that each actor addresses toward each target.

Thresholds of Violence: The proximity of an actor to war in its behavior toward a target within a span of time — a conflict 'ceiling' for each actor-target pairing over some period. More so than normal conflict and cooperation levels, thresholds of violence are sensitive to the occurrence (or non-occurrence) of confrontations and crises among major powers.[2]

---

[2] Although highly sensitive to the occurrences of politico-military crises — and to the conflict spiral dynamics so characteristic of major power interaction in crisis — a threshold of violence does not necessarily denote a crisis.

Just as the attribute variables are associated with individual societies, so also are these conceptual variables partitioned as to their association with individual societies, dyads, and directed dyads.[3] Thus, one can conceive of Soviet, American, and Chinese expansion and military capabilities; Sino-American, Sino-Soviet, and Soviet-American intersections and provocations; and normal conflict and cooperation and thresholds of violence from China toward the US, from the US toward China, from the US toward the USSR, and so on. In total, there are twenty-four endogenous conceptual variables in this study.

To represent these conceptual variables, including societal attribute variables, a large data collection has been assembled.[4] Excluding transformations, it now includes metric and metricized annual time-series data for some fifty different variables for each of the three societies.[5] It also includes additional series to represent events and attributes for other societies and geographic regions. All money series (e.g., gross national product, total trade, arms aid) have been converted to constant 1970 dollars in order to facilitate cross-national comparison and to rule-out inflation-induced bias.[6]

Wherever possible, alternative measures for each concept (and alternative estimates on each measure) have been assembled. The necessity of assembling these alternatives stems from an important characteristic of the conceptual framework. Unlike theories that treat concepts as atomistic 'data containers,'[7] the framework presents most of its concepts in *relational* terms. Technology, for example, is not discussed as a conceptual box that might contain and be exactly represented by data on, say, tools, machines, or economic output. It is, rather, presented relationally: as the application of knowledge and skills that is intended to serve objectified

[3] A 'dyad' is a two-nation pairing. In the Sino-Soviet-American triangle, there are three dyads: Sino-Soviet, Sino-American, and Soviet-American. A 'directed dyad' refers to a two-nation pairing wherein one nation is designated the 'actor,' the other is designated the 'target,' and attention focuses on actions directed by the actor toward the target. Thus, in the Sino-Soviet dyad, for instance, one distinguishes between Chinese actions toward the USSR (CPR → USSR) and Soviet actions toward the CPR (USSR → CPR) as two directed dyads. There are of course six directed dyads in the Sino-Soviet-American triangle.

[4] All data used in this study are available through the Inter-University Consortium for Political and Social Research at the University of Michigan, Ann Arbor.

[5] Metric data refer to naturally measurable phenomena, such as trade volume or men under arms. Metricized data are data developed through the use of systematic judgmental procedures to infer and assign values to dimensions that are not directly observable but are thought to be implied by observables.

[6] See Appendix C for further details.

[7] See G. Sartori, F. Riggs and H. Teune, *The Tower of Babel: On Definition and Analysis of Concepts in the Social Sciences* (Pittsburgh, Pa.: International Studies Association, 1975).

human purposes and that creates new demands and new 'needs.' In the same way, the concept of expansion is relationally presented as a manifestation of lateral pressure, a reflection of mounting demands combined with available specialized capabilities under environmental constraints. The relational character of the concepts implies that the validity of any measure cannot be predetermined on the basis of a one-to-one rule of correspondence between individual measure, on the one hand, and the definition of the concept in and of itself, on the other. Instead, in a way reminiscent of Donald Campbell's notion of 'criterion validity,'[8] a measure is said to validly represent a concept within some arena and during some historical period only if it empirically exhibits the relationships that are contained in the concept itself. This means that the empirical examination of relationships hypothesized in a model are at the same time tests of the adequacy of measurement. This also means that it is necessary to carefully evaluate the sensitivity of empirical results — at every stage — to the use of competing measures.

Table 2.1 shows the concept-to-measure linkages for the six classes of endogenous variables contained in the general model and examined in Part II of this book. It must be stressed that Table 2.1 is incomplete in one very important respect. It shows only those measures which appear in the most recent version of the general model and for which results are reported here. It neglects the many other measures, and combinations of measures, examined in the three-stage progression.[9]

While Table 2.1 reflects an attempt to construct and use the best measures possible, it would be a gross mistake to assert or believe that each measure is anything more than an approximation of the social processes conceptualized. In part, this is due to the fact that, as mentioned, the concepts themselves are relational. But in part, also, this is due to the inaccessibility of complete and cross-nationally comparable data series on alternative and in some ways preferable measures. For instance, the measures of expansion and intersections shown in Table 2.1 are based upon foreign trade data. As will be seen in Part II of this book, these measures do appear to reflect and express some of the relational properties attached to concepts of expansion and intersections in the conceptual framework. With respect to these concepts, though, it would have been very desirable to have also empirically examined alternative measures, such as direct and portfolio foreign investments, foreign aid, the foreign basing of men under arms, and so on. Unfortunately, such data could not

---

[8] Donald Campbell and Donald W. Fiske, 'Convergent and Discriminant Validation by the Multitrait-Multimethod Matrix,' *Psychological Bulletin*, Vol. LVI (1959).

[9] See the discussion in Appendix C.

Table 2.1   *The Concept-to-Measure Links*

Conceptual variable	Measure	Calculus*	Comments
Expansion	Trade Dispersion #2	Standard deviation across all R_i of A's % of each R_i's total trade (in US \$). $\dfrac{\text{Actor } A\text{'s Total Trade}}{}$	Reflects both aggregate intensity and dispersion across regions.
Intersection	A–B Intersection #2	$\sum_{i=1}^{N} (A$'s trade in $R_i) \times (B$'s trade in $R_i)$	Weights most heavily intersections in R_i of trading 'importance' to A and B.
Provocation	A–B Provocation #2	$\sum_{i=1}^{N} (A$'s trade in $R_i) \times (B$'s trade in $R_i)$ $\times$ (Number of Local Wars in R_i)	Weights wars as provocative depending on degree of intersection within a region.
Military Capability	Defense Expenditure	For US, official (constant 1970) dollar budgetary data are used. For CPR and USSR, annual defense expenditure figures derived from analysts' responses to question: how much would it cost, in US constant dollar equivalents, to develop, purchase, operate, and maintain military capability?	Extremely gross aggregates, but the only non-force-specific measures with capacity to gauge both military 'effort' and 'potential.'
Normal Conflict/Cooperation	Mean level of conflict, represented as $A \rightarrow B$ (Mean).	The mean across all conflict levels exhibited by A toward B within a one year period. Events scaled on 30-point conflict implications for violence scale.†	Sensitive to low and midrange as well as high conflict events.
Threshold of Violence	Peak level of conflict, represented as $A \rightarrow B$ (Peak)	Highest conflict level of A toward B within one year period. Events scaled on 30-point scale.†	Single highest point reached on the scale; may be viewed as a conflict 'ceiling.'

*'A' is an actor, 'B' is a second actor (or target), and R_i is a geographic region. Trade and defense expenditure data are in millions of constant 1970 dollars.

†On this scale, a score of '1' indicates very low conflict and high cooperation while, at the other extreme, a score of '30' represents very high conflict, usually escalating armed hostilities.

be obtained to span the full twenty-three year period for all three societies. As elaborated in Appendix C's discussion of these and related considerations, the issue of measurement remains highly problematical.

An important question can be raised in this regard: why use the same measures across all three societies, all three dyads, and all six directed dyads? Would not the use of different measures for different societies and dyads afford both sharper measurement and possibilities for better empirical fit? The answer cannot be phrased in terms of a desire for elegance or symmetry or the generalizability of theory. Instead, the answer is implicit in the conceptual framework and in the objectives of modeling. On this point, a brief digression is in order.

The relational concepts of the conceptual framework allow that various concepts can find expression in different modes or forms during different periods or junctures. As repeatedly stressed in Chapter 1, for example, lateral pressure can find expression in colonial expansion, foreign trade, foreign investment, travel, the activities of missionaries, ocean exploration, space flight, and much more. The *modal form* in which any one society exhibits lateral pressure, if at all, will be that form that is most expressive of (*a*) the kinds of demands it generates as combined with (*b*) the specialized capabilities it has previously developed under (*c*) environmental constraints on various kinds of activity. In addition, the concept of *equifinality* encourages one to think about a *dominant mode* of lateral pressure at the systemic level during any historical period. That is, to the extent that leading high capability, high lateral pressure societies engage in activities penetrating some region, the demands and capabilities of the region are likely to be affected over time, and societies of the region are likely to adapt to the forms of lateral pressure expressed by the leading, high lateral pressure society. When, in turn, other high lateral pressure societies are predisposed to expand into the same region or challenge the leadership of the first, they are likely to be largely limited to using kinds of specialized capabilities and to expressing modes of lateral pressure that are consonant with the region's previous social, political, and economic adaptations. In this way, one kind or mode of expansion and intersections can become and persist as dominant during some period of time or across some region of space. This is what Choucri and North mean when they say that 'During the period 1870–1914 the dominant mode [of expansion] among European great powers was colonial acquisitions.'[10] To use the same measures of expansion and intersections across all actors and dyads is simply to assert that the measures are or might be approximate

[10] Nazli Choucri and Robert C. North, *Nations in Conflict: National Growth and International Violence* (San Francisco: W. H. Freeman, 1975), p. 177.

reflections of the dominant mode of some period.

Moreover, given this conceptual background, the use of the same measures is essential to the pursuit of one important objective of modeling. As a kind of 'register' permitting the logical inference of causal connections from empirical data, *a model should help to identify the differential abilities of societies to shape the contexts of their mutual relations.* The question is not just, how do societies express lateral pressure? Nor is it simply, on what dimensions of activity do societies intersect? While these questions are important, another question needs to be addressed. In any historical juncture, what are the relative abilities of societies to shape and direct the dominant mode of expansion and intersections in the system? If, as the framework asserts, intersections can shape both integrative and conflictual opportunities, and if intersections can and do condition rivalry, provocations, and then confrontations, then this question directs attention to some of the critical loci of change in the system. It goes to the deeper meaning of power: the differential capacities of societies to shape the conditions, circumstances, and agendas of manifest interstate conflict. By using comparable measures in an integrated model, it becomes possible to use statistical results as a basis for inferring tentative answers to this question.

The normal conflict and cooperation measures and the thresholds of violence measures are constructed using metricized data.[11] They are based upon events culled from the *New York Times Index.* Using a procedure reported in Appendix C, each event was systematically coded as to 'actor' (initiator) and 'target' (recipient or object) nation. Each event was then scaled on a thirty-point scale of conflict and implications for violence developed by Lincoln E. Moses and others.[12] On this scale, a score of '1' represents very low conflict or high cooperation while, at the other extreme, a score of '30' represents very high conflict, usually war.[13] Researchers at Stanford Studies in International Conflict and Integration, working under the direction of Robert C. North, produced an early version of the conflict data for the Sino-Soviet and Sino-American dyads covering

---

[11] See n. 5, above.

[12] Lincoln E. Moses, Richard A. Brody, Ole R. Holsti, Joseph B. Kadane, and Jeffrey S. Milstein, 'Scaling Data on Inter-Nation Action,' *Science*, No. LVI (1967).

[13] Strictly speaking, this scale is not an equal interval scale. However, by convention, the data thus produced are treated as if they were in fact interval-scaled. See Choucri and North, op. cit. For related arguments see Sanford Labovitz, 'The Assignment of Numbers to Rank Order Categories,' *American Sociological Review*, Vol. XXXV (1972); and Robert Abelson and John W. Tukey, 'Efficient Conversion of Non-Metric Information into Metric Information,' in E. Tufte (ed.), *The Quantitative Analysis of Social Problems* (Reading, Mass.: Addison-Wesley, 1970).

1950–66. Subsequently, these data were rechecked, cleaned, and augmented for purposes of this study. The remainder of the conflict data — for the Soviet-American dyad, 1950–72, and for the Sino-Soviet and Sino-American dyads, 1967–72 — were produced especially for this research enterprise. The overall collection includes some 15,000 events.

Once the basic events collection was completed through 1972, these data were used to produce annual normal conflict and cooperation measures and annual threshold of violence measures for each of the triangle's six directed dyads. An annual normal conflict and cooperation measure is the *mean* conflict and cooperation level across all events exhibited by a single actor toward a single target over the course of one year. An annual threshold of violence measure is the *peak* or highest level of conflict exhibited by a single actor toward a single target during the course of a year. Figures 3.2, 3.3 and 3.4 in Chapter 3 plot these measures over the full twenty-three year period for each of the triangle's six directed dyads.

It has been indicated that all data, both metric and metricized, are annual aggregates. Each datum, each observation, represents a kind of 'trace' left by literally hundreds or thousands or even many millions of decisions. This is the case, not only of such measures as overall population or foreign trade, but also of measures of military capability building, normal conflict and cooperation, and thresholds of violence. While the latter reflect state decisions, it is a gross error to think of them as products of singular moments of purposive choice. Even thresholds of violence reflect the cumulative interplay of many governmental officials, advisors, and operatives, working within the limits of general sentiment and expectations, and establishing thereby a kind of 'ceiling' on the level of conflict exhibited toward another country. Such a level of aggregation must be borne in mind throughout this study. This book is concerned with long-term historical processes and trends. Its aim is not to explain or even describe discrete events.

III   THE GENERAL MODEL

A   Overall Form and Function of the Model

The general model is styled 'general' for two reasons. First, unlike other models preceding it in the three-stage modeling progression, the general model explicitly incorporates relationships representing all three classes of dynamics hypothesized in the conceptual framework: the unilateral dynamics of growth, the bilateral dynamics of rivalry, and the multilateral dynamics of balance of power. As in the framework's description of the modern security problematique, these three classes of dynamics are assumed to be poised in antagonistic relation. Second, the general model merits the label because, as noted above, it specifies identical relationships across all three societies and all three dyads.

In one most important respect the model is not 'general,' however. It will be recalled that the conceptual framework was developed with an eye to advancing a non-ahistorical story of the emergence, reproduction, globalization, and future passing of the modern security problematique. In contrast to this generality, the model represents the contemporary structural form of the security problematique as manifested in relations among China, the Soviet Union, and the United States. The model assumes that during the period examined some relationships are so very slowly changing as to be allowably treated as structural parameters. The model thus cannot be asked to account for the historical processes giving form and moment to the earliest historical expressions of the security problematique. Nor can it be asked to explain how the United States, the Soviet Union, and China have become heirs to the problematique as earlier experienced by Britain, France, Germany, and other powers examined in Choucri and North's *Nations in Conflict*. Nor can it be asked to explain the processes that will narrow the gap between the problematical, exploitative, violence-prone world that is and the preferred world that will be. To be sure, the model does allow for the idea that some relationships might be emergent, just as an aggregation of quantitative changes can give rise to qualitative changes. But on the whole, the general model is best seen as an incomplete representation of the highly structured processes that might account for the dynamics and reproduction of the modern security problematique among today's major military powers.

Nevertheless, as in Choucri and North's pre-World War I studies, a structural model does help one to see how an historical period can condense all history within its scope. According to the framework, the history of the modern security problematique is the story of the asynchronous, equifinal, irreversible, cumulative, and antagonistic joining of growth, rivalry, and balance of power within a widening geographic compass. It is the story of how differentially growing societies asynchronously adapt to their different experiences, collide in conflict as they seek to shape their worlds and one another as reflections of what they have become, and equifinally become part of a larger social unity in which phases of their historic pasts are cumulatively, irreversibly, and antagonistically poised in violence-prone relation. In an important sense, this story is never completed. Until accelerating differential growth reaches some limit in the world's capacities to sustain it, this story is likely to be endlessly repeated. Thus, from the standpoint of the framework, to view any period in the history of the problematique is to view its whole history telescoped, as it were, in a single moment.

Choucri and North's pre-World War I studies ably showed how a model can perform a *refractive function* and guide the interpretation of a particular period. By specifying a uniform model and modal measures across all actors analyzed, they specified the possible ways in which a story, prefigured by history, might have been manifested in the 1870–1914 period. Then they were able to use the model, in conjunction with empirical data, to infer differences in causal linkages — differences that helped them to identify how, amidst the possibilities, the story did in fact asynchronously and equifinally unfold during this period. The general model developed and used here is intended to perform the same refractive function in the empirical analysis of contemporary major power relations.

Apart from differences of measurement and functional form, the most noteworthy difference between the *Nations in Conflict* model and the present general model is that the latter integrates all powers, and their mutually directed behaviors, in a single representation. The Choucri–North model is a kind of single actor/generalized environment representation. In the Choucri–North work, the general form of one model is replicated as six distinct models: one for Britain, one for France, one for Russia, one for Germany, one for Austria-Hungary, and one for Italy. Each model is portrayed as a distinct system. Within each, the 'exogenous' activities and capabilities of other powers are distinguished only as to allies and non-allies, and the 'intersections' and 'violence behavior' of each state are measured in the aggregate, not with respect to particular powers. One therefore cannot meaningfully discriminate the processes contributing to, say, German 'violence behavior' against Britain from those influencing German 'violence behavior' against Russia. One cannot readily disentangle the effects of French and British arms building upon German arms building. And one cannot interpret how Anglo-German 'intersections,' as opposed to overall British 'intersections' or German 'intersections,' might have impacted upon British and German 'violence behavior' or 'alliances.'

Owing to a marriage of necessity and opportunity, the general model presented here does not have these limitations. The 'necessity' stems from three refinements in the conceptual framework as compared to the original Choucri–North proto-theory. The first is the framework's attempt to conceptualize balance of power dynamics more sharply. The second is the framework's attempt to further articulate the implications of symmetrical as opposed to asymmetrical intersections between societies. The third is the framework's discussion of bilateral provocations. In order to represent these revisions, it is necessary to specify distinctions among the other societies with which a single society might be interacting.

The 'opportunity' derives from the relatively small number of actors considered in this study. Choucri and North examined six in their pre-World War I studies. Consequently, were they to have tried to specify a unique relationship for each 'other actor,' they would have had to have included four additional terms in each equation for each 'influence of others' relationship. In their equation for 'violence behavior,' for example, there are five right-hand-side variable coterms, including 'military expenditures of nonallies' and 'violence of others.' To have broken these two terms down into variables for each of the five other actors would have required the net addition of eight coterms — an unwieldy and highly multicollinear thirteen in all. In this study, by contrast, the decision to discriminate among 'others' means the addition of only one term for each such relationship. In this respect at least, theoretical concerns can be realized in research practice without too great a loss of statistical power.[14]

B   Overview of a Block-Recursive Structure

The general model is a system of simultaneous equations. Within this system, each of the twenty-four endogenous variables appears as the left-hand-side or 'dependent' variable in one of twenty-four stochastic equations. The variation of each such endogenous variable is assumed to be explained by some combination of the weighted variation in right-hand-side or 'independent' variables, together with a constant and the influence of random error. The twenty-four stochastic equations, plus identity equations, make up the equation system.

The system conforms to what is called block-recursive form, a fact that requires a few words of elaboration. Because a variable that is 'dependent' in one equation is sometimes treated as 'independent' in another, one can speak of reciprocal interdependencies among variables: variation in one variable may be represented to both cause and be dependent upon variation in another, either directly or through some extended flow of dependency relations specified in the system. When such reciprocal interdependencies are specified to involve no leads or lags in time, then

[14] It should be noted that Choucri and North did initially specify and empirically estimate the parameters of what they called their 'long-form' equations. Their decision to employ the 'short-form' described above reflected the statistical considerations indicated in this paragraph. See *Nations in Conflict*, pp. 174–5, for a brief discussion.

the relationship is said to involve a simultaneous reciprocity or return effect. When, on the other hand, independent variables are not specified to be simultaneously and linearly determined by dependent variables, directly or indirectly (and assuming that the error processes exhibit certain properties), then the relationship is said to be recursive. In this light, to speak of the general model as a block-recursive system is simply to say two things. First, it is to say that the system contains 'blocks' of simultaneously and reciprocally determined variables. Within each block, dependent variables are or can be joined in relations of simultaneous reciprocity or can exhibit simultaneous return effects. Second, block-recursivity implies that relationships across blocks are recursive. That is, there are no simultaneous linear reciprocities or return effects across blocks. Across blocks, simultaneous relationships are one-directional only.

The twenty-four stochastic equations of the general model are contained in four blocks, as shown in Figure 2.1. Equations for each of the three countries' expansion, each of the three countries' military capability building, and each of the three dyads' bilateral intersections are contained in the simultaneously determined Block A. Block B contains equations

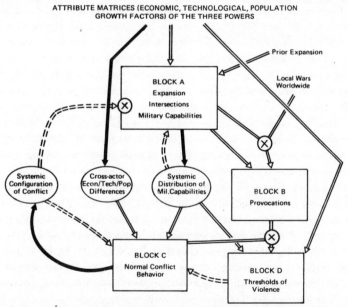

NOTE: The ellipses represent systemic/contextual factors (exactly defined), boxes indicate blocks wherein endogenous variables are simultaneously (and probabilistically) determined, dark arrows indicate definitional relationships, light arrows indicate main causal flows among blocks, dashed arrows indicate lagged relationships, and the symbol ⊗ indicates a nonlinear effect. See Fig. 2.2 for details and relationships within blocks.

Fig. 2.1 The general model: main causal flows among four blocks, with relationships to systemic-environmental factors.

for each of the three dyads' bilateral provocations. Equations for each of the six directed dyads' normal conflict and cooperation are contained in the simultaneously determined Block C. And equations for each of the six directed dyads' thresholds of violence are contained in the simultaneously determined Block D.[15]

The ellipses in Figure 2.1 are the loci of exactly determined systemic properties: the systemic configuration of conflict, the systemic distribution of military capabilities, and cross-actor economic, technological, and population differences. In the equation system, each ellipse is represented by a set of identity equations that exactly determines some aspect of a systemic property — say, the conflict configuration — in terms of combinations of variables at the foot of each dark arrow leading to an ellipse. Thus, for instance, aspects of the systemic military capability distribution are exactly determined by patternings of the three countries' military capability building, the output of Block A. In sum, the three ellipses are representations of the systemic context: aspects of an overall system that each society participates in shaping, to which all three might respond, but over which no single society has complete control.[16]

Figure 2.1 also affords a gross overview of the main causal flows specified across the four blocks. Factors predetermined with respect to Block A, including especially growth factors, impact upon mutually influencing patterns of Chinese, Soviet, and American expansion, bilateral intersections, and arms building. As specified, relationships *within* Block A to some degree depend upon their nonlinear interaction with the 'systemic configuration of conflict.' At the same time, the three societies' individual arms building, as determined in Block A, shapes the 'systemic distribution of military capabilities.' In Block B, in turn, patterns of bilateral provocations are shaped by the arms building of each power and by patterns of intersections combined interactively with (exogenous) total local wars worldwide. In Block C, simultaneously determined patterns of normal conflict and cooperation among the three powers are influenced by exogenously determined 'cross-actor socio-economic differences,' by aspects of the 'systemic distribution of military capabilities,' as well as by the effects of *prior* thresholds of violence. As shaped in Block C, the six directed dyads' normal conflict and cooperation then exactly determines the 'systemic configuration of conflict,' which, as indicated, conditions

---

[15] Relations within these four blocks are discussed in Section III.C , pp. 65–77.

[16] See Appendix E for the presentation of the identity equations, which involve simple arithmetic operations. The presentation of six basic stochastic equation forms in Section III.C reflects an attempt to make these arithmetic operations clear by fully expressing them within the right-hand-side coterms.

relations among expansion, intersections, and military capability building in Block A. In Block D, finally, thresholds of violence among the three powers are shaped by normal conflict and cooperation as combined interactively with current provocations, aspects of the 'systemic distribution of military capabilities,' and certain exogenous domestic factors. The reasoning behind this specification of a block-recursive structure becomes clear when one looks more closely at the specific relationships within each block.

C   Specific Postulated Relationships: Six Equation Forms

Figures 2.2A through 2.2D depict the specific postulated dynamics within Blocks A through D, respectively. In effect, Figures 2.2A through 2.2D are nested within the boxes or blocks of Figure 2.1. In each figure, those variables in boxes are the variables endogenous to the particular block shown. The label above the line in each box is the conceptual variable name. The label below the line identifies the corresponding measure from Table 2.1, above. This is the operational measure used in this study. In each figure, also, those variables with no boxes around them are predetermined (or exogenous) with respect to the block in question. One should note, however, that variables predetermined with respect to one block are sometimes endogenous elements of another block. Sometimes this is a direct linear relationship; for instance, predetermined defense expenditure terms in Block B (Figure 2.2B) are endogenous elements of Block A (Figure 2.2A). Sometimes more complex and nonlinear relationships are involved; for example, in Block A (Figure 2.2A) the relationship between any two countries' endogenous defense expenditures involves the nonlinear interaction or mediating effects of an aspect of the current 'systemic configuration of conflict,' which in turn is exactly determined by the normal conflict and cooperation variables that are endogenous to Block C (Figure 2.2C). For each relationship, an arrow away from a variable indicates that the variable is an 'independent' or right-hand-side variable in an equation meant to explain variation in the 'dependent' or left-hand-side variable at the head of the arrow.

The relationships depicted in Figures 2.2A through 2.2E are best described with reference to the equations corresponding to them. Although there are twenty-four endogenous variables in this model, this seeming complexity is due to the fact that the model joins all three actors and dyads in a single, integrated representation. There are only six classes of endogenous variables, and across endogenous variables of any class, all relationships are uniformly specified. There are, then, only *six basic*

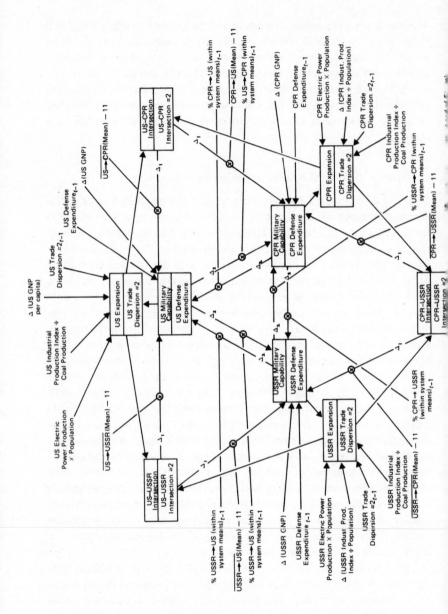

Fig. 2.2A   Block A: expansion, intersections, and military capabilities.

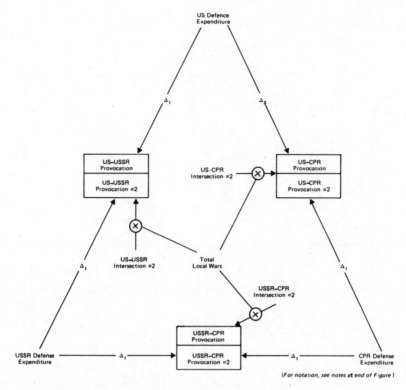

Fig. 2.2B   Block B: provocations.

equation forms. Appendix E presents the full system of equations, including identity equations. This discussion concentrates on the six basic equation forms.

The following discussion of the six equation forms requires the use of a simple notational convenience. That is, one makes each equation generalizable by referring to generic actors *A, B,* and *C.* In any of the following equation forms, actor *A* might be any one of the three actors, actor *B* might be either of the remaining two, and actor *C* would be the third actor. In these terms, an equation for *A*'s expansion applies uniformly for Chinese, Soviet, and American expansion. Similarly, an equation for *A–B* intersections or for *A–B* provocations applies uniformly for Sino-Soviet, Sino-American, and Soviet-American intersections or provocations. And in the same way, an equation for *A → B* normal conflict and co-operation or for *A → B* thresholds of violence would apply uniformly to US normal conflict or thresholds of violence toward the USSR, Chinese

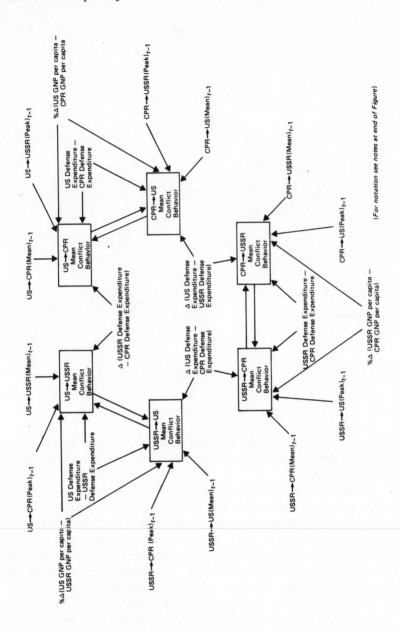

Fig. 2.2C   Block C: normal conflict and cooperation behavior.

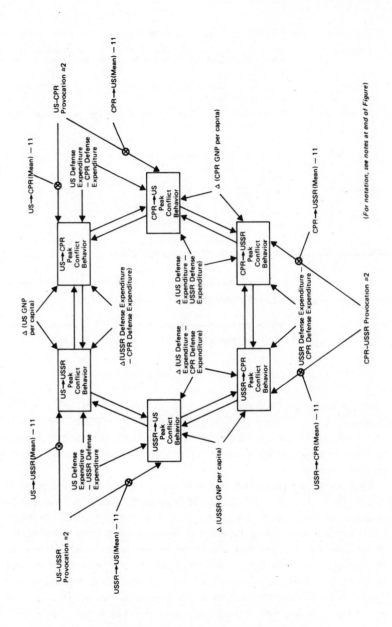

Fig. 2.2D   Block D: thresholds of violence

Symbol	Explanation
$A \rightarrow B$ (Mean)	'A' and 'B' are actors (like US, USSR, and CPR), '(Mean)' indicates a conflict level, and '$\rightarrow$' is read 'toward.' Thus, $A \rightarrow B$ (Mean) indicates 'A's mean level (or normal) conflict toward B.'
$A \rightarrow B$ (Peak)	Where $A \rightarrow B$ (Mean) indicates normal conflict, $A \rightarrow B$ (Peak) indicates 'A's threshold of violence toward B.'
$\overline{A \rightarrow B}$ (Mean) $- 11$	The bar over $A \rightarrow B$ indicates a three-year-lagged moving average; and 11 is a threshold level. Thus, $$\overline{A \rightarrow B} \text{ (Mean)} - 11 = \frac{\sum_{i=1}^{3} A \rightarrow B \text{ (Mean)}_{t-i}}{3} - 11.$$
% $A \rightarrow B$ (within system means)$_{t-1}$	The percentage of A's within-system normal conflict that is directed toward B, lagged one year: $$\frac{A \rightarrow B \text{ (Mean)}_{t-1}}{A \rightarrow B \text{ (Mean)}_{t-1} + A \rightarrow C \text{ (Mean)}_{t-1}}.$$
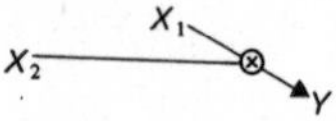 X_1 X_2 $\otimes$ Y	Indicates multiplicative interaction of X_1 and X_2 in their effects on Y. Alternatively, the effects of X_1 on Y depend upon the value of X_2.
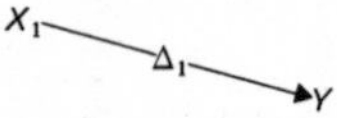 X_1 Δ_1 Y	Indicates that the one-year-change in X_1 (i.e., $X_{1_t} - X_{1_{t-1}}$) is entered in the equation for, and causally determines, Y.
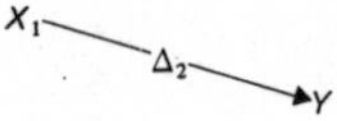 X_1 Δ_2 Y	Indicates that the two-year-change in X_1 (i.e., $X_{1_t} - X_{1_{t-2}}$) is entered in the equation for, and causally determines, Y.

Fig. 2.2E   Notation: symbols used in the model.

normal conflict or thresholds of violence toward the US, and so on. So expressed, each equation form is generalizable. To produce the twenty-four stochastic equations of the general model, one need only use the six basic forms discussed below and insert measures appropriate to the specific actor or actors involved.

Each of the six equation forms to follow conforms to the general linear model. There is, then, a left-hand-side dependent variable, Y, which is expressed as a linear function of (a) right-hand-side variables combined multiplicatively with unknown parameters, β; (b) the constant term, α; and (c) the disturbance term, μ. The task of regression analysis is to supply estimates of the βs, α, and μ in light of empirical data on left- and right-hand-side variables. The constant, α, represents the intercept of the regression function. It is an unknown parameter whose regression estimate is to be interpreted as the value that Y would assume were all right-hand variables to assume zero values — i.e., were the influences of right-hand variables somehow purged. The disturbance term, μ, represents the cumulative influences of error, principally from misspecification, measurement error, and random factors or chance. Complications of analysis surrounding these aspects of the analysis are mentioned later and are discussed at length in Appendix D.

With these notational features in mind, the six basic equation forms can be presented. The presentation proceeds block by block. The reader is urged to note the correspondencies between the equations described below and specific linkages shown in Figures 2.2A through 2.2D.

1. *Block A: Equations for Expansion, Intersections, and Military Capabilities*

Block A (Figure 2.2A) contains nine endogenous variables, and it is therefore represented by nine stochastic equations in the general model. However, these variables and equations correspond to only three basic forms: one for expansion, one for intersections, and one for military capabilities (defense expenditures).

The basic equation form for the three *expansion* equations is:

$$A\text{'s Trade Dispersion \#2} = \alpha_1 + \beta_1(A\text{'s Elec. Power Prod.} \times A\text{'s Population(1)} +$$

$$\beta_2\,[\Delta(A\text{'s Gross National Product} \div A\text{'s Population)}] +$$

$$\beta_3(A\text{'s Indust. Prod. Index} \div A\text{'s Coal Prod.)} +$$

$$\beta_4(A\text{'s Defense Expenditure)} +$$

$$\beta_5(A\text{'s Trade Dispersion \#2}_{t-1}) + \mu_1$$

The first variable coterm, (Electric Power Production $\times$ Population), represents the multiplicative growth of overall demands given mounting technology and population. The second coterm, Δ(GNP $\div$ Population), represents the proposition that population demands are subject to changing expectations as reflections of patterns of economic change.[17] The third coterm, (Industrial Production Index $\div$ Coal Production), introduces the important role of national resources: to the extent that they are domestically obtainable, inclinations toward expansion are likely to be reduced.[18]

---

[17] That is, as the *change* in per capita GNP mounts, the expectations of people regarding further growth are likely to increase accordingly, thereby contributing to current demands and expansionist dispositions. As will be noted in Chapter 4, the GNP component of this term is problematical in the cases of the USSR and the CPR, and consequently, this term has been revised for these two societies' expansion equations. This is the only case of a departure from basic equation form.

[18] It must be stressed that coal production is in many respects an inadequate measure of domestic resource availability, although it is one of the few resource

The fourth coterm is the defense expenditure term, another simultaneously determined endogenous variable of Block A. Military capabilities are specialized capabilities that can be exercised in the expression of lateral pressure; but the immediate development of military capabilities requires considerable investments of societal resources that can detract from a society's immediate capacities to engage in certain forms of foreign expansion. Finally, the fifth coterm, the one-year-lagged trade dispersion measure of expansion, expresses the proposition that expansionist activities, once underway, are likely to persist. Policies and expectations become established within governmental, industrial, and commercial bureaucracies; expansionist opportunities, once opened up, are more easily pursued; and commitments, once made, are difficult to foreclose.[19] All such relationships involve unilateral dynamics.

The basic equation form for the three *bilateral intersection* equations is:

$$A\text{–}B \text{ Intersection } \#2 = \alpha_2 + \beta_6(A\text{'s Trade Dispersion } \#2) +$$

$$\beta_7(B\text{'s Trade Dispersion } \#2) + \mu_2.$$

The relationships here expressed are straightforward. As indicated in the framework, any society's expansion, here measured as Trade Dispersion #2, makes collisions of interests and commitments — intersections — more likely. In the general model, no other factors are specified to *directly* influence overall bilateral intersections.

The third class of endogenous variables in Block A contains the military capability terms, here measured as total defense expenditures. The basic equation form for *military capabilities* is:

$$A\text{'s Defense Expend.} = \alpha_3 + \beta_8(A\text{'s Defense Expend.}_{t-1}) +$$

$$\beta_9[\Delta(A\text{'s GNP} \div A\text{'s Population})] +$$

measures for which complete, cross-nationally comparable time-series are available. Alternative measures have been experimentally employed for some actors over some periods, as noted in Chapter 4.

[19] Here, as in other equations involving lagged dependent variables to represent 'commitment-inertia,' it is necessary to underline the weakness of prior theory regarding the exact forms of time-dependent processes. One cannot be sure of the time lag, for example. However, on the basis of experimentation with competing lags through the three-stage modeling progression, it is possible to say that the strongest relationships are routinely evident over one-year lags as opposed to multi-year lags or extended moving average processes. On this, as on so many other aspects of the equation for expansion, further work is needed. As pointed out in Chapter 4, the expansion equation remains both problematical and highly tentative for several reasons.

$$\beta_{10}[\Delta(A\text{-}B \text{ Intersec. }\#2) \times [\overline{A \to B}(\text{Mean}) - 11]] +$$

$$\beta_{11}[\Delta(A\text{-}C \text{ Intersec. }\#2) \times [\overline{A \to C}(\text{Mean}) - 11]] +$$

$$\beta_{12}[(B\text{'s Def. Exp.}_t - \text{Def. Exp}_{t-2}) \times \% B \to A_{t-1}] +$$

$$\beta_{13}[(C\text{'s Def. Exp.}_t - \text{Def. Exp}_{t-2}) \times \% C \to A_{t-1}] + \mu_3,$$

where $\quad \overline{A \to B}(\text{Mean}) = \sum_{i=1}^{3} \dfrac{A \to B(\text{Mean})_{t-i}}{3}$,

$$\overline{A \to C}(\text{Mean}) = \sum_{i=1}^{3} \dfrac{A \to C(\text{Mean})_{t-i}}{3},$$

$$\% B \to A_{t-1} = \dfrac{B \to A(\text{Mean})_{t-1}}{B \to A(\text{Mean})_{t-1} + B \to C(\text{Mean})_{t-1}},$$

and $\quad \% C \to A_{t-1} = \dfrac{C \to A(\text{Mean})_{t-1}}{C \to A(\text{Mean})_{t-1} + C \to B(\text{Mean})_{t-1}}.$

Four of the terms are specified to reflect sensitivity to change in the systemic configuration of conflict — changes which are accounted for within other parts of the model. Unilateral, bilateral, and multilateral dynamics are represented in this equation.

The first variable coterm is the lagged dependent variable.[20] It represents the unilateral effects of prior commitments, previous rationalizations, and bureaucratic inertia. The second coterm, $\Delta(A\text{'s GNP} \div \text{Population})$, represents the impact of changing technology and economic resources upon defense expenditures. The third and fourth coterms express bilateral relationships involving the interaction of prior normal conflict and cooperation, above or below a threshold of eleven on the thirty-point scale,[21] with changes in bilateral intersections. The change terms are used, instead of absolute levels of intersections, in order to represent the actual current collisions of extended activities. The threshold value in the second part of these coterms is used to indicate that it is only when there is a sustained and relatively high degree of antagonism between

[20] As noted regarding the lagged dependent vaiable in the equation for expansion, the use of a one-year lagged coterm is an experimentally supportable but theoretically weak approximation of the effects of 'commitment-inertia.'

[21] The value of eleven on the thirty-point scale is theoretically 'neutral.' It stands between acts, lower on the scale that are manifestly dominated by cooperation and acts higher on the scale that are characterized by conflict. See Appendix C.

actors that intersections tend to amplify military competition.[22] The fifth and sixth coterms are the military competitive coterms, and they, too, are interactively specified. According to this representation, an actor's inclination to competitively respond to the arms building of another will reflect a multilateral 'threat assessment' logic. An actor will be inclined to competitively respond to a second's arms building to the extent that the first is the unique target of the second's conflict behavior in the overall system.[23] Military competitive processes are sensitive to and will reflect shifts in the multilateral configuration of conflict.

2. Block B: Equations for Provocations

Although Block B contains three endogenous variables and three stochastic equations, it is evident from Figure 2.2B that only one class of endogenous variables is involved: provocations. The basic form for the three *bilateral provocation* equations is:

$$A-B \text{ Provocation } \#2 = \alpha_4 + \beta_{14}\left[\Delta(A\text{'s Defense Expenditure})\right] +$$

$$\beta_{15}\left[\Delta(B\text{'s Defense Expenditure})\right] +$$

$$\beta_{16}\left[(A-B \text{ Intersec. } \#2) \times (\text{Number Local Wars})\right] + \mu_4.$$

In this equation, the first two variable coterms involve changes in the actors' military capabilities, their defense expenditures. Through developing and exercising their military instruments, it is hypothesized, states can to some degree influence the overall provocations they experience. Military capabilities may be used to promote or suppress destabilizing

---

[22] The use of the three-year moving average in this coterm is theoretically supported by the idea that sustained levels of conflict and cooperation, not transitory developments, are important in determining the implications of intersections for military competition. For purposes of analysis, and in order to avoid losses of precious degrees of freedom, it is assumed that normal conflict and cooperation levels for 1947, 1948, and 1949 equal normal conflict and cooperation for 1950. This assumption is built-in to the construction of the moving average term for the years 1950, 1951, and 1952.

[23] See Chapter 1, Section II.C, for further discussion of a 'threat assessment' balance of power logic. Note that the terms $\% B \rightarrow A_{t-1}$ and $\% C \rightarrow A_{t-1}$ refer to the percentages of prior 'within-system normal conflict' directed toward A by B and C, respectively. As, say, B increases its prior normal conflict toward C, while holding its prior normal conflict toward A constant, the $\% B \rightarrow A_{t-1}$ component is reduced in value, and it is assumed that A will reduce its competitive responses accordingly. Conversely, as B reduces its prior normal conflict toward C, while holding its prior normal conflict toward A constant, the $\% B \rightarrow A_{t-1}$ component is increased in value, and it is assumed that A will increase its competitive responses accordingly.

events and situations at points of intersection; or, alternatively, a power's increases or declines in military strength can incline it to promote or reduce local instability by other means. The third variable coterm is hypothesized to be the most important, however. It expresses a simple relationship. The more extensive and intensive are any two powers' bilateral intersections, the more likely it is that regionally destabilizing events (local wars) will occur at points of intense intersection and hence be provocative for the powers involved.[24]

3. *Block C: Equations for Normal Conflict and Cooperation*

Block C contains six endogenous variables and six stochastic equations.[25] There is, though, only one basic equation form for *normal conflict and cooperation* (mean conflict levels):

$$A \rightarrow B(\text{Mean}) = \alpha_5 + \beta_{17}[A \rightarrow B(\text{Mean})_{t-1}] +$$

$$\beta_{18}(A\text{'s Defense Expend.} - B\text{'s Defense Expend.}) +$$

$$\beta_{19}[\% \Delta(A\text{'s GNP/Population} - B\text{'s GNP/Population})] +$$

$$\beta_{20}[B \rightarrow A(\text{Mean})] + \beta_{21}[A \rightarrow C(\text{Peak})_{t-1}] +$$

$$\beta_{22}[\Delta(B\text{'s Defense Expend.} - C\text{'s Defense Expend.})] + \mu_5.$$

The first variable coterm is the lagged dependent variable, a representation of 'commitment-inertia' as an influence upon routine, day-to-day levels of conflict and cooperation.[26] The second coterm reflects the multidimensional character of competitive dynamics; it represents the hypothesis of 'compensatory dynamics' advanced in Chapter 1. An actor will tend to 'compensate' for felt physical weakness — as seen in the defense expenditure gap — with hostile assertions of strength and resolve. The third

---

[24] See Chapter 6 for a more extensive discussion. Strictly speaking, the three endogenous variables in Block B are not mutually dependent and the corresponding equations do not constitute a simultaneously determined block in the restrictive sense. One may think of Block B as containing three independent single-equation 'blocks' sharing some exogenous variables. The reference to these equations as comprising Block B is primarily a matter of presentational convenience.

[25] Owing to the absence of simultaneous reciprocities or return effects across dyads, Block C can be analytically decomposed into three independent two-equation subblocks: a Sino-Soviet subblock, a Sino-American subblock, and a Soviet-American subblock. The reference to a single Block C is a matter of presentational convenience.

[26] This specification is a product of both prior theory and preliminary empirical analysis. However, a one-year-lagged dependent variable remains at best a tentative approximation of complex memory functions and bureaucratic processes.

coterm is the percentage change in the per capita-GNP gap between two societies — an aspect of 'cross-actor economic, technological, and population differences.' As the gap widens in favor of a target nation, the actor will tend to increase conflict toward the target. However, since the term is a percentage change term, the relationship is such that constant changes in the size of the gap will have their greatest impacts when the gap itself is small.

The fourth term is the reciprocity term. It represents the hypothesis that actors will tend to respond in kind to the levels of conflict and cooperation directed toward them. The fifth coterm, an actor's prior threshold of violence (the conflict peak) toward a third actor, represents the possible influences of two multilateral balance of power logics: 'consistency maintenance' and 'isolation avoidance.'[27] A positive coefficient would reflect the operation of a 'consistency maintenance' logic, as an actor 'generalizes' from recent thresholds of violence in one direction to its normal conflict and cooperation in the other direction. Alternatively, a negative coefficient would reflect an actor's application of an 'isolation avoidance' logic — its attempts to reduce conflict in one direction as thresholds of violence mount in another direction. Finally, the sixth coterm represents the possible influences of a 'preponderance opposition' balance of power logic. An actor is hypothesized to attend to the changing gap between others and to reduce conflict with the 'weaker' among others as it increases conflict in opposition to the 'stronger.'

4. *Block D: Equations for Thresholds of Violence*

Like Block C, Block D contains six endogenous variables — in this case, one for each directed dyad's thresholds of violence — and six stochastic equations. As in Block C, all six stochastic equations conform to a single equation form. However, as stressed in Chapters 8 and 9, there are important differences between the hypothesized dynamics of normal conflict and cooperation specified in Block C and the hypothesized dynamics of thresholds of violence specified in Block D.

The basic equation form for *thresholds of violence* is:

---

[27] In preliminary analysis distinct terms to represent these two kinds of dynamics were employed — thus to allow for the possibility that the two kinds of dynamics might operate simultaneously, either congruently or antagonistically. However, owing to the fact that these theoretically distinct coterms were inescapably highly collinear, it was routinely impossible to parse out distinct effects, and other confounding statistical problems arose. As a result, the two terms are here collapsed into one.

$$A \rightarrow B(\text{Peak}) = \alpha_6 + \beta_{23}[\Delta(A\text{'s GNP} \div \text{Population})] +$$

$$\beta_{24}(A\text{'s Defense Expend.} - B\text{'s Defense Expend.}) +$$

$$\beta_{25}[(A\text{--}B \text{ Provocation \#2}) \times [A \rightarrow B(\text{Mean}) - 11]] +$$

$$\beta_{26}[B \rightarrow A(\text{Peak})] + \beta_{27}[A \rightarrow C(\text{Peak})] +$$

$$\beta_{28}[\Delta(B\text{'s Defense Expend.} - C\text{'s Defense Expend.})] + \mu_6.$$

The first variable coterm is the change in the actor's per capita gross national product. It represents the hypothesis that a society will tend to withdraw from external activities and at least temporarily avoid the risks of external confrontation when popular demands are most rapidly climbing relative to economic resources. The second coterm again represents the 'compensatory dynamics' hypothesis. The third coterm is bilateral provocations in interaction with normal conflict and cooperation above or below a threshold of eleven on the thirty-point scale. It is hypothesized that bilateral provocations can precipitate urgent, crisis-like confrontations when they occur in a context of intense normal conflict. However, provocations can lead to cooperative actions when normal conflict is very low — i.e., below the threshold on the thirty-point scale. The fourth coterm is the reciprocity coterm. Especially at threshold of violence levels, actors are expected to attend and respond in kind to the conflictual actions of others.

The fifth and sixth coterms reflect balance of power logics. The fifth coterm, an actor's current threshold of violence toward a third actor, represents the possible influences of 'isolation avoidance' or 'consistency maintenance' logics (as in the cases of negative or positive coefficients, respectively).[28] The sixth coterm is the change in the defense expenditure gap between others. The influence of a hypothesized 'preponderance opposition' logic is here represented, as it is in the equation form for normal conflict and cooperation.

Each of the six equation forms just introduced is discussed at greater length in Chapters 4 through 9. These chapters will consider in greater detail the development of each equation form, its implications for various theoretical traditions, problems of formulation that remain, and possibilities for refinement and reformulation. This chapter has assumed only the task of presenting the general model as it now stands.

In this presentation of the general model, as in all presentations of structural models, the discussion tends to advance incrementally through

---

[28] See p. 76, n. 27.

a set of particular, more or less constant relationships among variables. The limits of language make it difficult to convey how within constancy there is also immanent change and how within particulars there is also the whole. The limits of language make it likely that in the presentation of a model, the message will be subtly if mistakenly conveyed that reality can be finally segmented into the concepts used to describe it, finally captured in the symbolic relationships meant to represent it, and finally mastered in the minds that contemplate it. Against these tendencies, it is possible only to urge that medium is not message. Presentational convenience cannot be allowed to obscure the complexity, elusiveness, and dynamism of the interdependencies at work.

It must be remembered that each specified causal link is embedded in an equation. Each equation is an interdependent element of a block of simultaneous relationships. Each block is nested in an overall block-recursive system involving nonlinear return effects. The overall system is but an abstraction from structured relationships characterizing a period of time. And these structured relationships are prefigured and given form through the asynchronous, equifinal, cumulative, irreversible, and antagonistic combinations and recombinations of opportunities and limits among differentially growing societies throughout history. In the end, it is history that trims away some possibilities, denies the actualization of some relationships, makes it possible to meaningfully specify some causal linkages and exclude others, and permits the specification of an over-identified causal structure. It is a long history of social processes that determines whether or not the exclusion of a variable from an equation or the choice of a particular set of measures constitutes a correct specification of the processes at work. In using these equations as a basis for interpreting historical processes, it is therefore important to keep a humbling and self-critical idea in mind: what might be called the 'structuralist conceit' − the illusion that any term, any equation, any block, or any overall structural model can *capture* an aspect of history − such a conceit has it exactly backwards.

IV   SOME INTERPRETATIONAL ISSUES

The general model just introduced is a register designed to serve a refractive function with respect to historical data. In applying any such model, one hopes to find evidence partially corroborating the synthesis of traditions it represents. But one also hopes to expose to informed criticism those traditions that, in their ahistorical closure, deny cross-sectoral and through-time linkages that the model specifies. And perhaps most importantly, one hopes to uncover what might be called generative tensions between the model, on the one hand, and the reality it purports to represent, on the other. One hopes to discern tensions that drive a model-building program to a new stage of synthesis, lead it to expand the scope of its critical applicability, and thereby help to sharpen the depiction of complex, far-reaching global dilemmas.

This means that applying the model in empirical analysis is not just a confirmatory exercise. The most important function of systematic empirical analysis is that it anchors the desirable criticism-consciousness of an open-ended modeling enterprise in reality and does so in an operationally reproducible way. It permits one to interpret historical processes — and criticize human practices — while also exposing the act of interpretation to valued criticism.

This study uses econometric techniques and rules in order to sustain the operational reproducibility of empirical analysis. Consistent with econometric theory and practice, it uses regression analysis in order to test the 'fit' between specified relationships and empirical data. A number of statistical measures are used to determine the extent of this 'fit': (*a*) R^2, the amount of variance in the dependent variable accounted for by all of the right-hand variables combined; (*b*) the magnitudes of the unstandardized and standardized (beta) coefficients; (*c*) the t statistic, which indicates the 'significance' of individual coefficients; (*d*) the statistical significance of the overall equation, as indicated by the F ratio; (*e*) the partial correlation coefficient; and (*f*) the Durbin-Watson statistic, d, which indicates the degree of first-order serial dependence in the error term under some circumstances.[29] Taken together, these statistics permit one to interpret where and in what respects historical processes do or do not conform to relationships postulated in the general model. Whether they indicate good 'fit' or poor 'fit,' such statistics should always prompt one to ask, why?

Such statistics are rather straightforwardly produced given a simple recursive system. In this case, the single-equation estimation of parameters via ordinary least-squares would be appropriate. However, the general model is not of this simple form, and accordingly, the simultaneous

---

[29] As stressed throughout Part II, references to tests of statistical significance are matters of literary ease. It must be remembered that the data used in this study are not sampled from a population and that, therefore, statistical measures do not constitute tests of significance in the true sense of statistical theory. These measures should be understood to provide established, conventional, and operationally reproducible decision rules to guide processes of inference.

equation estimation strategy of two-stage least-squares has been employed.[30] Another complication stems from the recurring problems of time-dependence in error processes. That is, it is frequently the case that preliminary regressions produce estimates of the disturbances, the $\hat{u}$s, such that they are interdependent through time: $\hat{u}$ at time t for some equations is found to be related to some combination of the $\hat{u}$'s at prior times, say $t - 1$ or $t - 2$. This violates an important assumption underlying regression analysis and, if uncorrected, invalidates causal inference. It has therefore been necessary to (*a*) diagnose the error processes on the basis of estimates from empirical data and (*b*) employ generalized least squares, often in combination with two-stage least squares, in order to correct for the influence of the error process. The words AUTO1, AUTO2, MAV1, and MAV2 in this book's presentations of statistical results are shorthand references to different kinds of time-dependent error corrections imposed.[31]

Other serious problems must be borne in mind when interpreting results. Problems of data and measurement have already been discussed.[32] Here it is necessary only to underline the fact that faulty measurement — from choices of measures through biased coding schemes to typographical errors in data sources — can introduce serious bias into results. In the face of this, all that the researcher can do is exhibit caution and more caution in the collection, manufacture, and use of empirical data. Another serious problem is multicollinearity: high linear dependencies among right-hand-side variables. Extreme degrees of multicollinearity tend to reduce the precision of parameter estimates. In cross-sectional studies, multi-collinearity sometimes occurs. In time-series analysis, such as this, it is a pervasive problem. The issue is discussed in Appendix D.

Perhaps the most serious interpretational issues revolve around questions of 'fit' and 'invariance.' In one way or another, all of the statistical measures discussed above are tests of 'fit' between model and data. Each of the problems just mentioned is usually seen in terms of a tendency to jeopardize fit or tests of fit. In fact, regression algorithms involve

[30] See Appendix D for a discussion.

[31] See Appendix D.   [32] See Appendix C.

[33] See Mark S. Levine, 'An Evaluation of the Substantive Contributions of the Stanford Studies in Conflict and Integration,' in Francis W. Hoole and Dina A. Zinnes (eds.), *Quantitative International Politics: An Appraisal* (New York: Praeger, 1976). Levine explicitly criticizes the Choucri–North World War I studies for the 'absence of invariance' in their parameter estimates across actors and over periods of time. He is not alone in this attitude. However, the attitude betrays the domination of thought by the forementioned 'structuralist conceit' and reveals a fundamental misunderstanding of the role of a structural model in Choucri and North's analysis of historical processes.

'fitting' a model to data so as to reduce the ratio of unexplained to explained variance: they involve minimizing the sum of squared residuals around the regression line. This emphasis upon empirical fit is emblematic of a strong interpretational predisposition among social scientists. To many, empirical fit is the paramount criterion of a model's empirical adequacy.

Closely associated is the question of 'invariance.' Taking their cues from positivist philosophers' reconstructed models of natural science as the uncovering of invariant laws, many social scientists would gauge a model in terms of the cross-sectional and through-time invariance of parameter estimates. In these terms, a model would be judged good if, as fitted to historical data, it exhibits invariance in the parameter estimates across space and through time. In the eyes of many social scientists, an 'absence of invariance'[33] is a mark of a model's inadequacy and calls for a supratheory, an overarching structure-of-structures, that would explain why parameter estimates do vary.

From the standpoint of this study, such emphasis upon fit and invariance is misplaced and perhaps even scientifically pernicious. With regard to fit, one should perhaps worry more about obtaining too strong a fit than about obtaining a weak one. A very strong fit to some set of historical data suggests the possibility that a model is an ahistorical reflection of some period or some domain. Moreover, because there is little or no puzzling unexplained variation, a research program is purged of some of the valuable critical tensions that would animate its explorations of deeper, historical-contextualizing processes. With regard to invariance, the same idea applies. A model whose parameter estimates are invariant across all societies, for example, evidently affords little insight into the asynchronous and equifinal processes at work.[34]

This is not to say that fit is unimportant. It is only to say that criteria of a model's empirical adequacy must be expanded to embrace what might be called interpretational power and heuristic power. Regarding interpretational power, the question is: does the empirical analysis of a model improve one's ability to interpret historical processes within the context of the more general prior theory the model reflects? Regarding heuristic

---

[34] In a recent paper, Henry Teune has advanced an argument of relevance here. He argues that the 'task of comparative system analysis . . . would not be to find universal relationships but rather systems specific relationships, which fit with a general theory cast in one of several system languages.' See his 'Concepts of Evidence in System Analysis: Testing Macro System Models,' paper presented at the XIth Congress of the International Political Science Association, Moscow, USSR, August 1979, p. 5. This argument amounts to a reversal of the approach advocated by Adam Przeworski and Henry Teune in *The Logic of Comparative Social Inquiry* (New York: Wiley, 1970).

power, the question is: does the empirical analysis of a model uncover or sharpen the depiction of new research puzzles or further avenues of productive theoretical synthesis? A model-building program aspiring to meet these expanded criteria of empirical adequacy does aspire to 'goodness of fit,' but it is also disposed to deny the false and timeless sense of closure that too tight an empirical fit might imply.[35]

The presentation of empirical results in Part II proceeds, as it were, equation form by equation form. This approach permits the examination and interpretation of critical similarities and differences in parameter estimates across actors and across dyads. However, one must not lose sight of the fact that each equation is embedded in the general model just presented. In Part III, the pieces are reassembled, and the implications of the empirical analysis are interpreted at the level of the overall equation system.

In its conceptual and methodological arguments, this book has so far proceeded on a very abstract plane. Now, in turning to Part II's empirical analysis, it is useful to summon the recollection that China, the Soviet Union, and the United States are, after all, today's three major military powers. They are powers whose actions and interactions have been characterized by persistent conflict and recurring approaches to the brink of war. Chapter 3 thus commences the empirical analysis of Part II by performing this recall function. Using the normal conflict and cooperation and threshold of violence measures as guides, it very briefly retraces the history of Sino-Soviet-American interaction, 1950–1972.

---

[35] To phrase the argument in the stronger terms of Appendix A, the issues of fit and invariance should be *subordinated* to these other criteria in a theory-building program. Given a general model, one starts any analysis by *expecting* that there will be variation in empirical results across actors and periods of time. Unless one is terribly naive, one expects that empirical results will evidence some mix of strong and weak statistical fits and that inferred relationships will vary across actors and over time. One's prior theory should allow as much. Thus, it is logically impossible to equate tests of statistical fit with tests of prior theory. To infer from the former to the latter is a categorical error. At issue in the testing of prior theory is whether or not — and to what degree — it goes beyond permissively allowing such varied results. To what extent does prior, general, and historical theory predict to and permit the meaningful interpretation of varied statistical results across actors and over time (and without resort to *ad hoc* terms casually patched on to the original theory)? This is the key question.

PART II

CHAPTER 3

Traces of Conflict: Twenty-three Years of Systemic Interaction

Part II applies statistical techniques in the empirical analysis of the general model in order to illuminate the contemporary form of the modern security problematique. Specifically, it focuses on relations among China, the Soviet Union, and the United States. Chapters 4–9 concentrate upon systematic relationships accounting for expansion, intersections, provocations, military capability building, normal conflict and cooperation, and thresholds of violence among these three major military powers.

In focusing on these variables, Part II does not address specific events — for example, the opening of cultural exchanges, decisions to extend American trade to Eastern Europe, meetings at Geneva, angry charges regarding the Soviet Czechoslovakian invasion, the Soviet decision to build helicopter carriers, the signing of the partial test ban treaty, or Henry Kissinger's surprising first visit to Peking. Instead, the focus is upon long-range historical processes in which such events find their contexts and assume their immediate implications.

The purpose of this chapter is to introduce this empirical analysis, and sketch the historical context, by highlighting patterns of continuity and change in some of the key dependent variables. In particular, this chapter offers a descriptive accounting of patterns and trends in normal conflict and cooperation and in thresholds of violence among the CPR, the USSR, and the US from 1950 through 1972. Section I offers a *highly aggregated* view of the nature of relations in the Sino-Soviet-American triangle, emphasizing the strong and persistent currents of conflict and the frequent approaches to the brink of war. Section II briefly sketches the history of Sino-Soviet-American conflictual interaction using the conflict behavior data constructed for this study as a guide. One important sidelight of this sketch is to demonstrate the general correspondence between variation in the conflict and cooperation measures, on the one hand, and the changing tenor of relations among the three powers as journalists, historians, and traditionalist scholars might describe it, on the other. Finally, Section III suggests that a systematic, statistical analysis focusing on longer-range dynamics can *complement* historical/traditional approaches to the interpretation of unique events. In the words of Nazli Choucri and Robert C. North, 'these two approaches may be viewed as alternate, or even better, mutually supportive efforts at comprehending reality.'[1]

I   A SYSTEM OF CONFLICT

The Sino-Soviet-American triangle is a system of persistently intense conflict and perilously high implications for violence. As Figure 3.1 shows, high levels of conflict within the triangle have not been confined to a few brief periods. Indeed, the *average* systemic peak conflict level (threshold of violence) per year is scored approximately 25 on the 30-point scale[2] — *a score associated with preparations for imminent war and with explicit threats of war.* In thirteen of the twenty-three years examined at least one of the three dyads reached or exceeded this dangerously high level of conflict.

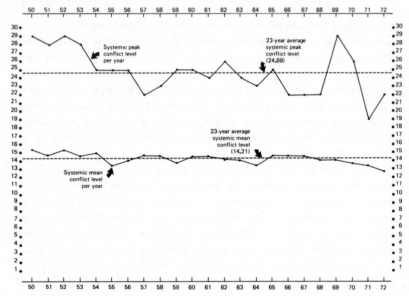

Fig. 3.1   Annual systemic mean and peak conflict levels, 1950–1972

[1] *Nations in Conflict: National Growth and International Violence* (San Francisco: W. H. Freeman, 1975), p. 10.

[2] See Chapter 2 and Appendix C for discussions of the events data, their sources and development, and the specific measures derived from them.

Though not as dramatically as systemic peaks, systemic mean levels of conflict also indicate that the triangle is a system of persistent hostility. The mean conflict level across all events since 1950, 14.2, is high when compared to a theoretical 'normal' level of interstate conflict of about 10 or 11.[3] On the 30-point scale, this 23-year average lies between a score of 14 — associated with such events as the introduction of new trade restrictions, the breakdown of talks, the extension of military aid to others' enemies — and a score of 15 — associated with events such as hostile criticism and direct accusations. That 14.2 is the systemic average assumes particular significance when one recognizes that this figure incorporates all six directed dyads in all years — even the early years of impressive Sino-Soviet cooperation and the more recent years of Soviet-American and Sino-American movement in the direction of detente.

As systemic aggregates, these figures are more remarkable for their relative stability than for any clear-cut upward or downward trends in levels of conflict. To be sure, systemic mean conflict levels have declined very gradually since 1967. But only in 1972 did the systemic mean finally reach an unprecedented low level.[4] And while 1971 saw a marked reduction in the upper bound of systemic conflict, 1972 witnessed an upward turn in this, the measure of the system's proximity to war.[5]

Of themselves, these gross figures can support only a most general impression: The triangle is a system of conflict — note the transitory, intermittent, or 'frictional' conflicts that occasionally mar the relations of otherwise friendly nations, but the persistent, deeply rooted conflicts over seemingly irreconcilable, highly valued ends that are manifested both in day-to-day suspicions and animosities and in disturbingly frequent decisions to risk, threaten, and sometimes apply force and violence.

II   SKETCHING THE PATHS OF DYADIC CONFLICT

A much richer picture — one permitting many more insights into the variations and trends of conflict and cooperation behavior· — can be obtained by turning from a focus on the system as a whole to a focus on

[3] This is a mean across all events, not a mean across annual directed dyadic means. On the thirty-point scale a score of eleven is generally, though not exclusively, associated with visible attempts to settle admitted differences by peaceful means. A score of ten assumes some success.
[4] The 1972 level was 12.76. The previous low systemic mean, 13.49, was reached in 1955.
[5] As mentioned later, this 1972 peak occurred when the US bombed Haiphong Harbor and damaged Soviet vessels.

annual measures of conflict *by dyad*. The figures presented in the follow-ing discussions will graphically depict the annual mean, peak, and low conflict levels for each of the triangle's six directed dyads — highlighting some of the major events and crises of the twenty-three years.

A   The Sino-Soviet Dyad

The most spectacular ranges of conflict are apparent in the Sino-Soviet directed dyads of Figure 3.2. Sino-Soviet interaction has ranged across twenty-eight of the thirty possible levels of conflict — from very high cooperation in the early 1950s to the violence of Damansky Island in 1969. It is likely that this wide range reflects a Soviet and Chinese awaken-ing to serious disputes — an increasing awareness of conflict occurring against a background of mutually perceived strong complementarities in the goals and objectives of two communist states.

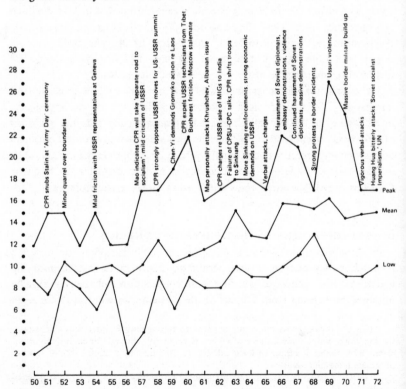

Fig. 3.2A   The Sino-Soviet dyad: CPR → USSR — crises and selected representative peak events — 1950–1972.

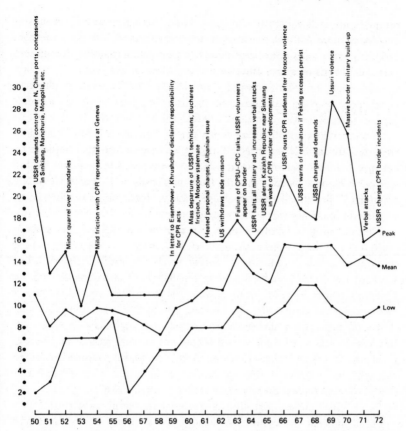

Fig. 3.2B The Sino-Soviet dyad: USSR → CPR — crises and selected representative peak events — 1950–1972.

If a turning point had to be identified within this twenty-three-year period, the conflict data seem to support the now customary dating of the Sino-Soviet split's emergence in the days of 1956 through 1958 (although movement in the direction of more conflictual modes of behavior is more immediately apparent in Chinese actions than in Soviet). As late as 1956, Sino-Soviet interaction could exhibit cooperative acts meriting scores as low as a two on the thirty-point scale. In 1957, the Soviets launched Sputnik and the Chinese claimed that the Soviets had promised to help China obtain a nuclear military capability. Yet the ensuing years saw the intensification of Soviet de-Stalinization;[6] the Soviets' formal abrogation of

---

[6] The policy can be dated to Stalin's death. But it did not receive formal sanction until Khrushchev's speech to the Twentieth Congress of the CPSU in 1956. On the

promises of nuclear help to China; numerous verbal attacks and counter-attacks at international communist meetings; heated bilateral meetings; and each actor's antagonistic attempts to gain partners among communist parties and regimes at the other's expense.[7] Clearly, the year 1959 marked the beginning of a long upward trend in the conflict levels of the two countries' day-to-day relations. And the following year, 1960, saw a simultaneous increase in all measures of conflict for both actors.

The year 1963 was the year of the partial Nuclear Test Ban Treaty and the year after the Cuban missile crisis. It was also a year that witnessed a collapse of talks between Soviet and Chinese party leaders and, in the words of Robert North, 'a shift from euphemistic polemics to public acrimony.'[8] For the first time, Soviet and Chinese mean conflict levels surpassed the twenty-three-year systemic average.

The following two years — years that saw the fall of Krushchev and the beginning of a rapid American build-up in Vietnam — were ones in which the upward climb in Sino-Soviet conflict levels was briefly suspended. But starting late in 1965 and continuing through 1966, the first year of the Chinese Cultural Revolution, mean Sino-Soviet conflict levels climbed to a new and higher plateau. It was a plateau of angry charges and recriminations, of rude, even terroristic harassment of diplomats, of property seizures, of less than thinly-veiled threats, of border tensions and border incidents. It was a plateau of intense conflict that both countries sustained through four years. With the violence along the Ussuri River in 1969, this period of most fervent Sino-Soviet conflict reached a climax.

But it was a climax that did not resolve. Both countries retreated from the brink in their thresholds of violence. And the wary Chinese answered the Soviets' stronger appeals to bargain peaceably with a reserved approach to the table. At least on the part of the Chinese, however, these moves are attributable more to the urgent necessity of avoiding a catastrophic Sino-Soviet war than to any desire to achieve a mutually accommodating settlement.[9] As indicated in the normal conflict and cooperation levels of Sino-

impact of de-Stalinization on Sino-Soviet relations, see Donald Zagoria, *The Sino-Soviet Dispute, 1956–1961* (Princeton, N.J.: Princeton University Press, 1962), especially Chapter 1.

[7] An excellent chronology of events in the 1957–63 period is provided in William E. Griffith's *The Sino-Soviet Rift* (Cambridge, Mass.: MIT Press, 1964). Events of 1962–63 are analyzed in some detail.

[8] Robert C. North, *The Foreign Relations of China* (Belmont, Calif.: Dickenson, 1969), p. 79.

[9] On both Chinese and Soviet motives see Thomas W. Robinson's penetrating 'The Border Negotiations and the Future of Sino-Soviet-American Relations,' P–4661 (Santa Monica, Calif.: Rand Corporation, August 1971).

Soviet relations for 1970, 1971, and 1972 — by far the highest in the system — the basic disputes, suspicions, and animosities that occasioned the violence of 1969 have not been extinguished.

B   The Sino-American Dyad

Where Sino-Soviet conflict behavior reflects in part the two actors' growing awareness of intersecting and inconsistent goals and objectives, Sino-American conflictual interaction (Figure 3.3) reflects the two actors' vivid recognition of one another as adversaries almost from the very outset. Shocked by the 'loss of China,' many Americans entered the 1950s viewing the newly established Chinese regime as an agent of an international

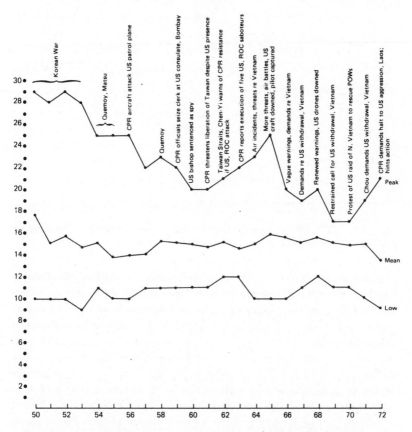

Fig. 3.3A   The Sino-American dyad: CPR → US — crises and selected representative peak events — 1950–1972.

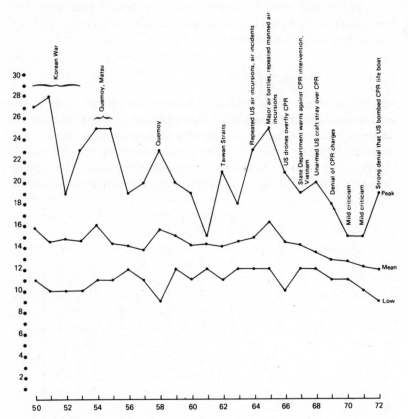

Fig. 3.3B   The Sino-American dyad: US → CPR — crises and selected representative peak events — 1950–1972.

communist conspiracy — an agent determined to enslave the Chinese people and extend communist control. Nevertheless, the American leadership was resigned to a policy of 'letting the dust settle in Asia.' 'Its expectation,' according to Louis Halle, 'was that Mao Tse-tung's new regime would inevitably complete its victory by the conquest of Formosa, and that in due course it would be proper for the United States to recognize the accomplished fact.'[10] Accordingly, the US reduced its commitment to Chiang Kai-shek, and President Truman announced a course of non-involvement in 'the civil conflict in China.'[11] For their part, the Maoist leaders of the mainland entered the decade viewing the United States as an

[10] Louis Halle, *The Cold War as History* (New York: Harper and Row, 1967), p. 212.
[11] *Department of State Bulletin*, January 16, 1950, p. 79.

alien foe — a view perfectly consistent with past American support for the Kuomintang and with the history of Western imperialism in Asia — but not as a particularly threatening foe.

The Korean War defined a very high initial ceiling of conflict and hardened the two countries' mutual enmity for years to come. In the eyes of American leaders, the CPR became an aggressive, expansionist state — one closely allied with the Soviet Union, bent on extending communist control throughout Asia, and capable of doing so because of its large and mobilizable population. If not checked by diligent American opposition — now including unbending support for the Republic of China — the CPR would surely realize its expansionist aims. In Chinese eyes, the United States became the world's leading imperialist power — an aggressive, reactionary power driven to expand its interests and influence in Asia and elsewhere, threaten Chinese security, and support the CPR's most bitter enemies.

For more than a decade after the Korean War, then, these positions and attitudes dominated the two countries' interaction. Normal levels of Sino-American conflict fluctuated to some extent but remained always above a very high plane. Repeatedly — in 1954–55, in 1958, and again in 1962 — the two countries confronted one another over the issues of Taiwan and the Offshore Islands. It is noteworthy, however, that through 1962 the implications for violence associated with these confrontations gradually declined.

As the year of the 'Gulf of Tonkin incident,' 1964 saw the first American bombing of North Vietnam, the beginning of the US build-up in Vietnam, and the return to relatively high thresholds of violence in Sino-American relations. This and the following year were ones of occasionally angry warnings, air and sea incidents, accusations, and recriminations. Significantly, though, 1965 marked the last year of very high thresholds of violence in Sino-American relations despite the continued escalation in Vietnam. In 1966, the US and CPR quietly initiated direct contacts in Warsaw (and, it is now known, American Ambassador Gronouski assured Chinese Ambassador Wang that the CPR should not consider itself threatened by the US build-up and that the US would not invade North Vietnam).

In fact, the years 1965 and 1966 witnessed the start of a long, gradual decline in the conflict content of American day-to-day behaviors toward China, as reflected in manner of normal conflict and cooperation. The US sustained this decline in normal levels at least through 1972. A reciprocal trend in Chinese behaviors is less perceptible: even as Chinese normal levels of conflict exhibited toward the United States have declined — at least since 1966, when Sino-Soviet conflict reached its highest plateau — the

pace of this decline has been excruciatingly slow. Not until 1972, the year
of Nixon's Peking visit, was the decline at all dramatic.

The year 1972 was one of unprecedentedly low conflict and high cooperation in Sino-American relations. For the first time, normal levels of
conflict for both Chinese behaviors toward the US and American behaviors toward the CPR fell below the twenty-three-year systemic average.
The dyad — which, in the 1950s and much of the 1960s, had rivaled the
Soviet-American dyad for the label of most hostile in the system — once
again rivaled the Soviet-American dyad, but this time for the distinction
of *least* conflictual.

C   The Soviet-American Dyad

Like the Sino-American patterns of conflict, Soviet-American conflict
patterns (Figure. 3.4) reflect the behaviors of two powers who, from the
outset, viewed one another as hostile adversaries. The cold war was well
under way as the United States and the Soviet Union entered the 1950s.
It had been four years since Winston Churchill's 'Iron Curtain' speech in
Fulton, Illinois, and George Kennan's first formulation of a concept of
containment in Moscow. The years from 1947 through 1949 had seen the
Greek–Turkish crisis and the enunciation of the Truman Doctrine, the
initiation of the Marshall Plan and the Soviet rejection of it, the creation
of the Cominform, the establishment of NATO, the reinstitution of con-
scription in the United States, the Berlin blockade and the Berlin airlift,
the communist seizure of Czechoslovakia, and the Soviet Union's explosion of its first atomic device. For each actor, these and other events in
part reflected and in part reinforced a conviction that the two powers'
ideological and nationalistic ambitions — so far seen to be intersecting
primarily in a European context — were strictly antithetical.

As in the case of the Sino-American dyad, the Korean War hardened
Soviet–American enmity. It also signaled a broadening of the cold war's
scope beyond the boundaries of Europe. Americans extended 'containment' to Asia and, seeing the war as a sign of Soviet intentions to apply
military force, began a rapid remobilization, a recruitment of Western
contributions to a NATO military force, and the acquisition of air bases
throughout the world.[12] Viewing this as threatening, the Soviets accelerated
their own conventional arms build-up — which they had commenced in
1948 — and began to expend greater energy and resources toward the end
of overcoming the American nuclear monopoly.[13] The cold war had

[12] See Halle, op. cit., Chapters 21 and 22.
[13] Adam Ulam, *Expansion and Coexistence* (New York: Praeger, 1969), pp. 497-9.

become an all-encompassing contest in which each actor viewed every possible gain for the other, or for the other's political and economic philosophies, as a loss for itself.

The year 1953 saw the inauguration of the Eisenhower administration; the death of Stalin and the ascent to power of the triumvirate of Malenkov, Beria, and Molotov; the Soviets' explosion of their first hydrogen bomb; and the signing of the Korean armistice. Despite the inflated rhetoric of 'liberation,' 'roll back,' 'brinkmanship,' and 'massive retaliation' that Dulles and Eisenhower brought to American foreign policy, and although Soviet–American relations by no means became cordial, 1953 did see the beginning of a brief decline in the levels of normal conflict exhibited in the two countries' day-to-day relations.

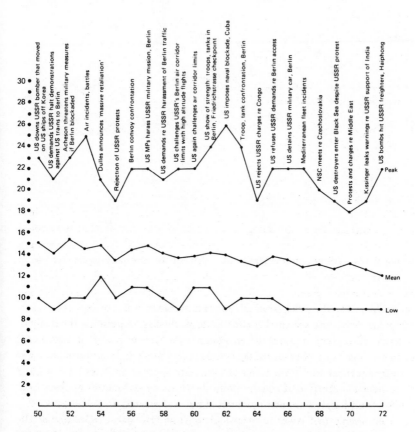

Fig. 3.4A   The Soviet-American dyad: US → USSR — crises and selected representative peak events — 1950–1972.

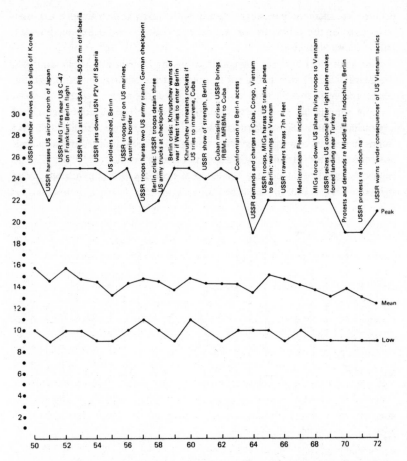

Fig. 3.4B   The Soviet-American dyad: USSR → US — crises and selected representative peak events — 1950–1972.

By 1955, the relaxation of postwar tensions was obvious and widely applauded. Although the US and USSR reached an impasse on the difficult subjects of Germany and disarmament at the Geneva conference for heads of the Big Four, this was a conference carried out in an atmosphere of at least superficial friendship. A conference of foreign ministers later in 1955 was equally amiable, if equally unproductive. Soviet-American normal conflict reached a low point which would not be repeated until 1963–64.

As the year of crises in the Middle East and Hungary, 1956 marked the end of what some would call the post-Stalin 'thaw' in Soviet-American relations. The following years, 1957 through early 1959, saw incidents on the access routes to Berlin, the Soviet launching of Sputnik and the alarm it aroused in the West, the Syria–Turkey crisis, the crisis in Lebanon and Jordan, and a Soviet threat to sign an agreement with East Germany allowing the East Germans the exclusive authority to negotiate (or unilaterally foreclose) allied rights of access to West Berlin. Normal levels of conflict remained high.

With the decade of the 1950s nearing a close, Soviet-American relations experienced another sudden 'thaw'. The Berlin crisis of the 1958–59 winter receded in the spring when Khrushchev relaxed his May deadline and declared his desire to negotiate a summit. In May of 1959 a foreign ministers' conference was convened in Geneva; and in August, just after the close of the conference, Eisenhower and Khrushchev announced their intentions to exchange visits. Khrushchev spent the last two weeks of September in the US. A summit conference — one that was widely expected to continue the 'spirit of Camp David' — was scheduled for May of 1960. Many observers foresaw in this summit the imminent demise of the cold war.

These visions of detente, however, departed more quickly than they had arrived. On May 5, 1960, just eleven days before the scheduled Paris summit, Khrushchev announced the shooting down of an American plane deep in Soviet territory. It quickly developed that the plane was a spy craft, that Khrushchev had evidence of the fact, and that its pilot had been captured alive. The summit collapsed in the midst of Soviet charges against the US and embarrassed American intransigence. Soon, Khrushchev repeated his threats regarding a treaty with East Germany. And shortly thereafter, the USSR threatened intervention in the Congo. The 'thaw' was over.

The first year of the Kennedy administration, 1961, witnessed the Bay of Pigs invasion and Soviet threats of retaliation to protect Cuba from 'aggressive bandit acts,'[14] still another Berlin ultimatum from Khrushchev, a consequent Berlin crisis in which both NATO and Warsaw Pact forces were partially mobilized, the construction of the Berlin wall, and the Soviet resumption of nuclear testing after a three-year tacit moratorium. But it was the following year, 1962, that witnessed 'the Gettysberg of the Cold War' — the Cuban missile crisis that Harold Macmillan, speaking before the House of Commons, called 'one of the great turning points of history.'[15]

[14] Significantly, this threat came *after* most of the action was over and more direct US involvement seemed unlikely. See Adam Ulam, *The Rivals* (New York: Viking Press, 1971), pp. 319–20.

[15] Quoted in Theodore Sorenson's *Kennedy* (New York: Harper and Row, 1965), p. 719.

As shown in Figure 3.4, the Cuban crisis did mark a turning point of sorts. In 1963 there was a brief Soviet-American confrontation on the access routes to Berlin, but it also saw the US and USSR sign the partial test ban treaty. In 1964, Khrushchev fell from power, and — as normal levels of Soviet-American conflict declined — the two countries imposed new, much lower threshold of violence ceilings on their relations. This post-Cuban crisis dampening of conflict was most impressive in Soviet behaviors toward the US: through 1962 annual Soviet thresholds of violence toward the US averaged about twenty-four on the thirty-point scale (a level associated with events such as armed confrontations), but after 1962 they averaged nearly three points lower (a level associated with harsh but not explicitly threatening demands).[16]

However, this reduced conflict ceiling apparently reflected a heightened mutual awareness of the dangers inherent in high level conflict — a mutual desire to avoid the newly underscored risks of miscalculation and over-commitment that attend activities approaching the brink of war — more than it reflected an absence of Soviet-American competition, antagonism, and friction. As repeatedly evidenced in the ensuing years, the two countries remained adversaries. The difference now was that each leadership was acutely aware of the frightening costs that might be realized if it chose to pursue contested goals by means of direct confrontation.

Thus, as the two actors encountered crises, each generally attempted to avoid those volatile, highly conflictual moves that might invite hasty counteractions and countercommitments by the other. Soviet responses to the American escalation in Vietnam, while frequently heated and some-times vaguely ominous, were never explicitly suggestive of a direct Soviet-American confrontation. Continued Soviet harassment of allied movement along the Berlin access routes was sporadic — intended to remind the West of an outstanding issue, not to decide it. During the Middle East's six-day war of 1967, each actor cautiously surveyed the other's activities, but each also tried to avoid any direct confrontation by informing the other of its own non-exploitative intentions. The United States eschewed belligerent posturing during the 1968 Soviet invasion of Czechoslovakia and confined its attacks to comparatively mild verbal ones, primarily in the UN forum. Occasional incidents, like accidental overflights, were received firmly but without the inflamed rhetoric that accompanied similar events in earlier years.

Beneath this lowered threshold of violence ceiling, normal levels of

---

[16] A similar dampening is also noticeable in American behaviors toward the USSR, but the drop is not as large because average American peak conflict from 1950 through 1962 was not as high as its Soviet complement.

Soviet-American conflict began a steady decline only after 1965. In 1965, the American escalation in Vietnam became the subject of intense Soviet criticism. In that year the conflict content of Soviet behaviors far exceeded that of its dyadic complement. But, beginning in 1966, normal levels of Soviet behaviors toward the US steadily declined. In 1967, the nuclear non-proliferation treaty was signed. In 1968, Soviet normal conflict levels approached the lower American level. In 1969 the two countries initiated strategic arms limitation talks.

The year 1970 marked something of a reversal in this downward trend. For this was the year of riots in Poland, the Cambodian incursion, a new flare-up in the Middle East (where Israeli air raids over Egypt encountered Soviet-piloted craft), renewed harassment on the West Berlin access routes, and noticeably increased Soviet submarine activity in the Caribbean near Cuba. The reversal, through, was short-lived. In 1971, as Sino-American conciliatory moves became public, the US and USSR joined in the quadri-partite agreement on Berlin, and in 1972, despite American bombing and mining of North Vietnam, Nixon visited Moscow where he and Brezhnev signed the SALT I and other agreements.

By 1972, both Washington and Moscow seemed committed to policies of detente and to actions conforming to the policies. A test of this commitment came in the last two weeks of the 7,401 days examined here when the United States commenced extremely heavy bombing of North Vietnam. In the process (and presumably by mistake) Soviet vessels were damaged. Brezhnev and Kosygin, as well as the Soviet media, angrily denounced the Christmas bombing campaign. Yet the injury of Soviet vessels — something that might have been received as a serious provocation a few years earlier — now was virtually ignored.

III BEYOND DESCRIPTION

This brief summary has been meant to (*a*) introduce the conflict behavior variables of each directed dyad, (*b*) underscore the persistently intense conflict and strong implications for violence attending interaction among China, the Soviet Union, and the United States, and (*c*) demonstrate a general correspondence between the conflict behavior measures, on the one hand, and conventional-historical *descriptions* of the period, on the other. The question at this point is, how are the patterns so described to be explained?

The approach to explanation pursued in this book should by now be clear. This approach starts from the premises that events are not random;

that patterned regularities exist; that decision situations, although never identical across time and space, exhibit recurring close analogies; and that some situations make some kinds of decisions very likely. In turn, each decision is seen to cumulate with numerous others, form further trends, shape other situations, and influence still other decisions. In focusing upon such *historical processes*, moreover, this approach is informed by a conceptual framework positing relationships extending well beyond the domain of politico-military interaction and intimately joining the dynamics of growth as part of the modern security problematique. Within this overall approach, the empirical analysis of the general model represents an attempt to depict such far-reaching historical processes as they give form to the modern security problematique among China, the Soviet Union, and the United States. It is only within an overall network of relationships — a network entwining the long-term dynamics of growth with the more visible and volatile dynamics of rivalry and balance of power — that the patterns described in this chapter can be explained. Quite evidently, this emphasis upon long-historical processes and the use of systematic techniques contrasts sharply with conventional-historical and traditionalist approaches, both of which tend to emphasize the interpretation of unique events using principally verbal techniques.

The present approach does not displace the interpretational insights that historians and traditionalists might offer, however. What it does do is provide a means of focusing these insights. As noted in Chapter 1, and as stressed again in Chapter 2, the conceptual framework and the general model built upon it are products of synthesis. They reflect attempts to join insights from many sources, historians and traditionalist scholars among them. What is more, a review of concepts of asynchrony, equifinality, and so on (at the end of Chapter 1) implies an important continuing role for historians and traditionalists. Specifically, these concepts indicate that various processes posited in the framework are likely to be unevenly experienced among societies, that societies' adaptations to circumstances are likely to be varied and deeply sensitive to different historical experiences, that not even dominant relationships are likely to be uniformly expressed at any time, and that, overall, the several kinds of processes are likely to be poised in potentially antagonistic and possibly generative relationships. Put negatively, these concepts imply a warning against the expectation that any model, no matter how encompassing, can approach closure in capturing relationships bearing upon the security problematique. Put positively, these concepts imply that the general model should be seen as a representation of dominant or modal tendencies. It should be seen as both a general explanation and a kind of metric against which changes of patterns and departures from dominant tendencies can be effectively discerned. In the interpretation of these empirically discerned changes and departures, historians and traditionalists can offer invaluable insights, and can thereby help to carry the continuing process of synthesis forward. In this sense, at the very least, the present approach and approaches favored by historians and traditionalists are mutually complementary.

In order to sustain this complementarity, the chapters comprising the rest of Part II reflect an attempt to avoid 'speaking another language.' Even as techniques of econometrics are used, the attempt is made to present and interpret findings in straightforward verbal terms, emphasizing substance above technique. The attempt is made, not because technical issues are trivial, but because communication across scientific/traditional frontiers is crucial to the eliciting of informed criticism, the cumulation of knowledge, and the comprehension of the kinds of interdependencies and dilemmas this research has begun to uncover.[17]

The ordering of the presentation is simple enough. Each of the six chapters to follow concentrates upon the empirical analysis of dynamics underlying one kind of endogenous variable in the general model. The chapters focus on the dynamics of expansion, intersections, provocations, military capability building, normal conflict and cooperation, and thresholds of violence, respectively. Chapter 4 begins the presentation with the dynamics of expansion.

---

[17] Throughout Chapters 4–9 technical issues are referred to primarily in footnotes. But instances of some technical dubiety are also signalled, in the text, so that the reader not trained in econometrics will have a firmer foundation upon which to evaluate the work.

In addition, Appendix A describes the three-phase experimental process of model development, and Appendix D discusses experimental econometrics and associated problems. Appendix C takes up data and measures.

CHAPTER 4

Expansion: The Extension of Interests and Commitments

The conceptual framework defined expansion in terms of a society's outward manifestations of its extending interests, commitments, and psychopolitical borders. Clearly, these external activities can assume a number of modes. Choucri and North suggest that among European powers in the 1870–1914 period, the dominant mode of expansion was colonial acquisitions.[1] In more recent times, by contrast, modes of expansion would include such activities as trade, aid, investments, foreign basing of men under arms, and so on. This study has concentrated primarily on trade-based measures of expansion.[2] (Figures 4.1, 4.2, and 4.3 depict a 'trade dispersion' measure of commercial expansion for each of the three major powers over the 1950–72 period.) Over the course of the twenty-three years, all three societies have greatly increased and widened the distribution of their trading activity.

An important aspect of the analysis (reported later) is the effect that this expansion has had on conflict among the three powers. Indeed, the model presented in Chapter 2 indicates that expansion is a prime source of conflict: expansion increases the likelihood of intersections — regional collisions of interests and commitments — and these in turn spur competition and conflict, especially when provocations occur.

For now, however, the issue is not the effects of such expansion but the roots of expansion within the national society. At least some of the possible domestic sources of expansion are addressed by the conceptual framework and incorporated in the general model. Technology and population, independently and most pronouncedly in combination, generate demands

[1] Nazli Choucri and Robert C. North, *Nations in Conflict: National Growth and International Violence* (San Francisco: W. H. Freeman, 1975), Chapter 11.

[2] Specifically, this chapter reports results using trade dispersion #2, a trade-based measure that takes both intensity of total trade and geographic dispersion across regions into account. See Table 2.1, p. 56, for details.

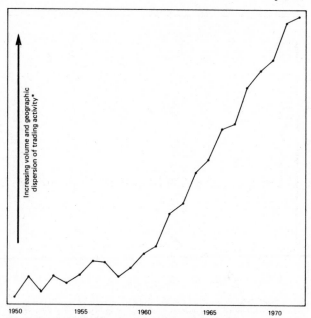

*See Table 2.1 of Chapter 2 for the calculus of this complex measure.

Fig. 4.1 US expansion (Trade Dispersion #2) 1950–1972.

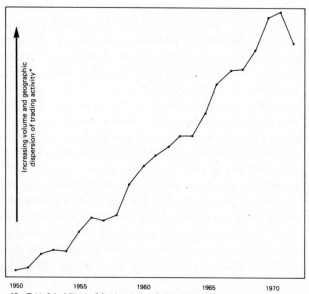

*See Table 2.1 of Chapter 2 for the calculus of this complex measure.

Fig. 4.2 USSR expansion (Trade Dispersion #2) 1950–1972.

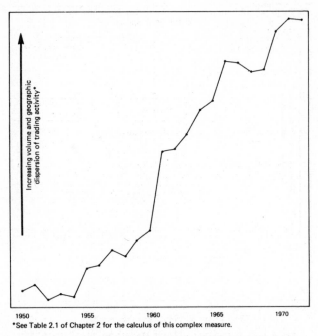

*See Table 2.1 of Chapter 2 for the calculus of this complex measure.

Fig. 4.3   CPR expansion (Trade Dispersion #2) 1950–1972.

for scarce resources — resources that can sometimes be obtained only externally. Popular demands, in particular, are subject to changing expectations based, in part, upon past levels of satisfaction that technology provides. When popular and technological demands combined with available specialized capabilities — military capabilities being one type[3] — external expansionist activity is a likely result. On the other hand, both the undertaking of expansionist activities and the construction of specialized capabilities require considerable investments of resources, so that (*a*) there may be some degree of immediate trade-off between the two and (*b*) a society having few or restricted specialized capabilities and confronted with a high ratio of demands to resources may be forced to lessen its expansion or turn inward. Finally, once expansionist activities are underway, they may be expected to persist: policies become established within governmental, industrial, and commercial bureaucracies; opportunities for expansion, once opened up, are more easily pursued; and commitments, once established, are difficult to foreclose. All such propositions address unilateral dynamics.

These propositions are reflected in the postulated dynamics of expan-

[3] See Chapter 6, below.

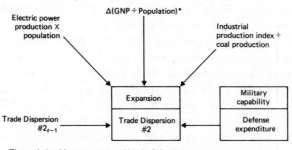

These relationships are represented by the following equation:

Trade Dispersion #2 = $\alpha_1 + \beta_1$(Electric Power Production X Population) +
β_2 [Δ(Gross National Product ÷ Population)] * +
β_3 (Indust. Prod. Index ÷ Coal Production) +
β_4 (Defense Expenditure) +
β_5 (Trade Dispersion #2$_{t-1}$) + μ_1

*In the equations for USSR and CPR expansion we substitute Δ (Industrial Production Index ÷ Population) for this term. When the original term, Δ(GNP ÷ Population), is used in the USSR and CPR equations, this term invariably loses significance in experimental regressions. The use of the industrial production index may be viewed as a means of eliminating the confounding effects of Soviet and Chinese agricultural reverses from this term. This, at least, is our interpretation. Future formulations might be improved by the addition of a term representing exclusively agricultural factors.

Fig. 4.4   The hypothesized dynamics of expansion.

sion shown in Figure 4.4.[4] A product of considerable experimentation using a variety of measures of *commercial* expansion, and using a variety of alternative measures and functional forms in the independent variables, this formulation is still quite provisional.[5] Parameters have been estimated on variants on these formulations over both the full period (1951–72) and subperiods; attention has been given to changes in parameter estimates across subperiods (see Appendix-B). The results of this experimentation must be generalized beyond commercial modes of expansion with extreme caution. Moreover, these results have revealed that subperiod parameter estimates are very unstable. And thus, while the findings reported below do show that external commercial activities are highly dependent upon internal factors, further refinement is necessary.

The difficulties of experimentation with this and similar formulations have been compounded by technical problems. One of these is inherent in the high linear correlations so often found among attribute variables; such multicollinearity can reduce precision of parameter estimates and lead to misinferences about causal relationships. The mix of functional forms has mitigated multicollinearity to some extent, but the problem persists nonetheless.[6] Another problem is that of high degrees of time-dependence

[4] The diagram, like those of following chapters, omits the intercept and error terms.

[5] See Appendix A on the development of this formulation.

[6] See Appendix A. Multicollinearity has been most troublesome for the Soviet Union equations.

among error terms, which can distort parameter estimates. Statistical corrections for such error processes have been essential.[7] Finally, these problems have been compounded still further by the inclusion of a lagged
dependent variable (trade dispersion #2 at $t-1$). The coincidence of lagged
dependent variables *and* serial correlation can yield exaggerated parameter
estimates and a tendency to inflate the significance of the lagged term
unless the analyst makes appropriate statistical adjustments.[8] The necessary adjustments have been made in this study. Nevertheless, it is essential
to base tentative conclusions, not on a single, unique formulation, but on
the full array of results within the experimental context.

From 1950 through 1972, all three societies have dramatically increased
their trading activity.[9] The (constant) dollar value of Chinese trade nearly
doubled during this period, the value of American trade nearly tripled, and
the value of Soviet trade grew by a factor of four. More impressive, perhaps, is the geographical dispersion of this trade. For example, while
American trade with Africa climbed only 11 percent over the twenty-three-
year period, Chinese trade in that region climbed by a factor of 8 and
Soviet trade grew by a factor of almost 10. And in the Middle East, the
value of American trade doubled as Soviet trade increased by a factor of 8
and Chinese trade climbed some 5,000 percent.[10] The United States, of
course, entered the period with a much larger base in the domain of trade:
the US total trade in 1950 was $34 billion compared to the Soviet Union's
$4 billion and China's $2 billion (in constant 1970 dollars). All three
societies have vastly broadened, as well as increased their trading activity.[11]

For the period covered in the quantitative analysis, the expansion (trade
dispersion #2) of all three countries is explained quite well by the unilateral
terms specified in Figure 4.4. (See Table 4.1.)[12] In various combinations,

---

[7] See Appendix D.   [8] See Appendix D.
[9] Imports plus exports. See Appendix C for sources of figures cited.
[10] Quite obviously, this increase was from a very small initial base. In 1972, Chinese
trade in the Middle East, imports plus exports, amounted to just over $88 million
(constant 1970). All statistics are based on the *United Nations Yearbook of International Trade Statistics*.
[11] Even so, it must be noted, only the Soviet Union has appreciably increased what
might be called its trading dominance across regions. When we take an actor's total
percentage of each region's total trade and then sum across all regions we call this
'aggregated regional trade dominance.' This measure for the US climbed through
1957 and then declined through 1972. For China, the measure has varied considerably
but today stands at the same level as in 1950. For the Soviet Union, the measure
climbed to a peak but has remained stable, with a slight downward trend, since then;
the 1972 measure is some 60 percent larger than the 1950 figure.
[12] In this table and all that report on regression results in the text we report actual
values of coefficient estimates, beta coefficients (standardized coefficients), t statistics, level of significance, and partial correlations *for significant* ($p < .10$) *coefficients
only*. We also report R^2, the F ratio, and Durbin-Watson statistic for the full

these terms account for 99 per cent of the variance in the trade dispersion of China, the Soviet Union, and the United States. Indeed, variants on these formulations have consistently accounted for better than 94 percent of the variance in trade dispersion. Yet, while this suggests that commercial expansion is well explained by domestic changes, and while each of the five terms is significant ($p < .05$) in at least two of the three full period regressions, specific parameter estimates differ markedly across actors — thus suggesting that each of the three actors' expansion might be affected by different dynamics. These parameter estimates deserve close attention.

In the case of the United States, the lagged endogenous 'commitment-inertia' term is but marginally significant ($p < .10$)[13] — as it has generally been throughout all phases of experimentation. Though regularly positive, the term frequently drops out of experimental equations. Clearly, given the diffusion of decision-making on commercial expansion in the United States, bureaucratic inertia has not been a dominant influence. Equally clearly, US commercial expansion has not been very susceptible to the commitments and barriers of the past.[14]

It is the electric-power-production $\times$ population and Δ (GNP $\div$ Population) terms, above all others, that appear to dominate US commercial expansion. The regular significance of these terms throughout the experimental analysis underscores the almost intuitive observation that it is the immense 'energy' generated by American economic and technological growth that largely accounts for the American presence, economic or otherwise, in the several regions of the globe. Similarly, the positive coefficient for the military capability (defense expenditure) term — also persistently significant in experimentation — suggests an equally familiar observation that the American military capability is, or is seen to be, an important instrument of commercial expansion.[15] The clear absence of a

equation. And we have included a short-hand expression linking the operational term to theoretical concepts.

[13] See n. 10 in Chapter 5, p. 118.
[14] This generalization requires testing with other, non-commercial measures of expansion — like foreign basing of men under arms, economic aid, and arms transfers, all of which are more centrally controlled.
[15] Perhaps a large American military capability encourages American industrial and commercial concerns to increase and widen their foreign commercial activities and commitments — in the belief, presumably, that a large capability can protect their expanded interests — while a reduced capability suggests a need to turn commercial interests homeward or toward the now restricted 'safe' or 'stabilized' regions of the world. Perhaps, alternatively, American commercial interests are more easily asserted when an American military presence (or potential presence) is most pronounced. And perhaps the persistent significance of a positive coefficient for this term is due to some combination of these and other factors. The measures used here do not permit a firm conclusion.

Table 4.1 Expansion (Trade Dispersion), 1951–1972: Results of Estimation from a Simultaneous Equation System*

Actor	R^2	F ratio	Durbin-Watson	Time-dependent correction	Variable: link to prior theory	Measure	Unstandardized coefficient	Standardized coefficient	Partial correlation	t statistic	Level of significance
US	.99	674.079 df = 5,16 p = .001	1.98	AUTO1	Constant	Constant	822993.4	.00	.44	1.99	.05
					Interaction of Technology and Population	Electric Power Production × Total Population	0.00155	.89	.80	5.36	.0005
					Changing Popular Expectations	Δ (Gross National Product ÷ Population)	1.83224†	.10	.74	4.36	.0005
					Technological Demands Relative to Resources	Industrial Production Index ÷ Coal Production	−1.01728‡	−.21	−.63	−3.28	.005
					Military Capability	Defense Expenditure	2.08503	.09	.50	2.33	.025
					Commitment-Inertia	Trade Dispersion$_{t-1}$	0.23998	.22	.37	1.57	.10
USSR	.99	1683.59 df = 5,16 p = .001	2.46	AUTO2	Technological Demands Relative to Resources	Industrial Production Index ÷ Coal Production	.638895	.57	.59	2.96	.005
					Military Capability	Defense Expenditure	−1.36650	−.41	−.93	−10.51	.0005
					Commitment-Inertia	Trade Dispersion$_{t-1}$	0.85902	.86	.95	12.09	.0005

CPR	.99	270.943 $df = 5,16$ $p = .001$	2.13	AUTO2	Constant				
					Constant	−1.37675†	.00	−.43	−1.89	.05
					Interaction of Technology and Population	Electric Power Production × Total Population	0.00331	.34	.56	2.69	.01
					Changing Popular Expectations	Δ (Industrial Production Index ÷ Population)	−5.89458†	−.10	−.50	−2.29	.025
					Technological Demands Relative to Resources	Industrial Production Index ÷ Coal Production	0.24527‡	.15	.51	2.37	.025
					Military Capability	Defense Expenditure	−30.5770	−.45	−.56	−2.67	.01
					Commitment-Inertia	Trade Dispersion$_{t-1}$	1.20680	1.18	.91	8.73	.0005

*All statistics refer to the simultaneous-equation-system estimates using both two-stage least squares and, as indicated in the time-dependent correction column, generalized least squares.

†Coefficient multiplied by 10^5.

‡Coefficient multiplied by 10^9.

negative relationship suggests, too, that for the US, military capability building does not detract from commercial expansion.

The most surprising aspect of the US equation is the negative coefficient for industrial production ÷ coal production. This unexpected result might be due to the confounding effects of collinearity or to a poor choice of indicators. The advanced US technology may be poorly represented by an industrial production index, and, as noted elsewhere,[16] no single measure of a society's resources, like coal production, can represent the full and increasingly diverse array of resources that an advancing society demands. Experimentation seems to support this interpretation. The substitution of alternative measures — oil production, for example — reveals remarkable sensitivity of this term to measures used.[17]

Combining these several observations, it would appear that American expansion, at least of the commercial variety, is far more responsive to shifting internal technological and economic factors than it is to bureaucratic decision-making patterns and international commitments of the past. Once again, this is most probably due to the diffusion of decision-making regarding foreign trade in the United States — a diffusion that thrusts direct control of this kind of expansion beyond the immediate grasp of political leaders.

In the Soviet Union, by contrast, decisions on foreign trade are centralized — and the dynamics of Soviet commercial expansion reflect this fact. 'commitment-inertia', measured as a lagged dependent variable, appears dominant in the USSR equation. The dominance of lagged endogenous terms, moreover, is a persistent feature of *all* experimental equations for the Soviet Union. Without question, Soviet commercial expansion has been extremely responsive to the commitments, policies, opportunities, and barriers of the past.

The second most powerful predictor of Soviet commercial expansion, military capability measured as defense expenditure, offers an even sharper contrast to the US case — while further corroborating the observation that Soviet expansion is dominated by bureaucratic patterns. Where the coefficient for American defense expenditures was significant and positive, the coefficient for Soviet defense expenditures is significance and negative — as it has been in all Soviet commercial expansion equations experimentally regressed over this period. A possible interpretation is that the Soviet military capability's role as an instrument of commercial expansion, to the

[16] See Appendix C.
[17] The substitution of oil production for coal production in the otherwise identical equation (estimated using MAV1) produces a positive, marginally significant ($p < .10$) coefficient. All other terms retain their approximate status, except that the lagged endogenous term drops out.

extent that such a role exists, is more than offset by its role as a competitor for scarce resources. Within the Soviet bureaucracy, increases in military capability building might detract, more or less directly, from the resources the Soviets require to engage in the expansion of commercial activity abroad.

The coefficient of the third statistically significant term — technological demands relative to resources measured as industrial production index ÷ coal production — is positive as expected, unlike the US case. Occasionally, in some experimental formulations, the term drops out.[18] But it is always positive. And it is often enough significant to suggest that the measures used here are perhaps more adequate representations of recent stages of Soviet technological development than they are in the US case.

As a society which, like the Soviet Union, manages its commercial expansion in a centralized way, China exhibits dynamics of expansion that are quite similar to those observed of the USSR. The dominant term in the equation for China, as in all experimental equations, is the lagged endogenous commitment-inertia term. The effects of previous decisions, prior commitments, and past barriers seem quite pronounced. Moreover, as in the Soviet equation, military capability (defense expenditure) appears to exert a strong negative influence on expansion — as if, given scarce resources, Chinese leaders have repeatedly confronted a necessary trade-off between commercial expansion and military capability building. That such trade-off relationships might exist lends further weight to the interpretation of Chinese expansion as bureaucratically dominated.

In addition, Chinese commercial expansion appears to be strongly and positively influenced by the growth of Chinese technology relative to resources, slow as this might be, and by the interaction of a rapidly growing population with a rising technological capacity. An influence in the other direction, however, seems evident in what was earlier called changing popular expectations: when industry is most rapidly advancing relative to population levels, commercial expansion tends to diminish. This may be a function of China's relative industrial impoverishment. Industrializing in large measure by importing technology, China may have needed trade least when industrializing the fastest. Put differently, it is precisely when China's industrial advancement most lagged behind the demands of a growing population that Chinese leaders felt the greatest need for infusions of technology from abroad.

The combination of parameter estimates for China is suggestively consistent with patterns conventionally associated with underdeveloped

---

[18] As when oil production is substituted for coal production in the otherwise identical equation.

countries. Given scarce resources, but confronted also with adversaries abroad, Chinese leaders have faced a most serious dilemma. To build military capabilities has apparent opportunity costs in the realm of commercial activity. Yet sacrificing international commerce has also meant a foregoing of one vehicle of technological development. Without infusions of technology from abroad, moreover, China has been inhibited in its efforts to sustain economic-industrial growth at a pace equal to the mounting of popular demands. And this, in turn, has meant persistently scarce economic resources. Not even China's reliance on a manpower-intensive military establishment has permitted an escape from the cycle generated by increased threats from abroad, which, to the extent that they require expensive military developments, make the cycle more vicious.

In general, then, these research findings are consistent with the propositions while also revealing some important differences in the dynamics of expansion associated with China, the Soviet Union, and the United States. To be sure, experimental work on expansion has been confounded by a number of technical problems stressed above. Certainly, too, extreme caution must be used in generalizing these findings beyond the commercial mode of expansion. The need to systematically consider other forms of external activity must be emphasized. And it is apparent from investigations into the stability of parameters across subperiods that significant changes — not represented in the formulation presented here — have occurred (see Appendix B). Nevertheless, this research has underscored the primacy of internal (unilateral) factors in explaining a society's international commercial expansion, and it has also suggested some intriguing cross-actor contrasts in the dynamics of expansion — some contrasts that also imply some very real dilemmas.

If, as discussed in following chapters, expansion increases the likelihood that interests will clash and competition and conflict will ensue, then the ability to manage external activity is to be valued. Yet these findings suggest that each of the three societies, in varying ways, vitally depends upon commercial expansion; and hence it seems evident that efforts to constrain or redirect commercial expansion can have severe domestic costs. Moreover, this analysis suggests that, even if national leaders want to assert control, they will encounter obstacles. In the case of the United States, control appears lost to diffusion of economic decision-making. In the cases of China and the Soviet Union, by contrast, control seems lost to centralized bureaucracies. These dilemmas will be considered again in Part III.

CHAPTER 5

Intersections: Collisions of External Activities

Bilateral intersections occur when the outwardly expanding activities of two societies collide. Expansion makes collisions of activities, interests, and commitments — intersections — more likely. The postulated dynamics for intersections, then, are as shown in Figure 5.1. Recalling from Chapter 4 that the roots of a society's commercial expansion are persistently within the society itself, the discovery of strong links from expansion to bilateral intersections will delineate a significant transition: the emergence of bilateral dynamics out of unilateral processes. The transition is all the more significant because, as stressed in the conceptual framework, intersections tend to be generative. To repeat the argument:

> . . . much of the generative quality of history — the tendencies of endur-
> ing historical trends and structures to converge, recombine, and produce
> a rich new set of relationships seemingly marking the opening of a new
> epoch — can be attributed to the emergent combinatorial possibilities
> that such intersections afford. Intersections always bear implications
> for both conflict and integration: integration proceeds through the

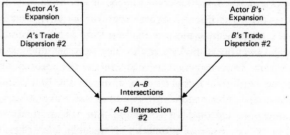

These relationships are represented by the following equation:
$$A\text{-}B \text{ Intersection \#2} = \alpha_2 + \beta_6 (A\text{'s Trade Dispersion \#2}) + \beta_7 (B\text{'s Trade Dispersion \#2}) + \mu_2$$

Fig. 5.1 The hypothesized dynamics of bilateral intersections.

creative working through of conflicts occasioned by historically emergent intersections. Conflict occasioned by intersections always results in
some degree of integration among as well as within the societies whose
activities collide.

The overall political and political-economic consequences of intersections largely depend upon the relative symmetry or asymmetry of the
intersections themselves. In order to simplify, the conceptual framework
has identified three general patterns: (1) *where a 'stronger' society's lateral
pressure generates expanding activities that encounter and penetrate the
domain of a 'weaker' society, a society having insufficient specialized
capabilities to resist;* (2) *where a society predisposed to lateral pressure
cannot express it due to obstacles posed by other societies;* and (3) *where
two societies having roughly equivalent specialized capabilities collide.* Section II.B of Chapter 1 elaborates at some length on the mix of integrative
and conflictual consequences likely to attend each of these patterns of
intersections. While all of these consequences must be borne in mind, two
consequences associated with the third pattern are given special attention.[1] First, intersections can engender antagonistic competition among
societies, which in turn can assume the form of military rivalry. Second,
intersections can establish the preconditions and territorial loci for provocations, those events and situations that can spark crises and high
thresholds of violence between nations. As will be discussed in later
chapters, these relationships are represented in the general model. They
have had an important bearing upon the course of Sino-Soviet-American
relations.

Within this context, then, key empirical questions in the analysis of
Sino-Soviet-American relations revolve around the issue of the relative
symmetry of intersections. In any bilateral relationship, are intersections
symmetrically determined? Or is the expansion of one society dominant in
determining the intersections it experiences with another? Positive answers
to the first question would indicate that the third pattern — and hence, the
preconditions of political-military rivalry, provocations, and confrontations
— might obtain. By contrast, positive answers to the latter question would
imply that conditions are more nearly those of the first or possibly the
second pattern of intersections. To be sure, totally unambiguous answers
to these questions are difficult to obtain. But just as surely, even weak
information on the issue of symmetry is valuable. For it helps to direct
analysis beyond the apparent relationships of power and influence in

---

[1] The reader not recalling the specific arguments is strongly advised to review
Section II.B of Chapter 1.

manifest rivalry and conflict to the deeper, less visible historical processes conditioning these relationships. In an important sense, to find that one society's expansion asymmetrically determines the intersections in which it becomes involved is to find that one society is dominant in determining the issues and arenas over which manifest conflict will be waged and to which explicit policies will respond.[2] The analysis of the dynamics of intersections begins to provide information in this regard.

It is clear from Figure 5.1 that intersections have so far been treated in a highly aggregated way.[3] Where expansion measures are actor-specific, intersection measures are dyad-specific. The concern is with the extent and intensity of Sino-Soviet, Sino-American, and Soviet-American intersections. Moreover, the intersection measures are global aggregates, as seen in Table 2.1 of Chapter 2. For the Sino-Soviet dyad, for example, the intersection measure is the sum, across all geographic regions, of the multiplicative products of Chinese and Soviet trade within each region. The measure increases in value as two actors tend to concentrate their trading activity in the same regions; and it diminishes as two actors tend to concentrate their trading activity in different regions.

To be sure, this measure has its limitations. First, like the expansion measure, it incorporates but one form of external activity: trade. It neglects foreign aid, basing of men under arms, military assistance, extensions of treaty commitments, foreign investments, and the many other forms of external activity that can project and reflect a society's extended interests and commitments. Second, being an aggregate, the measure precludes investigation of regionally-specific hypotheses. It is impossible, for instance, to examine the relationship between regional instability and major power intervention, the roles of local resources and the reevaluation of these, or the influences of regional colonial history, cold war alignment, culture, economic dependency, geography, and so on. Technical difficulties — particularly deficiencies in the available data base

---

[2] It should be evident that this argument resonates strongly with the notions of 'metapower' and 'relational control' as developed by T. Baumgartner, W. Buckley, and T. R. Burns. See their 'Relational Control: The Human Structuring of Cooperation and Conflict,' *Journal of Conflict Resolution*, Vol. XIX, No. 3 (September 1975).

[3] Note that the definition of intersections used in this study departs from the one used by Choucri and North. For them, for a given country, for any given year, the intersection variable is a 'metricized measure of violence in *intersections* (conflicts specifically over colonial crises) between major powers;' it is thus the single highest violence level registered between a power and *all others*, over a colonial issue, within a given year. By contrast, the intersection measures used here are dyad-specific and involve aggregate intensities of regional convergence in trading activity. See Nazli Choucri and Robert C. North, *Nations in Conflict: National Growth and International Violence* (San Francisco: W. H. Freeman, 1975), see Table 1.1 in Chapter 1 and Chapter 12.

— make it impossible to overcome these limitations at this stage of research.[4]

But put more positively, the measures do represent one important mode of intersections — intersections in commercial activity — and, as will be seen in later chapters, these intersections do appear to spur military competition while also making regionally destabilizing events more provocative for relations among China, the Soviet Union, and the United States. These measures also suggest that each of the triangle's three dyads has experienced a dramatic intensification of commercial intersections. Figures 5.2, 5.3, and 5.4 illustrate this rapid intensification over the twenty-three years.

These figures also suggest a deficiency in the simple formulation discussed here. The intensity of Soviet-American intersections wavers to some extent through 1958 but then begins a steady climb upward. By contrast, the increasing intensity of Sino-Soviet and Sino-American intersections is not nearly so smooth. Both Figures 5.3 and 5.4 exhibit sharp downturns

*See Table 2.1 of Chapter 2 for the calculus of this complex measure.

Fig. 5.2   Soviet-American intersections (Intersection #2) 1950–1972.

[4] To disaggregate the analysis of intersections, treating them region-by-region, would severely complicate the analysis beyond the limits of tractability. Moreover, the data base is not yet rich enough to sustain regional disaggregation. In saying this, however, it must be emphasized that systematic region-by-region studies would surely enrich understanding of the dynamics of bilateral intersections.

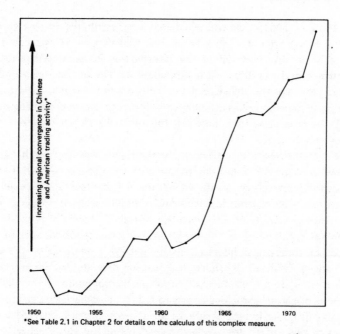

Fig. 5.3   Sino-American intersections (Intersection #2) 1950–1972.

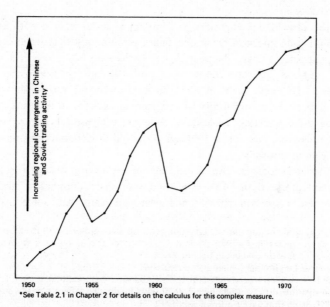

Fig. 5.4   Sino-Soviet intersections (Intersection #2) 1950–1972.

from 1960 to 1961 — downturns that can be attributed in part to the break in Sino-Soviet trading relations and China's slow adjustment. This sharp shift is also reflected in the investigation of parameter stability across subperiods, as discussed in Appendix B.[5] The present specification does not represent these changes, however. It does not because the attempt to maintain parsimony has meant the omission of terms representing trade *among* the three powers themselves. Further research must address this deficiency.

For now, however, it is evident that the simple formulation of Figure 5.1 does account for significant portions of the variance in each of the three dyad's intersections. As shown in Table 5.1, the formulation explains 99 percent of the variance in Soviet-American intersections, 92 percent of the variance in Sino-American intersections, and 85 percent of the variance in Sino-Soviet intersections.[6] In turn, the ability to explain so much of the variance in commercial intersections by exclusive reference to the unilateral and generalized dynamics of expansion suggests that intersections *of this variety* are not products of conscious manipulation — not, that is, the results of actors' conscious efforts to redirect commercial expansion so as to avoid or invade others' spheres of interests. Instead, bilateral intersections of this variety are largely the products of the actors' generalized, global expansionist energy. *The process appears to be stochastic, and the word 'collision' is apt.*

In the case of Soviet-American commercial intersections, both Soviet expansion and American expansion figure prominently. Yet American expansion appears to have dominated the relationship.[7] Moreover, the significant, negative constant term most probably reflects the Soviet and American tendency, early in the cold war, to concentrate trade within political blocs — a conformity of commercial patterns to political ones.[8] Only as these societies' expansionist energies propelled their commercial activities beyond and across cold war blocs did Soviet-American intersections begin to intensify.

Similar relationships are discernible in regression results for Sino-American intersections. Amercian expansion again dominates.[9] Indeed, the Chinese expansion term is not even significant. And once again, a

---

[5] Both analysis of full period regression residuals and application of the Chow test to subperiod regressions (1950–61 and 1961–72) for the Sino-Soviet formulation suggest very dramatic changes in parameters.

[6] All equations are significant at the .001 level.

[7] For US expansion, beta = .78; for USSR expansion, beta = .22.

[8] The significant ($p < .005$) negative constant might also reflect bureaucratic patterns of decision that have not been specified.

[9] For US expansion, beta = .77; for CPR expansion, beta = .07.

Table 5.1 *Bilateral Intersections, 1950–1972: Results of Estimation from a Simultaneous Equation System**

Dyad	R^2	F ratio	Durbin-Watson	Time-dependent correction	Variable: link to prior theory	Measure	Unstandardized coefficient	Standardized coefficient	Partial correlation	t statistic	Level of significance
US–USSR	.99	1099.01 $df = 2,20$ $p = .001$	1.55	AUTO2	Constant	Constant	−7.37217†	.00	−.98	−23.37	.0005
					US Expansion	US Trade Dispersion	238.796	.78	.93	11.44	.0005
					USSR Expansion	USSR Trade Dispersion	243.480	.22	.58	3.21	.005
US–CPR	.92	123.264 $df = 2,20$ $p = .001$	2.30	AUTO2	Constant	Constant	−1.39623†	.00	−.73	−4.75	.0005
					US Expansion	US Trade Dispersion	73.5541	.77	.91	5.35	.0005
CPR–USSR	.85	58.552 $df = 2,20$ $p = .001$	1.55	AUTO2	Constant	Constant	−0.25346†	.00	−.38	−1.84	.05
					CPR Expansion	CPR Trade Dispersion	−12.8929	−.47	−.33	−1.54	.10
					USSR Expansion	USSR Trade Dispersion	124.584	1.40	.71	4.45	.0005

*All statistics refer to the simultaneous-equation-system estimates using both two-stage least squares and, as indicated in the time-dependent correction column, generalized least squares. Bilateral intersections are measured as Intersections #2 (see Appendix C).
†Multiply the coefficient by 10^7.

significant, negative constant term — also most probably a product of early cold war patterns — is registered.[10]

For Sino-Soviet bilateral intersections, Soviet expansion is the dominant determinant.[11] The Chinese expansion term, in fact, assumes a negative, marginally significant coefficient in this formulation,[12] although the term frequently drops out in other experimental formulations. The constant term is again significant and negative. The latter, however, exhibits a far weaker relationship than is found for other dyads:[13] were it not for the expansionist energies of the two societies, particularly the USSR, intersections might never have occurred. But the kind of barriers separating American trade from regions of Soviet and China trade in the early cold war are absent in the Sino-Soviet case.

Thus, a comparison of regression results across all three dyads lends additional weight to the proposition that the roots of bilateral intersections are to be found in the unilateral dynamics of technology, resources, population, and expansion. *In each of the three dyads it is the expansion of the technologically and economically more developed society — the society richer in specialized capabilities — that dominates bilateral intersections.*[14] The United States, even in 1950, had a comparatively enormous technological and economic base. Hence, the expansion of the United States has been the prime source of Sino-American and Soviet-American commercial intersections. Similarly, compared to China, the Soviet Union also entered the period with a superior technological and economic base, and a more favorable ratio of resources to popular demands. Consequently, the expansion of the USSR has been the dominant determinant of Sino-Soviet intersections.

Viewed in the light of these empirical results, relations within the Sino-Soviet-American triangle can be at least tentatively situated with respect to the three patterns of intersections mentioned above and discussed in Chapter 1.[15] In its *asymmetrical* involvement in *Sino-Soviet and Sino-American intersections*, China can be seen to represent the case of a society whose domains of activity and interests are vulnerable to penetration, and whose own lateral pressure activities are obstructed, by the more rapidly mounting lateral pressure activities of the other two societies. According to the conceptual framework, were China in fact penetrated (i.e., were the first pattern fully realized), then the likely consequences would include the

[10] The constant is significant at the .0005 level.
[11] For USSR expansion, beta = .71; for CPR expansion, beta = −.33.
[12] $p < .10$.   [13] $p < .05$.
[14] Compare standardized regression coefficients in Table 5.1.
[15] Again, the reader is urged to review Section II.B of Chapter 1, which provides the basis for the following arguments and inferences.

skewing of China's social and economic structures in 'reflection' of the social and economic demands generated by the USSR, the US, and other societies having advanced specialized capabilities. However, at least since the mid-1950s, and up until quite recently, Chinese policy has demonstrated a political sensitivity to these possibilities. In a manner often associated with the second pattern of intersections, Chinese leaders have recognized the deep political implications of intersections, have sought to resist penetration, and have sought to limit 'encirclement.' As articulated in policies of self-reliance, the Chinese leadership has acted to limit foreign influence, mobilize social energies, restrict the immediate consumption of resources, and concentrate scarce resources on the building of specialized capabilities intended to confront and overcome obstacles of the present. For their parts, the US and the USSR have quite different roles with respect to Sino-American and Sino-Soviet intersections. If the conceptual framework is correct, then these societies, being asymmetrically dominant with respect to China, would be less responsive to the deep political implications of intersections, *per se*. American and Soviet policies toward China would be expected to respond, not so much to the fact of intersections, but to China's explicit attempts to mobilize resources, build capabilities, limit penetration, and resist American and Soviet expansion.

Being somewhat more symmetrical, *Soviet-American intersections* tend to exhibit relationships departing from those evidenced in the asymmetrical Sino-Soviet and Sino-American cases. There are similarities, to be sure. For in general, as indicated above, the symmetry of intersections is far from perfect, and US commercial expansion has been the dominant determinant of Soviet-American intersections. As in the case of China *vis-à-vis* the US and the USSR, therefore, the Soviet Union would be expected to resist the expansion of the United States and other high lateral pressure societies, limit foreign penetration, strengthen state apparatus, and extract societal resources in order to build specialized capabilities and overcome extant obstacles. In these terms at least, Soviet policies and capability building directed toward the US might be expected to be far more responsive to internal factors and the history of American dominance than to the immediate actions and attributes of the United States. At the same time, though, the empirical results suggest that conformity to this pattern might not be complete. The full period parameter estimates suggest that the Soviet position *vis-à-vis* the US, unlike that of China, has not been one of total impotence, and subperiod parameter estimates suggest that the relative importance of Soviet expansion in determining Soviet-American intersections has been increasing. Thus, in contrast to Sino-Soviet and Sino-American intersections, Soviet-American intersections more closely approximate the symmetrical pattern that is hypothesized to condition military rivalry, provocations, and confrontations. Overall, the picture conveyed by the analysis of the dynamics of Soviet-American intersections is a mixed and perhaps transitional one. Concepts of asynchrony, equifinality, irreversibility, cumulation, and antagonism all apply.[16]

All such inferences must be viewed with caution. The persistent significance of negative constant terms, particularly for Sino-American and Soviet-American intersections, suggests the very real possibility of misspecification in the simple formulation examined here. If, as inferred, these constants partially reflect cold war barriers, then (*a*) one might in the future incorporate a lagged endogenous term to represent the gradual breaking-down of barriers with time and (*b*) one might begin to view even the basic dynamics of intersections as influenced in part by global patterns of conflict and alignment. Both of these steps would involve complications of the model. The latter would require a richer data collection than is now available.[17]

For now, then, intersections are viewed primarily as collisions of expanding interests and commitments, efforts to delineate other factors determining intersections are postponed, and attention shifts to the empirical analysis of some of the consequences of intersections in the Sino-Soviet-American triangle. The next chapter, Chapter 6, addresses bilateral intersections as a basis for provocations.

---

[16] See Section III of Chapter 1.

[17] The efficient use of research resources indicates postponing consideration of these hypotheses until improved and alternate measures of expansion and intersections can be obtained.

CHAPTER 6

Provocations: Local Wars at Points of Intersection

As defined in Chapter 1, a provocation is an incident, event, or situation occurring at a point of intersection in the spheres of activities, interests, and commitments of two societies. Specifically, it is an event or situation that (a) poses a significant threat of sudden change in a region's internal political character, external orientation and alignment, and/or external economic relationships, and thus (b) poses a significant threat to the interests and commitments of one or both societies whose activities intersect. According to the definition, to qualify as a provocation with respect to the relations of two major powers a destabilizing event or situation must occur at a point of bilateral intersection. In the absence of intersecting activities, interests, and commitments, an event will not represent a threat of salience for the sovieties' mutual relations. Indeed, an event will tend to be provocative to the degree that intersections are intense.

Using the number of ongoing local wars per region as an indicator of destabilizing events,[1] the attempt to represent this conceptualization in a single measure of overall bilateral provocations involves (1) weighting the wars of each region by the intensity of bilateral intersections within each,[2] and then (2) summing across regions.[3] Figures 6.1, 6.2, and 6.3 depict one measure of bilateral provocations for each of the triangle's three dyads from 1950 through 1972. In each case, the intensity of overall bilateral provocations climbed rapidly through 1965 — reflecting in part the intensification of bilateral intersections within regions — and then dropped off thereafter — as the frequency of local wars has tapered-off, especially in regions of most intense bilateral intersections.

[1] See Appendix C for details.
[2] Intensity of intersection within a region is the product of each of two actors' total trade within a region.
[3] See p. 56, Table 2.1, for the exact calculus.

*See Table 2.1 in Chapter 2 for details on the calculation of this measure.

Fig. 6.1   Soviet–American provocations (Provocation #2) 1950–1972.

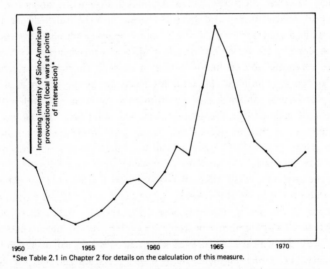

*See Table 2.1 in Chapter 2 for details on the calculation of this measure.

Fig. 6.2   Sino-American provocations (Provocation #2) 1950–1972.

By destabilizing regions and by threatening interests, provocations can precipitate urgent, crisis-like behaviors. When they see threats to their interests, actors may be inclined to directly intervene, to attempt to 'stabilize' (or, alternatively, to exploit)[4] a situation, and to engage in

---

[4] Whatever an actor's motives, a rival is likely to perceive them as exploitative.

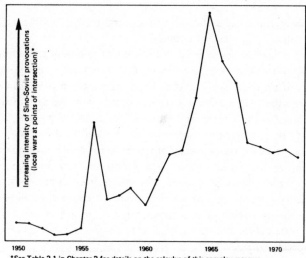

*See Table 2.1 in Chapter 2 for details on the calculus of this complex measure.

Fig. 6.3   Sino-Soviet provocations (Provocation #2) 1950–1972.

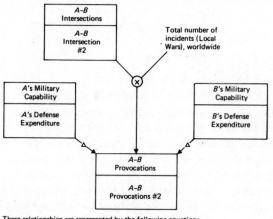

These relationships are represented by the following equation:

$A–B$ Provocation #2 = α_4 + β_{14} [Δ(A's Defense Expenditure)] +
β_{15} [Δ(B's Defense Expenditure)] +
β_{16} [($A–B$ Intersec. #2) × (# Local Wars)] + μ_4

Fig. 6.4   The hypothesized dynamics of bilateral provocations.

demonstrations of strength and resolve. These activities can heighten a rival actor's perception of threat and lead it to take counter-action — warnings, ultimata, and counter-demonstrations of commitment. When interlocked, these dynamics can quickly assume the form of a conflict spiral as each actor's range of options rapidly narrows to increasingly conflictual ones. Provocations make such dynamics very likely. In Chapter 9 these propositions are empirically examined.

At this point, the focus is upon the *sources* of provocations within the Sino-Soviet-American system. Figure 6.4 illustrates the hypothesized dynamics of provocations — a formulation that is the product of extensive experimentation. This experimentation began with the proposition that intersections, as they widen and intensify for a pair of powers, will serve to identify an ever greater proportion of the world's disputes, conflagrations, and incidents as potentially provocative for that pair of powers. The implication is that *the sources of these events and situations lie primarily outside of the triangular system.* The proposition itself is simple and stochastic: the widening and intensification of two actors intersections increases the probability that a given event or situation will occur at a point of intersection and hence qualify as a provocation. This proposition can be operationalized

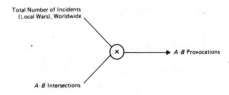

with all relationships expected to be positive.

Adding to this proposition, a number of other possible relationships were experimentally examined, as discussed in Appendix A.[5] While most relationships examined were found to be insignificant, support was found for one hypothesis: change in an actor's military capabilities (defense expenditures) will affect the bilateral provocations it experiences.[6] This additional hypothesis is reflected in the postulated dynamics of Figure 6.4.

Taken together, these several hypothesized relationships are simultaneously suggestive of the powers' abilities to influence the provocations they experience and of the degree to which these provocations are beyond

---

[5] Among the propositions considered: 'Bilateral provocations increase as a reflection of the change or rate of change in bilateral intersections' and 'Bilateral provocations increase as a result of the change and percentage rates of change in inividual actors' expansive activities.'

[6] The neutral 'affect' is used in lieu of the directional 'increase' or 'diminish' because, in the preliminary analysis, both positive and negative relationships were found. Moreover, experimentation was also undertaken with levels of defense expenditures, as opposed to changes; but, interestingly, change variables were found to be more regularly significant. In part, perhaps, this is due to collinearity introduced in the two level-of-defense-expenditure terms. See Appendix A. See Chapter 7 for related arguments regarding defense expenditures.

the immediate control of national leaders. To the extent that changes in military capabilities (defense expenditures) are found to be influential, one can infer (*a*) an actor's increasing inclination to use military capabilities or other means to incite or encourage provocative incidents as military capabilities increase, in the case of positive coefficients or (*b*) an actor's mounting inclination to use military capabilities or other means to stabilize or suppress conflict situations as military capabilities increase, in the case of negative coefficients. On the other hand, the salience of the interactive term would suggest an absence of immediate control. If this term is significant, then important sources of bilateral provocations can be traced back to collisions of interests — i.e., intersections — and then to the expansionist energies generated by advancing societies.[7]

Table 6.1 displays the regression results for each of the three bilateral intersections — Sino-Soviet, Sino-American, and Soviet-American — across the 1951 through 1972 period. These equations, it is clear, do not account for extremely large percentages of the variance in the three dyads' bilateral intersections. Between 50 and 79 percent of the variance in the provocation measures is explained. This might be an accurate representation. Provocative events, taken in the aggregate, might be largely random phenomena — or at least largely independent of the variables considered part of the Sino-Soviet-American system.[8]

Morevoer, in all three equations *one term, the multiplicative interaction of bilateral intersections and local wars, is both significant and the best predictor of bilateral provocations.* Widening, intensifying bilateral intersections do increase the probability that a local conflict will become a provocation for a pair of actors. And because commercial intersections are themselves products of stochastic processes — largely inadvertent collisions of two societies' outwardly expending activities[9] — provocations as defined here are in turn largely unintended consequences of growth and the expansion it generates.

But there is reason, too, to infer a modest role for military capabilities as means by which the actors assert some influence over the provocations they experience. In the case of Soviet-American bilateral provocations, the interactive term is clearly dominant (beta = .89). But the change in

[7] It must be stressed that these inferences are appropriate only to a high level of aggregation and refer only to vehicles of control associated with the variables explicitly incorporated in this analysis. With regard to particular local conflicts, it is clear, a number of strategies and tactics — to manipulate if not control — are available to the three actors.

[8] However, see Appendix B, which discusses different and often much better 'fits' over various subperiods. Hypotheses as to why this occurs are advanced below.

[9] See Chapter 5.

Table 6.1 Bilateral Provocations, 1951–1972: Results of Estimation from a Simultaneous Equation System*

Dyad	R^2	F ratio	Durbin-Watson	Time-dependent correction	Variable: link to prior theory	Measure	Unstandardized coefficient	Standardized coefficient	Partial correlation	Level of significance	t statistic
US-USSR	.79	22.099 df = 3,18 p = .001	1.83	MAV1	Intensifying Intersections Given Incidents & Situations	US-USSR Intersection #2 × Total Local Wars	0.03358	.98	.89	8.23	.0005
					Change in USSR Military Capability	Δ (USSR Defense Expenditure(1))	−1353.53	−.18	−.39	−1.78	.05
US-CPR	.50	5.951 df = 3,18 p = .01	1.95	AUTO2	Constant	Constant	8.89007†	.00	.49	2.41	.025
					Intensifying Intersections Given Incidents & Situations	US-CPR Intersection #2 × Total Local Wars	0.03315	.57	.62	3.32	.005
					Change in CPR Military Capability	Δ (CPR Defense Expenditure)	5859.65	.19	.32	1.42	.10
CPR-USSR	.69	13.071 df = 3,18 p = .001	2.10	None	Intensifying Intersections Given Incidents & Situations	CPR-USSR Intersections #2 × Total Local Wars	0.02011	.59	.64	3.56	.005
					Change in CPR Military Capability	Δ (CPR Defense Expenditure)	2701.55	.47	.45	2.15	.05
					Change in USSR Military Capability	Δ (USSR Defense Expenditure)	−292.702	−.44	−.40	−1.84	.05

*All statistics refer to the simultaneous-equation-system estimates using both two-stage least squares and, as indicated in the time-dependent correction column, generalized least squares. Provocations are measured as Provocation #2 (see Appendix C).

†Multiply coefficient estimate by 10^6.

Soviet defense expenditures also figures significantly in this equation — with a *negative* coefficient. One possible interpretation, mentioned above, is that the Soviet Union has effectively applied its capabilities to the end of controlling or suppressing conflicts within its areas of commercial interests. Another interpretation — more plausible, perhaps — is that the inclination of Soviet leaders to support, incite, or encourage local violence, by a number of means has declined as Soviet military capabilities have increased.

In the case of Sino-American provocations, once again, the interactive term is dominant (beta = .62); yet unlike the Soviet-American case, the change in neither actor's defense expenditure predicts negatively and strongly to bilateral provocations. (Indeed, over the 1951–65 subperiod, both the change in American defense expenditures and the change in Chinese defense expenditures predict significantly and positively to Sino-American provocations.)[10]

Finally, Sino-Soviet provocations, like the others, are dominated by the interactive term (beta = .64). Here, however, the changes in both actors defense expenditures figure prominently, although their effects are contrasting. As in the case of Soviet–American intersections, the change in Soviet defense expenditures apparently exerts a negative influence on provocations; but here, the change in Chinese defense expenditures is a significant, positive predictor of provocations. The effect of increases in Chinese expenditures appears to be greater intensity in provocations experienced.

According to the analysis so far, more generally, the provocations experienced by pairs of triangular actors are largely beyond the actors' immediate control. The equations account for significant portions of the variance in the provocation measures, yet a large part remains unexplained. Moreover, in explaining what they have of bilateral provocations, these equations indicate that intersections assume dominant roles; and this means that the actors' control of provocations, to the extent that it can be asserted, would largely involve the immense cost of restricting and/or redirecting their expanding activities so as to avoid intersections. To be sure, the actors' changing defense expenditures have been found to influence the provocations they experience. Their capabilities might be used as spurs to or constraints on provocations within intersections. Or, alternatively, an actor's felt strength or weakness, as reflected in its military expenditures, might affect its efforts to spur or constrain provocations by other means. But it has also been found that, compared to other

---

[10] See Appendix B.

factors, the impact of actors' changing defense expenditures is a minor and irregular one.

In reaching these conclusions, though, several additional points need to be emphasized. First, the measures used here for total destabilizing incidents and situations, intersections, and provocations are not wholly independent of one another. In view of this, the discovery of significant relationships among them is not surprising. This, however, is as true of the conceptualized relationships as it is of the measures. It is important to remember that the analysis focuses upon a simple probabilistic relationship.

Second, the provocation concept, as articulated, is almost a theory of itself, and as a result, the validation of any provocation measure is a most problematical issue. That is, the provocation concept (like others in this study) is *relationally* defined. It expresses possible relationships between combinations of intersections and local events, on the one hand, and major power confrontations and thresholds of violence, on the other. Moreover, as a relational concept, it must be understood within the overall historical context involving the lateral pressure sources of expansion, the patternings of intersections themselves (as discussed in Chapters 1 and 5), the politicization of intersecting activities, and many other factors considered in the conceptual framework. All of these contextual factors, in combination, are conceived to determine whether or not the particular mix of intersecting activities and local events that is represented in the provocation measure would in fact be provocative — would in fact tend to provoke confrontations and increasing thresholds of violence. For present purposes, the implications for the validation of the provocation measure are two. One implication is that the empirical analysis of provocations *as variables impacting upon thresholds of violence* will be critical to the assessment of measurement validity. In other words, since the concept is relational, validation depends not so much on rules of correspondence between conceptualized things and empirical referents but on the capacity of the measure to relate to other terms as the concept suggests it would.[11] The second implication is that, in so assessing the validity of provocation measures, different historical-contextual relationships — at least those implied by different patternings of intersections — must be borne in mind.[12] These implications are considered again in Chapter 9, where the

[10] See Appendix B.

[11] This statement suggests the applicability of Donald Campbell's notion of 'criterion validity.' See his 'Recommendations for APA Test Standards Regarding Construct, Trait, or Discriminant Validity,' *American Psychologist*, Vol. XV (1960), pp. 546–53.

[12] Specifically, as presented in Chapter 1 and reviewed in Chapter 5, the three patterns of intersections are likely to have quite different implications for the societies

provocation terms appear as right-hand side variables in equations for thresholds of violence.

Third, the three bilateral intersection and provocation measures have been discussed as if they refer to distinct geographic regions when in fact they are in large part overlapping. The most obvious example is Asia, where all three powers have had strong and increasing economic ties. The consistent reference to *bilateral* intersections and *bilateral* provocations is wholly a product of prior theory. As articulated in Chapter 1, the conceptual framework does not expressly anticipate trilateral intersections. The possibility of revisions on this point deserves to be considered later in the research enterprise.[13]

Fourth, further research into the probabilistic relationships addressed here can both benefit from and contribute to the investigations of the cyclical, periodical, regional, cross-national, and dyadic incidence of wars as exemplified by the works of Pitrim Sorokin,[14] Lewis Richardson,[15] Quincy Wright,[16] and, most recently, J. David Singer and Melvin Small.[17] These important works offer a host of propositions, insights, and analytic approaches regarding the distributions of violent conflicts over both the temporal and spatial domains. The work reported in this chapter represents a concern for the same kind of questions but with (*a*) a special interest in potentially changing and intensifying regions and (*b*) an allowance for the causal influences of other variables on the incidence of wars within regions. In addition, the conceptual framework has articulated, and later chapters of this study will examine, the potentially important roles of provocations, like local wars, as contributors to conflict among major

and their interactions. These implications are likely to extend to the impacts of provocations upon any bilateral relationship. For example, where intersections are highly asymmetrical, local destabilizing events and situations are likely to be seen as threatening instances requiring interventionist responses *only by the dominant party to the intersection*. For the lagging party, local destabilizing events and situations may be looked upon, not as threats, but as opportunities to alter or remove the 'oppressive,' expansion-limiting dominance in a region of the leading party. After all, given the historic patterns giving rise to intersections, it is the asymmetrically dominant society that has most to lose.

[13] The identification of trilateral intersections (as in Asia) is potentially informative as to regional or national 'balancing' patterns — the kind identified by Donald Zagoria in his *Vietnam Triangle* (New York: Western Publishing, 1967).

[14] Pitrim Sorokin, *Social and Cultural Dynamics* (New York: American Books, 1937), Volume 3, *Fluctuation of Social Relationships, War and Revolution*.

[15] Lewis Richardson, *Statistics of Deadly Quarrels* (Pittsburgh: Boxwood Press, 1960).

[16] Quincy Wright, *A Study of War* (Chicago: University of Chicago Press, 1942), revised edition 1965.

[17] J. David Singer and Melvin Small, *The Wages of War, 1816–1965* (New York: Wiley, 1972).

powers. In short, further work along the lines reported here can draw more extensively upon these earlier research enterprises and, at the same time, give them additional meaning.[18]

Finally, as discussed in Appendix B, it is apparent that breakpoints have occurred in the dynamics postulated and examined above. This, in fact, has been the case for all three dyads. The Sino-American and Soviet-American regressions, it has been found, exhibit the best 'fits' for the earlier of two subperiods (1951–65) while the Sino-Soviet regressions exhibited the best 'fit' for the later subperiod (1961–72).[19]

These shifts may well be attributable to factors lying beyond the system of variables identified by the conceptual framework — to the creation of newly independent states, for example, or to the emergence or decay of a kind of 'war contagion' or 'demonstration effect' in, say, Africa and Asia. But such shifts might also be attributable to factors included as parts of the triangular system, and a variety of *ad hoc* hypotheses to this effect can be put forth. For instance, it can be hypothesized that widening and intensifying bilateral intersections most readily occasion local provocations when the two actors whose interests are intersecting are themselves in conflict. When the two actors' mutual behaviors are more cooperative than conflictual, they may be less inclined to induce or support and more inclined to cooperate in the abatement and settling of local disputes.[20] Another hypothesis is that actors' attitudes toward local provocations will become increasingly negative — and hence they will act to constrain such events — as their respective leaderships *learn* to appreciate the potential consequences of the major power crises such events can precipitate. Yet, even though such hypotheses are plausible, they lie beyond the scope of the conceptual framework. Examination of them will have to await later stages of the research enterprise.[21]

Expansion, intersections, provocations — these are the variables considered so far. It has been seen that the first of these, expansion, is deeply

[18] With regard to relationships through time, it should be noted that a variety of time-dependent processes appear to be operative for the residuals of the regressions. See Table 6.1, for instance. However, no attempt has been made to model total wars as an autoregressive process.

[19] The 'best-fitting' subperiod parameter estimates, however, are not identical across dyads in the kinds of dynamics they reveal; see Appendix B.

[20] Viewed from the perspective of local parties, this hypothesis can be put in somewhat different terms: when two conflicting actors' interests and commitments intersect, local parties to a dispute can 'play one actor off against the other' in obtaining material and political support for their interests, thereby possibly prolonging local conflict and increasing the probabilities of violence.

[21] As noted before, the efficient use of research resources indicates postponing consideration of these hypotheses until improved and alternate measures of expansion, intersections, and provocations can be obtained.

rooted in unilateral dynamics, in the domestic growth of national societies. It has been seen, too, that expansion projects activities and interests outward where they collide with those of others to identify areas and intensities of intersecting interests and commitments. Once these intersections occur, provocations are extremely likely. And to the extent that these intersections and these provocations foster suspicions, antagonisms, competition, and conflict, the nature of the Sino-Soviet-American relations can be attributed in part to the demands and constraints of national growth.

The general picture so far, then, is one of dynamics unintended and relationships uncontrolled. The next chapter, Chapter 7, takes up one of the ways that actors attempt to assert control: their efforts to protect interests, meet threats, prevail in conflict, and sustain systemic balance by building military capabilities.

CHAPTER 7

Military Capability: The Capacity for Force and Violence

In military capabilities one finds at once the capacity to take, punish, and destroy and the capacity to defend, deter, and stabilize. It is this dual capacity of military capabilities — the security they connote to those who possess them and the insecurity they portent for other actors — that make military capabilities such dominant features of the international landscape, such important variables in the relations of nations. Military capabilities are among the prime referents and paramount instruments of national leaders as they interact, encounter conflicts, and seek to assert control.

Among the major influences on any one nation's capability building, it is frequently proposed, are the increasing, possibly threatening capabilities of others. Lewis Fry Richardson built his seminal investigations of arms races upon just this premise.[1] For Richardson, the rate of change in a nation's military capability building (its military budget, more precisely) could be viewed as a mathematical function of its defensiveness and grievances, its domestic economic constraints, its own level of expenditure, and the level of its rival.[2] A rival's capabilities connote insecurity, Richardson hypothesized, insecurity that can be minimized only by building capabilities of one's own. And it is because such perceptions are mutual — because the expression 'one nation's security is another's insecurity' is interchangeable — that spiraling arms races result. In seeking control

---

[1] Lewis Fry Richardson, *Arms and Insecurity* (Pittsburgh: Boxwood Press, 1960).
[2] In his two-actor formulation, Richardson represents an arms race by:

$$dx/dt = ky - ax + g$$
$$dy/dt = lx - by + h,$$

where t = time, x = the defense expenditure of nation A, y = the defense expenditure of nation B, k and l are positive *competition* coefficients, a and b are positive *fatigue* coefficients, g is a constant representing A's *grievances* with respect to B, and h is a constant representing B's *grievances* with respect to A. Ibid., p. 13.

over their respective nations' fates, the leaders of two nations contribute to a process that no one controls.

Now extended, the classic Richardson hypothesis is best seen in multi-dimensional terms. Nazli Choucri and Robert C. North have proposed that 'between rivals, any increase in the strength and effectiveness in one country along a critical dimension is likely to generate new demands in the other, and create a disposition among its leaders to increase national capabilities, either on the same *or a different dimension.*'[3] In their examination of the four decades prior to World War I, moreover, Choucri and North have shown that such dynamics are best understood within a complex network of relationships among a number of variables, including expansion, clashes over external interests, alliances, and violence behavior. They have shown, too, that an actor often responds to the capabilities (defense expenditures) of others, not necessarily with capability building, but with violence behavior — and that such behavior can spark further violence behavior from rivals, thus setting off a conflict spiral.[4] And they have found that domestic factors play immensely important roles. Technology combined multiplicatively with population and bureaucratic patterns of decision-making are among the dominant influences on defense expenditures.[5]

The research reported in this book has found strong support for the Choucri–North revisions, and it has extended the Richardson hypothesis still further. This and the two chapters to follow investigate the roles of military capabilities. Here the determinants of capability building (defense expenditures) are considered. Chapters 8 and 9 show that the distribution of capabilities has important effects on both normal conflict behavior and thresholds of violence. Throughout, attention focuses upon the unilateral dynamics of growth and the bilateral dynamics of rivalry. As in the work of Choucri and North, the dynamics of competition are found to be multi-dimensional, and bureaucratic patterns of decision-making are found to contribute to these dynamics. But the analysis weighs multilateral balance of power dynamics as well. And in so doing, it begins to show how each state's efforts to build arms and maintain security within a multi-actor system serve to project the dynamics of growth and rivalry beyond any one nation's actions or any one pair of nations' relations. Indeed, although the relationships are complex, *even systemic balance of power dynamics can be understood as an extended Richardson process.*[6]

[3] *Nations in Conflict: National Growth and International Violence* (San Francisco: W. H. Freeman, 1975), p. 203, emphasis in original.
[4] Ibid., pp. 249–53.   [5] Ibid., especially Chapter 13.
[6] This proposition is best understood in light of the full system of relationships. Chapter 10 presents a synthesis and elaborates on this proposition among others.

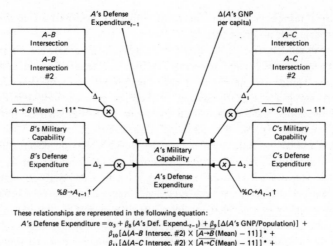

These relationships are represented in the following equation:

$$A\text{'s Defense Expenditure} = \alpha_3 + \beta_8\,(A\text{'s Def. Expend.}_{t-1}) + \beta_9\,[\Delta(A\text{'s GNP/Population})] +$$
$$\beta_{10}\,[\Delta(A\text{-}B \text{ Intersec. \#2}) \times [\overline{A\rightarrow B}(\text{Mean}) - 11]]\,^* +$$
$$\beta_{11}\,[\Delta(A\text{-}C \text{ Intersec. \#2}) \times [\overline{A\rightarrow C}(\text{Mean}) - 11]]\,^* +$$
$$\beta_{12}\,[(B\text{'s Def. Expend.}_t - \text{Def. Expend.}_{t-2}) \times \%B\rightarrow A_{t-1}{}^\dagger] +$$
$$\beta_{13}\,[(C\text{'s Def. Expend.}_t - \text{Def. Expend.}_{t-2}) \times \%C\rightarrow Z_{t-1}{}^\dagger] + \mu_3$$

$$^* \;\overline{X\rightarrow Y}(\text{Mean}) - 11 = \frac{\displaystyle\sum_{i=1}^{N} X\rightarrow Y(\text{Mean})_{t-i}}{3} - 11,$$

where X and Y are actors analogous to actors A, B, and C in the diagram.

$$^\dagger \;\%X\rightarrow Y_{t-1} = \frac{X\rightarrow Y(\text{Mean})_{t-1}}{X\rightarrow Y(\text{Mean})_{t-1} + X\rightarrow Z(\text{Mean})_{t-1}}$$

where X, Y, and Z are actors analogous to actors A, B, and C in the diagram.

Fig. 7.1   The hypothesized dynamics of Military Capability (Defense Expenditure)

The hypothesized dynamics of military capability building (defense expenditures) are shown in Figure 7.1. The specification of this equation is the product of extensive experimentation in three distinct research phases.[7] It also reflects attention to changes in parameters discerned in earlier formulations and efforts to represent these changes.[8] Four of the terms are specified to reflect sensitivity to change in intensities of normal conflict or change in the multilateral conflict configuration — changes which are explained within the context of the overall model. In this way at least, *the triangle is viewed as a system capable of the self-transformation of critical relationships.*

The first variable coterm in this formulation is the lagged dependent variable, representing the effects of 'commitment-inertia.'[9] The second coterm, the change in a society's GNP, represents the impact of changing technological and economic resources on defense expenditures. The third and fourth coterms — the interaction of prior normal conflict, above

[7] See Appendix A.   [8] See Appendix B.
[9] This, it will be recalled from Chapter 4, is a shorthand term that encompasses the effects of prior commitments, previous allocations, and bureaucratic patterns of decision-making.

or below a threshold level,[10] with the changes in bilateral intersections[11] — represent the competition-exacerbating influence that collisions of interests can exert. The threshold term is important: it is only when there is a relatively high degree of historically established suspicion and antagonism between actors[12] that intersections give rise to a perception of threat and a felt need to build capabilities. If prior suspicions and antagonisms are relatively low,[13] intersections can actually have an integrative influence.

Finally, the fifth and sixth coterms, the military-competitive coterms, are also interactively specified. Choucri and North refined the conventional unidimensional specification of such terms by incorporating instead the military expenditures *of nonallies.* In so doing they sought to incorporate the effects of one kind of breakpoint — a breakpoint that occurs as a nation allies with another nation that might otherwise have been perceived, and responded to, as a rival.[14] In the same vein, the military-competitive coterms of Figure 7.1 are multidimensionally specified. An actor is assumed to be guided by a 'threat assessment model' in its responses to others' capability increases.[15] Such a model guides an actor to increase its proportional responses to others' capability advances as the actor is increasingly the unique target of others' conflict behavior within the system.[16] As the conflict configuration changes, so also does an actor's felt need to respond to variation in others' capabilities.[17]

Figures 7.2, 7.3, and 7.4 plot the annual defense expenditures of the United States, the Soviet Union, and China over the 1950 through 1973 period. American defense expenditures have ranged from a low in 1950 of about $23 billion to a high in 1968 (the peak of US Vietnam involvement) of approximately $90 billion. Since 1968, American defense

----

[10] The threshold level — eleven on the thirty-point scale of conflict and implications for violence — is experimentally determined. It also connotes a theoretically 'neutral' level of the scale, dividing conflict dominated acts from cooperation dominated ones. See Appendix A. Regarding the scale, see Chapter 2 and Appendix C.

[11] Changes in bilateral intersections are used to represent the actual collisions.

[12] i.e., when normal conflict is above eleven on the thirty-point scale.

[13] i.e., below eleven on the thirty-point scale.   [14] op. cit., p. 204.

[15] See Section II.C of Chapter 1, where the threat assessment model, a balance of power model, is presented.

[16] That is, the coterm pre-multiplies the two-year change in actor B's military expenditures by the proportion of B's within-system-normal-conflict that is directed toward *A*, lagged one year. In this way, should *B* increase its conflict toward *A*, the coterm increases in value; should *B* increase its conflict toward third actor *C*, the coterm decreases in value.

[17] The use of changes in others' defense expenditures reflects both experimentation with the data and an effort to avoid the multicollinearity that including three level-of-defense-expenditure terms on the right-hand side would introduce. Two-year changes are empirically indicated. See Appendix A.

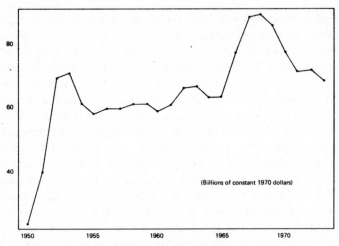

Fig. 7.2   US Defense Expenditure 1950–1973

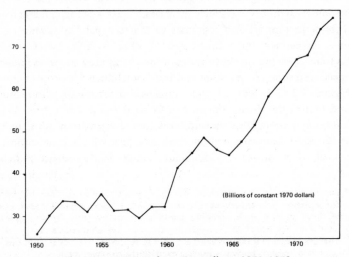

Fig. 7.3   USSR Defense Expenditure 1950–1973

expenditures declined to a figure of $69 billion in 1973.[18] The Soviet Union's defense expenditures have climbed, with several apparent reversals, from a low of about $26 billion in 1950 to a high of nearly $78 billion in 1973. And China's defense expenditures, after hovering above $2.5 billion through 1960, turned sharply upward in 1961 and reached a peak of about $10 billion in 1973. Despite this rapid climb, China's military expenditures

---

[18] All defense expenditure figures are in constant (1970) US dollars.

Fig. 7.4   CPR Defense Expenditure 1950–1973

remain minute compared to those of the two superpowers. In fact, China's total increase over a quarter of a century was more than tripled in a US increase in a single year, 1950–51. How well does the equation formulation account for these patterns?

Table 7.1 presents the regression results for this formulation, over the 1952 through 1972 period, for the defense expenditures of each of the three powers. As shown, the equation accounts for 78 percent of the variance in US defense expenditures, 93 percent of the variance in Chinese defense expenditures, and 99 percent of the variance in Soviet defense expenditures. In all three cases both foreign and domestic factors contribute significantly to the explanation.

The regression results suggest that over the last quarter century American defense expenditures have been dominated by two factors: bureaucratic patterns of decision-making and the growth of the Soviet military capability. The significance of the lagged dependent variable (defense expenditures of the previous year) most probably reflects a tendency noted by a number of analysts:[19] a nation's policies and budgetary

[19] See, e.g., Graham T. Allison and Morton H. Halperin, 'Bureaucratic Politics: A Paradigm and Some Policy Implications,' in Raymond Tanter and Richard Ullman (eds.), *Theory and Policy in International Relations* (Princeton, N.J.: Princeton University Press, 1972); Aron B. Wildavsky, *The Politics of the Budgetary Process* (Boston: Little, Brown, 1964); Otto A. Davis *et al.* 'A Theory of the Budgetary Process,' *American Political Science Review*, Vol. LX, No. 3 (1966), pp. 529–47.

Table 7.1 Military Capability (Defense Expenditure), 1952–1972: Results of Estimation from a Simultaneous Equation System*

Actor	R^2	F ratio	Durbin-Watson	Time-dependent correction	Variable: link to prior theory	Measure	Unstandardized coefficient	Standardized coefficient	Partial correlation	t statistic	Level of significance
US	.78	8.902 $df = 6,14$ $p = .001$	1.99	AUTO2	Constant	Constant	28224.8	.00	.73	3.75	.005
					Commitment-Inertia	US Defense Expenditure$_{t-1}$	0.52464	.57	.79	4.78	.0005
					Changing USSR Military Capability, Given Configuration of Conflict	(USSR Defense Expenditure$_t$ − USSR Defense Expenditure$_{t-2}$) × %USSR → US$_{t-1}$†	1.69420	.49	.74	4.36	.0005
					Changing CPR Military Capability, Given Configuration of Conflict	(CPR Defense Expenditure$_t$ − CPR Defense Expenditure$_{t-2}$) × %CPR → US$_{t-1}$†	4.00509	.15	.37	1.49	.10
USSR	.99	167.544 $df = 6,14$ $p = .001$	1.95	AUTO2	Constant	Constant	9309.75	.00	.55	2.47	.025
					Commitment-Inertia	USSR Defense Expenditure$_{t-1}$	0.94172	.83	.95	11.31	.0005
					Changing Economic Resources	Δ (Gross National Product)	−5.12708	−.22	−.72	−3.89	.005

			Variable	Coefficient				
CPR	.93	29.630 df = 6,14 p = .001	1.81	None					
			Changing CPR Military Capability, Given Configuration of Conflict	(CPR Defense Expenditure$_t$ − CPR Defense Expenditure$_{t-2}$) × %CPR → USSR$_{t-1}$†	9.51700	.20	.44	1.85	.05
			Constant	Constant	1169.80	.00	.49	2.12	.05
			Commitment-Inertia	CPR Defense Expenditure$_{t-1}$	0.62075	.57	.76	4.37	.0005
			Changing Economic Resources	Δ (Gross National Product)	70.6154	.20	.51	2.19	.05
			CPR–USSR Collisions of Interests, Given Prior Sino-Soviet Conflict	Δ (CPR–USSR Intersections) × $\overline{\text{CPR} \rightarrow \text{USSR}}$ (mean)‡	45.4232§	.56	.72	3.92	.005
			CPR–US Collisions of Interests, Given Prior Sino-American Conflict	Δ (CPR–US Intersections) × $\overline{\text{CPR} \rightarrow \text{US}}$ (mean)‡	−4.67046§	−.27	−.40	−1.64	.10
			Changing USSR Military Capability, Given Configuration of Conflict	(USSR Defense Expenditure$_t$ − USSR Defense Expenditure$_{t-2}$) × %USSR → CPR$_{t-1}$†	0.199937	.21	.45	1.88	.05

*All statistics refer to the simultaneous-equation-system estimates using both two-stage least squares and, as indicated in the time-dependent correction column, generalized least squares.

†See p. 134, Fig. 7.1, n. †.   ‡See p. 134, Fig. 7.1, n. *.   §Multiply the coefficient by 10⁻⁵.

allocations, once set, are usually changed in but an incremental way. Bureaucracies resist 'root' reassessments and instead revise policies and allocations by 'branching' from previously established ones.[20] Moreover, bureaucracies, once established, tend to find means of justifying their continued existence — and their sustained funding.

The changes in Soviet capability building have been an additional impetus for American defense expenditures. Although the change in Chinese defense expenditures are marginally significant, it is the change in defense expenditures of the Soviet Union — the nation most challenging American military supremacy throughout the period — that has captured the attention of American leaders and most influenced US defense expenditures.[21]

In the case of the Soviet Union, one again finds that domestic factors, the change in Soviet GNP and bureaucratic 'commitment-inertia,' are influential. The lagged dependent variable dominates the USSR equation, again reflecting the tendencies of bureaucracies to sustain prior policies and previous commitments. Indeed, so strong is the lagged endogenous term — and so strong have these terms been in all experimental full period and subperiod regression equations for USSR expenditures — that one must at least hypothesize a persistent and uniquely potent role for the Soviet military bureaucracy.[22] Once a course is set, the decision-making machinery would seem to be nearly imperturbable.

Yet, at least one external factor does play a role: the change in Chinese defense expenditures interacting with the mounting levels of Sino-Soviet conflict. As the Sino-Soviet schism has deepened, and as Chinese normal conflict within the system has increasingly come to focus on the USSR, the Soviet Union has responded to changes in Chinese defense expenditures with expenditures of its own.

Chinese defense expenditures are influenced by a number of factors, both internal and external. China, like both the United States and the Soviet Union, is apparently strongly influenced in its defense expenditures by the policies and allocations of the past. Here, as for the other actors, 'commitment-inertia' is immensely, influential. In addition, the change in China's GNP, its economic resources available for investment, is a strong positive predictor of China's defense expenditures. In this resource-

[20] Charles E. Lindblom, 'The Politics of Muddling Through,' *Public Administration Review*, Vol. XIX (Winter 1959), pp. 79–88.

[21] Note that the coefficient estimate for change in Soviet-American intersections is greater than the standard error, but not quite marginally significant. The term, however, is sometimes significant in other experimental formulations. See Appendix A.

[22] Beta = .83.

constrained society, more so than in the USSR and the US, defense expenditures strain the limits of the economy.

Among external influences on China's defense expenditures, collisions of interest with the USSR (i.e., changing intersections) are clearly dominant. With mounting Sino-Soviet conflict, China has come to view Sino-Soviet commercial intersections, primarily in Asia, as threatening; and China has responded with military capability development.[23] China has responded as well to increases in Soviet defense expenditures. Over the full period, it would appear, Chinese domestic factors and the mounting Soviet threat have most influenced Chinese capability building.

This mix of internal and external influences on capability building, more generally, is consistent with, and further substantiates, Choucri and North's revision of the classic Richardson hypotheses. In no case is an actor's capability building wholly a response to the military capabilities of others. All three actors' decisions are profoundly influenced by bureaucratic-inertial tendencies; and in at least two cases, China and the Soviet Union, changing domestic economic conditions have an important impact. Among external influences, moreover, an actor's collisions of interests with those of a rival are sometimes more influential than the growing capabilities of the rival. This is not to say that direct military competition plays no part: the analysis shows that the US has responded to the rapid climb in Soviet arms and that China and the Soviet Union have been mutually responsive. But it is to say that such influences are but some among many, and that even military competition is best understood in light of a changing, multilateral configuration of conflict.[24]

In reaching this conclusion, four points merit attention. First, a number of technical difficulties attend any analysis such as this. These equations are part of a simultaneous system involving reciprocal relationships and simultaneous feedback loops, multicollinearity has been a problem, degrees of freedom are limited, and a lagged dependent variable is represented in each equation.[25] Insofar as possible, adjustments have been made to avoid any bias, inconsistency, or loss of precision that these problems

---

[23] The changes in Sino-American intersections are marginally significant and predict negatively to Chinese arms expenditures. Perhaps this reflects a Chinese perception of American involvement in Asia as a counterweight to increasing Soviet involvement.

[24] When all military-competitive coterms are specified unidimensionally — when, that is, the interactive conflict component is omitted from each — these terms dropout of the USSR and CPR defense expenditure equations. This is a partial corroboration of the hypothesis that the overall configuration of conflict is crucial to military competitive dynamics.

[25] See Appendix D for a discussion of these problems.

might introduce;[26] and, just as importantly, conclusions are based, not on the regression results for any single equation, but on the cumulation of results in a lengthy progression through experimental research phases.[27] Nevertheless, caution is surely warranted in interpreting results.

Second, it is noteworthy that the terms for changing intersections (in interaction with prior normal conflict levels) are so infrequently significant in these equations. Only in the case of the equation for Chinese defense expenditures are these terms significant: Chinese defense expenditures appear to be strongly and positively influenced by mounting Sino-Soviet intersections (and weakly, but negatively,[28] influenced by Sino-American intersections). In some respects, this is to be expected. For as suggested in Chapter 5, Sino-Soviet and Sino-American intersections are asymmetrically determined by Soviet and American expansion, respectively. Accordingly, Chinese leaders, as leaders of the lagging society most negatively affected, would be most inclined to sense and respond to the political implications of these asymmetrical intersections; for their parts, Soviet and American leaders would be inclined to respond, not to intersections, *per se*, but to China's explicit, politicized attempts to limit Soviet and American expansion into Chinese areas of activity and interest. However, the same reasoning would seem to call for Soviet responsiveness to Soviet-American intersections, and evidence of such responsiveness is distinctly absent from full-period regression results.[29] Perhaps the absence of a significant relationship here reflects some error of measurement. Perhaps the present measure of *commercial* intersections fails to tap aspects of Soviet and American expansion and collisions — such as, say, foreign aid or the foreign basing of troops — that do have political implications for Soviet-American relations and hence arms building. In any case, this gap between theory-based expectations and empirical results represents one more critical tension that should motivate further research.

Third, it is important to avoid leaving the impression that neither the Soviet Union nor China has responded directly to American capability advances. This analysis has concentrated upon defense expenditures, the

[26] Specifically, the estimation strategy has involved the use of instrumental variable/two-stage least squares combined with generalized least squares, and the competitive coterms have been specified as change variables, as opposed to levels, so as to limit multicollinearity. See Appendices A and D.

[27] See Appendix A.

[28] See n. 23, above, for one possible interpretation of this negative relationship.

[29] But see Appendix B, where subperiod regression results are discussed. While the evidence is still very weak, it does suggest that Soviet arms building might have been responsive to mounting Soviet-American intersections in early parts of the period examined here — that is, when American expansion most dominated the shaping of these intersections.

most general of military capability measures. And it remains possible — indeed, it seems likely — that both the Soviet Union and China have responded to changes in various specific components of the American force structure: ICBMs, the basing of men under arms, the stationing of naval fleets, and so on.[30]

Fourth, it must be emphasized that the full implications of these findings cannot be appreciated by reference to any one class of dependent variables alone. The Sino-Soviet-American triangle is a complex system. In the next chapter, Chapter 8, it will be seen that the distributions of military capabilities are among the crucial determinants of conflict behavior. It will be seen, more specifically, how an actor's changing capabilities can affect this distribution and lead others to adjust directions and intensities of conflict behavior in order to sustain balance. And it has already been seen that conflict within the system can feed back and help to transform capability building dynamics. Thus, even though an actor's capability building might not elicit an immediate, direct capability building response from a rival, the first actor's capability advance can have an immense, albeit indirect, impact on others' capability building.[31] This is but one example of an extended Richardson process — an extended process in which the dynamics of growth, rivalry, and balance are all critical elements.

[30] Moreover, in this type of analysis, results are extremely sensitive to full model specification and analytic techniques. For some contrasting findings regarding Soviet-American military competition, see, e.g., Richard P. Lagerstrom, 'The Arms Race that Wasn't' (unpublished manuscript, Institute of Political Studies, Stanford University, 1971).

[31] For example, in the next chapter it will be seen that Sino-Soviet conflict is in part responsive to US defense expenditures (relative to Soviet and Chinese expenditures). And because, as just discussed, Sino-Soviet conflict helps to shape Sino-Soviet arms competition, US defense expenditures can be said to have *indirectly* affected Chinese and Soviet arms building.

CHAPTER 8
Normal Conflict Behavior

In Chapter 3 it was observed that the Sino-Soviet-American triangle is a system of persistently intense conflict and dangerously high implications for violence.[1] Over the course of the 1950–72 period all three dyads — the Sino-Soviet, the Sino-American, and the Soviet-American — have repeatedly approached the brink of war. Apart from these peaks of hostility, it was also observed that the normal, day-to-day level of conflict and cooperation characterizing each of the three dyads' relations has undergone considerable change: the Sino-Soviet dyad has replaced the Soviet-American and Sino-American dyads as the most intensely conflictual of the system.[2]

This chapter attempts to explain this variation in normal conflict behavior — a concept that is measured as the mean conflict level across all recorded events exhibited by an actor nation toward a target nation in the course of a year.[3] This measure is a general one — sensitive to activities at the low, midrange, as well as high levels on the thirty-point scale of conflict and implications for violence. It can be said to reflect the degree

[1] Across all six directed dyads, and over the full twenty-three-year period, the average mean conflict level is about fourteen or fifteen on the thirty-point scale — a score associated with such events as the introduction of trade restrictions, the breakdown of talks, open criticism, and the extension of aid to others' enemies. See Appendix C regarding this scaling procedure.

[2] See Figures 3.2, 3.3, and 3.4 of Chapter 3 for plots of the annual conflict measures across the 1950–72 period for each of the triangle's six directed dyads. Chapter 3 also provides a brief descriptive treatment of the three dyadic conflicts.

[3] See Table 2.1 in Chapter 2. See also Appendix C. In focusing on annual aggregates, it must be stressed, no attempt is made to explain or predict discrete events — like the Soviet Union's withdrawal of advisers from the CPR, the Warsaw meetings of Chinese and American ambassadors, or Soviet criticism of American initiatives in the Middle East. Instead, the concern is with more general trends and fluctuations in the level of conflict characterizing the routine day-to-day interactions of nations. See below.

of trust/distrust, amity/enmity, and perceived interest complementarity/incompatibility affecting one actor's behavior toward a second.

In focusing on directed, normal conflict behavior, then, this analysis makes two kinds of distinctions. First, it distinguishes among the possible targets of an actor's behavior. To be sure, an actor's overall level of outward hostility varies to some extent from year to year.[4] But this analysis is especially concerned with how and why an actor's hostility varies *with respect to particular target nations*. This distinction among targets will permit deeper insight into the nature of bilateral and multilateral dynamics. Hence, the focus is upon normal conflict behavior in six 'directed dyads': CPR → US (read CPR conflict behavior toward the US), CPR → USSR, USSR → CPR, USSR → US, US → CPR, and US → USSR.

Second, this analysis distinguishes between the dynamics of normal, day-to-day conflict and cooperation, the present focus, and the dynamics of thresholds of violence, the annual peaks of conflict behavior upon which the next chapter concentrates. There is strong empirical support for this distinction: *the experimental research progression has begun to uncover dynamics of normal conflict behavior that differ in many important ways from the dynamics of thresholds of violence.*[5] As indicated in the general model, normal conflict and cooperation and thresholds of violence are causally related but distinct variables.[6]

Within the context of the modeling effort, uncovering the determinants of normal conflict and cooperation is doubly important. On the one hand, the normal conflict behavior variable is substantively intriguing in itself. Where thresholds of violence reflect the often spectacular, sometimes crisis-like confrontations, ultimata, warnings, charges, and demonstrations of strength that have too frequently punctuated the last quarter century, the normal conflict behavior variable reflects the tenor of relations within a span of time. 'Cold war,' 'thaw,' 'rift,' 'tension,' 'spirit of Camp David,' 'peaceful coexistence,' 'era of negotiation,' 'detente,' 'the opening to China' — much that these general words and phrases connote is represented in the normal conflict and cooperation measure. On the other hand, explaining variation in normal conflict is important because *changes in normal conflict can help to transform dynamics within the system.* As seen in the last chapter, normal conflict and cooperation behavior,

---

[4] See, e.g., Nazli Choucri and Robert C. North, *Nations in Conflict: National Growth and International Violence* (San Francisco: W. H. Freeman, 1975), especially Chapter 15. Choucri and North focus on generalized peaks of 'violence behavior.'

[5] Compare Figure 8.1 of this Chapter with Figure 9.1 of Chapter 9.

[6] See Appendix A, where development of the model is described and the empirical basis for distinguishing the dynamics of normal conflict behavior from the dynamics of thresholds of violence is discussed.

above or below certain thresholds, helps to determine the impact of inter-sections on arms building. As also seen, changes in the systemic configura-tion of normal conflict behaviors influence each actor's assessment of the threat inherent in others' capability building. Moreover, it will be observed in the next chapter that the normal conflict and cooperation levels help shape the impact of provocations on thresholds of violence. To explain variation in normal conflict behavior, then, is to begin to explain how and why the processes at work in the Sino-Soviet American triangle have changed through time.

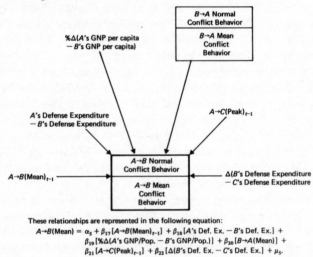

These relationships are represented in the following equation:

$$A{\rightarrow}B(\text{Mean}) = \alpha_5 + \beta_{17}[A{\rightarrow}B(\text{Mean})_{t-1}] + \beta_{18}[A\text{'s Def. Ex.} - B\text{'s Def. Ex.}] + \\ \beta_{19}[\%\Delta(A\text{'s GNP/Pop.} - B\text{'s GNP/Pop.})] + \beta_{20}[B{\rightarrow}A(\text{Mean})] + \\ \beta_{21}[A{\rightarrow}C(\text{Peak})_{t-1}] + \beta_{22}[\Delta(B\text{'s Def. Ex.} - C\text{'s Def. Ex.}] + \mu_5.$$

Fig. 8.1   The hypothesized dynamics of Normal Conflict Behavior

The postulated dynamics of normal conflict and cooperation are shown in Figure 8.1.[7] Unilateral, bilateral, and multilateral dynamics all contri-bute to normal conflict. The first variable coterm, the lagged dependent variable, represents the unilateral impact of 'commitment-inertia'. For thresholds of violence, it will be seen in Chapter 9, 'commitment-inertia' has little influence.[8] But for normal, routine, or day-to-day conflict and

[7] This formulation is a product of extensive experimentation. As described in Appendix A, hypothesized links from bilateral intersection and bilateral provocations to normal conflict behavior have been examined. It was found, however, that these hypothesized links are generally insignificant across all six directed dyads. Although such findings were surprising — strong links from bilateral intersections to conflict behavior were expected — these findings are reflected in the specification of the general model.

[8] Indeed, on the basis of experimental research, lagged dependent variables in the threshold of violence equations are not specified. Preliminary results showed that such terms are regularly insignificant.

cooperation behaviors, experimentation has begun to suggest that prior policies, habit, and routinization sometimes have a profound influence.

The second, third, and fourth coterms represent various bilateral relationships and, at the same time, they underscore once again the multidimensional character of competition.[9] Implicit in the second coterm is the hypothesis of 'compensatory dynamics': an actor's tendency to compensate for felt physical weakness — as when it lags behind another in a widening capability gap — with hostile demonstrations of strength and resolve.[10] The third coterm, the percentage change in a per capita GNP gap between actor nation and target nation, reflects the hypothesis that, even among allies, a gross and growing discrepancy on economic, technological, and other dimensions can awaken actors to the proposition that theirs is not a partnership of equals. The use of the *percentage change* in the gap will mean that the term itself will decline in value as a gap widens by constant increments. Thus, the functional form reflects the belief that changes in this kind of gap will have their greatest impact when the gap itself is small.[11] The fourth variable coterm reflects a hypothesis that actors are likely to respond with highly conflictual behaviors to highly conflictual behaviors directed at them and with more cooperative behaviors to cooperative behaviors directed at them. Actors, put briefly, are likely to respond in kind.[12]

Finally, the fifth and sixth coterms represent multilateral balance of power dynamics. It will be recalled from the conceptual framework that, at some point in the histories of their development, societies and states are likely to look outward upon the international system and try to know and order their responses to it on the basis of various balance of power models.[13] The fifth coterm reflects the possible influence of an actor's

[9] See Chapter 7. See also Choucri and North, op. cit., Chapters 13, 15 and 16.

[10] This hypothesis reflects prior experimentation, as described in Appendix A, plus the findings of Choucri and North. In their study of dynamics prior to World War I, they found that the 'military expenditures of nonallies,' whenever significant, predict positively to a nation's 'violence behavior' but that a nation's own military expenditures, whenever significant, predict negatively to its 'violence behavior.' op. cit., Chapter 15.

[11] And once two actors are very 'distant' in terms of this measure, even major changes may have little effect. On this basis, one might expect the term to be insignificant for Sino-American normal conflict.

[12] There is a growing literature on the so-called 'reciprocity' effect. It extends across a number of behavioral dimensions, not just conflict. See, e.g., Warren R. Phillips and Robert C. Crain, 'Dynamic Foreign Policy,' in *Sage International Yearbook of Foreign Policy Studies*, Vol. II (1974); and Warren R. Phillips, 'The Dynamics of Behavioral Action and Reaction in International Conflict,' *Papers of the Peace Research Society (International)* (1971).

[13] See Chapter 1, Section II.C.

Table 8.1   Normal Conflict Behavior (Mean Conflict Levels), 1951–1972: Results of Estimation from a Simultaneous Equation System*

Directed dyad	R^2	F ratio	Durbin-Watson	Time-dependent correction	Variable: link to prior theory	Measure	Unstandardized coefficient	Standardized coefficient	Partial correlation	t statistic	Level of significance
US → USSR	.80	10.159 $df = 6,15$ $p = .001$	2.32	None	Commitment-Inertia	US → USSR(Mean)$_{t-1}$	0.44274	.43	.62	3.08	.005
					% Change in Soviet-American Technological/Economic Gap	% Δ (US GNP Per Capita − USSR GNP Per Capita)	−4.61689	−.26	−.47	−2.03	.05
					Reciprocity	USSR → US(Mean)	0.76521	.70	.65	3.30	.005
US → CPR	.92	27.755 $df = 6,15$ $p = .001$	2.23	AUTO1	Constant	Constant	−4.32870	.00	−.36	−1.50	.10
					Commitment-Inertia	US → CPR(Mean)$_{t-1}$	0.31565	.29	.61	3.00	.005
					US-CPR Military Capability Gap	US Defense Expenditure − CPR Defense Expenditure	−3.15081†	−.25	−.57	−2.72	.01
					Reciprocity	CPR → US(Mean)	0.83129	.48	.77	4.66	.0005
					US Threshold of Violence Toward USSR$_{t-1}$	US → USSR(Peak)$_{t-1}$	0.18317	.34	.71	3.86	.005
					Changing Sino-Soviet Capability Gap	Δ (USSR Defense Expenditure − CPR Defense Expenditure)	−16.2963†	−.46	−.75	−4.42	.0005

	R^2	F				Coef.			t	p
USSR → US	.78	9.058 $df = 6,15$ $p = .001$	1.98 AUTO2	Constant	Constant	9.51223	.00	.66	3.40	.005
				Commitment-Inertia	USSR → US(Mean)$_{t-1}$	−0.36631	−.36	−.51	−2.30	.025
				US-USSR Military Capability Gap	US Defense Expenditure − USSR Defense Expenditure	2.31428†	.35	.43	1.84	.05
				Reciprocity	US → USSR(Mean)	0.65163	.71	.72	4.05	.0005
				Changing Sino-American Capability Gap	Δ (US Defense Expenditure − CPR Defense Expenditure)	2.31178†	.28	.41	1.73	.10
USSR → CPR	.96	61.423 $df = 6,15$ $p = .001$	2.01 AUTO2	Constant	Constant	−16.8093	.00	−.71	−3.95	.005
				USSR-CPR Military Capability Gap	USSR Defense Expenditure − CPR Defense Expenditure	20.1332†	.90	.71	3.94	.005
				% Change in Sino-Soviet Technological/Economic Gap	% Δ (USSR GNP Per Capita − CPR GNP Per Capita)	64.5814	.50	.70	3.79	.005
				Reciprocity	CPR → USSR(Mean)	0.36889	.34	.42	1.82	.05
				USSR Threshold of Violence Toward US$_{t-1}$	USSR → US(Peak)$_{t-1}$	0.48499	.37	.68	3.58	.005
				Changing Sino-American Capability Gap	Δ (US Defense Expenditure − CPR Defense Expenditure)	9.85094†	.31	.62	3.03	.005

continued

Table 8.1 continued

Directed dyad	R^2	F ratio	Durbin-Watson	Time-dependent correction	Variable: link to prior theory	Measure	Unstandardized coefficient	Standardized coefficient	Partial correlation	t statistic	Level of significance
CPR → US	.73	6.900 $df = 6,15$ $p = .01$	1.74	AUTO2	US-CPR Military Capability Gap	US Defense Expenditure − CPR Defense Expenditure	1.87366†	.26	.40	1.69	.10
					Reciprocity	US → CPR(Mean)	0.43876	.77	.69	3.65	.005
					CPR Threshold of Violence Toward USSR$_{t-1}$	CPR → USSR(Peak)$_{t-1}$	0.13310	.74	.61	2.96	.005
					Changing Soviet-American Capability Gap	Δ (US Defense Expenditure − USSR Defense Expenditure)	4.17763†	.55	.54	2.49	.025
					Constant	Constant	7.47415	.00	.49	2.19	.05
CPR → USSR	.95	44.551 $df = 6,15$ $p = .001$	1.89	AUTO2	USSR-CPR Military Capability Gap	USSR Defense Expenditure − CPR Defense Expenditure	8.46670†	.41	.40	1.75	.05
					% Change in Sino-Soviet Technological/Economic Gap	% Δ (USSR GNP Per Capita − CPR GNP Per Capita)	24.9640	.21	.33	1.36	.10

CPR Threshold of Violence Toward US$_{t-1}$	CPR → US(Peak)$_{t-1}$	−0.19370	−.27	−.44	−1.91	.05
Changing Soviet-American Capability Gap	Δ (US Defense Expenditure − USSR Defense Expenditure)	6.22873†	.21	.38	1.61	.10

*All statistics refer to the simultaneous-equation-system estimates using both two-stage least squares and, as indicated in the time-dependent correction column, generalized least squares.
†Multiply coefficient estimate by 10^{-5}.

'consistency maintenance' and 'isolation avoidance' models.[14] A positive coefficient would most probably reflect the operation of the former, an actor's tendency to 'generalize' from recent heated conflict in one direction to its normal conflict in another.[15] A negative coefficient would most probably reflect an actor's efforts to 'avoid isolation' by reducing normal conflict in one direction when recently engaged in conflict on the brink of war in another direction.[16] The sixth coterm reflects the influence of an actor's 'preponderance opposition' model: an actor's calculated efforts to reduce conflict and join with the weaker among others in opposing the proto-preponderant stronger.[17]

Table 8.1 displays the regression results, over the 1951–72 period, for this formulation for each of the triangle's six directed dyads.[18] As shown, this formulation explains between 73 percent and 96 percent of the variance in normal conflict and cooperation behavior.

For US normal conflict and cooperation behavior toward the Soviet Union, the formulation accounts for 80 percent of the variance, primarily by reference to the lagged dependent term,[19] the percentage change in the Soviet-American per capita GNP gap,[20] and Soviet normal conflict behavior toward the United States.[21] Taken together, the two most significant variables – the lagged endogenous variable and Soviet normal conflict and cooperation toward the US – suggest that American day-to-day actions toward the USSR have been dominated by a combination of bureaucratic-inertial decision-making and reactive tendencies. From the significance and negative sign of the term, the changing per capita GNP gap, one can infer a tendency of American conflict toward the USSR to rise when the Soviet Union most challenges American economic-technological supremacy. Balance of power considerations apparently have not had any *direct* impact upon American normal conflict and cooperation behavior toward the Soviet Union.

But American behaviors toward China are another matter. Here, 92 percent of the variance is explained by the equation. Next to Chinese normal conflict behavior toward the US[22] – a term whose significance is again a reflection of American reactive tendencies – the most powerful

---

[14] Preliminary research involved experimentation with unique terms for each of these two possible models. It was found, however, that it was impossible to specify these so as to avoid statistically confounding effects. Collinearity was a frequent problem. In addition, one more term would further strain degrees of freedom.

[15] See Chapter 1, Section II.C.   [16] See Chapter 1, Section II.C.

[17] Chapter 1, Section II.C, describes the rationale in further detail.

[18] See Appendix B regarding regression results for subperiods.

[19] Beta = .43 ($p = .005$).   [20] Beta = $-.26$ ($p = .05$).

[21] Beta = .70 ($p = .005$).   [22] Beta = .48 ($p = .0005$).

explanations of US conflict behavior toward the CPR are to be found in (a) the change in the Sino-Soviet defense expenditure gap[23] and (b) the previous US threshold of violence toward the USSR.[24] The negative sign for the first of these would appear to reflect a US effort to 'oppose preponderance' by reducing conflict toward China as the Soviet capability most rapidly climbs. The positive sign for the latter suggests an American tendency to (psycho-logically) generalize from its thresholds of violence with the USSR to its normal conflict toward the CPR.[25] The significant, negative coefficient for the Sino-American defense expenditure gap[26] most probably reflects 'compensatory dynamics,' a US tendency to substitute hostile assertions of strength and resolve for physical strength when the Sino-American capability gap is the narrowest. Lastly, the inertial character of American foreign policy decision making can again be seen in the significant, positive lagged endogenous term.[27]

Soviet normal conflict and cooperation toward the US — for which the equation accounts for 78 percent of the variance — is best explained by the constant,[28] the lagged endogenous term,[29] and American normal conflict behavior toward the USSR.[30] Like its dyadic complement, routine Soviet behavior toward the US is largely reactive in character. The *negative* lagged dependent term is particularly intriguing: combined with a strong, positive constant term it suggests a Soviet tendency to reverse or moderate extremely high conflict levels of the previous year.[31] In addition, the positive coefficient for the Soviet-American defense expenditure gap term[32] is consistent with the compensatory dynamics hypothesis: when US spending (and capabilities, presumably) most outdistance Soviet spending, the Soviet Union is increasingly disposed to conflictual assertions of its interests and commitments. And there is some sign, too, that the Soviet Union has heeded a 'preponderance opposition' model; the last significant, positive term — the change in the Sino-American defense expenditure gap[33] — supports this hypothesis.

The equation explains 96 percent of the variance in Soviet normal conflict and cooperation toward China — a directed dyad which has

---

[23] Beta $= -.46$ ($p = .0005$).   [24] Beta $= .34$ ($p = .005$).

[25] This suggests that the American image of a Sino-Soviet 'monolith' might in fact have influenced American behavior toward China. Interestingly, though, the analogous term is not significant in the equation for US normal conflict behavior toward the USSR.

[26] Beta $= -.25$ ($p = .01$).   [27] Beta $= .29$ ($p = .005$).

[28] $p = .005$.   [29] Beta $= -.36$ ($p = .025$).

[30] Beta $= .71$ ($p = .0005$).

[31] As if, perhaps, to confine Soviet-American conflict to 'safe' limits.

[32] Beta $= .35$ ($p = .05$).

[33] The term is but marginally significant. Beta $= .28$ ($p = .10$).

evidenced the extremes of cooperation and conflict.[34] The strong, negative constant term[35] is indicative of the generally cooperative spirit with which the Soviet Union approached China in the early 1950s. It also suggests that, were it not for a number of conflict-inducing factors specified in the model, cooperation might have prevailed. But these other factors are strong indeed. More specifically, the wide and widening military and technological–economic gaps between the two communist societies have been the dominant, positive influences on Soviet normal conflict behavior toward China.[36] As Soviet military capabilities have climbed relative to those of China, as the highly industrialized Soviet Union has rapidly outstripped the massively populated CPR in per capita GNP, *and* as the Soviet Union has responded in like fashion to Chinese normal conflict behavior toward the USSR,[37] Soviet conflict behavior toward China has quickly climbed. In addition, multilateral dynamics have had an important impact. The Soviet Union appears to have generalized from its recent thresholds of violence toward the US to its current normal conflict behavior toward the CPR.[38] And, contrary to the 'preponderance opposition' hypothesis, the USSR has increased normal conflict toward China as the US has most outpaced the CPR in defense expenditures.[39] One can only conjecture that the issues of (*a*) how to deal with American conflict (the Berlin crisis, the Quemoy crises, the Bay of Pigs, the Cuban missile crisis, and so on) and (*b*) how to deal with mounting American capabilities (particularly the capability increases attending US involvement in Asia) have severely strained Sino-Soviet relations.

In the case of Chinese normal conflict and cooperation toward the United States, the formulation accounts for 73 percent of the variance. This variance is best explained by US behavior toward China, prior Chinese thresholds of violence toward the USSR, and the changing Soviet-American defense expenditure gap.[40] The strength of the first of these suggests that, like US behavior toward China, Chinese normal conflict and cooperation toward the US is largely reactive. The strong, positive coefficient for prior Chinese thresholds of violence toward the USSR, once again, most probably reflects a tendency to generalize conflict behavior

[34] See Figure 3.2 in Chapter 3.   [35] $p = .005$.
[36] For the Sino-Soviet defense expenditure gap, beta $= .90$ ($p = .005$). For the change in the Sino-Soviet per capita GNP gap, beta $= .50$ ($p = .005$).
[37] For CPR normal conflict behavior toward the Soviet Union, beta $= .34$ ($p = .05$).
[38] For the USSR threshold of violence toward China, lagged one year, beta $= .37$ ($p = .005$).   [39] Beta $= .31$ ($p = .005$).
[40] Respectively, beta $= .77$ ($p = .005$), beta $= .74$ ($p = .005$), and beta $= .55$ ($p = .025$).

across possible target nations. And from the significance of the changing Soviet-American defense expenditure gap one can infer a Chinese effort to oppose preponderance. One can infer an initial Chinese tendency to oppose a proto-preponderant United States followed by a reduction of Chinese normal conflict behavior toward the US as the 'west wind' of American power gave way to the 'east wind' of Russian power and the threat of Soviet 'hegemonism.' There is some evidence, moreover, that a compensatory dynamic has operated: when the Sino-American defense expenditure gap widens, China tends to conflictually assert interests and resolve.[41] And finally, it is important to note the insignificance of both the constant term and the lagged endogenous term. Contrary to conventional wisdom, and unlike its dyadic complement, Chinese normal conflict behavior toward the United States has not been dominated by the decisions and policies of the past. To be sure, Chinese normal conflict behaviors toward the US varied very little until late in the twenty-three-year period examined. But this analysis finds little support for the proposition that Chinese behavior toward the US is dominated by either bureaucratic inertia or ideological intransigence.

The equation explains 95 percent of the variance in Chinese normal conflict behavior toward the Soviet Union. Neither the lagged dependent variable nor (importantly) Soviet normal conflict behavior toward China is significant, but all other variables are at least marginally significant. The constant term is positive,[42] perhaps revealing latent Chinese dissatisfaction with their early dependence upon the USSR and latent Chinese resentment regarding, for instance, the independence of Outer Mongolia and other territorial issues. The widening Sino-Soviet defense expenditure gap appears to have contributed to Chinese normal conflict toward the USSR,[43] just as it did in the case of Soviet normal conflict toward China. The marginally significant term, the percentage change in the Sino-Soviet per capita GNP gap, might also reflect the strain introduced by heightening differences in two societies' technological and economic standards.[44] Moreover, change in the Soviet-American defense expenditure gap, also a marginally significant term,[45] reflects the impact of multilateral dynamics. The positive sign for this term, however, is inconsistent with the 'preponderance opposition' hypothesis, as it also was in the case of Soviet normal conflict behavior toward China. And another multilateral dynamic appears to have been operative: the negative sign for prior Chinese thresholds of violence toward the US most probably reflects a Chinese effort to avoid

---

[41] The term, though, is only marginally significant: beta = .26 ($p = .10$).
[42] $p = .05$
[43] Beta = .41 ($p = .05$).
[44] Beta = .21 ($p = .10$).
[45] Beta = .21 ($p = .10$).

isolation — an effort to moderate conflict with the USSR when thresholds of violence with the United States are most threatening.[46]

Taken dyad by dyad, these several findings are extremely suggestive. With respect to *Sino-American relations*, for example, it would appear that China has been potentially more open to change — and was open to change at a far earlier date — than usually suggested. Far from being ideologically entrenched or bureaucratically immobilized, and despite persistent slogan-eering, China has been positively responsive to American actions. While the US, too, has been responsive to Chinese initiatives, it has been America's China policy, not China's US policy, that has been most mired in yesterday's decision and bureaucratic politics. The same can be said of *Soviet-American relations*. The two nations are mutually responsive, but the conflict behavior of only one, the United States, seems to build cumulatively on past policies and prior commitments.[47] Moreover, Soviet normal conflict behavior toward the US is *positively* influenced by increases in American defense expenditures — at least insofar as these increases translate into a wider American-Soviet defense expenditure gap. Rather than deterring Soviet conflictual assertions of interests and commitments, American capability building appears to have contributed to them. In the case of *Sino-Soviet relations*, finally, one must observe the importance of multidimensional competition. One must note how, between two allies, the dynamics of antagonistic comparison generate conflict. As differences widened and interests changed, it became increasingly difficult for Chinese leaders to apply 'lessons from the Soviet experience'; and it became ever more difficult for Soviet leaders to reconcile China's revolutionary ambitions with their own increasingly strong desires to consolidate gains and assure stability.

But even more provocative insights are to be found in viewing the three dyads as a system. Indeed, one conclusion of the analysis is that the three dyads *must* be viewed in this way. Sino-Soviet relations are dependent upon American behaviors and American capabilities. Sino-American relations reflect the role of the Soviet Union. And Chinese behaviors and capabilities impact upon Soviet-American relations. Primarily in their efforts to oppose others' preponderance and in their psycho-logical tendencies to generalize from one conflict to another, all three actors have evidenced multilateral dynamics in their normal conflict behaviors; and in so doing, they have assured that the unilateral and bilateral

---

[46] Beta $= -.27$ ($p = .05$).

[47] Recall that the coefficient of the lagged dependent variable in the equation for USSR normal conflict behavior toward the United States is both significant and negative.

dynamics affecting any one nation's conflict behaviors or any one nation's capability building will be transmitted across all three bilateral relationships.

In this light, one can better discern this study's further extensions of the Richardson hypothesis, as first noted in Chapter 7. There the dynamics of capability building were examined, the multidimensionality of competitive dynamics was observed, and it was found that the actors' defense expenditures are attributable to a combination of unilateral, bilateral, and multilateral dynamics. Here it is again found that competition is multidimensional. Specifically, it is observed that the defense expenditures of the several actors, and the capability distributions they generate, strongly influence normal conflict behavior. For example, actors often 'compensate' for felt physical weakness with increasingly conflictual behavior. It has been found, too, that one actor's conflict behavior toward a second usually gives rise to a conflictual response. In these statements alone there is corroboration for Choucri and North's extension of the Richardson hypothesis.[48] But it is extended still further. For once capabilities are influenced, or once conflict behaviors change, the effects tend to reverberate throughout the system. In fact, once normal conflict behaviors are influenced, important relationships throughout the system can be transformed. Owing to multilateral dynamics, in short, the effects of growth and rivalry cannot be confined to any one nation's actions or to any pair of nations' relations.

Here as elsewhere in this study the provisional nature of conclusions must be stressed. The analysis of normal conflict behavior has encountered many of the technical problems discussed earlier.[49] Moreover, it would have been preferable to have specified unique terms to represent both 'isolation avoidance' and 'consistency maintenance' dynamics.[50] This, however, proved impossible given limited degrees of freedom. And finally, precisely because of the few degrees of freedom, the analysis of subperiod parameter shifts (see Appendix B) has not been as informative as might have been hoped. In view of these problems, conclusions must be viewed within the full experimental context of the analysis reflected here

[48] Consider the following statement by Choucri and North: 'military expenditures . . . often evoke a violent response from rival powers (though not necessarily an increase in military spending). This response, in turn, evokes violence-behavior by the first country. This action–reaction process, so characteristic of major power interaction, partially validates and partially modifies Richardson's hypothesis.' Op. cit., p. 278.

[49] i.e., simultaneous relationships and a coincidence of serial correlation and lagged endogenous terms. Appropriate statistical adjustments have been made.

[50] See p. 152, n. 14.

— and they must be viewed cautiously. It must be remembered that the equations analyzed here are the products of extensive experimentation in three research phases.

The Sino-Soviet-American triangle, it was said at the outset, is a system of persistently intense conflict and one of dangerously high implications for violence. Here the focus has been on explaining variation in normal conflict behavior — the variable that characterizes the general tenor of relations and that reflects in part the general suspicions, antagonisms, and perceptions of conflict that have long been part of Sino-Soviet-American relations. In the next chapter attention turns to thresholds of violence — the variable that indicates a directed dyad's proximity to war.

CHAPTER 9

Thresholds of Violence

In any given year, one nation can initiate a variety of actions toward another, and these actions can range from extremely cooperative ones to acts of outright physical violence. The variable examined in the last chapter, 'normal conflict behavior,' represents an annual central tendency for one nation's acts toward another. Here though, attention focuses on the 'peak' conflict level per year. In a sense, this measure indicates a directed dyad's annual proximity to war. It indicates how close, given the full repertoire of acts at its disposal, one nation came to using force and violence against another within the course of a year. In this study these variables are called 'thresholds of violence.'[1]

Where normal conflict behavior variables, being annual means, reflect low and mid-range as well as high conflict levels, thresholds of violence reflect only the highest conflict level exhibited by one nation toward another.[2] Consequently, *it is in thresholds of violence that one expects to see the dynamics of crisis — threat, counterthreat, and demonstrations of resolve — most clearly manifested.* At the same time, however, it must be understood that an annual threshold of violence does not necessarily connote the occurrence of a crisis and that, in attempting to explain variation in thresholds of violence, this analysis does not try to illuminate the short-range dynamics of crisis or crisis decision-making.[3] Instead, the emphasis

---

[1] Figures 3.2, 3.3, and 3.4 in Chapter 3 plot these measures across the 1950–72 period for each of the triangle's six directed dyads. These figures also include representative peak conflict events.

[2] For details on these variables and the scaling procedure, see Appendix C.

[3] See, e.g., Ole R. Holsti, *Crisis, Escalation, and War* (McGill–Queen's University Press, 1971); Eugenia V. Nomikos and Robert C. North, *International Crisis: The Outbreak of World War I* (McGill–Queen's University Press, 1975); Charles A. McClelland, 'The Communist Chinese Performance in Crisis and Non-Crisis: Quantitative Studies of the Taiwan Straits Confrontation, 1950–1964,' Naval Ordnance Test Station, China Lake, California, Report N60530–11207; Charles F. Hermann, *Crisis*

is on those longer-range dynamics that incline national leaders to expand or constrict their repertoires of action so as to include or exclude actions approaching the brink of war. Put differently, the interest is in those longer-range processes that eventuate in the raising or lowering of what might be called conflict 'ceilings.'[4]

Efforts to explain normal conflict and cooperation are distinguished among the triangle's six directed dyads.[5] Here the distinction is again made — and for essentially the same reasons. This chapter is particularly concerned with how and why each actor's thresholds of violence vary with respect to particular targets. This distinction among targets will permit deeper insight into the nature of bilateral and multilateral dynamics.

The hypothesized dynamics of thresholds of violence differ substantially from those postulated for normal conflict and cooperation. Preliminary experimentation focused upon a wide variety of measures, functional forms, and equation formulations for both normal conflict and thresholds of violence, and it was found that relationships often significant for one conflict variable are regularly insignificant for the other. *Though some similarities were found, distinct processes appear to be at work.* The model specification reflects these findings.[6]

Most of these differences can be seen in an inspection of the general model,[7] but one deserves particular emphasis. Thresholds of violence — the annual peak measures of conflict that are most sensitive to the dynamics of crisis, threat, and preparation for imminent war — are less susceptible than normal conflict behaviors to the effects of habit, routinization, and bureaucratic decision-making, *at least insofar as these effects can be captured by a one-year-lagged dependent variable.*[8] It was seen in Chapter 8 that the normal conflict behaviors of both the United States and

---

in *Foreign Policy: A Simulation Analysis* (Indianapolis: Bobbs-Merrill, 1969); and articles in Charles F. Hermann (ed.), *International Crisis: Insights from Behavioral Research* (New York: Free Press, 1972).

[4] In saying this, the need to allow for error must be underscored. The peak conflict level event of any year, often being a single event, is particularly susceptible to error, miscommunication from central authority to field operatives, and the operatives' misinterpretation of orders — a point emphasized by both Graham T. Allison and Glen D. Paige. See Allison, 'Conceptual Models and the Cuban Missile Crisis,' *American Political Science Review*, Vol. LXIX (1969), pp. 689–718; and Paige, *The Korean Decision* (New York: Free Press, 1968).

[5] See Chapter 8.

[6] In addition, as pointed out below, even where the specified terms are similar, the parameters estimated often differ substantially.

[7] See Chapter 2. See also Chapter 10 for a verbal description.

[8] This finding does not rule out strong links among elements of crisis decision-making and behavior (a) extending from crisis to crisis even as these are widely and irregularly spaced over time and (b) within individual crises. Again, a threshold of violence does not necessarily connote a crisis.

the Soviet Union are closely linked to prior conflict behaviors. Such links, however, regularly dropped out of experimental threshold of violence equations. *At peak conflict levels, in short, no cumulative, incremental, or 'snowballing' effect can be discerned.*[9]

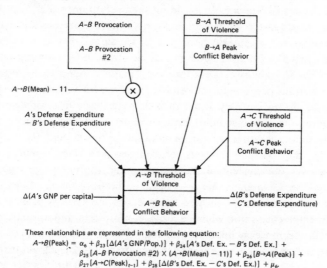

These relationships are represented in the following equation:

$$A{\to}B(Peak) = \alpha_6 + \beta_{23}[\Delta(A\text{'s GNP/Pop.})] + \beta_{24}[A\text{'s Def. Ex.} - B\text{'s Def. Ex.}] +$$
$$\beta_{25}[A\text{-}B \text{ Provocation #2}] \times (A{\to}B(\text{Mean}) - 11)] + \beta_{26}[B{\to}A(\text{Peak})] +$$
$$\beta_{27}[A{\to}C(\text{Peak})_{t-1}] + \beta_{28}[\Delta(B\text{'s Def. Ex.} - C\text{'s Def. Ex.})] + \mu_6.$$

Fig. 9.1   The hypothesized dynamics of Thresholds of Violence

Figure 9.1 displays the hypothesized dynamics of thresholds of violence.[10] Unilateral, bilateral, and multilateral dynamics are specified. The one strictly unilateral term, the first variable coterm, is the change in a society's per capita gross national product. Implicit in this term is the hypothesis that a society will tend to withdraw from external activities, at least temporarily forsaking the extension and conflictual assertion of interests, and at least temporarily avoiding the risks of external confrontation, when its capacity to satisfy internal demands is most constrained — or when popular demands are most rapidly climbing relative to economic resources.

The next three terms represent bilateral dynamics. The second coterm, the gap between the defense expenditures of actor and target, reflects the

[9] This finding, for measures of directed peak conflict levels, resonates with Choucri and North's observation for generalized peak conflict in the four decades prior to World War I. Nazli Choucri and Robert C. North, *Nations in Conflict: National Growth and International Violence* (San Francisco: W. H. Freeman, 1975), especially Chapter 15.

[10] As in the case for all of the equations in the general model, this formulation is a product of extensive experimentation in three research phases. See Appendix A.

hypothesis of compensatory dynamics — an actor's tendency to 'compensate' for relative military weakness with hostile expressions of strength and resolve.[11]

The third coterm is bilateral provocations interacting with normal conflict above or below a threshold on the thirty-point scale.[12] It is hypothesized that bilateral provocations threaten actors' interests and commitments at points of intersection; and in so doing, they can precipitate urgent, crisis-like behaviors. Actors may be tempted to intervene in order to exploit or stabilize a situation; they may be tempted to engage in demonstrations of strength and resolve. However, such dynamics are likely to be set in motion only when there is some basic level of distrust or antagonism (above a threshold) between actors. If normal conflict is below this threshold, provocations can have an integrative effect.[13] Moreover, in assessing the possible impacts of provocations, the overall context provided by the conceptual framework — and the derivative arguments developed in Chapters 5 and 6 — must be borne in mind. As explicitly argued late in Chapter 6: where intersections are asymmetrical, it is the leading actor (the actor whose expansion most determines intersections) that will be most inclined to respond to local destabilizing events as threatening and hence provocative. By contrast, the lagging actor may in fact be inclined to view provocations as opportunities to reverse asymmetrical relationships, escape subordination, and enhance its own latitude to expand.

The fourth coterm, the reciprocity term, is representative of actors' tendencies to respond in kind to conflict behaviors directed at them. Indeed, when interests are perceived to be at stake, an actor will be inclined to answer threat with counterthreat, demonstration of commitment with demonstration of resolve — always to make clear that it will not retreat in the face of threats while it prepares to meet a contingency increasingly seen to be likely: war.[14]

The last two coterms in the formulation represent multilateral dynamics. The fifth coterm, an actor's current threshold of violence toward a 'third actor,' reflects the hypotheses of 'isolation avoidance' and 'consistency maintenance' dynamics — two kinds of relationships that

[11] See Chapter 8, where this hypothesis is examined for normal conflict levels.

[12] As elsewhere (see Chapter 7), this threshold is set at a theoretically 'neutral' value of eleven on the thirty-point scale.

[13] As specified, the coterm takes on a positive value when normal conflict behavior is above eleven on the thirty-point scale and takes on a negative value when normal conflict is below eleven on the scale.

[14] The reciprocity relationship is also examined for normal conflict behavior. See Chapter 8.

can emerge when an actor is guided in part by balance of power models.[15] As with normal conflict, a positive coefficient for this term would suggest that an actor is guided by a psycho-logical 'consistency maintenance' model, that an actor tends to generalize from thresholds of violence in one direction to thresholds of violence in the other. A negative coefficient, on the other hand, would suggest that an actor heeds an 'isolation avoidance' model. An actor following this model tries to avoid simultaneous, two-front confrontations.[16] The sixth coterm is the change in the defense expenditure gap between 'others.' Here one expects to see 'preponderance opposition' dynamics reflected.[17]

Over the 1950 to 1973 period, Sino-Soviet thresholds of violence have ranged from a low of ten on the thirty-point scale to a high of twenty-nine with the violence along the Ussuri River in 1969.[18] Sino-American thresholds of violence have ranged from a high of twenty-nine during the Korean War to a low of fifteen, connoting such events as mild but direct criticism, in 1971. And Soviet-American thresholds of violence were regularly high through the 1950s, reached a peak of twenty-six in 1962 with the Cuban missile crisis, and generally declined thereafter. The lowest Soviet-American threshold of violence during this period is scored eighteen on the scale. How well do the equations account for this variation?

Table 9.1 displays the full period regression results for each of the triangle's six directed dyads.[19] As shown, the formulation explains between 81 and 95 percent of the variance in thresholds of violence.

In the case of US thresholds of violence toward the USSR the equation accounts for 83 percent of the variance. The dominant term is Soviet thresholds of violence toward the US.[20] As at normal conflict levels, American thresholds of violence toward the USSR are in very large part reactive. They are also responsive to Soviet-American provocations, given current levels of normal conflict behavior, and to the Soviet-American defense expenditure gap.[21] Regarding the latter, the negative coefficient is

[15] See Chapter 1, Section II.C.
[16] Similar relationships were examined in Chapter 8. As noted there, it would have been preferable to have specified unique terms — one for 'isolation avoidance' and one for 'consistency maintenance' dynamics. In fact, on the basis of prior experimentation with such terms it was found that degrees of freedom are too few and that the addition of an extra term introduces severe confounding effects.
[17] See Chapter 1, Section II.3, for a description of preponderance opposition dynamics. See also Chapter 8 where these dynamics are examined with respect to normal conflict and cooperation.
[18] These figures refer to both directed dyads within any dyad.
[19] See Appendix B regarding analysis over subperiods.
[20] Beta = .93 ($p = .0005$).
[21] Beta = .19 ($p = .05$) and beta = $-.33$ ($p = .025$), respectively.

Table 9.1 Thresholds of Violence (Peak Conflict Levels), 1951–1972: Results of Estimation from a Simultaneous Equation System*

Directed dyad	R^2	F ratio	Durbin-Watson	Time-dependent correction	Variable: link to prior theory	Measure	Unstandardized coefficient	Standardized coefficient	Partial correlation	t statistic	Level of significance
US → USSR	.83	12.149 df = 6,15 p = .001	1.76	AUTO2	Changing Economic Resources	Δ (GNP Per Capita)	3.45225	.17	.33	1.34	.10
					US–USSR Military Capability Gap	US Defense Expenditure − USSR Defense Expenditure	−6.21554†	−.33	−.51	−2.32	.025
					US–USSR Provocations, Given Normal Conflict	(US–USSR Provocation #2) × [US → USSR(Mean) − 11]	6.07486‡	.19	.41	1.79	.05
					Reciprocity	USSR → US(Peak)	0.92162	.93	.89	7.97	.0005
					US → CPR Threshold of Violence	US → CPR(Peak)	0.16686	.28	.46	2.02	.05
US → CPR	.93	32.880 df = 6,15 p = .001	2.27	MAV2	Constant	Constant	19.2368	.00	.72	3.98	.005
					Changing Economic Resources	Δ (GNP Per Capita)	18.4022	.54	.68	3.59	.005
					Reciprocity	CPR → US(Peak)	0.56148	.55	.84	5.91	.0005
					US → USSR Threshold of Violence	US → USSR(Peak)	−0.44243	−.26	−.62	−3.08	.005

Relationship	R^2	F		Predictor	Variable					
USSR → US	.81	10.633 $df = 6,15$ $p = .001$		Changing Sino-Soviet Military Capability Gap	Δ (USSR Def. Expend. − CPR Def. Expend.)	−52.0808†	−.49	−.66	−3.37	.005
			AUTO2	Constant	Constant	15.1598	.00	.66	3.39	.005
				Changing Economic Resources	Δ (GNP Per Capita)	−37.6897	−.50	−.51	−2.31	.025
				US–USSR Military Capability Gap	US Defense Expenditure − USSR Defense Expenditure	12.6935†	.68	.74	4.31	.0005
				Reciprocity	US → USSR(Peak)	0.36116	.36	.48	2.11	.05
				USSR → CPR Threshold of Violence	USSR → CPR(Peak)	−0.08662	−.20	−.31	−1.35	.10
				Changing Sino-American Military Capability Gap	Δ (US Defense Expenditure − CPR Defense Expenditure)	−6.63680†	−.28	−.43	−1.86	.05
USSR → CPR	.95	50.749 $df = 6,15$ $p = .001$	AUTO2	USSR-CPR Military Capability Gap	USSR Defense Expenditure − CPR Defense Expenditure	12.8006†	.33	.53	2.40	.025
				USSR-CPR Provocations, Given Normal Conflict	(USSR-CPR Provocation #2) × [USSR → CPR(Mean) − 11]	165.189‡	.34	.63	3.16	.005
				Reciprocity	CPR → USSR(Peak)	0.54086	.48	.74	4.24	.0005

continued

Table 9.1 *continued*

Directed dyad	R^2	F ratio	Durbin-Watson	Time-dependent correction	Variable: link to prior theory	Measure	Unstandardized coefficient	Standardized coefficient	Partial correlation	t statistic	Level of significance
CPR → US	.85	13.779 df = 6,15 p = .001	1.73	None	Constant	Constant	26.8269	.00	.81	5.34	.0005
					Changing Economic Resources	Δ (GNP Per Capita)	70.3923	.20	.41	1.76	.05
					Reciprocity	US → CPR(Peak)	0.21993	.22	.37	1.53	.10
					CPR → USSR Threshold of Violence	CPR → USSR(Peak)	−0.43819	−.54	−.70	−3.80	.005
					Changing Soviet-American Military Capability Gap	Δ (US Defense Expenditure − USSR Defense Expenditure)	11.7888	.30	.54	2.49	.025
CPR → USSR	.90	23.164 df = 6,15 p = .001	2.08	AUTO2	Constant	Constant	27.8731	.00	.78	4.85	.0005
					Changing Economic Resources	Δ (GNP Per Capita)	67.0245	.15	.43	1.84	.05
					USSR-CPR Military Capability Gap	USSR Defense Expenditure − CPR Defense Expenditure	−9.83456†	−.29	−.45	−1.95	.05
					Reciprocity	USSR → CPR(Peak)	0.53678	.61	.70	3.78	.005
					CPR → US Threshold of Violence	CPR → US (Peak)	−0.68640	−.55	−.68	−3.59	.005

*All statistics refer to the simultaneous-equation-system estimates using both two-stage least squares and, as indicated in the time-dependent correction column, generalized least squares.

†The coefficient is multiplied by 10^{-9}.

consistent with the hypothesis of compensatory dynamics but inconsistent with the predictions of deterrence theory: increase in Soviet defense expenditures relative to those of the United States appear to spur *higher* American thresholds of violence toward the USSR. Moreover, US thresholds of violence toward the USSR are not independent of Sino-American relations: American peaks of conflict toward the CPR are a positive influence.[22] As if operating under the image of a Sino-Soviet monolith, the United States appears to have generalized from its thresholds of violence toward the CPR to its peaks of conflict toward the USSR.

The equation explains 93 percent of the variance in US thresholds of violence toward China. The constant term is significant and positive, with a value of about nineteen on the thirty-point scale.[23] This high constant — corresponding to such events as strong demands and warnings — might reflect the high 'ceiling' of conflict at which the US and China entered the 1950s together with the persistent American belief, throughout most of the period, that China is an aggressive power that must be contained. This interpretation is at least partially supported by the significance and strength in the equation of Chinese thresholds of violence toward the US.[24] The US has readily reacted to peaks of Chinese conflict directed at it. Moreover, the significance and positive sign of the change in US per capita GNP is consistent with the hypothesis that societies, when lagging in their capacities to satisfy internal demands, tend to withdraw from external confrontation.[25] As at normal conflict levels, finally, multilateral dynamics play an important role. As at normal levels, and consistent with the 'preponderance opposition' hypothesis, the US appears to have reduced peak conflict toward China as the Sino-Soviet defense expenditure gap has most rapidly widened.[26] In addition, the US has tended to *reduce* its thresholds of violence toward the CPR when engaged in high peaks of conflict with the USSR.[27] The latter relationship is consistent with the hypothesis of 'isolation avoidance' dynamics, the hypothesis that actors will seek to avoid simultaneous, two-front confrontations.

For Soviet thresholds of violence toward the United States the equation explains 81 percent of the variance. The dominant term here — again contrary to the prediction of deterrence theory — is the American-Soviet gap in defense expenditures.[28] Consistent with the compensatory dynamics

[22] Beta = .28 (p = .05).
[23] For the constant term, p = .005.
[24] Beta = .55 (p = .0005).
[25] Beta = .54 (p = .005).
[26] Beta = −.49 (p = .005).
[27] For US thresholds of violence toward the CPR, beta = −.26 (p = .005). At normal conflict levels, the apparent US tendency was to generalize across targets of conflict; see Chapter 8.
[28] Beta = .68 (p = .0005).

hypothesis, the Soviet Union has tended to *increase* its thresholds of violence toward the US when American defense expenditures are most outpacing those of the USSR. Soviet thresholds of violence toward the United States are also positively responsive to their dyadic complement, American thresholds of violence toward the Soviet Union,[29] but this reciprocity dynamic is not nearly so important a contributor to Soviet thresholds of violence as it is to American. Indeed, this observation coupled with the strong, positive constant term[30] suggests the interpretation that the Soviet Union has been the most frequent initiator of Soviet-American confrontations. There are also negative influences on Soviet peaks of conflict toward the United States, however. Unlike relationships for American and Chinese behaviors, increases in Soviet per capita GNP appear to have a negative impact upon Soviet thresholds of violence.[31] The widening defense expenditure gap between the US and China, contrary to the 'preponderance opposition' hypothesis, takes on a negative coefficient.[32] And mounting Soviet thresholds of violence toward China take on a negative, albeit marginally significant, coefficient;[33] possibly Soviet leaders have been guided in part by an 'isolation avoidance' model.

The equation accounts for 95 percent of the variance in Soviet thresholds of violence toward the CPR principally in terms of three variables: the Sino-Soviet defense expenditure gap, Sino-Soviet provocations, and Chinese peaks of conflict toward the USSR.[34] The Sino-Soviet defense expenditure gap takes on a positive coefficient, as it did for Soviet normal conflict behavior toward China. Sino-Soviet provocations, with the increase in Soviet normal conflict toward the CPR, have apparently become strong, positive influences on Soviet thresholds of violence toward China. The strongest influence, however, is to be found in the reciprocity term. The Soviet Union has responded strongly and positively to Chinese thresholds of violence toward the USSR.[35]

In the case of Chinese thresholds of violence toward the United States the formulation explains 85 percent of the variance. The constant term is significant, positive, and very high, assuming a value of twenty-seven on the thirty-point scale.[36] Clearly, while normal conflict levels are

---

[29] Beta $= .36$ ($p = .05$).

[30] For the constant term, $p = .005$.

[31] Beta $= -.50$ ($p = .025$).

[32] Beta $= -.28$ ($p = .05$).

[33] Beta $= -.20$ ($p = .10$).

[34] Respectively, beta $= .33$ ($p = .025$), beta $= .34$ ($p = .005$), and beta $= .48$ ($p = .0005$).

[35] Interestingly, Soviet thresholds of violence toward China appear to be independent of direct multilateral, balance of power dynamics.

[36] For the constant term, $p = .0005$.

independent of prior values,[37] thresholds of violence appear to be dominated by the initially strong level of hostility characterizing Sino-American
relations in the early 1950s — a level of hostility that has been almost
ritualized since. At the peak conflict level, China has been but weakly
responsive to American thresholds of violence toward the CPR.[38] Nevertheless, Chinese thresholds of violence toward the United States have
apparently been constrained by a number of factors. One of these is the
slow growth of the Chinese economy: China tends to increase peaks of
conflict behavior when its per capita GNP is most rapidly growing,[39]
yet this growth has evidenced a number of reversals. Another constraint is
the influence of a 'preponderance opposition' dynamic: as the Soviet
Union has narrowed the Soviet-American defense expenditure gap, the
CPR has been increasingly inclined to reduce thresholds of violence toward
the US — as if to turn attention and capabilities toward the proto-
preponderant Soviet Union.[40] In fact, the dominant negative influence is
to be found in the escalating Sino-Soviet conflict. Chinese peaks of
conflict toward the USSR have a strong, negative impact upon Chinese
thresholds of violence toward the United States.[41]

Finally, the equation explains 90 percent of the variance in Chinese
thresholds of violence toward the USSR, with the significant influences
being the constant term,[42] the Sino-Soviet defense expenditure gap,[43] the
change in the Chinese per capita GNP,[44] Soviet thresholds of violence
toward the CPR,[45] and Chinese thresholds of violence toward the United
States.[46] Of these, the most significant is the positive, high constant term
— from which one might infer Chinese leaders' latent anti-Soviet hostility,
from the outset, despite the apparent early cooperation. The slow Chinese
economic growth — the change in per capita GNP — appears to have constrained outward manifestations of this hostility. Even more constraining,
apparently, have been the widening Sino-Soviet defense expenditure gap
and China's conflict with the United States. Regarding the latter, Chinese
peaks of conflict toward the USSR have been strongly and negatively
influenced by Chinese thresholds of violence toward the US — again,
as if China has sought to avoid isolation in a two-front confrontation
with both superpowers. The one strong positive influence is inherent in
the reciprocity term: just as the Soviet Union has responded to Chinese

[37] Recall that neither the constant nor the lagged endogenous term was significant
in the equation for Chinese normal conflict behavior toward the United States. See
Chapter 8.
[38] Beta = .22 (p = .10).
[39] Beta = .20 (p = .05).
[40] Beta = .30 (p = .025).
[41] Beta = −.54 (p = .005).
[42] For the constant, p = .0005.
[43] Beta = −.29 (p = .05).
[44] Beta = .15 (p = .05).
[45] Beta = .61 (p = .005).
[46] Beta = −.55 (p = .005).

actions, China has responded strongly and positively to Soviet thresholds of violence toward the CPR.

More generally, these findings further illuminate the differences between the dynamics of normal conflict behavior and the dynamics of thresholds of violence. Beyond the experimentally indicated differences in specification, for example, it is apparent that reciprocity relationships are generally much stronger among thresholds of violence than they are among mean conflict levels. The powers, it would seem, increasingly attend to and respond to actions at or approaching the brink of war. Furthermore, it is evident that, where multilateral 'consistency maintenance' dynamics generally dominate 'isolation avoidance' dynamics at normal conflict levels, the reverse is more often the case for thresholds of violence.[47] Actors, one can conjecture, will often generalize their conflict behaviors among others, but they are also sufficiently alert to the risks of war attending high thresholds of violence that they will consciously seek to avoid simultaneous, two-front confrontations.

At the same level of generality, the hypothesized role of provocations in the system seems to have found at least partial corroboration. To be sure, the term (provocations interacting with prior conflict) is significant in only two of the six full period regressions. Provocations appear to have contributed significantly and positively only to US thresholds of violence toward the USSR and to Soviet thresholds of violence toward the CPR.[48] In other equations for other dyads the provocation term does not significantly contribute to the variance explained. At the same time, though, these 'negative results' are largely consistent with the reasoning advanced in Chapter 6 and repeated a moment ago. In view of the extreme asymmetries of intersections empirically discerned in Chapter 5,[49] only leading actors whose expansion dominates intersections are likely to identify and respond to provocations as threatening events requiring explicitly political, often confrontational responses. Lagging actors are much more likely to view provocations as opportunities to alter existing relations of domination and subordination that limit their own latitude to grow and expand. In these terms, then, the absence of significant provocation coefficients in

[47] American thresholds of violence toward the USSR are the only exception: in this case, the US appears to have reflected a tendency to generalize from one communist adversary to another.

[48] Although the coefficient estimate for US–CPR provocations is slightly larger than the standard error of the estimate in the equation for US thresholds of violence toward China, it is not statistically significant at the .10 level.

[49] From Chapter 5 it will be recalled that US expansion asymmetrically dominated Sino-American and Soviet-American intersections and that the expansion of the Soviet Union asymmetrically dominated Sino-Soviet intersections.

equations for CPR-toward-US, CPR-toward-USSR, and USSR-toward-US thresholds of violence is to be expected.

A review of the findings supports still other propositions, while also raising some serious questions. If the model is correct, then it appears that there are strong links from a society's changing technological/economic capacity to satisfy internal demands, on the one hand, to its thresholds of violence, on the other. Most often, these links are positive.[50] Additional support is found, too, for the proposition that actors attempt to adjust to the systemic capability distribution and oppose proto-preponderant others. But most importantly, these findings raise serious doubts as to the adequacy of a deterrence theory that would emphasize superiority in capabilities above all else. Here, as in the analysis of normal conflict behavior, support has been found for the compensatory dynamics hypothesis, wherein it is proposed that an actor lagging in defense expenditures will be inclined to increase the levels of conflict inherent in its behavior toward the leading actor. Admittedly, this analysis has dealt with aggregate defense expenditures; and the longer range dynamics of normal conflict behavior and of thresholds of violence are not generalizable to the short-range dynamics of crisis.[51] Yet the aggregate relationships discerned here would seem to suggest that the mounting superiority of a rival, even if deterring an actor from a calculated decision to initiate war, might at the same time dispose an actor to introduce increasingly conflictual actions into its repertoire — to take steps approaching the brink.[52]

As in the last chapter, moreover, empirical evidence supports a view of the triangle as a tightly integrated system. Multilateral, balance of power dynamics are strong. They bind all three dyads together, so that no one bilateral conflict can be treated in isolation from the capabilities and behaviors of a 'third actor.' It is these multilateral links, primarily, that account for the triangle's internal dynamism, its identity as a system. And it is these multilateral links that assure that the effects of growth and rivalry will ramify beyond any one nation's actions and any one pair of nation's relations.[53]

Chapter 4 initiated Part II with a brief, descriptive review of Sino-Soviet-American conflictual interaction. Chapters since have examined

---

[50] Positive links are consistent with the hypothesis that actors troubled by an inability to satisfy internal demands will often turn inward, withdrawing from external confrontations. [51] See n. 3, above.

[52] This proposition can be generalized to encompass a superior actor confronted by a challenger. See A. F. K. Organski, *World Politics*, second edition (New York: Knopf, 1968).

[53] In this one finds further corroboration of the proposition that balance of power dynamics are extended Richardson processes. The point, first made in Chapters 7 and 8, is amplified in Part III.

a constellation of factors and relationships that have contributed to conflict and implications for violence among China, the Soviet Union, and the United States after 1950. Expansion, intersections, provocations, military capabilities, normal conflict behavior, and thresholds of violence — these are the variables analyzed here. By focusing on dynamics underlying one of these six variables, each of the six chapters has sought to (a) identify and interpret correspondencies between hypothesized relationships and historical patterns and (b) highlight critical gaps between theory and model, on the one hand, and available historical evidence, on the other. Overall, it is not too much to say that the correspondencies have helped to strengthen prior information for further research and that the gaps have helped to identify some worthy topics upon which further research might profitably focus.

Yet if the presentation strategy ordering Part II has been valuable in this regard, it must also be said that this strategy is largely contrary to an overall theme of this book. The theme is the modern security problematique. The theme, more specifically, is that the security problematique finds its form and tragic dynamism in the recurrence of fragmented attempts to confront and resolve the particular problems and issues it generates. Derived from this theme is the general methodological heuristic that has motivated this study: approaches to objective understanding of contemporary security dilemmas require synthesis — the persistent attempt to critically and systematically join insights and propositions from competing vantage points on reality. Against the backdrop of this theme, the contradiction implicit in Part II's presentation strategy is clear. In effect, this strategy has involved fragmentation. In focusing on distinct equations and particular terms, it has shifted attention away from the larger, open-ended whole in which these terms find their meaning. It has invited the misapprehension that the security problematique can be adequately known almost atomistically — by breaking it down into its components. In pointing to 'confirmatory evidence' for particular relationships, this strategy might even be said to nurture the dangerous belief that a complex, dynamic, and elusive reality can be finally and segmentally mastered.

Thus, the task before Part III is to restore the context in which each sentence of Part II must be viewed. As a synthesis, Chapter 10 will attempt to integrate the results just reported so as to more sharply depict the modern security problematique. As will be argued, the Sino-Soviet-American triangle must be understood in terms of the asynchronous, equifinal, irreversible, cumulative, and antagonistic joining of growth, rivalry, and balance of power. As such, the triangle bears within it the history and future of the modern security problematique. Following this attempt at synthesis, Chapter 11 then considers theoretical implications. In effect, it employs the overall synthesis in a kind of refractive function — using it as a basis for criticizing several theoretical vantage points whose insights are joined within it. This criticism is largely positive. For it involves an attempt to identify critical tensions that might animate productive research within each of the traditions considered.

PART III

CHAPTER 10
Elements of the Modern Security Problematique

Part II of this book has just examined a brief episode in the story of the modern security problematique. It is an episode, not yet concluded, involving relations among China, the Soviet Union, and the United States. The objective and the strategy of the empirical analysis should be clear. The objective is to begin to illuminate the contemporary form of the modern security problematique as it finds expression among today's major military powers. The strategy of analysis involves the construction of the general model as a kind of 'register.' The model portrays some of the possible ways in which historical processes identified in the framework might be manifested in the Sino-Soviet-American triangle. When analyzed in light of empirical data, the model then provides a basis for discerning how these processes have in fact unfolded and how the three societies are differentially situated amidst them. It becomes possible to see how the three classes of dynamics are intertwined. It becomes possible to identify some of the long-historical and far-reaching sources of constraints on effective action. And it becomes possible to trace the compound relationships through which well-intended attempts to answer demands, solve particular problems, or exert control in individual sectors of activity might reverberate through time and across sectors to sharpen other dilemmas and yield unwelcome outcomes. To discern these relationships is to begin to identify the broader proportions of the modern security problematique.

In reporting upon empirical results, however, Part II did not carry this strategy to completion. Each of the last six chapters has concentrated upon a particular equation form, a particular class of endogenous variables, in the model. The discussion in these chapters has often tightly focused on individual terms in these equations and on individual hypothesized causal links. One advantage of this approach has been that it permits the direct comparison of relationships at work across societies and dyads. It permits the interpretation of each link in terms of the cumulative traces of environmentally and institutionally constrained people — citizens and leaders — attempting to make rational choices, solve problems, and shape their futures. One disadvantage of this approach is that it neglects the overall network of relationships in which each rational choice implicates all others. Obscured from view amidst the detail are the complex, far-reaching causal connections that join fragmented attempts to assert rational control in a violence-prone system whose scope is beyond rational control.

The purpose of this chapter, then, is to illuminate the broader proportions of the security problematique by systematically assembling the results reported in Part II and by assessing their implications for the search for a lasting peaceful order. It proceeds in three steps. The first section offers a brief overview of the empirical results reported in Part II. It identifies and assembles significant links in the general model. Relying on the conceptual framework, it situates China, the Soviet Union, and the United States as societies asynchronously and equifinally reflecting the processes portrayed.

The second section then presents three sets of propositions informed by the empirical analysis. As will be seen, these propositions express the intimate intertwining of unilateral, bilateral, and multilateral processes. As will be seen, also, these propositions suggest that growth and differential growth have some serious long-term implications for security and peace and that manifestly politico-military responses to security dilemmas are likely to prove inadequate if not counterproductive over the longer term. The same propositions additionally submit that the dynamics and dilemmas of growth and differential growth will be unmanaged and unmanageable so long as societies are organized to answer insecurity through politico-military action. It is in the overall picture conveyed in these interdependent propositions that the modern security problematique finds its sharpest definition.

Finally, the third section considers implications for practical action. The discussion regarding practical action is lengthy, at times philosophical, and almost certainly controversial. For its starting point is within the second section's depiction of the security problematique as an all-pervading, ineluctable system. It starts with a system that differentially confronts people with specific problems requiring specific rational responses and takes its tragic dynamism from people's fragmented rational attempts to solve the problems they confront. The more people struggle to manage aspects of the problematique within their immediate reaches, the more the dilemmas of the security problematique tighten upon all who would escape them. The discussion thus takes up the meaning of rational action. It distinguishes rationality proper from technical rationality, and it argues that the latter is a dominant grammar of thought that today infuses all aspects of life and frames the choices giving form to the antagonistic dynamics of growth, rivalry, and balance of power. Section III argues that if the tragic logic of the security problematique is to be escaped, human beings must find means of subordinating technical rationality to rationality proper, a grammar of thought that acknowledges the inescapable dependence of each person and social group on its environment. An appropriate point of departure for practical action toward that end, it argues, is to be found in the transnational community of social science.

I SIGNIFICANT LINKS IN THE GENERAL MODEL: THE THREE POWERS AMIDST LONG-TERM PROCESSES

As just stated, the general model is a kind of 'register' that draws upon the conceptual framework to specify some of the *possible* ways in which postulated historical processes might find expression among today's major military powers. The estimation of parameters and the application of statistical measures then provides a basis for inferring which variables are in fact causally connected, how hypothesized processes are expressed, and where in the system the dominant determinants of conflict and violence are located during the period examined. Importantly, the same results help to situate the three societies amidst long-term processes that none can fully control. Viewed in light of the conceptual framework, the results provide a basis for interpreting how the societies are differentially positioned with respect to processes of growth, expansion, and intersections — and how, accordingly, developments in their internal structures and external postures are likely to be differentially influenced and constrained.

In employing the general model in this way, the conceptual framework's emphasis upon the asynchronous and equifinal character of international processes must be kept in mind. 'Asynchrony' implies that, among societies, occurrences of the progression from growth and expansion through rivalry to balance of power are unlikely to begin at the same historical moment or proceed at the same pace. 'Equifinality' implies that among societies starting from different historical conditions and entering a system at different times, there are likely to be marked differences in their relative tendencies and capacities to shape and adapt to the overall system and in the ways in which they express its dominant dynamics.

Such considerations are plainly reflected in Figure 10.1, which represents statistically significant causal links in the general model for the period 1950–72. As an assembling of results reported and discussed in Chapters 4

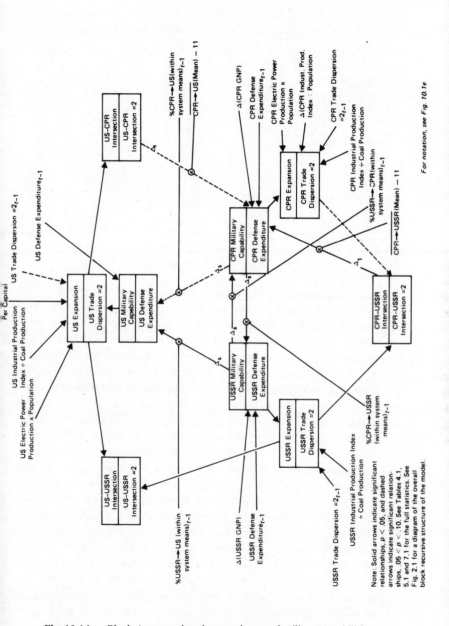

Fig. 10.1A Block A: expansion, intersections, and military capabilities

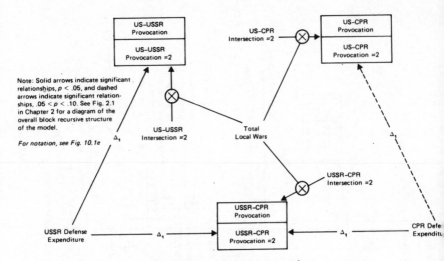

Fig. 10.1B   Block B: provocations

through 9, Figure 10.1 must be cautiously viewed and interpreted in light of the commentary and provisos advanced in those chapters. In this kind of analysis, problems of measurement, specification, and parameter estimation are never inconsequential.[1] It must be stressed that the processes at work are much more complex and elusive than either the model or the framework might seem to imply. Based as it is on the block-recursive general model, furthermore, Figure 10.1 requires a meticulous examination. It is difficult to identify the compound causal paths — the extended multivariate causal paths delineated by joinings of individual causal links — as these cut across blocks of the model. Section II, below, will therefore trace some of these paths in its development of some specific propositions.

Even prior to such a tracing, however, Figure 10.1 does begin to convey an overall picture of the asynchronous and equifinal processes underlying Soviet-American, Sino-American, and Sino-Soviet patterns of conflict. Consistent with the observations advanced in Chapter 3, significant relationships immediately bearing on Soviet-American and Sino-American normal conflict and thresholds of violence reflect the high levels of conflict already reached by 1950. The influences of the progression from growth and expansion through intersections and provocations to arms building and conflict behavior are weak on the whole, although occasional significant relationships are detected. By contrast, as shown in Section II, the progres-

---

[1] See Chapter 2 and Appendix D. As there stressed, the measures used are not strictly speaking tests of significance. They are used in this study as valuable decision rules.

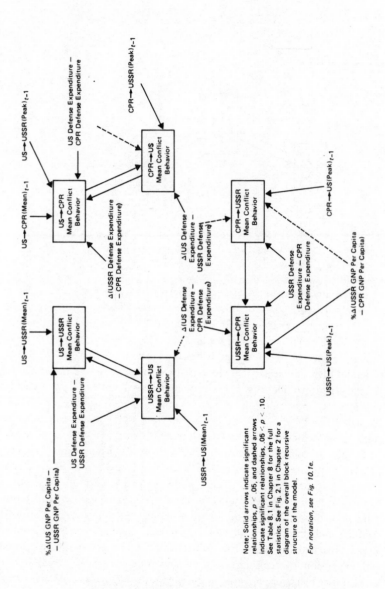

Fig. 10.1C Block C: Normal conflict and cooperation

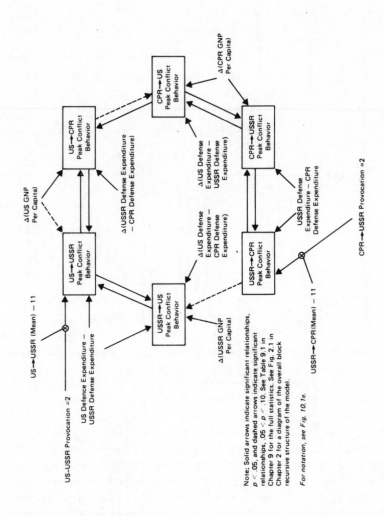

Fig. 10.1D   Block D: Thresholds of Violence

Symbol	Explanation
$A \rightarrow B$(Mean)	'A' and 'B' are actors (like US, USSR, and CPR). '(Mean)' indicates a conflict level, and '$\rightarrow$' is read 'toward.' Thus, $A \rightarrow B$(Mean) indicates 'A's mean level (or normal) conflict toward B.'
$A \rightarrow B$(Peak)	Where $A \rightarrow B$(Mean) indicates normal conflict, $A \rightarrow B$(Peak) indicates 'A's threshold of violence toward B.'
$\overline{A \rightarrow B}$(Mean) $- 11$	The bar over $A \rightarrow B$ indicates a three-year-lagged moving average; and 11 is a threshold level. Thus, $$\overline{A \rightarrow B}\text{(Mean)} - 11 = \frac{\sum\limits_{i=1}^{3} A \rightarrow B\text{(Mean)}_{t-i}}{3} - 11$$
%$A \rightarrow B$(within system means)$_{t-1}$	The percentage of A's within-system normal conflict that is directed toward B, lagged one year: $$\frac{A \rightarrow B\text{(Mean)}_{t-1}}{A \rightarrow B\text{(Mean)}_{t-1} + A \rightarrow C\text{(Mean)}_{t-1}}$$
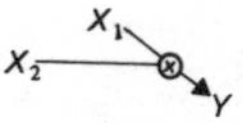 $\begin{matrix} X_1 \searrow \\ X_2 \rightarrow \otimes \\ \qquad \searrow Y \end{matrix}$	Indicates multiplicative interaction of X_1 and X_2 in their effects on Y. Alternatively, the effects of X_1 on Y depend upon the value of X_2.
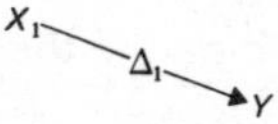 $\begin{matrix} X_1 \searrow \\ \quad \Delta_1 \rightarrow Y \end{matrix}$	Indicates that the one-year-change in X_1 (i.e., $X_{1_t} - X_{1_{t-1}}$) is entered in the equation for, and causally determines, Y.
 $\begin{matrix} X_1 \searrow \\ \quad \Delta_2 \rightarrow Y \end{matrix}$	Indicates that the two-year-change in X_1 (i.e., $X_{1_t} - X_{1_{t-2}}$) is entered in the equation for, and causally determines, Y.

Fig. 10.1E   Notation: symbols used in the model

sion plays a very important role in the one dyad that entered the period exhibiting low conflict and high cooperation: the Sino-Soviet dyad.

As underscored in the propositions put forth below, this does not mean that Sino-American and Soviet-American relations have been immune to the impacts of growth and differential growth. Far from it. What it does mean is that during this relatively brief period and among the powers examined, the asynchronously recurring progression described in the framework has most fully registered its impact upon the one pair of nations which, at the beginning of the period, exhibited the strongest signs of enduring peaceful relations. By 1950, one can conjecture, American expansion and intersections with the other two societies had already occasioned Sino-American and Soviet-American conflict and competition at levels that further intersections might reinforce but could hardly increase. In effect, for these two dyads, the irreversible implications of the progression had already been realized.

What is more, the overall results summarized in Figure 10.1 begin to illuminate how the three societies might be differentially positioned to express and reflect the processes at work. All three societies' domestic growth factors have contributed to their tendencies to expand.[2] All three pairs of societies have experienced increasing intersections and increasing provocations. But as the significant causal paths record, the three societies are far from equal in their relative abilities to contribute to and alter these long-term processes that so strongly influence the patterns of conflict among them.

More specifically, while both Soviet expansion and American expansion have contributed to Soviet-American intersections and then provocations, it is the expansion of the technologically more advanced United States that has principally determined in what regions and at what intensity Soviet-American intersections have been experienced. Even more clearly, Sino-Soviet and Sino-American intersections have been principally determined, not by the underdeveloped CPR with its low technological base and enormous population demands, but by Soviet and American expansion.

Such assembled findings go a long way toward effectively situating the three societies in terms of their *relative* lateral pressure. In turn, when read in light of the conceptual framework, the relational positionings of the three societies bear implications for their internal developments as well as their external practices.

That the *United States* has dominantly (though not exclusively) determined the intersections and provocations it has experienced suggests that the United States is, relatively speaking, a high-lateral-pressure society. According to the conceptual framework, a high-lateral-pressure society with long experience in relatively unrestrained expansion is likely to assume expectations, values, and an overall societal order predicated on sustained growth and expansion in the future. Having long witnessed other societies' adaptations to and dependencies upon their own extended activities and involvements, people and groups of such a society are likely to see their own characteristic social, economic, and political forms as somehow superior and worthy of fostering and protecting. Having long invested resources, energies, and symbolic rationalizations in state instruments and institutions intended to foster and protect these extended activities — not only for the society itself but also allegedly to the benefit of all humankind — the same society is likely to become socially, politically, economically, and ideologically ordered in ways that tend, on balance, to promote further investments in the future. In short, having wielded power, the society orders and reproduces itself as *a power*. According to the conceptual framework, such tendencies are common to high-lateral-pressure

[2] See Chapter 4 for the full period parameter estimates for the equations on expansion.

societies in general. According to empirical results, the United States is a high-lateral-pressure society.

In sharp contrast, the expansion of the *Chinese People's Republic* has had relatively little influence over when and where its intersections with others have occurred. This fact helps to situate China as, relatively speaking, a constrained, low-lateral-pressure society. Such a society, the framework suggests, might disintegrate in the face of mounting demands and diminishing or unobtainable resources. Or, as is more often the case, it might surrender its autonomy in interaction with high-lateral-pressure societies. It might become a dependent reflection of the activities penetrating its social, economic, and political fabric. As a third alternative, leaders of such a society might seek to mobilize popular support, dampen material expectations and demands, close-off foreign influences, adopt postures of self-reliance, and invest in the development of specialized capabilities required to overcome external obstacles of the present and future. Insofar as empirical results situate China as such a society, they also identify China as a society whose fears of foreign 'encirclement' and policies of self-reliance are far from surprising. According to the empirical results, long-expressed Chinese fears of Soviet and American 'encirclement' are anything but illusory extrapolations from nineteenth-century experience. For China is in fact a vulnerable, low-lateral-pressure society. In their references to the expansionist tendencies of others — be they phrased in terms of 'capitalist imperialism' or 'socialist imperialism' — Chinese leaders are struggling to articulate the vulnerability of China and other countries to the expansion of a few high-lateral-pressure societies.

The empirical results situate the *Soviet Union* between the extremes of the United States and China. On the one hand, Soviet expansion is to some degree subordinated to American expansion in determining Soviet-American intersections. *Vis-à-vis* the United States, the Soviet Union is, relatively speaking, a low-lateral-pressure society. On the other hand, Soviet expansion dominates Sino-Soviet intersections. *Vis-à-vis* China, the Soviet Union is a relatively high-lateral-pressure society. According to the framework, a society so positioned is likely to order itself as a power as it relates to low-lateral-pressure societies. Its interactions with low-lateral-pressure societies — societies having fewer specialized capabilities and unable to effectively resist its expansion — are likely to confirm and reproduce values of sustained growth and expansion. In its political forms and economic commitments, it is likely to internalize the notion that the currents of collective human progress are borne in its own expansion and extended influence. At the same time, the framework also suggests that the people and leaders of such a society are likely to view their social, political, and economic systems as vulnerable to the sustained expansion of societies exhibiting higher lateral pressure and dominating the contemporary international order. Even as they conceive of their society as a benevolent power with respect to the weak, they are likely to conceive of this status as fully obtainable only by overcoming the constraints upon growth and expansion entailed in the stronger society's continued lateral pressure. The combination invites tendencies to strengthen state apparatus and instruments, proscribe foreign influence, extract increasing resources at home, and exploit the low-lateral-pressure societies with which it interacts. It invites such developments in the name of a collective and progressive challenge to the dominant and always threatening conditions shaped by the stronger. The empirical results situate the Soviet Union as a society for which such tendencies are likely.

Other results portrayed in Figure 10.1 at once corroborate and refine this attempt to situate the three societies amidst the historical processes conceptualized in the framework. For instance, statistically significant military competitive relationships suggest that, once the overall conflict configuration is taken into account, American arms building is responsive to sustained Soviet military development and to sustained Chinese military development.[3] While the Soviet Union and China are mutually responsive, neither state's arms building is significantly responsive to sustained American arms building. Such findings suggest an ordered relationship among the three societies that is consonant with their relative levels of lateral pressure — the relative abilities of the societies' foreign expansion to determine the intersections they experience. The high-lateral-pressure United States is at once the most rapidly growing society, the society with the greatest resources for investment in arms building, and the society with the greatest latitude to determine how much to invest in military responses to others' activities and capabilities. It is also the society whose continued growth and development as a self-acknowledged 'power' most depends upon the sustained expansion to which others' increasing armaments might constitute serious threats. By contrast, the two relatively low-lateral-pressure societies, the USSR and the CPR, are the societies that have sought to extract the maximum resources from the economy, to mobilize human energies, to build the state and its military instruments, and to overcome the obstacles and threats posed, not so much by American arms, but by sustained American lateral pressure. Having committed resources to the fullest extent possible, and having already mobilized every aspect of their economies and societies to meet a continued external threat, these societies have little latitude to respond to the acts and capability building of the high-lateral-

[3] See Chapter 7.

pressure United States. While the strong do what they can, in short, the weak have already committed themselves to doing what they 'must.'

Still other results align with these. In the Sino-Soviet relationship, it is principally the Soviet Union, the relatively high-lateral-pressure society of the two, whose thresholds of violence reflect provocations. In the Soviet-American relationship, it is principally the United States — again, the relatively high-lateral-pressure society — whose thresholds of violence reflect provocations.[4] In the Sino-Soviet and Sino-American dyads, furthermore, changes in arms building of the relatively low-lateral-pressure CPR exhibit significant and positive influences on provocations, while changes in Soviet and American arms building do not exhibit positive influences upon provocations.[5] Such relationships are consistent with the vision of relatively high-lateral-pressure societies politicizing expanded activities, seeing threats in regional instability, and mobilizing state instruments to sustain the dominant relationships upon which their statuses as 'powers' are founded. Such relationships are equally consistent with the vision of low-lateral-pressure societies mobilizing instruments of state in attempts, not to directly and politically confront dominant societies, but to encourage change in the relationships that reflect and are necessary to the continued dominance of high-lateral-pressure societies.

If such descriptions seem to fit the societies addressed, it must be remembered that the descriptions are implied, not by characteristics specific to each of the societies, but by an interpretation of empirically discerned relationships among them in light of the conceptual framework. In their external policies and in what they internally become, China, the Soviet Union, and the United States — indeed, all societies — equifinally reflect the long-term transnational processes in which they are engaged.

II   SOME SPECIFIC PROPOSITIONS: ELEMENTS OF THE MODERN
      SECURITY PROBLEMATIQUE

To situate societies amidst long-term processes is to infer from systemic patterns to likely local expressions of those patterns. It is not yet to describe or define the overall system that is produced and reproduced as individual societies equifinally reflect long-term processes and interact in their attempts to preserve and extend what they have become. It is not yet to describe how, among a multiplicity of societies, the dynamics of growth, rivalry, and balance of power are antagonistically joined in the modern security problematique.

[4] See Chapter 9.   [5] See Chapter 6.

This section undertakes a definition of the security problematique. The strategy of definition is to offer a number of propositions informed by empirical results as interpreted within the concepts of the framework. In particular, these propositions are intended to synthesize information regarding extended causal sequences in the model and their implications for international conflict and its management. Although the limits of ordinary language require that these propositions be individually and sequentially presented, each is, as it were, an abstraction from the definition of the problematique. As definitional elements, they must be read as inextricably interconnected. It is in the interconnections that the antagonisms are revealed.

Three sets of propositions are offered. *The first set refers exclusively to the dynamics of rivalry and balance of power.* Making no reference to the dynamics of growth and differential growth, this first set of propositions is consistent with classical expressions of security dilemmas. The picture is one of a politico-military system whose shifting patterns of conflict and capability are at once attributable to and managed by the rule-guided choices of security-interested states. Yet this picture, the classical image of security politics, is incomplete — as the second set of propositions indicates. Reflecting a tracing of significant causal paths from unilateral factors to politico-military variables, *the second set of propositions underscores the ways in which long-term processes of differential growth condition, disturb, and constrain high political actions and outcomes.* If security and peace are to be maintained over the longer-term, this set of propositions implies, then the dynamics of differential growth, as well as the dynamics of rivalry and balance, must be effectively monitored and managed. *The third set of propositions thus points to some of the obstacles and dilemmas likely to be encountered in attempts to manage growth processes in the interest of peace and security.* As will be seen, these dilemmas reflect the intimate intertwining of unilateral, bilateral, and multilateral dynamics. Owing to these confounding interrelationships, modern security questions are much more intricate and extensive in scope, much more deeply embedded in multiple domains and levels of human activity, much less susceptible to diplomatic-military intervention and manipulation, and much more tightly bound to sharpening international dilemmas of welfare, equity, national autonomy, and the natural environment than is ordinarily assumed.

A   **Rivalry and Balance of Power in Sino-Soviet-American Relations:**
    Propositions Regarding the Visible Elements of the Modern Security
    Problematique

When one thinks of military security questions, one's mind is nearly inevitably drawn to dynamics of rivalry and balance of power. Antagonistic comparison, competition, clashes of interests, confrontations, crises, the systemic distribution of military capabilities, and the overall configuration of conflict — these are the sorts of variables and relationships that come to mind. Similarly, issues of security management — issues of deterrence, arms control, alliance policy, crisis manangement and the like — are conventionally characterized with reference to these same variables, and options and outcomes are generally portrayed with reference to the visible, highly manipulable activities and instruments of soldiers and diplomats. Even in a period widely proclaimed 'an age of interdependence,' the dynamics of military rivalry and balance of power are the immediate focal points of security policy debates.

When attention is restricted to statistically significant relationships among politico-military variables in the general model, this conventional image of security politics would seem to find ample support. Phrased in the broadest terms, empirical results strongly indicate the manifestation of the bilateral dynamics of rivalry and the multilateral dynamics of balance of power in Sino-Soviet-American relations.

Three propositions usefully summarize the potent roles of political-military rivalry among China, the Soviet Union, and the United States.

A.1   *In the Sino-American and Soviet-American dyads, and at both normal conflict and cooperation and threshold of violence levels, relationships of reciprocal interaction are clearly evidenced.* In each case, actors tend to answer heightened levels of conflict with heightened levels of conflict and reduced levels of conflict with reduced levels of conflict. Especially for threshold of violence levels, such simultaneous, positive return effects imply the emergence of a potentially explosive *conflict spiral* once one actor's conflict behaviors toward another begin to increase toward hostile action.

A.2   *Across all three dyads, there is evidence of military competitive relationships, although not all actors are equally responsive to the military capability increases of all others.* Allowing for the influences of shifts in the overall conflict configuration (see proposition A.6, below), the United States has tended to increase its capability building (arms expenditures) in response to both Soviet and

Chinese increases, the Soviet Union has tended to increase its capability building (arms expenditures) in response to Chinese increases, and China has tended to increase its capability building (arms expenditures) in response to Soviet increases. As a result of these relationships, the capability building of each state is at least partially influenced by factors affecting the capability building of its rivals.

A.3 *For any pair of actors, patterns of mutual conflict behavior tend to be sensitive to the military capability gap between them.* More often than not, these relationships are contrary to a 'superiority deters' version of deterrence theory. In all three dyads, the normal conflict behavior of the militarily lagging actor tends to *increase* as the gap in military expenditures widens and tends to *diminish* as the gap narrows. As suggested by the framework, a 'compensatory' relationship appears to operate: lagging actors tend to behave as if to compensate for felt military weakness with open, often conflictful assertions of strength and resolve. In turn, such assertions can lead to concentrations of conflict in the dyad, mounting military competition, and (under proposition A.1) the reciprocal, potentially explosive dynamics of the conflict spiral.

Left unmanaged, the bilateral dynamics expressed in these propositions have potentially serious implications. They can contribute to intensifying conflict, increasing military expenditures, and mounting propensities toward violence.

Within the Sino-Soviet-American triangle, however, the bilateral dynamics of rivalry occur in a multilateral context. Given this extended context, the actors' observance of a balance of power rule system might effectively dampen tendencies toward violence between rivals. Concentrating upon the multilateral dynamics of balance of power, the following four propositions identify some of the possibilities.

A.4 *At threshold of violence levels, all three actors have tended to avoid isolation by reducing peak levels of conflict in one dyad when engaged in high thresholds of violence in another.* The United States, for example, has tended to reduce thresholds of violence exhibited toward China at times of higher thresholds of violence toward the USSR. The Soviet Union has exhibited a weak tendency to reduce conflict toward the United States as its thresholds of violence toward the CPR have mounted. And China has tended to reduce thresholds of violence toward the United States as conflict with the USSR has climbed. Consistent with an 'isolation avoidance' logic,[6] such relationships (negative across dyads) tend to have equilibrating effects. To the extent that they are joined by reciprocity relationships within dyads (see proposition A.1), they reduce tendencies to identify a single state as the unique target of others' conflict in the system.

A.5 *To some significant degree, actors tend to oppose others approaching military preponderance in the system.* Chinese normal conflict and thresholds of violence toward the United States, for instance, have been positively responsive to the change in the American-Soviet military capability gap. As this gap widened in favor of the United States, China acted in increasingly conflictful ways toward the United States; as the gap has narrowed, and as Chinese perceptions of Soviet hegemony have sharpened, China's conflict behavior toward the United States has diminished. In the same way, United States behaviors toward China have reflected the Sino-Soviet military gap. And Soviet normal conflict and cooperation toward the United States has reflected the Sino-American military capability gap. Consistent with a 'preponderance opposition' logic,[7] such patterns tend to have an equilibrating effect. To the extent that they occur, these patterns reduce the likelihood that a clearly dominant coalition will emerge to easily overwhelm the weakest of several actors.

A.6 As a refinement of proposition A.2, above, *the military competitive responses of all three actors are sensitive to the overall configuration of conflict in the system.* Consistent with a 'threat assessment' logic,[8] all three actors condition their military responses to the arms building of others on the degrees, directions, and dyadic concentrations of conflict in the system. Thus, for example, Sino-Soviet mutual arms competition emerged only as the Sino-Soviet dyad became a locus of concentration in the overall conflict of the system. As argued by Karl W. Deutsch and J. David Singer some years ago, such tendencies in a multipolar system have a stabilizing effect.[9]

A.7 *All three actors have exhibited tendencies to maintain consistency in the overall configuration of conflict, even though these tendencies have sometimes contradicted their avoidance of isolation in the*

---

[6] See Chapter 1 for a discussion of this and other balance of power logics.
[7] See Chapter 1.　　　　　　　　　　　　　[8] See Chapter 1.
[9] Karl W. Deutsch and J. David Singer, 'Multipolar Power Systems and International Stability,' in James N. Rosenau (ed.), *International Politics and Foreign Policy*, revised edition (New York: Free Press, 1969).

system. For example, US normal conflict toward the CPR tended to increase shortly following high US thresholds of violence toward the Soviet Union — as if the US were generalizing across two adversaries perceived as mutually cooperative. Unlike isolation avoidance tendencies, such patterns are generally disequilibrating. They have the effect of rigidifying polarized situations.

Taken together, these propositions point to mixed evidence regarding the Sino-Soviet-American triangle's capacity to manage conflict through the exercise of balance of power logics. On the positive side, the significant degree to which all three powers appear to have observed balance of power logics would seem to substantiate the existence of a shared rule system — a multilateral balance of power regime or quasi-regime. Moreover, as indicated in propositions A.4, A.5, and A.6, the observance of some of these logics would tend in general to moderate the violence-prone tendencies born of bilateral rivalries within the system. Owing to the multilateral linkages transcending strictly bilateral relationships, hostilities between any two powers tend to be muted to some degree by the observance of logics incorporating the third.

At the same time, other evidence signaled by these propositions is clearly negative. First, and most obviously, propositions A.4, A.5, and A.6 refer to general tendencies involving model-guided choices, not to uniform, nearly automatic relationships across all actors and dyads. Several multilateral relationships specified in the model are not statistically significant, thus indicating that the logics of balance of power are far from uniformly observed.[10] In the Sino-Soviet-American triangle, therefore, balance of power is best understood as a *weak* quasi-regime.

Second, as proposition A.7 implies, the logics of balance of power, even when observed, do not necessarily tend toward the reduction of tension and conflict between nations. The evidence of consistency maintenance tendencies cited in proposition A.7 reflects sources of rigidity seriously limiting the adjustment capacities of the Sino-Soviet-American system.

Third, and most importantly, the conflict management potential of balance of power clearly depends upon the establishment of interdependencies, and the displacement of conflict, across dyadic relationships. Propositions A.4, A.5, and A.6 imply that observance of certain balance of power logics may moderate the conflict potential of bilateral rivalry, not through the resolution of differences, but through the involvement of third actors and the consequent dispersal of conflict that would otherwise remain concentrated in the dyad. Each actor thus becomes entangled in,

[10] Consult the statistical results reported in Chapters 7, 8, and 9.

and experiences the reverberations of, the others' mutual conflicts. So long as the logics are adequately observed and stability is maintained, the security of all may benefit. But should any one of the three dyadic relationships experience an escalation of conflict toward war, the web of multilateral interdependencies is likely to draw all into the hostilities.

From the conventional vantage point on security politics, these descriptive statements may be seen to have normative implications. In particular, these statements invite the prescription of policies aimed toward (*a*) the further articulation of a balance of power quasi-regime whose rules tend to foster both the regularization of states' politico-military actions and the maintenance of systemic stability and (*b*) the eliciting of the three states' acknowledgement of and conformity to these rules. In these terms, the strengthening and further legitimation of the balance of power quasi-regime may be said to be in the collective interest of all. Its success may be seen as a collective good; its failure, a collective bad.

B From Growth to Conflict in Sino-Soviet-American Relations: Propositions Regarding the Deeper Elements of the Modern Security Problematique

Yet if the general model presented here represents important relationships underlying major power conflict and violence, then prognoses and policy based upon conventional perspectives are incompletely informed. As an examination of other statistically significant causal paths in the general model will indicate, the dynamics of differential technological, economic, and population growth are very much a part of the security problematique. The propositions presented below set the dynamics of rivalry and balance of power in the context of these longer-term processes.

The first three propositions identify some, but not all, of the statistically significant causal paths from growth to conflict.

B.1 *In all three dyads, the normal conflict behavior of at least one of the two actors is sensitive to the changing technological/economic gap (measured as the percentage change in the difference between the two countries' GNPs per capita) between them.*[11] The proposition refers to causal paths of the form shown in Figure 10.2.

B.2 *In all three dyads, the thresholds of violence of at least one of the two actors is sensitive to its own tendencies toward economic growth, with rapidly growing societies tending in general to behave at higher thresholds of violence.*[12] Causal links of the form shown in Figure 10.3 are identified.

[11] See Chapter 8.   [12] See Chapter 9.

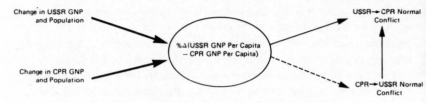

Fig. 10.2   Significant links illustrating Proposition B.1
(Excerpted from Figure 10.1a — 10.1d)

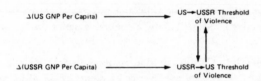

Fig. 10.3   Significant links illustrating Proposition B.2
(Excerpted from Figure 10.1a — 10.1d)

B.3 *The arms building of each of the three powers is sensitive to and constrained by the unilateral dynamics of technological, economic, and population growth.* When this proposition is joined with A.3, above, causal paths of the form shown in Figure 10.4 are identified.

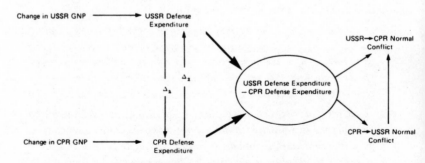

Fig. 10.4   Significant links illustrating Proposition B.3
(Excerpted from Figure 10.1a — 10.1d)

In turn, these propositions converge to substantiate a more sweeping generalization:

B.4 *Among the three major powers of contemporary international politics, the dynamics of rivalry and balance of power are disturbed and constrained by processes of domestic growth and their consequences.*

As actors seek to build arms and direct their high political actions in response to threats of their rivals and the logics of balance of power, each also confronts emergent sources of conflict born of differential growth across actors (proposition B.1) while constrained within the technological, economic, and demographic limits its own growth helps to shape (propositions B.2 and B.3).

What is more, when propositions B.1 through B.4 are combined with propositions A.1 through A.7, the dynamics of rivalry and balance of power are cast in a different light. The dynamics of rivalry and balance of power are not only disturbed and constrained by the concurrent influences of the long-term dynamics of growth. They also assume the function of transmitting growth's security-political impacts throughout the system:

B.5 *Owing to the bilateral dynamics of rivalry (see propositions A.1 through A.3), growth's security-political impacts can be confined to no one nation's actions.*

B.6 *Owing to the multilateral dynamics of balance of power (see propositions A.4 through A.7), growth's security-political impacts can be confined to no one pair of nations' relations.*

That bilateral and multilateral dynamics serve to transmit the political reverberations of growth and differential growth is illustrated by the diagrams of statistically significant causal paths shown in Figures 10.5 and 10.6. As Figure 10.5 indicates, American arms building and American behaviors toward the Soviet Union are indirectly impacted by unilateral Soviet processes underlying Soviet behavior. More strikingly, as Figure 10.6 indicates, Soviet-American relations are indirectly influenced by the unilateral Chinese processes underlying Chinese behavior. *These relationships are not unique.* Figures 10.5 and 10.6 are illustrative of recurring causal sequences by which the political impacts of growth and differential growth, occurring anywhere within the system, reverberate throughout — effectively transmitting disturbances to which other largely constrained actors must then respond.

As they relate to the dynamics of rivalry and balance of power, furthermore, the dynamics of growth have a deeper historical significance. In

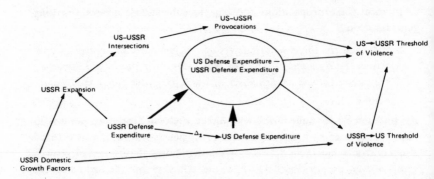

Fig. 10.5   Significant links illustrating Proposition B.5
(Excerpted from Figure 10.1a — 10.1d)

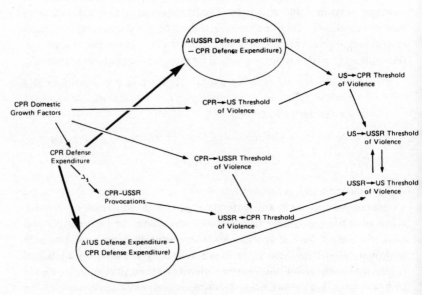

Fig. 10.6   Significant links illustrating Proposition B.6
(Excerpted from Figure 10.1a — 10.1d)

particular, both China's increasing conformity to balance of power logics
and the emergence of Sino-Soviet conflict lend corroboration to the following two propositions:

B.7   *In long-historical perspective, the dynamics of growth and differen-*

*tial growth can cue, condition, or accentuate the dynamics of rivalry
and balance of power among societies.*

B.8 *As growth propels the expansion of the system, and as formerly
external societies are drawn within, the dynamics of rivalry and
balance of power tend to elicit these societies' adaptations to the
requisites of participation, thereby reproducing these dynamics
through time and across societies.*

These two propositions find support, first of all, in a tracing of statistically significant causal paths underlying the transformation of Sino-Soviet
relations from highly cooperative to intensely conflictful. Although the
emergence of the Sino-Soviet dispute is conventionally analyzed in terms
of diplomatic events, exchanges of public charges, and border confrontations, Figure 10.7 suggests that these historical tracings are largely reflections of deeper growth-rooted changes. Omitting relationships bearing
upon the United States, Figure 10.7 identifies significant causal paths from
Chinese and Soviet domestic growth factors to their mutually exchanged
normal conflict and thresholds of violence.

The lower part of the diagram concentrates on the long-term processes
accounting for the mounting of Sino-Soviet military rivalry and normal
conflict: widening gaps in both military capabilities and technological/
economic development — both largely attributable to differentials in the
two societies' domestic growth — contribute to increasing normal conflict.
With increasing normal conflict in the dyad, the two powers become increasingly competitive in their arms building (note the nonlinear return
effects). And in turn, further differential arms building generates still
higher levels of normal conflict.

The upper part of the diagram in Figure 10.7 concentrates on long-
term processes accounting for increasing thresholds of violence in Sino-
Soviet relations: the differential growth of the two societies contributes to
their expansion. The more rapid expansion of the Soviet Union is largely
responsible for the intensification of Sino-Soviet intersections, principally
as Soviet activities extend more deeply into prior areas of Chinese activity
and interest. With increasing Sino-Soviet normal conflict, the increases in
these intersections spur Chinese arms building. Both Sino-Soviet intersections and increasing Chinese arms building contribute to the intensification
of Sino-Soviet provocations, despite the dampening effects of Soviet arms
building. And finally, increasing Sino-Soviet provocations tend to generate
higher thresholds of violence toward China, especially as normal conflict
levels climb. In short, the emergence and intensification of Sino-Soviet
rivalry and conflict are largely (although not exclusively) due to patterns

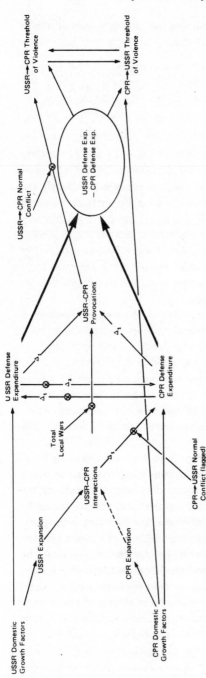

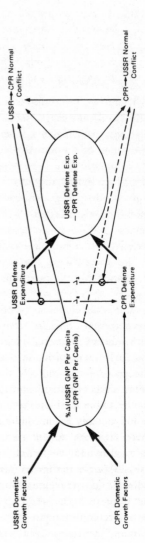

Fig. 10.7   Significant causal paths from Growth to Conflict: the Sino-Soviet dyad*
*Excerpted from Figure 10.1a – 10.1d. Relationships bearing on the United States omitted.

of differential growth and expansion between the Chinese People's Republic and the Soviet Union.

Additional evidence for propositions B.7 and B.8 is found, not in the full period parameter estimates reported in Part II of this book, but in the changes of estimated parameters over shorter subperiods: 1950–63 and 1960–72.[13] Especially regarding China's normal conflict and thresholds of violence, quite different dynamics appear to be at work in the two subperiods. Specifically, China's behaviors toward the United States and the USSR in the later subperiod, much more than the former, tend to be consistent with balance of power logics of 'isolation avoidance' and 'preponderance opposition.' Only with the intensification of Sino-Soviet conflict – conflict largely occasioned by differential Sino-Soviet growth and Soviet penetration into Chinese areas of activity and interest – did China begin to adapt its policies and behaviors, bringing them into close conformity with balance of power logics that had long been evidenced in the actions of the United States and the USSR.

The evidence, it must be stressed, is very far from conclusive. Further investigation involving techniques of far more subtlety than the econometric analysis of aggregate annual time series data is required. Nevertheless, empirical results so far are consistent with the historical interpretations implicit in propositions B.7 and B.8. Initially cooperative, Sino-Soviet relations came to exhibit intense conflict and rivalry as rapid Soviet growth, together with lagging technological growth and massive population demands in China, contributed to widening gaps, Sino-Soviet intersections, and Sino-Soviet provocations. Initially a large revolutionary society, antiimperialist internationally and pursuing a nativist socialist road domestically, China eventually confronted the 'imperatives' of balance of power as manifested in the increasing Soviet threat.

Individually and in combination, the several preceding propositions imply that policies and designs intended to manage security solely by regulating the political dynamics of rivalry and balance of power are, at best, extremely risky. To be sure the 'deradicalization' of China and the strengthening of a balance of power regime among China, the Soviet Union, the United States, and other powers might be celebrated *over the next few years* as major diplomatic accomplishments – as solutions to persistent problems. *For a time*, certainly, patterns of differential growth within and across nations might afford leaders the latitude to observe the rules of a strengthened multilateral relationship that moderates bilateral rivalries. The attitude of guarded optimism fostered by conventional security perspectives might prevail *for a time*.

---

[13] See Appendix B for a discussion of the subperiod analysis. As there stressed, all results must be regarded as very tentative.

*Yet when set in the long-term context of sustained growth and differen-
tial growth, even the most successful high political designs reside, as it
were, on the infirm outcroppings of a far deeper, less tractable glacier of
change.* With time and movement in these deeper processes, the relationships posed in the preceding propositions are likely to find expression once
more. These processes are likely to give form to new intersections, expose
major power relations to intense provocations, configure new conflict in
the system, propel formerly external societies into the contest, and sharply
limit the powers' latitude to maintain stability according to dominant rule
systems.

At such a moment, it would be too late to effect the management of
deep socio-economic processes that both security-interested state actions
and multilateral high political regimes had previously neglected. Here, at
the moment of crisis, the costs of deep societal adaptations would
probably appear intolerable. Caught in dilemmas between serious socio-
economic dislocations and risks of war, leaders might perceive little choice
but to exercise the few manipulable instruments at their disposal —
political-military instruments. They might perceive little choice but to
pose ultimata, issue threats, and prepare for the use of force. At such
a moment, the once celebrated collective solution to security problems —
the network of multilateral relationships binding the several societies
within a common regime — would become itself a collective problem.
Assuring system-wide reverberations among actors too constrained to
adapt, the onetime collective solution can entrap all in violence and war.

C　Limits to the Management of Growth: Some Propositions Regarding Obstacles and Dilemmas in the Management of Technology, Resources, and Population

The implication of the immediately preceding propositions is unmistak-
able. *Politico-military designs, no matter how carefully deliberated, will
not suffice to assure lasting peace. So long as the dynamics of differential
growth remain unmanaged, it is probable that these long-term processes
will sooner or later carry major powers into war. With the continued
acceleration of processes of differential growth, the 'lead time' for effective adaptations is shrinking.* The question thus emerges with some ur-
gency: how can these long-term processes of growth and differential
growth be managed?

In this regard, the general model does highlight a number of points at
which, in principle, interventions might be undertaken. It does identify a
number of variables that are 'in principle' susceptible to informed

manipulation. Diplomatic and political actions, for example, represent highly manipulable variables. A nation's leaders might be able to restrain investments in arms building or other specialized capabilities to some extent. Patterns of foreign trade and foreign investment might be limited or redirected to some degree so as to avoid conflict-inducing intersections. Technology transfers from one society to another might alter prevailing patterns of growth and expansion to some extent. Various policies might be undertaken to diminish reliance upon certain resources, to dampen rates of growth, or to redistribute access to resources among participants in any society. Many other opportunities for intervention are apparent.

If opportunities for intervention are apparent, though, it must also be observed that the choices involved cannot be considered in isolation from one another. When sights are lifted from particular variables and specific causal links to the larger network of relationships, it becomes plain that efforts at intervention will encounter obstacles and costs. Propositions advanced below identify some of the dilemmas and obstacles likely to be encountered in attempts to manage growth and its consequences in the interest of peace and security.

Some of the obstacles are found in domestic structures of decision making. In particular, the empirical results point to a classic dilemma encountered in the assertion of centralized state control over societal behaviors. On the one hand, there is the first proposition, which addresses American foreign economic expansion.

C.1 *Aggregate patterns of American commercial expansion are dominated by changing economic conditions — growing demands and resource constraints, more specifically — and exhibit little in the way of incremental or inertial development.*[14]

American expansion, in other words, represents the aggregate traces of decisions sometimes diffused throughout the economy and sometimes concentrated among major corporations that are responsive to external market conditions (and hence to decisions throughout the world). Yet while such a system's aggregate economic behaviors tend not to evidence bureaucratic inertial influences, precise state control can be exerted only through the exercise of crude instruments: tariffs, quotas, export licensing, taxation policy, and so on. Even then, the exercise of these instruments is encumbered by the domestic political interplay of competing groups whose activities would be regulated or affected.[15]

---

[14] See Chapter 4.
[15] See Chapter 11, Section IV, for a further discussion of how a balance of power regime restricts such state practices.

On the other hand, the expansion of state authority does not guarantee the enhancement of precise state control:

> C.2 *Across all societies, patterns of military expenditure (which in turn affect patterns of expansion) and patterns of normal conflict and cooperation behavior exhibit signs of inertia — the persistent, unwieldy influences of prior decisions and previous commitments in large state bureaucracies.*[16]

Of itself, this proposition implies serious unilateral limits — products of centralized decision-making structures — on states' capacities to act responsively in the management of their politico-military relations. Such bureaucratic influences, though, are not necessarily limited to the politico-military domain. They extend as well into the socio-economic domain for societies dominated by socialist movements:

> C.3 *In China and the Soviet Union, bureaucratic-inertial tendencies are as apparent in patterns of growth and expansion as they are in politico-military affairs.*[17]

Bureaucratic centralization, rationalized as a means of asserting precise control over large aggregate processes, does not guarantee rational control. Instead, it can involve the substitution of one kind of unwieldy process for others.

Domestic obstacles to the management of growth's political consequences are best identified, though, not in terms of absolute structural impediments, but in terms of the time-frames and costs of bringing about change. In this respect, the present analysis has not specified causal relationships among variables within societies; and consequently, it cannot offer systematically and empirically informed insights. Nevertheless, so important are these relationships to the definition of the security problematique that three general propositions merit attention, further empirical research, and refinement for concrete cases.

> C.4 *The domestic costs of redirecting or limiting a society's technological, economic, and population growth are likely to escalate, becoming less and less bearable to the society, as time constraints are shortened.* That is, the adaptations that would entail deep and far-reaching societal disruptions if undertaken within one or a few years might be more or less smoothly undertaken within evolving domestic structures over a decade or more.

> C.5 *The domestic costs of redirecting or limiting a society's technological,*

---

[16] See Chapters 7 and 8.   [17] See Chapter 4.

economic, and population growth will tend to reverberate well beyond the target sectors to which instruments of control are directed. For example, the costs of redirecting or limiting a society's international commercial activities can involve environmental as well as economic effects if, as a result of such limits, participants must substitute new forms of energy for those formerly obtained beyond national boundaries.

C.6 *The costs of redirecting or limiting a society's technological, economic, and population growth are likely to be unevenly felt; accordingly, such interventions are likely to have potent domestic political ramifications, especially to the degree that differential costs coincide with preexisting social cleavages.*

In short, considerations of time, scope, and distribution of costs — perhaps far more than the net societal deprivations involved — lend an unyielding, cumbersome complexity to the domestic management of growth.

Even if domestic costs could be borne and state authority could be responsively wielded, furthermore, other obstacles to managing growth and its political implications are to be found in relations *among* societies. While the sovereignty of an individual state is territorially bounded, more specifically, the socio-economic-environmental processes of growth, expansion, and intersections are global in scope, largely transnational in causal linkages, and enormously sensitive to international conditions, including market conditions, over which even paramount states have limited influence. The important role of international markets, and the state control-obstructing problems of capital internationalization, are not adequately modeled here. But because the general model does portray relationships across societies and dyads, the empirical analysis has informed the following proposition:

C.7 *Very few of the causal paths from growth to conflict are composed entirely of variables potentially under the exclusive control of a single state.* Cross-actor economic and technological gaps, the systemic military capability distribution, the overall configuration of conflict, intersections, and provocations — these and many other variables and relationships are influenced or defined by the activities, attributes, and patterns of growth among two or more societies.

As in imperfect markets, it is true, the analysis indicates politically salient asymmetries in actors' relative capacities to effect change in crucial relationships.[18] Yet the analysis also points to a proposition that is

[18] This is the relational difference between high and low lateral pressure societies.

reminiscent of recent thrusts in international political economy research:

> C.8 *The effective management of growth in the interest of peace will require the establishment of multilateral regulative norms; uncoordinated, strictly unilateral attempts to grasp control are unlikely to find long-term success.*

Indeed, as suggested by propositions B.1 through B.6, above, strictly unilateral interventions might prove counterproductive. They might constitute serious disturbances which, in turn, would reverberate throughout the system, calling upon other tightly constrained actors to respond.

Success, in any case, cannot be gauged with respect to collective international values of peace and security alone. Although proposition C.8 implies a need to collectively regulate the dynamics of growth in the interest of peace, it has long been clear that growth is a central, controversial concern in other international issue areas. A variety of other values obtain — as theorists of integration, dependency, neocolonialism, imperialism, structural violence, neomercantilism, liberal economics, system dynamics, and interdependence have emphasized. Values of welfare, equity, national autonomy, and the natural environment join in the definition of complex, multi-level dilemmas whenever theorists and policy makers weigh the implications of altering or sustaining prevailing patterns of growth.

Thus, in emplacing security issues within an international political economy context, propositions C.8 implies still additional complexities to be encountered in the security-interested management of growth:

> C.9 *Long-term security outcomes are on the 'hidden agenda' even when formal deliberations among states and their agents concentrate on welfare, equity, national autonomy, and ecological issues.*

> C.10 *Conscious attempts to collectively regulate growth in the interest of peace and security are likely to involve the establishment of cross-issue linkages in processes of multilateral consensus-building and norm-setting.*

These propositions suggest, for example, that multilateral efforts to reshape or reform patterns of growth and interchange in a New International Economic Order, perhaps far more than collective consensus building on disarmament questions, can have profound long-term implications for peace and security. They suggest, as well, that processes of creating a peaceful order among major powers might well require the genuine participation of states whose political strengths are found, not so much in the military domain, but in their critical loci within a world economic system that sustains differential growth. And they also suggest that efforts to negotiate the establishment of a lasting peaceful order will potentially telescope within them all of the complexities, mixed interests, transaction costs, learning, and mislearning evidenced in efforts to come to grips with all other growth-related collective outcome dilemmas. In their linkages to differential growth, in short, dilemmas of poverty, exploitation, economic instability, dependence, environmental destruction, *and war* are joined as one.

The joining, it should be clear, cuts two ways. On the one hand, the increasing political salience of welfare, equity, national autonomy, and natural environmental issues — and the echoing of 'imperatives' to the effect that these issues must be collectively resolved — may signal new opportunities for the management of growth, and hence insecurity. Despite the complexities, the joining of issues would seem to point to indirect avenues of access to global security management.

On the other hand, a counter-proposition must also be seriously weighed:

C.11 *Propelled by differential growth to global scope, the dynamics of rivalry and balance of power contribute to the shaping of political conditions that potentially obstruct the collective management of growth for whatever purpose.*

As stressed above (see propositions B.7 and B.8), the dynamics of rivalry and balance of power tend to perpetuate and extend the political conditions of their own existence. Extended outward by differential growth, they draw formerly external societies within, creating 'imperatives' for these societies' adaptations to the requisites of participation in a balance of power regime. They make 'imperative' — they in some sense legitimate — the investment of societal resources and energies in the support of state agencies and instruments that claim autonomy with respect to domestic demands and sovereignty *vis-à-vis* externally imposed limits as they seek to answer the threats of rivals and observe the rules of balance. Such adaptations become deeply bound within the *raisons d'être*, the very identities, of these agents of state. In effect, the regime of balance of power becomes *interiorized* within the self-definitions of these agents. And the image of external anarchy, the illusory face of this regime, becomes critical to the continued rationalization of what these agents of state have become.

For each state, therefore, opposition to multilateral limits on state autonomy represents an expression of aspects of its deeply structured identity. To the extent that this 'high political' identity pervades and finds expression in all domains of activity — to the extent that it is dominant —

states are likely to resist the imposition of multilateral regulative norms, not only in the politico-military domain, but also in the domains of technological, economic, and population growth. And this aspect of each state's identity is likely to be dominant, not always, but whenever processes of growth and differential growth generate escalating competition, military rivalries, recurring provocations, disturbances in the balance of power, increasing propensities toward vioence, and renewed prospects that conflict will spiral beyond control and toward war.[19]

The propositions describing the modern security problematique thus come round an eclectic and vicious circle. The assembled propositions do not portray a harmonious set of relationships. They do not portray a set of relationships wherein conflict and violence are either anomalous or attributable to some easily managed, potentially arrestable set of causes. Quite the contrary. It is to the overall network, the parts and their interdependencies through time, that one must look.

Within this network, growth and differential growth historically condition and contemporaneously disturb and constrain the violence-prone dynamics of rivalry and balance of power. With sustained growth and expansion, the dynamics of rivalry and balance of power reproduce the political conditions of their existence and draw societies within. The effective management of insecurity thus requires the management of growth. Yet within the same network of relations, the pervasiveness of rivalry and balance of power invites adaptations of societies and states, constrains choices, and impedes growth's collective control.

The circle closes, then, embracing tragedy within it. It captures even those who would alter the system, even those who would seek to escape. While much differs, the parallels between the pre-World War I European system investigated by Choucri and North and the contemporary system are all too clear.

And that, perhaps, should not be surprising. For the vicious circle of today's security problematique is best seen, not as a stationary system, but as another revolution in an historic, ever-widening spiral of growth and conflict. It is a spiral initially swept forward through time and upward toward global scope by Europe's accleration of differential growth and expansion. It is a spiral whose swirling vortex today captures not only developed capitalist societies, such as the United States, but also developed and underdeveloped socialist societies, such as the Soviet Union and China. In an important sense, the world is today heir to the economic legacy of Europe's successful growth, and due to that growth, the world has inherited Europe's sorry political legacy as well. The spiral continues,

[19] This argument is further elaborated in Chapter 11.

recreating its requisite elements through time.

III PRACTICAL ACTION AND THE FUTURE

'Ineluctable' means that which cannot be gotten out of, and the picture of the security problematique presented in the preceding propositions certainly seems to portray an ineluctable system. It is a violence-prone system. It is an irrationally destructive system. And it is a system from which there appears to be no rational course of escape. As the preceding propositions suggest, the modern security problematique spans all sectors and levels of human activity. It has expanded over several centuries to embrace all societies within its geographic compass. As the foregoing propositions also suggest, no matter where one begins in the system to undertake practical action toward change, one will find oneself situated amidst problems and constraints given form through the cumulative problem-solving efforts of the participants and their forbears. And as the tracings of causal paths suggest, no matter how wise, rational, and well-intentioned one's attempts to solve immediate problems might be, the attempts to behave rationally within the constraints of the moment will cumulate with numerous others, form trends, and reverberate through time and across sectors to reproduce and sharpen the dilemmas that others are left to rationally solve.

In short, there is no rational avenue of escape. No escape exists because rational action involves people's attempts to solve the problems they confront, because the problematique asynchronously and unevenly confronts people with specific problems in particular sectors and locales, and because the problematique takes its tragic dynamism from the antagonistic joining of people's fragmented and equifinal attempts to solve the practical problems before them. To answer Ernst Haas's question, there is no 'hole in the whole.'[20]

There is, then, a basis for profound pessimism in the picture of the security problematique presented so far. It is a pessimism tinged with an ugly irony that, unlike the irony of Greek tragedy, ensnares even those who perceive it. In Greek tragedy, the irony resides in the fact that the players make speeches and do things whose meanings are plain to the audience but are not grasped by the players themselves. The audience

[20] Ernst Haas, 'Is There a Hole in the Whole? Knowledge, Interdependence, and the Construction of International Regimes,' in *International Responses to Technology*, a special issue of *International Organization*, Vol. 29, edited by John G. Ruggie and Ernst B. Haas (1975).

can reason that, were the players privy to its own level of understanding, the irony would dissolve, and so would the dramatic tension that carries the play toward its tragic conclusion. By contrast, the irony of the modern security problematique entangles the audience as well as the players. For were the informed members of the audience to join the players — as in fact they must — how could they do any better than to behave rationally within the fragmented problem situations that a history of fragmented rational decisions shapes for them? How could they possibly find a rational solution to a security problematique that they can confront only in parts — a problematique that takes its dynamism from people's attempts to be rational in parts? The answer is that they cannot. Practical action can mean only complicity. The problematique, again, is ineluctable.

But is it? A careful reading of the preceding statements reveals that they rely upon but do not define the concept of rational action. The force of the argument depends upon an implicit agreement on what rational action is. It depends upon an agreement that the patterns and processes described in this study's depiction of the problematique reflect cumulations of constrained human choices that can be taken for granted as rational. And it assumes that, even after it is seen that these rational choices contribute to the production and reproduction of a violence-prone system, one is still unable to imagine any practical alternatives to the rational logics one shares with other participants in the tragedy. It is upon this agreement, unspoken as it is, that the argument that the security problematique is ineluctable depends.

But what if the agreed-upon understanding of rational social action were in some sense false or too restrictive? What if natural human capacities to develop knowledge and skills and to communicate might bear the possibility of another logic, a more expansive rational logic, that is in some ways different from the logic so far equated with rationality and shared with participants in the tragedy of the problematique? What if this 'other' rational logic, this less confining logic, could in principle orient practical action toward change? Would it not then be the case that people attempting to come to grips with the security problematique, including social scientists, are doubly trapped — trapped by the conditions of their positions within the system and trapped, too, by the restrictive grammars of thought in which they conceive of those conditions? Could it not then be said that part of what imprisons people in an ineluctable problematique is their confinement in a false rationality that denies them the full exercise of their natural human capacities to build knowledge and communicate? Would it not then be true that the first practical step toward 'getting out of' the problematique is to find some way to 'get out of' this restrictive grammar of thought?

These, to be sure, are abstract — some would say, metaphysical — questions. No amount of evidence could ever afford final answers to them. At the same time, though, they are essential questions. Answering them, if only broadly, is essential to any reasonably complete definition of the security problematique. Only by setting the logics actually at work in the context of logics denied does it become possible to see how the processes of the problematique repress — and are contingent upon the repression of — human potentialities. More than that, answers to the questions posed above are essential to any attempt to find a form of responsible, practical social action that might transcend the tragic logic of the security problematique. At the very least, to ask the questions is to search for a grammar of thought in which practical action does not necessarily mean resignation to complicity.

An important clue to the answering of these questions is contained in an excerpt from the first paragraph of the lateral pressure 'theory kernel,' as presented in Chapter 1. It is repeated here:

> *Among the natural characteristics of the human being — characteristics that link humankind to nature in unyielding interdependence — are capacities to develop knowledge and skills and to communicate.* These capacities may be exercised to sustain manifest relations of oneness among human beings and between society and nature. That is, they may be exercised to interiorize within each social unit, from the individual to the social organization, a sense of identity between each unit's immediate fulfillment of itself and the realization of socio-environmental potentialities of the present and future. On the other hand, knowledge, skills, and capacities to communicate may also be used *technologically*. They may be used by human beings to objectify their 'environments,' including one another, as elements of life external to themselves — elements to be managed, manipulated and controlled through the application of knowledge and skills. . .

What is important in this excerpt is that it conveys the possibility that human thought and interaction might not involve the full exercise of human capacities to develop knowledge and skills and to communicate. Human thought and interaction, it implies, might instead be confined within a narrow aspect of these capacities: the technological. Indeed, the remainder of the theory kernel, the story told in the conceptual framework, and the preceding section's propositions all assume that this technological aspect of natural human capacities can become and has become dominant. The story of the modern security problematique, to revise Richardson, is the story of 'what happens when people don't stop to exercise their natural human capacities to the fullest.' More accurately, it is the story of what happens when 'stopping to think' is reduced to the exercise of technological capacities alone.[21]

Here, in the theory kernel, is the skeleton of a response to the questions just posed regarding the meaning of rational action and the ineluctability of the modern security problematique. Specifically, the theory kernel suggests that one might usefully consider two distinguishable (but overlapping) logics or grammars of rational social action, both of which are within human capacities. First, the grammar of thought framing strictly technological action might be styled *technical rationality*. This, as the preceding comments imply, is today the dominant grammar of thought. It is the grammar of rational action underlying the choices that cumulate to shape the antagonistic processes of the security problematique. Insofar as one's contemplation of the problematique is confined within this technical rational grammar, one will find the claim of the problematique's ineluctability to be thoroughly warranted. Means of escaping the tragic irony of the security problematique will be unimagined and unimaginable.

However, there is also a second, far richer grammar to be considered. Termed *rationality proper*, the latter is a grammar wherein human capacities to develop knowledge and skills and to communicate can find their fullest expression. The full dimensions of rationality proper do not find expression in the dynamics of the problematique. They are in fact repressed in the face of technical reationality's dominance. Nevertheless, within the emancipatory logic that is rationality proper, it is possible to contemplate forms of social action that do not participate in the reproduction of the problematique — that hold out some promise that the security problematique might somehow be peacefully transcended.

The pages to follow are meant to fill out this skeleton of a response by elaborating upon the two forms of rationality just mentioned: technical rationality and rationality proper. The latter, it will be argued, might represent a way of thinking whose time is at last approaching. Social scientists having some hope for the emergence of an epoch of peace might do well to show the way by orienting their scholarly practices and normative concerns within the grammar of rationality proper. Indeed, it will be contended that the transnational communities of social science represent a particularly likely point of departure for emancipatory praxis so oriented.

[21] See Lewis Fry Richardson, *Arms and Insecurity* (Pittsburgh: Boxwood Press, 1960).

This argument takes time to relate, and in some eyes, the somewhat philosphical threads of the argument may seem to weave a tapestry that is wholly unrelated to the main focus of this chapter: the hard realities of the modern security problematique. Such objections are perhaps especially likely to be raised when the argument turns to consideration of scientific practice. Again, though, the depiction of the security problematique cannot be complete until its relation to human potentialities is explored. After all, as Quincy Wright reminds us, international reality contains the possible as well as the actual.[22] To understand the 'is' in any objective sense one must see it in the context of the 'is not but might be.' Science, moreover, is inescapably a part of this same reality. If scientists set about exploring more than the actual — if they strive to discern and exercise the possibilities for change immanent in human capacities to build knowledge and communicate — then their participation can be a liberating force *within* the system. If they do not, then at best, their activities will constitute a force for resignation.

A   Technical Rationality

The label, 'technical rationality,' is particularly appropriate. For the grammar of thought to which it is attached conceives of reality as essentially consisting of sequences of more or less discrete problem-solving episodes in which problems are met and possibly solved by the exercise of means under the tutelage of knowledge and skills. More specifically, a problem situation involves people confronting certain obstacles to the realization of their purposes, certain limits on their abilities to satisfy needs, or certain actual or possible events that might have costly effects in terms of their purposes. Technical-rational action then involves people's attempts to apply knowledge and skills, survey actual or possible means available to them, and make choices and employ means so as to 'solve problems' — that is, serve purposes by overcoming obstacles and limiting costs. If all rational action is subsumed under the technical rationality rubric, then rational action *is* problem-solving behavior. There is no rational purpose for knowledge and skills except insofar as they orient the development, application, or strategic manipulation of means to solve poblems and serve ends.

[22] Quincy Wright, *The Study of International Relations* (New York: Appleton-Century-Crofts, 1955), p. 11 and Chapters 8–11. More specifically, Wright distinguishes the 'actual' (corresponding to history), the 'possible' (corresponding to art), the 'probable' (corresponding to science), and the 'desirable' (corresponding to philosophy) as aspects of reality.

To identify rational action with technical rationality is thus to celebrate human autonomy by denying any form of historical-processual determinism. After all, a technical-rational grammar of thought tends to conceive of life as consisting of so many more or less discrete problem situations; and problem situations are defined in terms of certain given purposes or needs, certain obstacles to or limits on the realization or satisfaction of these, and certain means by which the obstacles and limits can or might be overcome. Accordingly, such a grammar tends to take for granted and hence disregard those slowly changing aspects of life that, relative to immediate purposes or needs, are too costly to manipulate. It tends also to leave unquestioned the boundaries of the immediate problem, how obstacles and limits might be given form by choices and actions in other sectors of life, and how attempts to solve the immediate problem might reverberate through time and impact upon other sectors. Most importantly, it takes purposes and needs for granted. It does not question the sources of the purposes and needs against which actors evaluate events and outcomes and define problems. To borrow the words of Spinoza, people guided by such a grammar 'think themselves free inasmuch as they are conscious of their volitions and desires, and as they are ignorant of the causes by which they are led to wish and desire, they do not even dream of the existence of these causes.'[23]

Moreover, this technical-rational grammar is extraordinarily robust in defense of the idea of human autonomy. It is robust even in the face of serious challenges. When it becomes evident, for example, that a given problem, as bounded, cannot be solved at acceptable costs by accessible means, then this grammar points to the extension of control — and with it, the boundaries of the problem situation — so that effective means can be accessed. When, alternatively, it becomes evident that events external to a problem situation confound solutions, then this grammar indicates action aimed toward either bringing externalities under control or hardening the boundaries of effective action. And when it is evident that two or more sectors of problem-solving activity are mutually confounding, then this grammar of thought redefines the original problem as one collective problem to be solved through the establishment of some coordinating rules or overarching regulating institutions.

As this discussion suggests, a technical-rational grammar not only celebrates autonomy but also gives it a very special meaning. A social unit — whether an individual or the whole world as one society — is said

---

[23] From Baruch Spinoza, the *Ethics*, Appendix, and reproduced in Stuart Hampshire (ed.), *The Age of Reason* (New York: Mentor, 1956), p. 123.

to be autonomous to the extent that it can technically-rationally solve problems. A social unit is said to have no autonomy when it cannot develop and apply knowledge and skills to solve problems and must accommodate itself entirely to the problem situations it confronts — when it must be and become a reflection of its environment. A social unit has absolute autonomy when it can persistently develop and apply knowledge and skills to solve problems and assert control over its environment — and need never adapt its purposes to changes in its environment. Within a technical-rational grammar, in short, *concepts of autonomy, knowledge, and power are soldered into one.*

The assertion that the modern security problematique reflects the cumulative actions and interactions of rational people rests on an equation of rationality with technical rationality, as just described. In fact, this study's approach to hypothesizing the dynamics of growth, rivalry, and balance of power *begins* with the assumption that human choices have come to be dominated and framed by this technical-rational grammar.

The approach to hypothesizing key dynamics begins, in other words, in a way very much akin to a methodology that Karl Popper calls 'situational analysis.' This methodology involves the asumption of human technical-rational problem-solving in certain problem situations. In particular, by situational analysis Popper means

> . . . a certain kind of tentative or conjectural explanation of some human action which appeals to the situation in which the agent finds himself . . . Admittedly, no creative action can ever be fully explained. Nevertheless, we can try, conjecturally, to give an idealized reconstruction of the *problem situation* in which the agent found himself, and to that extent make the action 'understandable' (or 'rationally understandable'), that is, adequate to his situation as he saw it. This method of situational analysis may be described as an application of the *rationality principle.*[24]

In much the same way, this study has proposed and treated the dynamics of growth, of rivalry, and of balance of power as processes reflecting the cumulative rational choices of people set in certain kinds of recurring problem situations. Thus, for instance, the dynamics of growth and expansion are posited to reflect the cumulative choices of countless people at several levels attempting to solve problems and answer demands born of technological and population growth by mobilizing certain

---

[24] Karl R. Popper, 'On the Theory of the Objective Mind,' Chapter 4 of his *Objective Knowledge: An Evolutionary Approach*, revised edition (Oxford: Oxford University Press, 1979), p. 179.

specialized capabilities. The dynamics of rivalry and balance of power are similarly described. Furthermore, as seen in Section I of this chapter, significant relationships in the general model are interpretable in just these terms. Once the societies are situated among long-term processes of differential growth, expansion, and intersections, remaining links in the model are interpreted in terms of leaders' constrained attempts to respond to their different problem situations, solve problems, and assert control. At base, then, the general model assumes — and results seem to corroborate — the tendency of social processes to behave as if the choices involved are framed within a technical-rational grammar.

This assumption is not uncommon in the study of international relations For example, Hans Morgenthau argues for an approach in which we

> . . . put ourselves in the position of a statesman who must confront a certain problem of foreign policy under certain circumstances, and we ask ourselves what the rational alternatives are from which a states-man may choose who must meet this problem under these circum-stances (presuming he acts in a rational manner), and which of these circumstances, he is likely to choose. It is the testing of this rational hypothesis against the actual facts and their consequences that gives theoretical meaning to the facts of international politics.[25]

As Graham Allison has pointed out, Stanley Hoffmann's 'imaginative reconstruction' and Thomas Schelling's 'vicarious problem solving' involve essentially the same assumption and the same approach.[26] And to Allison's list of Morgenthau, Hoffmann, and Schelling one might add Ernst Haas and his assumptions about welfare-oriented technocrat-politicians; Lenin with his assumptions about the problem-solving responses of financiers in the face of the contradictions of capitalism; Adam Smith and David Ricardo with their hypothetical 'primary acting units;' Keohane and Nye with their arguments about the choices of state bureaucracies en-gaged in transgovernmental politics; and even Allison himself with his attempt to locate rationality, not in a monolithic government, but in each of many bureaucratic 'players' in a 'central, competitive game.'[27]

[25] Hans Morgenthau, *Politics Among Nations: The Struggle for Power and Peace*, fifth edition (New York: Knopf, 1978); p. 5.

[26] See Graham Allison, *Essence of Decision: Explaining the Cuban Missile Crisis* (Boston: Little, Brown, 1971), pp. 11–14. See also Stanley Hoffmann, *Contemporary Theory in International Relations* (Englewood Cliffs, N.J.: Prentice-Hall, 1960); and Thomas Schelling, *The Strategy of Conflict* (New York: Oxford University Press, 1960).

[27] See Ernst Haas, *Beyond the Nation State* (Stanford, Calif.: Stanford University Press, 1964); V.I. Lenin, *Imperialism: The Highest Stage of Capitalism* (New York: International Publishers, 1939); Robert O. Keohane and Joseph S. Nye, Jr., *Power and Interdependence* (Boston: Little, Brown, 1977).

While different social scientists find the locus of rational choice in different sectors or levels of human activity, it is evident that most share with this study the premise that the actualities of international relations can to a large extent be understood in terms of the interactions, aggregations, and recombinations of individual technical-rational choices.

What may be less evident is that most social scientific vantage points are in many ways little different from those of the participants whose practices social scientists examine. Social scientific vantage points may be more sweeping, more abstract, and at least somewhat more self-consciously systematic. But in general, the difference between the vantage points of social scientists and those of the participants they study is that the former tend to focus their own technical-rational grammars of thought upon somewhat more general and generalizable problem situations. The social scientist's grammar of thought is no less a technical-rational grammar simply because it is applied at a different level of generality. For to the extent that social scientists see their task as one of theoretically capturing social laws or general social principals, they, like the participants they study, celebrate their autonomous capacities to solve (analytical) problems, close (theoretical-empirical) gaps, and bring social reality (intellectually) under control. To the extent that social scientists additionally assume that the knowledge they build can or should orient and inform attempts to solve particular social problems, the technical-rational character of their thinking is all the more plain.

In view of the pervasiveness of this technical-rational grammar of thought, it is small wonder that this study's depiction of the modern security problematique would be read as a portrait of an ineluctable system. This study has done little more than attempt to systematically join insights from several different traditions, each focusing upon particular sectors or levels of activity, and each offering generalizing knowledge claims regarding certain patterns and processes. Each assumes that the patterns it identifies reflect the technical-rational choices of people acting within certain kinds of problem situations. Each further assumes that, as knowledge of its particular domain is enhanced and applied, people will be better able to make rational choices that solve or manage the problems that beset them. And those few traditions that do look across sectoral boundaries tend to assume that, with improved knowledge or with more resolute application of available knowledge, cross-sectoral effects can be controlled or subordinated within a more encompassing political order.

Yet while this study incorporates a kind of situational analysis approach, it is not confined to situational analysis. It attempts to see how recurring problem situations might be interlinked in giving form to interacting social processes, and hence it tells a different kind of story. Diverse processes addressed by diverse traditions are antagonistically poised. The problem situations recurring within them are at once mutually confounding, mutually perpetuating, and insusceptible to piecemeal resolution. So encompassing is the network of relationships, in fact, that there is no way, literally no way in the world, that the conflicts born of these antagonisms can be peacefully brought under technical-rational control.

Within a technical-rational grammar of thought, there is only one imaginable way out, and that is a path that carries the story of the modern security problematique to the logical conclusion toward which it has long been moving. The path, in a sense, is the path of least resistance. For it is a path prepared by a long history of technical-rational solutions. It is a path to some form of world empire, and it is a path whose traversal involves the deadly application of the most destructive of human technologies. World empire via massive violence — this is the acme of technical-rationality. The story of the modern security problematique is but the protracted climactic scene in the tragic drama of technical rationality's ultimate failure. Technical-rational action has brought progress — progress toward the destruction of all it has built.

If this suggests that technical rationality is a false logic, the dimensions of its falsity need to be made plain. It is a false logic because it is at once a creative logic and a logic that is totally in awe of its creations. It is a false logic because it serves human purposes without questioning their sources and creates new needs in ways it refuses to see. It is a false logic because it cannot acknowledge that people and organizations can to a large extent become what they do and because it disallows their reflexive examination of what they are and might otherwise be. It is a false logic because it orients attempts to solve problems in fragments, frames social action such that it institutionalizes limitlessness in society's manifest structures and forms, and thereby implicates all aspects of a finite world in every seemingly isolated problem situation. It is a false logic because it equates autonomy with an unobtainable independence of and mastery over the environment, because it frames the mobilization and commitment of resources on the assumption that this autonomy is everlasting, and because it makes likely the explosive breaking down of social barriers whenever the assumption evidently fails. It is a false logic because, in a finite world of differential growth and asynchronous experiences, it frames every choice in a way that creates new needs and new capabilities and sets human beings on collision courses. And it is a false logic because, in its celebration of autonomy and its equation of autonomy with power, it finds lasting success only by persistently subordinating the many to the solutions of the few.

In an important sense, though, this false logic is also 'true,' and its 'truth' resides in the fact that people are differentially situated today amidst confining material conditions and crying needs given form through a long, cumulative history of technical-rational choices. People are differentially situated, too, amidst a variety of specialized capabilities — and capabilities for creating capabilities — that have been technically-rationally built and that hold out the promise that, with further commitments of resources and resolve, solutions can be found. In effect, technical rationality is a false logic that is also 'true' because technical rationality is embedded, layer upon layer, in society's manifest structures and forms. It is sedimented as well in the purposes and plans of those who have succeded in its light. It is thus a 'true' logic because people have purposes and needs, because people are situated amidst constraints and confront immediate problems, and because *some people* at any time are able to mobilize capabilities and solve the immediate problems they confrtont.

To be sure, some people are not able to do so. It is their lot, situated as they are, to be part of others' solutions. And from their perspective there could be no logic more false. Yet as the strong do what they can and the weak suffer what they must, it is the technical rationality of the strong that dominates and shapes the 'truth' of immediate experience. The grammar of technical rationality is 'true,' then, because it is dominant, because those who succeed in its light are free for a time in the technical-rational meaning of freedom, and because their version of truth, a projection of their immediate problems upon all, subordinates all others.

To see the modern security problematique as ugly testimony to the failure of technical rationality thus does not set one free of its grip. To note that technical rationality is a false logic — an ideology — is not to deny that it is an ideology-*qua*-material force. Indeed, one may rightly reason that the individual, group, or society that refuses to try to solve problems or exert control will soon be in jeopardy of being reduced to a part of others' solutions.

The question thus emerges: is there within human capacities a grammar of thought that can contain technical rationality but go beyond it to search for a deeper meaning of autonomy? The answer is yes. Rationality proper is such a grammar. It is a grammar of thought that can orient attempts to solve problems while also problematizing the attempts in light of the following proposition: *in what it is and will become, every social unit is profoundly and inescapably dependent upon its environment, including all other units that inhabit it.* In rationality proper, the search for rational solutions and human autonomy begins, not ends, with this proposition. The search begins, not ends, with the acknowledgement of the interdependence of humankind and of humankind and nature.

B   Rationality Proper

Technical rationality proclaims human freedom by denying the deterministic influences of historical processes, and in so doing, it is entrapped in complicity with the historical processes it is unable to imagine or criticize. Rationality proper commences the search for human freedom by allowing that human beings, in their thinking as in their choices, are distinctly unfree of historical-processual influences. Technical rationality sees history episodically, as a sequence of discrete, and discretely analyzable, problem situations. It see reality as segmentable in principle into a number of bounded or boundable problem domains. It accepts purposes and needs as unquestioned givens, and its aim is to orient the use of means on the environment to serve purposes and satisfy needs. Rationality proper sees history processually. It allows that the segments of reality are processually created, interdependent, and susceptible to change. It seeks to uncover the deeper values and needs hidden beneath layers of contingent necessities and ephemeral values shaped by choices of the past. Technical rationality assumes the autonomy of systematic knowledge, sees truth in the actual dominant patterns of the historical moment, and denies the truth of realities that are not but might have been. Rationality proper strives for autonomy and truth by seeking after an intersubjective consensus through the non-coercive exchange of communications and criticisms among people and groups differentially situated within, and having varying vantage points upon, the whole of actual and possible human experience.

It is this last aspect, perhaps more than the others, that distinguishes the operational form of rationality proper from technical rationality. Where technical rationality seeks to focus knowledge and skills on specific, bounded problem situations, rationality proper starts from the premise that knowledge and skills so focused are not and cannot be autonomous of the historical processes giving the problem situation its manifest form. *The task within rationality proper is to begin with the specific problem situation and attempt to 'import' the larger historical reality within it.* This attempt is made, not by invoking the assumption that there exists some fixed, final, and potentially knowable structure predominating over the whole of reality, but through the attempt to engage, criticize, and synthesize competing vantage points associated with other aspects of reality as these do or might relate to the specific problem situation.

In a way, this appraoch is reminiscent of peace researchers' long-standing, if weakly articulated, predisposition in favor of taking 'symmetrical' as opposed to 'strategic' viewpoints on international processes. At the very least, this approach shares the view that rationality requires something more than a one-sided attempt to strategically subordinate others' interests in order to solve problems for a particular aspect of reality with which one happens to identify. But rationality proper goes further. Within rationality proper, autonomy of historical processes is something that can be obtained, and then only partially, only through the continuous seeking of autonomy — only through the continuous attempt to engage, criticize, and excavate the self-critiques immanent in competing vantage points that are reflective of a differentiated reality.

Rationality proper thus does not reject the problem-solving orientation of technical rationality. Instead, rationality proper embeds and subordinates technical rationality within a richer logic that problematizes the elements of technical-rational problem-solving. Purposes, needs, obstacles, costs, prior commitments, means, likely consequences, and the definition and boundaries of the problem situation — none of these elements is taken for granted. The acting social unit, within rationality proper, cannot even accept unquestioningly its immediate definition of self as something distinct from its environment. On the contrary, within rationality proper, the acting unit is persistently committed to finding the deeper meaning of itself, not by identifying its immediate appearances and structures, but in the reflexive attempt to understand how, through time, it relates to, interiorizes, and implicates the aspects of reality with which it is interdependent. It is this *commitment* — born of the sense that a social unit is inescapably dependent upon its environment — that permits rationality proper to subordinate technical rationality.

It should be clear, then, that rationality proper admits a form of practical action that technical rationality does not allow. Technical rationality allows as practical only those kinds of action that involves the application of means on an objectified environment in order to solve problems, satisfy given needs, and serve given purposes. Rationality proper does not rule out the possibility that such action might be practical. But because rationality proper problematizes questions regarding purposes, needs, and the distinction between social unit and environment, rationality proper also admits into the realm of practical action a form of action that technical rationality denies: *adaptation*. Within a technical-rational logic, a social unit either dominates its environment or submits to it against its will. Within the logic of rationality proper, a social unit may also engage in adaptation as a conscious expression of its quest for that form of human autonomy that can only be realized through the unit's attempt to acknowledge and interiorize the interdependence of itself and the larger, changing socio-natural whole.

This means that, within rationality proper, practical action is not reduced to the play of power between the unit and its environment, including other units. In fact, within rationality proper, to confine practical action solely to the exercise of power — even if the power of a unit is in some sense predominant — is to surrender real autonomy. Within rationality proper, it can be said, the most powerful social unit of any time — the unit best able and most inclined to technically-rationally solve its problems and bend others to its solutions — may also be the least autonomous. For it alone is unable to see and is inclined to deny what is often plain to those it subordinates: its profound dependence upon its environment.

Captivated by the momentary appearance that it is an autonomous thing that dominates others, the unit is likely to make technical-rational commitments and assume norms and values that reduce its capacity to learn and adapt — that restrict its practical latitude to the realm of technical-rational action. For a time, to be sure, such a unit may be able to develop and apply technologies, make commitments, solve problems, and disguise from view the reactive character of its technical-rational actions. Within rationality proper, though, one can be certain that the illusion is at best temporary, that a growing social unit in a world of change cannot for long disguise its dependence upon its environment, and that uncritical technical-rational solutions of the moment are likely to lock even the now powerful unit onto a reckless course toward disaster.

One may object, of course, that these are quaint but largely irrelevant arguments. After all, did not the depiction of the dynamics of growth, rivalry, and balance of power start from the premise that long-term, aggregate social processes reflect the cumulative traces of people confronting problem situations within technical-rational grammars of thought? Did not the interpretability of empirical results lend some support to this premise? Is it not likely that people situated amidst pressing problems whose roots they do not know will continue to make technical-rational choices whose consequences they cannot foresee? And is it not likely too, that people having varied vantage points consistent with their varied positions in a complex, differentiated reality would encounter serious obstacles and incommensurabilities in their attempts to communicate and import the whole into each problem situation?

The answer to each of these question is, in general, yes. Empirical results do tend to substantiate the argument that significant trends and relationships in international politics reflect the dominance of technical rationality.[28] Moreover, it is likely that this technical-rational grammar of problem-solving will be dominant for some time and that, so long as it is, patterns of choice will contribute to the partitioning of social reality and the hardening of sectoral, political, and other boundaries across which communication is difficult indeed. Clearly, the objections phrased above are not without merit.

C Convergent Trajectories of Change

In the face of these objections, though, one should not concede too much. For recent trajectories of change in international relations might be read to suggest that rationality proper, long suppressed in the face of technical rationality's dominance, might someday find improved means and greater latitude for effective expression. In particular, one can point to (*a*) possible revolutionary developments in technologies of communication and information processing, (*b*) mounting signs of global interdependence and their implications, and (*c*) the growth of a multifaceted, transnational social scientific community that is already exhibiting a modest commitment to the seeking of autonomy through the criticism-conscious pursuit of some intersubjective consensus across social, political, and economic divides. These developments surely do not guarantee the generalized global subordination of technical rationality to rationality proper within the next years or decades. But *taken in combination*, they do hold out opportunities unlike any previously experienced in the history of humankind. Accordingly, some brief elaboration is in order.

1. *Technological Developments: Emergent Opportunities for the Expression of Rationality Proper*

In his book, *The World That Could Be*, Robert C. North identifies five great 'system breaks,' or revolutions of technology, occurring in the course of human development. As he notes, 'Each of these has involved a

---

[28] However, the full historical argument makes two additional points. First, the dominance of technical rationality is something that emerged at a certain juncture and was then carried toward global scope as an expression of the contradictions in the grammar's logic of environmental domination. Second, that technical rationality is dominant does not mean that anywhere and everywhere it is the only grammar of thought finding expression.

transformation in the way people have perceived the universe, their assumptions about their relationship to it, the values they have professed and/or invoked, and the ways people have expected to relate to one another.' Indeed, he says, 'we can almost imagine "human nature" itself undergoing significant modifications during each of these great technological revolutions.'[29]

The first of these system breaks occurred early in the Paleolithic Age, as humans learned to make and use stone tools. The second system break identified by North involved humans learning to control fire. The third was the Neolithic revolution, which 'involved a transformation from hunting and gathering as the prevailing technology to the mastery of agriculture by societies in many parts of the world.'[30] The fourth, beginning in the late eighteenth century and continuing into the present, was a revolution of technological, economic, and political components marked by a change from agriculture to industry.

A fifth great system break is occurring today. It is 'the computer revolution — the transition from industry as the prevailing technology to cybernation — which is almost certain to involve a rapid and epic revolution in technological, economic, political and social dimensions that will transform the ways people live throughout the world.'[31] What new possibilities will be opened up by these revolutionary changes in technologies of communication and information processing?

At the very least, these changes will permit the rapid, near instantaneous assembling, recombination, and wide dispersion of information regarding aspects of social relations and the natural environment. As capacities increase and technologies improve, moreover, the immediate costs of communication and information processing are likely to continue to rapidly decline. In fact, now, for the first time in history, one can envisage the possibility of a cybernetic system — global in scope and involving the participation of people in all levels and sectors — to monitor patterns of change in socio-environmental conditions, conditions that all help to shape.

As with all technological changes, this cybernetic revolution bears some frightening prospects. The continuing pervasiveness of technical rationality augers the likely increasing concentration of cybernetic control in autocratic centers. One can imagine secret computerized data banks on individuals and groups, the proliferation of electronic surveillance, and the centralized cybernetic control of information as an instrumentality of social, political, and economic domination. In this anti-utopian

[29] Robert C. North, *The World That Could Be* (New York; Norton, 1978), p. 16.
[30] Ibid., p. 17   [31] Ibid., p. 17.

view, the cybernetic revolution opens the way for effective totalitarian world empire — the logical end of technical rationality.

Such tendencies, however, are not characteristic of the technologies themselves — only of the logic that frames their use. In fact, some of the most recent and projected strides in the cybernetic revolution open the way for the development of forms of social organization that can be at once differentiated, coherent, and non-hierarchical. There is, for example, no necessity that communication systems be organized according to the design of so many spokes linked to a single central hub. There is no necessity that all levels, regions, and sectors be tied into a single, fixed model of the system through which all inputs from local nodes are processed and out of which all information to local nodes is then disseminated. It is entirely possible, instead, that each node would be able to access all others directly, giving form to a vital grid of information flows that can be fluidly configured and reconfigured with (and in anticipation of) changes in material conditions and flows of resources. It is entirely possible, too, that each node would be able to develop its own models of the larger whole, access others, note contradictions between its own and others' projections and corresponding plans, employ competing sources of evidence, and alter its own models in light of communications with others. In this way, the several models would not be subordinated to some centralized, dominant, unyielding model of the whole system. On the contrary, each node would be able to import the whole within itself. And through interaction, self-reflection, and systematic argumentation, the several might be continuously in motion toward some non-coercively achieved consensus about their collective past and future. Such, at least, are the possibilities.

As stressed, though, whether or not these possibilities are realized depends upon the grammars of thought that frame their use. And technical rationality, whose surge to global dominance coincides with the globalization of the industrial revolution, remains dominant today. Yet due in part to the welling influence of the fifth great system break — the revolution in information processing and communication — this robust grammar of thought is subjected to new challenges. The challenges are contained in people's increasing sensitivity to the deeper meaning of interdependence.

2. *Interdependence: A Basis for Commitment*

Interdependence, it is clear, is a term that is at once in vogue, highly ambiguous, and, owing in part to its celebrity and ambiguity, subject to much controversy. The concept evidently calls to mind both political and economic relationships among societies and with respect to their common environment. But the exact meaning of the concept is not uniformly acknowledged by all who use it. It is common for analysts to try to qualify and sharpen their usages by referencing many special forms of interdependence. And no matter what special form is distinguished, there is always some significant controversy over whether societies are in fact more or less interdependent than at other times and what this fact implies.

Regarding interdependence, however, one fact is neither ambiguous nor subject to serious controversy: more than before in recent times, people of leading industrial societies find reason to use the word as a descriptor of the conditions in which they find themselves. While some would like to dismiss recurring references to 'spaceship earth, the shrinking planet, our global village, and international interdependence' as so much self-amplifying indulgence in fashionable clichés,[32] one really should not stop short of asking: why now? What is it about contemporary conditions that people are trying to articulate — or reacting to — in resorting to such terms?

Part of the answer is that 'interdependence' connotes a generalized sense that '. . . old slogans are uninstructive' and 'old solutions are unavailing.'[33] It is a way of phrasing the idea that people of leading industrial societies can no longer take entirely for granted their autonomy of foreign influences, can no longer be so confident as before that their tried and once reliable means of solving problems and asserting control over their environments will be effective. Indeed, arguments about increasing interdependence very often carry with them a deep uncertainty as to whether or not there is room for any more technical-rational, cost-minimizing solutions of any kind.

Thus, for example, recurring references to a 'shrinking world' imply more than the observation that people seem to be drawn closer together. They also imply that the fragmentation, complication, and bureaucratization born of a history of mutually implicating solutions have entangled people in a knot that evidently tightens on all as any one struggles for freedom. And the same references also imply that the costly effects of even rich societies' solutions can no longer be exported over the horizon and out of sight. In the same way, recurring references to the 'acceleration

---

[32] Kenneth N. Waltz, *Theory of International Politics* (Reading, Mass.: Addison-Wesley, 1979), p. 141.

[33] Henry A. Kissinger, 'A New National Partnership,' speech by the Secretary of State, Los Angeles, News Release, Office of Media Services, Department of State, p. 1.

of history' imply something more than the increasing pace of change. They imply also that people are less and less able to sustain the illusion of technical-rational solutions by postponing the associated costs to subsequent generations. Increasingly, the costs of people's technical-rational solutions fold back on them so quickly that the roots of the costs in their own 'solutions' are more and more plain. In short, references to interdependence often bespeak a kind of malaise of impotence — a sense of powerlessness confined within a grammar of thought that can conceive of practical social action only in terms of power and weakness.

Herein, though, there is also a basis for emancipation. Herein is a necessary starting point for the subordination of technical rationality to rationality proper. For the acknowledgement of interdependence implies consciousness of the social unit's dependence upon its environment. It implies the unit's acknowledgement that it is not autonomous of social processes ongoing among it, other social units, and their natural surroundings. In turn, from this acknowledgement can stem the commitment that strengthens rationality proper in relation to technical rationality. It is a commitment to the seeking after the only kind of autonomy that human beings are naturally able to know: the autonomy found in the exercise of knowledge, skills, and capacities to communicate in reaching toward some intersubjective consensus regarding the history and future of the human condition. This, it can be said, is the deeper meaning of interdependence.

The case, however, must not be overstated. As noted earlier, technical rationality is a robust grammar of thought. It fends off challenges to its adequacy by bending them into the form of problems requiring technical rational solutions. Even mounting signs of interdependence are often read, not as signals of humans' dependencies upon their environments, but as problems in their own right to be solved. Thus, for example, a Henry Kissinger can speak at length of interdependence and then ask: 'In what other country could a leader say, "We are going to solve energy; we're going to solve food; we're going to solve the problem of nuclear war," and be taken seriously?'[34] In the face of this robust grammar of thought, the challenges contained in currently available evidence of interdependence may be somewhat stronger than challenges of the past. But they are still too weak. They are still too weak to generate the kind of widely shared commitment that is essential to the global subordination of technical rationality to rationality proper.

But is there a way in which people can learn now to see the deeper

---

[34] Quoted in Waltz, *Theory of International Politics*, p. 154.

meaning of interdependence, acknowledge the falsity of technical-rationality, grasp hold of unfolding technological possibilities, import the future into the problems of the present, and project their choices outward in reaching toward a collective future that all genuinely prefer? Must people await the future occurrence of the welling hurtful consequences of their technical-rational acts before learning? Or is there now, amidst present actualities, a community where such learning can at least begin?

3.   *Transnational Social Science: A Point of Departure*

Speaking of social scientific communities as a point of departure immediately summons the specter of technocracy. The specter emerges, though, only because the idea of social scientists having a significant role to play in change toward the future is usually interpreted within a technical-rational grammar of thought — a grammar in which knowledge, if relevant, means power. Within rationality proper, a technocratic role for social scientists is only one among many possible roles. It is a possibility that takes form only when scientists somehow lose their humility, assume that their ideas and choices reflect some totally autonomous 'third world' of objective knowledge,[35] see knowledge building as 'capturing' some fixed, lawful structure or structures, and greatly constrain the kinds of criticism that they will entertain as valid. It is a possibility that is realized, in other words, only when scientists themselves are captives of a technical-rational grammar. Often they are — too often.

Yet what are recognized as social scientific communities, perhaps more than other identifiable communities, also tend to exhibit critical tensions whose full expression would mean the subordination of technical rationality to rationality proper. It is this potential, born of critical tensions, that sets scientific communities slightly apart from the rest, that makes scientific communities slightly more likely points of departure for responsible, rational practical action.

What are these critical tensions? Scientists aspire to some objective knowledge of reality, some form of knowledge that is more than personal belief, but responsible scientists remain always skeptical of assertions that knowledge claims constitute unassailable truth. Scientists concern themselves with discerning order, but responsible scientists desallow the claim that a form of order discerned is the only form that could be or might have been. Scientists seek to discern regularities of life, but responsible scientists allow that the regularities discerned are at least possibly

[35] See Popper, *Objective Knowledge*, Chapters 3 and 4.

contingent, emergent, and susceptible to change. Scientists seek to uncover and articulate general social principles, but responsible scientists are wary of the possibility that they might falsely generalize from fragments of time, space, and experience. Scientists employ instruments to observe, establish, and discern order, but responsible scientists recognize that their instruments cannot be hypostatized, that all instrumentalities bear within them the whole problematical history of theoretical development that led them to regard their instruments as reliable. Scientists seek to resolve problems residing in anomalies to their theories, but responsible scientists allow that the problematical anomalies are seen as such from the vantage points of theories and instruments that have been developed through sequences of problem solutions; they concede that current solutions will contribute to the generation of still more problems. Scientists strive to understand the regularities and rhythms of the natural and social phenomena they study, but responsible scientists understand that they and their theories are profoundly dependent upon nature, society, and the vantage points in which nature and society situate them. Scientists recognize that scientific knowledge can orient practical social action, but responsible scientists also know that scientific knowledge claims, deprived of their critical context, can rationalize distorted conditions, foster errant practices, and immunize against criticism all those practices and institutions subsumed in their *ceteris paribus* clauses. Scientists who study social relations attempt to understand how purposes are reflected in action, but responsible scientists always ask whence the purposes. Scientists struggle for parsimony of conceptualization and precision of measurement, but responsible scientists strive also for a kind of theory that exposes and can express the recombinatorial possibilities among the many aspects of global systems. Scientists seek communicable knowledge and intersubjective consensus about the world they study, but responsible scientists seek a form of consensus that is neither encumbered by coercive influences nor the captive of momentary patterns of political and economic domination.

As each of these statements suggests, scientific communities engage in practices and have aims that are framed by technical rationality, but they also exhibit strains toward the kind of commitment that is the basis for embedding technical rationality in rationality proper. At least somewhat more than other communities, scientific communities continuously engage in criticism, and a large part of that criticism surrounds the likelihood that knowledge claims and practices having pretensions to generality are in fact dependent expressions of influences of which scientists might not be conscious. This fact is immensely important.

For what it records is each scientist's commitment to the self-reflexive examination and explication of preassumptions deeply embedded in every scientific act. It records a widely shared determination to expose unseen influences through the creative act of communication and criticism among scientists having varied vantage points upon the reality they commonly inhabit and study.

Through communication and argument among scientists who bring to bear different models, theories, assumptions, and concepts, each becomes cognizant of the fact that, from one's own vantage point on the world, the knowledge claims of others are disturbingly unwarranted. And while some scientists might simply dismiss others' seemingly unwarranted knowledge claims out of hand, responsible, self-reflexive scientists are disposed to try to see how their own and others' vantage points might be mutually implicating, mutually contextualizing, or possibly relativized in a shared understanding of the larger whole their assertions commonly reflect. The tendency, overall, is to commit scientific practice to the kind of emancipatory aim that is the aim of rationality proper. Technical rationality persists and finds a place in scientific practice, but among communicating scientists, rationality proper can in principle subordinate each technical-rational act by embedding it within a community-wide quest for some consensually shared understanding.[36]

Such tensions, it must be said, are not unique to any one brand or philosophy of social science. True, it is fair to say that some adherents to some philosophies are somewhat more inclined than others to strive toward self-reflection, criticism-consciousness, and the building of intersubjective consensus through argumentation. But if, say, a negative Hegelian philosophy, with its dialectical character, seems strongly associated with this form of scientific practice, it can be noted that positivism, too, strains in this direction. After all, one need look no further than Auguste Comte to see that positivism presses toward the breaking through of political and disciplinary boundaries that might compartmentalize scientific practice. For Comte, all humanity is the *être suprême*, the real universal, the only reality worthy of scientific reverence.[37]

---

[36] As should by now be evident, the writings of Jürgen Habermas and T.W. Adorno, among others, exert an important influence on arguments present in the text. In brief, the arguments point to a 'dia-logical' community of science. See Jürgen Habermas, *Legitimation Crisis* (Boston: Beacon Press, 1975) and Habermas, 'The Analytical Theory of Science and Dialectics,' in T.W. Adorno, *et al.* (eds.), *The Positivism Controversy in German Sociology* (Boston: Beacon Press, 1976), pp. 131–162.

[37] See Auguste Comte, *Systeme de Politique Positive* (Paris: 1890), Volume 1, especially as discussed in Herbert Marcuse, *Reasons and Revolution* (Boston: Beacon Press, 1960), pp. 340–360.

What is more, these tensions of science occur today amidst the two other trajectories of change identified above. More than before, scientists of different countries are cognizant of the interdependencies joining the problems that they have long confronted separately. More than before, also, scientific communities have available — and are rapidly developing — technologies of information processing and communication that permit them to systematically explore complex relationships transcending geographic, political, sectoral, and disciplinary boundaries. Using these technologies, they are able in principle to develop and employ communication networks through which to sustain continuous contact, continuing access to one another's work, and continuing exchanges of information and criticism relevant to models and designs sometimes separately and sometimes cooperatively undertaken. For the first time, it will be possible to realize in practice what has long been at best an ideal: the ideal of a truly integrated transnational scientific community — a community integrated by virtue of its capacity to sustain the critical tensions that are the hallmark of rationality proper.

Transnational social scientific communities are thus positioned to engage in an important, participatory experiment in social change. As elaborated in Appendix A, this experiment can be understood in terms of transnational social scientific communities becoming, as it were, a microcosmic and anticipatory form of a social order organized through each participant's expression of rationality proper. Within such an order, each participant, each tradition, each program, or each node makes use of advancing technologies. Each takes as its task, not the subordination of the whole to its will, but the attempt to import the past and the future into the present and the whole within itself and its immediate problems. Each is engaged in a continuing reflexive struggle, and each is aided through communication and criticism across the problematic boundaries between itself and others.

Scientific communities, in this view, are not engaged in an isolated 'communal' experiment, deliberately apart from the rest of reality. The experiment, instead, is participatory. For each node or each tradition is cognizant of its inescapable dependence upon the larger socio-natural environment, is aware that its ideas and plans might somehow be captive expressions of this or that aspect of life. Each, moreover, is continuously engaged in attempts to uncover, expose, and criticize the limits and extended consequences of technical-rational actions and institutions in a reality that can never be finally partitioned. With time, with continuing and broadening sensitivity to the meaning of interdependence, and with increasing sensitivity to the hurtful costs of technical-rational actions, aspects of society not now classed as scientific might be increasingly inclinded to join the experiment. With more time, the microcosmic experiment might engage all aspects of life, and the experiment might thus become the whole. In short, the experiment beckons not a technocratic but a scientific world — a world wherein natural human capacities to develop knowledge and skills, to communicate, and to reach toward consensus and autonomy can be fully expressed.

This study is intended to be part of that experiment. The conceptual framework and the depiction of the security problematique represent modest attempts to reach across and synthesize insights and propositions from competing, seemingly incompatible traditions — each of which is linked to particular domains, levels, or classes of problem situations, and all of which are linked to insecurity. The modeling of Sino-Soviet-American relations represents an attempt to employ systematic research technologies in order to uncover long-term, far-reaching processes — and in order to expose and criticize the technical-rational patterns of choice underlying these processes. And this whole book is an attempt to use quite conventional means to communicate results and invite criticism.

To the extent that what has been attempted here is communicable and understandable, this study might have helped to show that social science can in principle proceed along the lines of the forementioned experiment. If, in addition, this book inclines even a few people even slightly more toward acknowledging the non-autonomy of even the most powerful leaders of the most powerful nations, then it has succeeded in showing that people need not necessarily await cataclysmic war before coming to grips with the falsity and violence-proneness of technical-rational ideology and all institutions it rationalizes.

Science and scientific communities can to some extent succeed in importing history and the future into the present and the whole into the parts. To some extent, science can invite people to learn of how they and their purposes are situated amidst long-historical processes, how their participation in these processes implicates other aspects of life and the future as well, and how their choices and failures to choose might lead to disaster. To the degree that people, upon confronting the preceding arguments, are more inclined to contemplate these things, this book will have succeeded. It will have succeeded in that people who think about these things are already struggling toward autonomy. They are already struggling to find within themselves and their relations to others the 'hole in the whole' of the modern security problematique.

VI SUMMARY AND CONCLUSION

The arguments contained in this lengthy chapter have ranged widely across many topics — some might think too widely. Not once, however, have they ranged beyond topics relevant to the reproduction and possible passing of the modern security problematique. Section I began by situating the three major military powers of contemporary times amidst long-term processes of differential growth, expansion, and intersections. In so doing, it showed that in many respects the policy orientations and purposes, internal characteristics, and security-political relations of these powers can be interpreted as reflections of their asynchronous and equifinal adaptations to long-term processes that they can express but never fully govern.

Section II then presented three sets of empirically informed propositions which, taken together, portray a complex network of intertwined dynamics and reproducing dilemmas. It is a network of relations whose scope embraces all aspects of life and exceeds the reaches of even the most powerful leaders. This network of relationships, the contemporary expression of the problematique, presents people in general and leaders in particular with recurring problems. It joins attempted solutions in the reproduction of long-term processes of growth, rivalry, and balance of power. And it poises these processes in violence-prone antagonism.

Finally, the third section confronted the seemingly ineluctable character of the modern security problematique. It argued that the system is indeed inescapable so long as people's consciousnesses — then their choices and then the processes at work — are framed by a technical-rational grammar of thought. It argued that, nevertheless, the security problematique is not necessarily ineluctable when seen within the grammar of rationality proper — a grammar that acknowledges the dependence of all human beings and all social organizations upon their environments and the social processes of which they are parts. And it has argued that three now converging trends might open the way for the full expression of rationality proper. The first is the cybernetic revolution. The second is increasingly widespread sensitivity to the deeper meaning of interdependence. The third is the strengthening of a transnational scientific community bearing certain critical tensions that make it a likely point of departure for the exercise of rationality proper.

The last few comments have gone to the point that this community might play an important, non-technocratic role in the subordination of technical rationality to rationality proper, the transformation of international relations, and the transcendence of the modern security problematique. Indeed, it can be argued that participants situated in this community have a special responsibility. They have a responsibility born of the scientific quest for autonomy and intersubjective consensus. So far, though, the special role is a matter of potentiality, not actuality.

If the overall picture leaves room for optimism, therefore, it is, to use Kenneth Boulding's term, a *despairing* optimism. At the very moment that technological developments are making room for social action framed by rationality proper, and at a time when some people sense in interdependence a dim glimpse of the failure of their long-unquestioned ways of thinking, technical rationality remains dominant, the modern security problematique persists, and people confront problems that invite their mobilization of resources and their commitments of themselves to specific solutions. People persist in making technical-rational choices that freeze commitments fractionate reality, and set its fragments on collision courses that the people do not see. And scientists persist in forms of analysis that lend legitimacy to the fragments, apologize for the choices, and celebrate the commitments as lawful tendencies.

The deplorable possibility is thus also the probable possibility: the tragic dynamism of the modern security problematique will be carried forward through time, destructive violence, and widespread human misery to the ultimate end of technical rationality. Only then, only in the self-destructive demonstration of humanity's interdependence, will technical rationality finally be falsified.

This, it would seem, is the logic at work. It is a logic that scientists of all traditions would presumably want to stop. Whether or not they are responsible enough to try is an empirical question only scientists, in their work, can answer. How social scientists of various theoretical traditions might contribute to its answering is the subject of the concluding chapter.

CHAPTER 11

Implications for Theory

This chapter reviews and criticizes a number of competing theoretical traditions in light of this study's depiction of the modern security problematique. In particular, it addresses traditions of (1) balance of power theory, (2) integration theory, (3) Marxian imperialism theory, and (4) liberal and neomercantilist international political economic theory. In greater or lesser degree, each of these and other traditions has had an influence upon this study. Each finds some degree of resonance in the conceptual framework and in the discussion of the modern security problematique. Although none of these traditions is given anything like a full airing in all of its richness, each is reinterpreted, relativized, and accorded partial expression in light of the long-historical perspective that the lateral pressure concept affords.

There are two reasons for reviewing and criticizing these traditions. First, the argument presented in this book, being the result of synthesis, is somewhat complex, and the exposition of that argument will benefit from the attempt to contrast it with competing vantage points. As will quickly become evident, the present synthesis has done more than simply add together insights from competing traditions. Instead, synthesis involves a creative joining of ideas such that the meaning of each proposition is understood in terms of the ways in which it implicates, depends upon, and hence contains all others. By bringing the present treatment into confrontation with competing traditions, it thus becomes possible to draw out contrasts. It becomes possible to show how the present treatment significantly, if sometimes subtly, departs from and revises the more familiar ideas upon which it draws.

Second, Chapter 10's argument regarding the important participatory role of critical social science in international processes is intended quite seriously, and critical engagement across competing scholarly vantage points is essential to the realization of this role. Such engagement, it is frequently noted, tends to be impeded by communication-disrupting differences among competing traditions — differences in social-normative, epistemological, ontological, and other commitments. It often appears as if different traditions address, and inhabit, different worlds. Arguments that are deemed rational and warranted in one community are often taken to be irrational and unwarranted by another. It therefore becomes difficult to realize in practice one of the scientific maxims born out of a commitment to rationality proper: every human attempt to gain mastery over a domain of activity, including intellectual mastery over some scholarly domain, is profoundly dependent upon the environment beyond, including processes addressed by competing communities of scholars. Consequently, the search for scholarly autonomy requires, at a minimum, an unceasing effort to confront viewpoints associated with seemingly distinct aspects of life, to surface hidden interdependencies among aspects, and to thereby import the larger whole into each domain.

There is no claim here that the synthesis presented in this book finally uncovers the essential interdependencies among the aspects of international relations addressed by competing traditions. What is claimed, instead, is only that this study has attempted to engage in synthesis. Accordingly, it has begun to uncover some of the cross-sectoral and cross-level inter-dependencies that transcend theoretical domains, and it has raised questions about others. More importantly, in order to make even these modest strides, it has necessarily confronted and partially explicated some of the social-normative, epistemological, and ontological commitments upon which traditions differ. These are far from breathtaking accomplishments. But they do begin to shed light on some of the lines of engagement among competing traditions. In some small degree, they do begin to prepare the way for a kind of process that is essential to the search for human freedom: the struggle for noncoercively established intersubjective consensus about the interdependent human condition through the waging of controversy among competing vantage points.

The reader should be warned at the outset that the arguments to follow are sometimes complex, often repetitious, and frequently harshly critical. The repetitious character of the arguments derives from the fact that the aspects of reality addressed by competing traditions are overlapping. To use a crude analogy, what follows is a little like explaining how four different bodies of theory help to illuminate the dynamism of a turbulent ocean whirlpool, where each of the four bodies of theory addresses one of four currents, and each current at once helps to shape and is bent within the whirlpool itself. The contribution of no one theoretical tradition can be understood apart from the others.

The arguments will also sometimes be harshly critical — or at least, some will so judge them. This is because this study does not accept the widely shared idea that scientific theory can be somehow set neutrally apart from the realities addressed. Theory cannot be gauged solely in terms of its truth, objectivity, or empirical fit. Theory is always a participatory activity — a fact that Keynes acknowledged when he took note of 'academic scribblers' imprisoning policy makers and Marx acknowledged when he observed that theory can become a 'material force.' As a result, theorists and theoretical traditions have social responsibilities. They can be guilty of complicity in tragic processes. They can present theoretical statements that, as uncritical ideologies, rationalize and apologize for the reproduction of violence-prone and exploitative conditions. They can invent concepts that ensnare and cripple attempts to contemplate and exercise human potentialities. And they can even parade as radical theorists of human liberation while immunizing the liberating vanguard's most alienating practices from radical criticism. Many people who are accustomed to Popperian notions of scientific criticism will look askance at the use of such terms as these. To accuse a tradition, not just of being empirically mistaken, but of being, say, an ideology that rationalizes violence — such assertions will for some seem to strike below the scientific belt. Yet, from the perspective of this book, the view of science that is offended by such criticism is itself an ideology, although it masks itself as the end of ideology. It is a view of science embedded in technical rationality. It is a view that exalts scientific knowledge as somehow occupying an autonomous and objective 'third world' that is securely apart from the rest of reality and powerful enough to make reality in its light.

If the arguments to follow appear offensively harsh to some, however, it must be stressed that they are also intended to have a positive effect. Criticism should be a productive enterprise. If even a few proponents of the various traditions addressed below do more than reject the criticisms out of hand, if they respond scientifically to the arguments regarding interdependencies transcending their various theoretical domains, then something productive might occur. Somewhat more than before, a few social scientists might be disposed to examine how some of their unquestioned preassumptions and time-honored knowledge claims implicate and depend upon processes ongoing seemingly beyond the horizons of their respective domains. Somewhat more than before, social scientists might approach engaging in a 'dialogical,' criticism conscious enterprise apropos of a dialectical reality.

The discussion begins, appropriately enough, with what is perhaps the most honored, enduring, and widely disputed of all theoretical perspectives on international relations. It begins with a theoretical perspective corresponding to the third stage of the three-stage historical progression described in the conceptual framework. It begins with balance of power.

I   BALANCE OF POWER THEORY

Referring to a body of research and theory from Machiavelli to Morgenthau and Riker, Karl Deutsch asserts that balance of power theory goes far to illuminate 'the politics of appropriation' but fundamentally ignores 'the politics of production, of cooperation, and of growth.'[1] Deutsch's assertion is correct. For since Machiavelli, balance of power theorists have held to the explicit assumption of 'the autonomy of the political sphere.'[2] Political standards, not social or economic ones, are argued to be the exclusive gauges of international political praxis.

The assumption takes undeniable force when coupled with the appropriate ontological fix: the world consists of a multiplicity of individual *states* having certain given characteristics; i.e., they are unitary actors seeking their own preservation. Usually the identitites of states are given in these terms even before their actual and possible relationships are considered. Next, the ordinary line of thought moves to consideration of the conditions of states' coexistence: (*a*) the absence of any supranational agent that can effectively limit the political use of force and (*b*) the actual or possible absence of any preponderant state among the several. Unregulated competition is thus likely — and in fact generates certain necessities of policy. Given the assumed primacy of survival motives, these necessities dominate all others. Balance of power derives from the technical-rational actions and interactions of states calculating policies on the basis of these necessities. In these terms, extra-political concerns can be effectively purged from consideration as contingent reflections of balance of power.[3]

To be sure, this description is an oversimplification of a rich and controversial arena of theory. As Kenneth Waltz points out, for example,

[1] Karl W. Deutsch, *The Analysis of International Relations*, second edition (Englewood Cliffs, N.J.: Prentice-Hall, 1978) p. 174.

[2] Hans Morgenthau, *Politics Among Nations: The Struggle for Power and Peace*, fifth edition, revised (New York: Knopf, 1978), pp. 11–14.

[3] Probably the sharpest statement of this hard core position is contained in Kenneth N. Waltz, *Theory of International Politics* (Reading, Mass.: Addison-Wesley, 1979).

theorists of balance of power, including Kissinger and Morgenthau, admit considerations of national attributes into their perspectives.[4] Morgenthau also admits considerations regarding the individual human being's alleged desire for power and the projection of this desire, via the state, upon the international scene. Both Morgenthau and Kissinger concern themselves with the potential effects of 'revolutionary' or 'imperialistic' states by way of addressing systemic questions of 'moral consensus' and 'legitimacy.'[5] Yet, while many balance of power theorists would elaborate upon the 'hard core' depiction of the previous paragraph, few would dissent from it as a description of the main properties of balance of power.

The analysis presented here challenges the ontological base of this impeccable logic. It starts, not with states, but with individuals and groups having in principle all sorts of recombinatorial possibilities among them. It starts with individuals and groups who are profoundly dependent upon their environments and who have capacities to develop knowledge and skills and to communicate. These capacities can be exercised reflexively and critically in striving toward some intersubjective consensus

---

[4] Ibid., pp. 62–5. Waltz is referring to Morgenthau, *Politics Among Nations*, and Henry A. Kissinger, *A World Restored* (New York: Grosset and Dunlap, 1964).

[5] This, however, does not make them 'reductionist,' not even by Waltz's own definition of the reductionism: 'Theories of international politics that concentrate causes at the individual or national level are reductionist; theories that conceive of causes operating at the international level *as well* are systemic.' Waltz, *Theory of International Politics*, p. 18, emphasis added.

Unfortunately, despite his own definition, Waltz claims that these and other theorists who admit attributes other than political capabilities as well as systemic factors are engaging in reductionism. For Waltz, apparently, all theories of balance of power are reductionist save those, such as Waltz's own one-sided vision of structural dominance, that reduce explanations to referencing behavior under conditions of anarchy. Theorists are of course free to use terms in any way that they please. But one wonders what has happened to language when a theory that reduces explanation to a single, unproblematical, uncriticized systemic attribute, anarchy, is said to be less reductionist than theories that try to enrich the concept with reference to societies' interiorizations of the requisites of participation under conditions of anarchy.

In fact, as it turns out, Morgenthau and Kissinger are applying or attempting to apply a way of thinking that Waltz's essentially (Comtean) positivist perspective can never comprehend: the balance of power systemic 'whole' is or can be *within* the 'parts.' When they speak of 'moral consensus' or 'legitimacy,' this is what they mean. For them, 'revolutionary' or 'imperialist' societies are those that lag in their equifinal adaptations to the precariously dominant properties of the system, and to the extent that they have not adapted to and interiorized the requisites of participation, they threaten the system's capacity to function in a predictable, behavior ordering way. This view, it should be clear, does not deny the causal significance of dominant ordering principles of the system. It says only that these principles are always problematical given the mutual determination of parts and wholes.

about society and its relations to nature. Or, alternatively, they can be used uncritically — that is, technologically — to assert mastery and control over human environments, including other human beings. According to the conceptual framework, states can emerge when patterns of population and technological growth and environmental change open the way for the technological exercise of knowledge and skills, leading to differential growth and accumulation, leading to competition, and leading to further opportunities and motives for uneven technological growth and accumulation of rewards. States, as emergent political systems, require such a process so that they can extract from accumulated wealth the energies of their existence. And if the processes are to be sustained, then states are required to regulate competition and maintain patterns of social stratification.

It must be stressed that this shift of perspective does not deny the reality of states or of balance of power. It is simply a matter of denying the ontological status of states and asserting instead that the state is a historically emergent structuration. It is a structuration that, like all social structurations, has the general effect of limiting human choices, human interaction, and social possibilities. This ontological shift is all that is necessary to begin to join other perspectives with and within balance of power. It is all that is necessary to begin to articulate a meaning of political autonomy in a world wherein politics can never be independent of natural constraints and varied and changing human wants and needs.

What results is a view of balance of power as a historically *emergent* and now deeply structured regime of international reality. 'Deeply structured' here means that the rules and institutions of human and social interaction now generally (and by and large unquestioningly) presuppose a world order wherein states will interact according to balance of power principles. It means, among other things, that relations among people and societies have come to be widely ordered under the presupposition that human choices will routinely regenerate the social structurations of states in apparent anarchy. Balance of power theory simply records the manifest appearances of these historically-wedded deep structures. Insofar as balance of power theory additionally assumes or asserts that these appearances are natural lawful and inescapable — and insofar as it lends states, and hence anarchy, an ontological status and denies the fact that they are emergent and transformable — it also apologizes for all aspects of life that the regime and associated structurations help to reproduce.

Among the aspects of life reproduced are states prepared for war. This much has been strongly emphasized in the conceptual framework, and this much has been argued in balance of power theory as well. But the framework, with the human being as its ontological base, is also capable of addressing the political autonomy question that most balance of power theory simply assumes away. Specifically, it is able to bring to bear insights — for example, insights from imperialism and integration theory — regarding the socio-economic-environmental complexities of the politicization process and regarding transnational communication and interaction. The result of the joining is that the balance of power regime is seen to (*a*) reproduce states and strengthen states' claims to political autonomy; (*b*) enhance the state's capacity to defend social stratifications, discipline domestic competition, accelerate growth, extract resources, and make commitments; while thereby (*c*) contributing to the long-term, highly differential amplification of socio-economic-environmental demands and transnational pressures that are unmanageable within an international regime predicated on political autonomy principles. How, more precisely, the regime does these things is described at length in Section IV, below.

Balance of power thus does more than contribute to the reproduction of states prepared for war. Viewed over the longer term it also contributes to the generation of the preconditions of political rivalries, conflict, crisis, and war itself. It contributes to the shaping of environmental conditions that disturb the 'balance of power system' and limit the states' abilities to effectively adapt and avoid war.[6]

Small wonder that balance of power theorists have little trouble finding evidence that international relations are anarchical and violence-prone. For balance of power theory is within states, almost as a material force. And as such, its prophecy of violence is self-fulfilling.

If this means that balance of power theory offers inadequate guidance for the search for peace, however, it does not mean that balance of power theory can be safely ignored. Rather, the implication is that balance of power theory needs to be reexamined with an eye to treating the balance of power regime as a historically emergent open system. In this way, one can still note that peoples and leaders have increasingly succumbed to principles of political autonomy and the primacy of high politics ever since these principles were first invoked to bolster and justify the absolutist state-building of absolutist monarchs. In this way, also, one can still note with Waltz and others how the coexistence of several states so ordered might configure a prisoner's dilemma to which states tend to adapt their policies. But by treating balance of power as an open system,

---

[6] A more systematic elaboration of this argument is found below in Section IV's treatment of liberal and mercantilist political economy.

one can also avoid making theory an accomplice in the further mystification of the short-sighted quest for unlimited power.

How does the strengthening of states in answer to the created necessities born of a created anarchy contribute to the reproduction of political conditions in which differential growth is the dominant pattern? How does differential growth within societies, as well as among them, contribute to disturbances in the overall balance of power and constrain states' attempts to respond? To what extent do highly uneven flows of resources and information across national boundaries generate relations of inter-societal dependency — relations that limit the latitude of states to act in accordance with the logics of balance of power? To what extent are societies differentially positioned amidst and affected by these flows, and how do these differential positions affect (*a*) their roles within the balance of power and (*b*) tendencies toward bipolarity and multipolarity in the overall system? To what extent do societies' different positions within the overall balance of power — and different patterns of polarity — affect societies' capacities to shape flows of resources and information and configurations in these flows? In light of answers to these questions, how might a balance of power regime be adapted, elaborated, or transformed? To ask these questions is to begin to treat the systemic balance of power as an open system. As will be seen in the discussion of other traditions below, the same questions are raised from a variety of theoretical vantage points.

Among some balance of power theorists, such questions might seem pointless, and the arguments behind raising these questions might seem misguided. Kenneth Waltz, for example, might see these arguments as 'reductionist' to the extent that they submit that domestic attributes play a significant part in determining systemic outcomes. He might assert that the 'argument confuses theory with reality and identifies a model of a theory with the real world' by suggesting that balance of power theory should account for relationships across boundaries of political and economic systems.[7] He might cite general systems theorist W. Ross Ashby and assert that 'the problem . . . is how to find out what we really want to know without being overwhelmed with useless detail.'[8]

If one is to agree with Ashby, however, one ought also to note that his is hardly the advocacy of theories of closed systems. Such systems, i.e., closed systems, are prone toward entropy, toward maximal disorder, and this is not how balance of power theorists want to describe the balance

---

[7] Waltz, *Theory of International Politics*, p. 38.

[8] Ibid., p. 4. Waltz is quoting from W. Ross Ashby, *An Introduction to Cybernetics* (London: Chapman and Hall, 1964), p. 113.

of power system. To say that balance of power has long endured as a highly structured system is in fact to deny that it has reached or approached this maximally disordered state. In turn, if one is to acknowledge the openness of a balance of power system, one must also allow for flows of energy and information from the environment — from those aspects of reality not presumed to be part of the ordered balance of power system.

To allow for such flows is not to engage in reductionist reasoning unless one commits one of two errors. One error is to assume that the systems comprising the environment of a balance of power regime are themselves closed systems or somehow operate in ways totally independent of the balance of power system: they 'drive' balance of power but are impervious to its changes. The questions outlined above, taken together, do not contain this assumption and do not commit this error. The second error is to assume that the balance of power system predominates over other systems comprising its environment in ways that wholly determine flows of energy and information from the environment. The questions outlined above do not commit this error either, although it is an error tantamount to an assertion of closure and often implicit in the balance of power theorist's arguments regarding the primacy and autonomy of the political sphere.

The questions phrased above do little more than invite attention to the basic systems theoretical notion of *feedback* across system boundaries: two-way feedback, as each of several open systems equifinally responds and adapts to other systems comprising its environment. Even if one wants only to explain manifestly political outcomes in terms of manifestly political causes, one must minimally allow for the possibility that the overall relationship might involve complex patterns wherein political changes contribute to economic conditions that in turn have political effects.

Such arguments do not 'confuse theory with reality' or identify 'a model of a theory with the real world.' It is balance of power theorists who commit this error. For what they fail to see is that this impeccable logic, with its celebration of anarchy, is already a theory-*qua*-material force. In their onesided abstraction of systemic patterns from all relationships that do or might exist, they abstract out exactly those apparent patterns that powerful participants are prone to see and, in the seeing, are prone to reproduce. Yes, part of 'the problem . . . is how to find out what we really want to know without being overwhelmed with useless detail.' But if we ask more of knowledge than the ideological rationalization of inhumane human creations, then questions that go to the ways in which such creations emerged, are reproduced, and might be transcended can hardly be said to address useless detail.

II   INTEGRATION THEORY

'As for balance of power in our age, let it rest in peace.' So wrote Ernst Haas by way of expressing his conviction that theories of balance of power represent 'obscurities enshrined' and that functionalist logics, though flawed, help to identify important possibilities for international socio-political change toward a peaceful order.[9] The insights of neo-functionalist integration theory find room and partial expression within the conceptual framework. The framework is equally open to a Deutsch-like perspective on integration, a perspective that emphasizes communication flows having social effects and giving form and boundaries to national and international communities.[10] The framework is open to both of these perspectives, and is able to accommodate some of their insights, because the conceptualization of lateral pressure contains an assumption that both of these perspectives share: human beings are able to communicate, learn from experience, alter their values, shift their loyalties and identifications, and change their social groupings and political patterns (albeit *never* with full and objective understandings of themselves and their circumstances, devoid of habit, and free of political, social, economic, and environmental limits shaped through historical processes).

In terms of the lateral pressure argument, though, there are subtle but important distinctions to be made between the communication-theoretical emphasis of Deutsch and the neofunctionalist perspective of Haas. A communication-theoretical perspective can and does stress integration as, in part, a kind of 'inner' relation.[11] It is a relation wherein people (*a*) interiorize a sense of the larger community within their symbolic definitions of self and (*b*) through interaction and communication within certain changing, possible unevenly felt conditions, are able to sustain, for a long time, their sense of community and of 'institutions and practices strong enough and widespread enough to assure . . . dependable expectations of peaceful change.'[12] Such a perspective also accommodates,

[9] *Beyond the Nation State* (Stanford, Calif.: Stanford University Press, 1964), especially p. 76.

[10] See, e.g., Karl W. Deutsch, *et al.*, *Political Community and the North Atlantic Area* (Princeton: Princeton University Press, 1957); and Karl W. Deutsch, *Nationalism and Social Communication* (Cambridge, Mass.: MIT Press, 1953).

[11] See Appendix A for a discussion of the distinction between 'internal' and 'external' relations.

[12] Deutsch, *et al.*, *Political Community*, p. 5.

and holds in continuing tension, the possibility that such relations might cooccur at at least two mutually implicating levels: the level of the 'amalgamated' and 'pluralistic' security communities. And such a perspective is at once dialectical and historical in that it allows for the fact that communications can produce (often simultaneously) potentialities for both conflict and cooperation or differentiation and identity; these possibilities are embedded in memories, recombined with new experiences, and find expression in the communication patterns and contents of any moment. In all of these respects, adherents to a communication-theoretical perspective anticipate and have sometimes answered (although not always self-consciously) the full implications of the lateral pressure argument.

Neofunctionalists, on the other hand, have grasped but part of the argument and remain unknowing captives of the larger whole. For them, the interdependence of integrative processes is principally an 'external' relation. The processes discussed involve people acting pragmatically — that is, to serve unquestioned purposes through the applications of specific technical means upon their objectified environments. Learning is seen to consist principally of people coming to recognize that some organizational commitments serve their interests better than others. In short, the neofunctionalist tends to assume that participants are confined within a technical-rational grammar of thought, and so, the neofunctionalist's integration logics are confined there too. Thus, although the neofunctionalist tends to emphasize (almost exclusively) the positive side of differential growth and lateral pressure, he, like so many others, is unable to get outside of the processes of the modern security problematique.

While proponents of communication-theoretical perspectives might find things of interest in the criticisms to follow, then, the criticisms themselves are addressed principally to neofunctionalist thinkers. What do the latter emphasize in their searches for peace?

As Ernst Haas puts it, 'The dominant desire of modern students of regional integration is to explain the tendency toward the voluntary creation of larger political units each of which self-consciously eschews the use of force in relations between the participating units and groups.'[13] Haas thus points to the main *normative* reason for studying regional integration:

---

[13] Ernst B. Haas, 'The Study of Regional Integration: Reflections on the Joys and Anguish of Pretheorizing,' in Leon Lindberg and Stuart Scheingold (eds.), *Regional Integration: Theory and Research* (Cambridge, Mass.: Harvard University Press, 1971), p. 4.

The units and actions studied provide a living laboratory for observing the peaceful creation of possible new types of human communities at a very high level of aggregation and of the processes which may lead to such conditions. *The study of regional integration is concerned with tasks, transactions, perceptions, and learning, not with sovereignty, military capability, and balances of power. It refuses to dichotomize the behavior of actors between 'high' political and 'low' functional concerns; it is preoccupied with all concerns of actors* insofar as they can be used for sketching processes of adaptation and learning free from coercion.[14]

In turn, the normative concerns serve to define a primary theoretical focus:

The study of regional integration is concerned with explaining how and why states cease to be wholly sovereign, how and why they voluntarily mingle, merge, and mix with their neighbors so as to lose the factual attributes of sovereignty while acquiring new techniques for resolving conflict between themselves.[15]

To underscore the boundaries of this theoretical focus, Haas states that 'the study of regional integration is unique and discrete from all previous systematic studies of political unification because it limits itself to *non-coercive* efforts.' 'Our task,' he continues, 'is to explain integration among nations without recourse to [historical catalytic agents using force] not because they have not been important but because they make the explanation too simple and too time-bound.'[16] Not all work on regional integration theory conforms to Haas's statements of direction, but it is fair to say that he points up the main tendencies among neofunctionalist thinkers.

When these tendencies are refracted through this study's conceptual framework, two criticisms emerge. The first goes to the familiar issue of regionalism versus globalism as perspectives on the maintenance of international peace. The second relates to the tendency of neofunctionalist theory to ahistorically neglect the socio-economic determinants of insecurity politics.

The first criticism, regarding regionalism versus globalism, has two sides. On the one hand, the theoretical perspective developed here implies that it is within regional boundaries that integrative momentum is most likely to begin. Why? The answer is that the 'background conditions' for economic and political integration among societies, such as those identified by Haas, are themselves reflections of the historical, asynchronous, and equifinal ebb and flow of differential growth and lateral

[14] Ibid., emphasis added.   [15] Ibid., p.6.   [16] Ibid., p.4.

pressure throughout the world: differential movements of populations; uneven transmissions of knowledge and skills; intersections of peoples, cultures, and environmental circumstances; and resulting localized commonalities of historical experiences, including historic patterns of (and adaptations to) conflict and violence. In these terms, were one to imagine replications of Bruce Russett's factor analytic approach to regional identification throughout history, century by century, the resulting sequence of changing clusterings would be seen to provide a kind of 'newsreel' account of how differential growth and lateral pressure has formed and reshaped 'regions' throughout time.[17] At any historical moment, the framework implies, it is mainly within such regions that partially shared historical experiences will have established norms, values, symbols, expectations, forms of political organization, and lines of social stratification of sufficient commonality and potential interdependence to make likely, at least for a time, non-coercive functional engagement.

On the other hand, the historical dynamism of the framework implies not only change in the historical 'configurations' of regions but also a kind of principle of *supplementarity* for any region at any moment.[18] That is, if regions are constantly changing, on geographic and other dimensions, then they are also at any moment 'reaching out' beyond themselves and toward what they are not but will or might become. This means that (1) regions and the political units comprising them are individuated — i.e., given form as identifiable regions and units meriting attention as reasonable boundaries and possible partners in integration — only because of differential, unevenly felt, and still occurring historical experiences among peoples and over territory. This means (2) that such identifiable configurations of any moment are, as it were, 'supplemented' by other possible configurations, some of which are in the process of becoming, and others of which are being denied.

The point of such abstractions is that the strictly regional focus of regional integration theory always risks hardening down the regional boundaries of any historical moment by limiting the search for supplementarity to the actual and possible interdependencies among units

---

[17] Bruce M. Russett, *International Regions and the International System* (Chicago: Rand-McNally, 1967).

[18] The notion of supplementarity is due principally to Jacques Derrida. For an English-language introduction to his writings see Gayatri Cahakavravorty Spivak's preface to her translation of *Of Grammatology* (Baltimore and London, New Left Books, 1976), pp. ix-lxxxvii. As a concept, if one can privilege it by calling it a concept, 'supplementarity' functions to question the status of any central or dominant concept by revealing what it leaves out, represses, or has yet to express.

within those boundaries. That is, while states comprising a regional system are regarded as mutually implicating open systems, the regional system is itself regarded as closed.

Serious consequences follow. The political units within a region, being individuated as units in the first place because of their partially unique but interdependent histories, always bear potentialities of mutual conflict as well as cooperation in their growth and in the lateral pressure they express. If the boundaries of the region have in fact been so hardened as to demarcate a closed regional system, then the partially conflicting aspects of each unit's lateral pressure will intersect with other units of the same region in ways generating tendencies toward exploitation, differential growth, the politicization of transactions, conflict, and disorder. If, by contrast, regional boundaries are open enough to permit each unit's externalizations of costs beyond the region, then political relations within the region are made dependent upon externalities over which the regional decision-making apparatus may have little control. Still further, even if a regional grouping succeeds in turning all mutually productive expressions of lateral pressure within the region and all potentially exploitative expressions outward — even if the differential growth within the grouping is somehow minimized while overall growth is accelerated — this will mean that the integrative possibilities within other regional groupings outside the first will be restricted by the limited kinds of intersections it can have with the first. (The historical 'cases' of the European Economic Community and the Latin American Free Trade Area are not distinct 'laboratory experiments' in any sense.)

Evident in this first criticism is the same systems theoretical reasoning earlier applied in the discussion of balance of power. To treat a regional system as in fact closed, and hence bounded in a way impermeable to exchanges of energy and information with other regions comprising its environment, is to submit that it will exhibit entropy — tendencies toward maximal disorder. To treat it as an open system but not to allow for its adaptations with respect to its environment is to submit that it predominates over and determines the ways in which energy and information are exchanged with the environment; and this is tantamount to saying that systems comprising the environment are subordinate with respect to and cannot determine the same flows.

Insofar as they concentrate upon regional integration among developed societies, regional integration theorists tend to implicitly assume that the latter is in fact the case. What they fail to see is that in one region's ability to extract order from its environment in exchange for disorder expelled, other regional systems comprising the environment are thereby reduced to extracting order, not from the first, but only from other systems, including especially the *natural* environment.

This bears an important implication: *neofunctionalist notions of regional integration among developed societies contain as a hidden premise the idea of exploitative growth amidst center-periphery relationships.* Symmetrical integrative possibilities of the kind described by regional integration theorists exist only in the center and imply the subordination of semi-periphery and periphery. Semi-peripheral economies can progress only through the subordination of the periphery. The periphery can progress, if at all, only through the subordination of material resources accessible in its natural surroundings. At the periphery, in fact, human systems are reduced to extracting only the most basic forms of ordered energy from the environment and to reproducing themselves by the most basic means. To the extent that integrative momentum accelerates at the center, integrative possibilities among peripheral societies are denied.

The second criticism emerging from the framework stresses another partitioning problem in integration theory. But this one is more conceptual and historical than geographical. Specifically, the arguments developed in the framework would endorse Haas's *expressed* belief that one cannot 'dichotomize the behavior of actors between "high" political and "low" functional concerns.' One cannot because in long historical perspective, the emergence of dynamics of rivalry and balance of power — indeed, the creation of the 'actors' entangled in these dynamics — is largely a product of people, groups and classes engaged in 'tasks, transactions, perceptions, and learning' and thereby accelerating competition for resources and positions. One cannot dichotomize, furthermore, because rivalry and balance of power are among the processes by which social forms, stratifications, material human values, and 'the factual attributes of sovereignty' are shaped and limited.

What the arguments contained in the framework cannot endorse is the contradictory negative heuristic that Haas somehow derives: 'Our task is to explain integration among nations without recourse to [historical catalytic agents using force] . . . because they make the explanation too simple and too time-bound.' Such a heuristic *implicitly* urges research practices that Haas *expressly* opposes. It 'dichotomizes.' It leaves aside 'sovereignty, military capability, and balances of power' as if they stood mysteriously beyond the kind of dynamic historical explanation that neofunctionalists would marshal for peaceful change. In so doing, it joins the balance of power theorist in investing in these realities an ontological primacy they do not merit.

It is not enough for the analyst to skillfully dismember balance of power theory, impale it on its flaws, and read *requiescat in pace* over its grave. It is not enough when the specter of balance of power – the specter of international violence amidst anarchy – remains a deeply structured aspect of social organization and a prime source of motivating tension for integration theory itself. It is not enough because the dynamics of rivalry and balance of power are produced and reproduced as the dark 'other side' of the very processes upon which neofunctionalists pin their hopes for peace.

In an important sense, balance of power is a form of integration among societies. It is a realization of differential growth and interdependence among societies, albeit one expressed in the individuation and reproduction of violence-prone social structurations called states. Some years ago, Quincy Wright reached the same conclusion:

> It is important to emphasize . . . that whenever maintenance of the balance of power becomes a guide to the policy of a government, that government is on the threshold of conceding that stability of the community of states is an interest superior to its domestic interests. Doubtless it concedes this only because it believes that stability is a *sine qua non* of its own survival. The concession is, however, an enlightenment of self-interest which approaches altruism or submergence of the self in a larger whole.[19]

Just how integrative is the balance of power regime is further discussed in Section IV, below.

It is perhaps instructive to remember that de Gaulle was not a mysterious external actor entering the stage of European integration to dramatically disrupt the play short of its climax. He acted within the latitude that history allowed him and using a language of 'French grandeur' generated by a grammar that history had long followed. His words and his deeds had effect, not only because of the presence of the man, but also because they carried the whole weight of the French history of growth and expansion, of involvement in military rivalries, and of deep societal adaptations to the requisites of participation in a European balance of power. They had effect beyond France because other European societies share aspects of this same history. De Gaulle's words and deeds evoke, or should evoke, the proposition that in passively 'forgetting' these 'time-bound' concepts, integrationists' active attempts to steer and redirect

---

[19] Quincy Wright, *A Study of War* (Chicago, University of Chicago Press, 1964 abridged), p. 119.

processes of growth and interchange are likely to bring these same concepts conflictually to the fore.

These two criticisms can be combined to suggest that neofunctionalist integration theory, far from constituting a design for peace, bears within itself the sources of its own demise. In partitioning reality both geographically and historically, in failing to acknowledge principles of supplementarity in open systems and the historical socio-economic sources of the processes it would overcome, it urges policies and practices that foster inequality, conflict, and the reinvigoration of power politics. If balance of power theory is self-fulfilling, neofunctionalist constructions of integration theory tend to be largely self-denying.

This negative critique also has its positive side. What is needed are two heuristics. The first would poise in continuing dialectical tension (*a*) the attempt to explain the tendency toward the voluntary creation of larger political units and multilateral regimes that are capable of guaranteeing for a long time peaceful change and (*b*) the attempt to explore, expose, and criticize those patterns, programs and practices of exchange and communication (as well as strictly politico-military practices) that might sharpen security dilemmas, generate military rivalry, strengthen state sovereignty, increase probabilities of violence, and foreclose opportunities for peaceful change. The second would poise in continuing dialectical tension (*a*) the attempt to locate possible regional integrative opportunities and describe/prescribe the processes and their likely regional consequences and (*b*) the attempt to discern the actual and possible extra-regional constraints on and consequences of regional integration. The two heuristics implicate one another and, as such, seriously problematize research on integration. Yet unless neofunctionalist integration theory draws these critical tensions within itself, it will never transcend what it has long been: one more expression of a technical-rational quest for problem solving and the abatement of conflict through terminal closure.

III   MARXIAN IMPERIALISM THEORY

It has been said repeatedly that the concept of lateral pressure constitutes the hard core conceptual anchor of this study's approach to synthesis. Few readers of this book — and of the writings of Choucri and North before it — will have failed to notice a resemblance between the concept of lateral pressure, on the one hand, and the concept of imperialism, on the other. Many will have asked, is not the term 'lateral pressure,' with its connotations of expansion, simply a synonym for 'imperialism'? Is not the whole of the theoretical synthesis really nothing more than an extension or generalization of one or another version of imperialism theory? These questions have been raised before about the work of Choucri and North. This book might again elicit such questions.

The answer to the first question is no, 'lateral pressure' and 'imperialism' are not synonyms. The intended relationship between the two terms, instead, is that lateral pressure represents a generic, timeless social process, potentially evidenced by all living systems at all levels, of which processes Marxists call 'imperialism' represent a specific, historically dependent form.

There are similarities, surely, between the two terms and the reasoning behind their use. Like much of Marxist-Leninist imperialism theory, the concept of lateral pressure is developed as an expression of a dialectical logic of crititical social consciousness. As Joan Robinson has put it, 'the function of social science is quite different from that of the natural sciences — it is to provide society with an organ of self-consciousness.'[20] Like much of Marxist-Leninist imperialism theory, too, the concept of lateral pressure has been developed with an eye to the orienting of what might be called emancipatory social praxis. The aim is to construct a form of theory that can do more than explain and steer action to reproduce the world as it is. Theory should also (*a*) set the 'is' amidst the 'is not' and 'could be' and (*b*) leave room for responsible action that might effect the transcendence of actual conditions.

There are, however, important differences between 'lateral pressure' and 'imperialism' as concepts. Unlike much of imperialism theory, the concept of lateral pressure, being generic and non-ahistorical, can claim to accomplish the forementioned tasks, at least potentially, without immunizing emancipatory social praxis from criticism. Those who would find guidance in lateral pressure thoery in their attempts to alter dominant patterns are not exempted from the social critique contained in the concept of lateral pressure itself. As will be made clear below, the same cannot be said of most Marxian treatments of imperialism.

This, then, is the force of Robert North's gesture toward developing a non-ahistorical concept in light of general systems theoretical insights. The thrust is two-fold. First, it is to develop a theoretical synthesis that not only orients individual and collective action aimed toward the transcendence of existing conditions but also contains concepts that allow for the effective criticism of practices so oriented. Second, it is to construct a concept, applicable at several interconnected levels of analysis, that

[20] Joan Robinson, *Freedom and Necessity* (London: Allen and Unwin, 1970), p. 120. Robinson is a Keynesian, but her statement would be accepted by most Marxists.

allows for the emergence of social units at higher levels out of processes below, admits the mutual determination of wholes and parts, and hence can expose and criticize the determinism of emergent systems without losing sight of individual responsibility. The two thrusts are really one. For without the retention of individual responsibility, critical theory becomes a one-sided theory of system dominance, and what is meant to be critical dissolves into a rationalization of individual complicity.

Thus, although the concept of lateral pressure may be said to 'contain' the Marxist-Leninist concept of imperialism, the former also contains a critique of theoretical perspectives that would be slavishly wedded and confined to the latter. How this is so is best stated by reviewing the lateral pressure argument. More specifically, it is instructive to do three things: (1) summarize the basic lateral pressure argument as it might relate to any single level of social units; (2) allow for the possibility of emergent, higher-level social units to regulate processes below; and thereby (3) develop a simplified understanding of the emergence, reproduction, and transcendence of the multilayered system here described as the modern security problematique. With this background established, it will then be possible to criticize two approaches to the study of imperialism as expressed in Marxian analysis. One is a 'subsystem dominance' approach, as associated with the writing of V.I. Lenin, and emphasizing contradictions in the national capitalist economy.[21] The other is a structuralist, or 'system dominance,' approach, as associated with the explicit theory of Immanuel Wallerstein and also reflected in Marxian dependency literatures.[22]

A   A Summary of the Lateral Pressure Argument

Although, as indicated, lateral pressure can occur at multiple, interconnected levels of analysis, the basic argument is best phrased, at least initially, with reference to a single level of like social units. The argument is this:

Lateral pressure reflects the growth of a social unit's population and technological demands (*a*) as these exceed the capacities of a unit's immediate resources to satisfy them and (b) as these combine with previously developed specialized capabilities. A unit thus reaches out

[21] V.I. Lenin, *Imperialism: The Highest Stage of Capitalism* (Moscow: Progress Publishers, 1967).

[22] See especially Immanuel Wallerstein, *The Modern World System: Capitalist Agriculture and the Origins of the World Economy in Sixteenth Century* (New York: Academic Press, 1974).

to overcome obstacles, subordinate its environment, and satisfy internally generated demands. In the process, new demands and 'needs' are generated. Among the aspects of each's environment potentially subordinated are other social units, especially low lateral pressure social units. Relationships of inequality thus emerge.

Among two or more high lateral pressure units — two or more units having roughly equal specialized capabilities — competition is likely. Competition and inequality are unstable relationships, though. They can be sustained only so long as the expansion of each high lateral pressure competitor can be projected outward, and not toward other high lateral pressure units. Once a limit to the outward expansion of the domain of competition is reached — once, say, the expanding units encounter obstacles that cannot be technologically surmounted — their lateral pressure tends to be mutually directed. Each aims to directly subordinate the other. Violence and the eventual subordination of the whole domain to the demands and capabilities of one is the long-range tendency.

As this tendency advances, extreme pressures for redistribution begin to mount. Conditions of relative equality are then restored. Conditions of inequality cannot and do not emerge again until there occurs some change in environing factors or available technologies (knowledge and skills) that (*a*) permit some minority of social units a differential ability to overcome previous environmental limits, (*b*) generate new, differentially felt demands, and thereby (*c*) open the way for and extend the domain of competition.

As this brief argument suggests, conditions of equality (but not necessarily the absence of conflict) are to be taken as basic, normal, and representative of asymptotic tendencies in all systems. Conditions characterized by protracted competition, social stratification, hierarchical social control relations, and high degrees of material inequality are to be taken as emergent and transitory. Here, the debt to systems theoretical thinking should be clear. As can be said of growth in all open systems, a growing system made up of many social units at any level can sustain such hierarchical 'order' among units only to the degree that it can continuously maintain or expand its access to resources and energies from its environment. Once it reaches an environmental limit, growth ceases, this hierarchical order cannot be sustained, and the system moves toward a kind of thermodynamic equilibrium among units.

It should be evident that the argument just presented preassumes the important role of technical rationality at the individual level.[23] The lateral pressure expressed at the individual level is in part a function of basic biological needs and available specialized capabilities. In larger part, though, the extent to which any individual expresses lateral pressure reflects the joining of biological needs and specialized capabilities with the demands generated by the history of its interactions *as remembered and ordered in a hierarchized, technical-rational logic of environmental domination*. It is in this logic that emergent technological demands are unquestioningly accepted as new 'needs' tantamount to environmental necessities. It is the dominance of this logic that accounts for the failure of participants to fully exercise their natural human capacities to develop knowledge and skills, communicate, and adapt. And it is this failure that makes it possible to adequately describe the dynamics of social systems as very similar to the dynamics at work in natural living systems. Contrary to what one might expect, technical rationality's dominance reduces human systems to operating in ways tantamount to growth processes in nonintelligent organisms. The analogy to natural living systems holds precisely because the technical-rational logic that acclaims human mastery over nature also denies the full exercise of those human capacities that distinguish humans from other forms of life.[24]

It should also be evident that the argument just advanced, though addressed to a single level of social units, already prefigures the notion of emergent, higher order units. Differential growth, lateral pressure, and competition at the individual or any other level implies the at least momentary emergence of higher level systems of relations that are recognizable

---

[23] See Chapter 10's discussion of technical rationality.

[24] The point to be stressed is that the logic of technical rationality does not involve — or represses — rationality proper. Human knowledge, skills, and capacities to communicate are used, not self-reflectively, but as instrumentalities of problem-solving, control, and domination. This is why the logic of lateral pressure tends to be cumulatively expansionist and explosive.

Recall the analogy to Lewis Fry Richardson's research orienting query — what happens when decision makers don't stop to think? — as drawn in Chapter 10. The overall lateral pressure argument is a response to the question: what happens when human thought and interaction is captive of a technical-rational grammar? Or, what happens when people don't stop to fully exercise their capacities for knowledge and communication? The reference is to Lewis Fry Richardson, *Arms and Insecurity* (Pittsburgh: Boxwood Press, 1960).

Jürgen Habermas puts it well when he states that 'What raises us out of nature is the only thing whose nature we can know: *language*. Through its structure autonomy and responsibility are posited for us. Our first sentence expresses unequivocally the intention of universal and unconstrained consensus.' *Legitimation Crisis* (Boston: Beacon Press, 1971), p. 314. The point is that, in technical rationality, these natural human capacities are denied full expression.

in terms of a stratified order among units at the first level. If such a system effectively regulates and sustains relations below — thereby protracting competition and forestalling violence and the asymptotic tendency toward equality — then the system can itself be called a higher order social unit. *It may itself be said to exhibit lateral pressure.* If there are several such higher order units — whose expressions of lateral pressure are potentially mutually implicating — then one can refer to a higher order level of analysis. One can say that, at this higher level, the single level argument advanced above again applies.

The conceptual framework, to simplify, can be said to address three levels of social units. First, and most basically, there is the level of *individual human beings*, which can evidently combine and recombine into all manner of social groups and patterns of interdependence: families, ethnic groups, social classes, parties, peoples, nations, corporations, and so on. Emerging out of the first level, as one among many possibilities, is the second level, the level of *states*. These are the territorially identified political agencies and instrumentalities claiming and enforcing monopolies on the legitimate use of violence within some geographic areas. States may of course combine and recombine into various groups with various patterns of interdependence. Or they may be relatively isolated from and indifferent to one another, in which case, each is the highest possible level of unit, and each is the equivalent of an empire. At the third level, emerging out of the interactions and interrelations among units at the second, is the possible kind of social unit called an *interstate system* and characterized by the existence of weak or strong regulative *regimes*. Quite evidently, the existence of this third level presupposes the existence of a multiplicity of states (at the second level) which are actually or potentially interdependent.

In considering these three levels, two points must be borne in mind. First, all units at all levels above the individual are abstractions in the sense amplified in Appendix A. Though real, social units at the second and third levels owe their existences to the fact that people are situated amidst social processes and environmental limits such that they are inclined to make choices (or not make them) in ways that produce and reproduce states and regimes. Second, the three levels are therefore mutually implicating and innerrelated.[25] The processes of units at any one level presuppose more or less normal processes at the others. Where the domain of possible human interaction transcends state boundaries, for example, the choices, actions and interactions among individuals tend to preassume not only the existence of the state but also the

[25] Again see Appendix A.

operation of systemic regulative regimes that to some degree constrain what states are and can do. In the same way, the effective operation of a systemic regime tends to presuppose human choices reaffirming the existence of states as social forms regulated in accordance with the regime itself. In these terms, in fact, the third level, that of regimes, is *within* the second, that of states, insofar as individuals tend to make choices and invest energies in ways producing and reproducing a multiplicity of states as things that tend to behave in accord with the regime.

The conceptual framework presents these three levels in the order of their emergence. It begins with individuals and societies as they experience differential growth, lateral pressure, and tendencies toward competition under certain circumstances. This, it argues, makes possible the emergence of the second level unit, the state, to regulate and perpetuate competition, sustain social stratifications, and assure the differential return of rewards and privileges to those members of society who legally own or otherwise control certain resources and capabilities. The third level of social unit, the interstate system, then emerges only when these processes take form at a multiplicity of centers which bear actual and potential interdependencies and are carried into sustained interaction. Through sustained interaction, the *regime of balance of power* emerges and is deeply structured within states.

This progression, according to the argument, has unfolded many times, but only once has it reached the third level of a strong interstate regime. Most often it has stopped at the second level, with the emergence of strong but lone states. These, as empires, have expanded to some limit of a technological reach and then have degenerated under some combinations of internal pressures for redistribution and external challenges. Occasionally, this progression has approached the third level, but even then, interdependencies among states were typically so weak, and interactions therefore so shallow, that the regime of balance of power was not deeply structured within what states became.

Only once has the progression completely unfolded. Only in Europe, with the uneven end of feudalism and the emergence of capitalism against the background of residual socio-cultural influences of the Roman Empire, did processes of differential growth, expansion, and state building surface at a multiplicity of centers in ways that were mutually implicating and hence productive of a balance of power regime. Here, for the first time, was the creation of the modern security problematique.

The importance of this event goes beyond the fact that the inherently unstable competitive dynamics born of differential growth and lateral pressure at the first level were immediately regulated and protracted by states at the second. This had occurred before. What is particularly important is that people associated with the several states were joined in degrees of interdependence such that the life of any state structuration, as an abstraction, depended greatly upon processes extending across boundaries among states. Actually and potentially, differential growth and lateral pressure among the several centers were mutually implicating. This in turn forced upon states accommodations to their sustained coexistence in a community. It forced upon them a protracted and difficult period in which, gradually, each would reconcile what it was and could become with the needs of a larger community of which it was a part. Thus was the balance of power regime to take form.

Its formation was critical. For it had the effect of limiting any one state's rapid movement toward transforming the whole into empire. It had the effect, too, of enlisting the compliance of even those people, groups, and classes, at the first level, who might have benefited by overturning the whole. It had the effect of confronting societies yet to adapt to the system with serious dilemmas of insecurity and prospects for violence which made them likely to create such states and reproduce the system in wider scope. And it had the effect of assuring that when one state failed and fell to violence, others succeeded, gained strength, and were able to sustain competition all the more.

Here, for the first time, was differential growth, lateral pressure, and competition doubly regulated. Political violence and war may have been no less terrible than before. But now they had become parts of a kind of 'fail safe' mechanism in a system of differential growth. Institutionalized within the balance of power regime, war became a means by which every failure of states (at the second level) to hold competition in check (at the first) would be bent into a reaffirmation of the balance of power regime (at the third). Forces that would ordinarily challenge and ultimately weaken individual states now had the effect of strengthening the political apparatus, the regime, of the overall system.[26]

If this helps to account for the extraordinarily robust and sustained character of differential growth and competition in the modern world, though, it does not in any sense imply that the relationships can go on forever. In this regard, what needs to be stressed is this: *a social unit at any level can effectively regulate and hence preserve differential growth, lateral pressure, and competition at the next lower level only to the extent that it can generate and express lateral pressure of its own relative to other units at the same level.*

[26] The character of the balance of power regime is discussed at length in Section IV, below.

The point can be made with respect to both states and the overall system. Once any *state* is unable to foster relations with and among other states such that its own subunits at the first level can express lateral pressure beyond its boundaries, the lateral pressure of these subunits will be differentially expressed *within* its bounds, the competitive relations within its bounds will tend toward extreme concentrations of wealth and power in the hands of the few, and then pressures for redistribution will intensify. This, clearly, is the position of most peripheral states today; and it helps to explain why, for peripheral societies, growth is rarely development and state regulation is frequently repressive. This, however, is generally not the position of the high lateral pressure societies often described as 'core' powers. Similarly, once the *overall system* ceases to expand and subordinate other contesting societies beyond — once the overall system comes up against obstacles that deny the further expansion of states, their subunits, and the scope of the systemic regime — the competitive dynamics among states will tend toward violence, conquest, and the domination of the one over the many. At this point, the regime is in jeopardy of giving way to world empire, and to consequent pressure for redistribution at the global level.

This line of argumentation suggests that what has here been called the modern security problematique is a system predicated on its own expansion, its own lateral pressure. *It is therefore a system whose transformation is implicit in the fact that, in a finite world of finite resources, its expansion cannot go on forever.* War and conquest are among the mechanisms of its transformation once the limits of its growth are reached, approached, or become too costly to overcome. World empire created through massive violence — this, as said in Chapter 10, is the end of technical rationality and the violence-prone form of lateral pressure it frames. This, according to the logic of the system, is the path that must be traversed in the search for an end to collective insecurity and the beginnings of global equality. The logic applies so long as technical rationality prevails.

This last point underscores the non-ashistorical and criticism-conscious character of the overall argument as a guide to emancipatory practice. If one accepts the argument, then one must also accept the idea that the trajectory of change toward massive violence and global empire cannot be deflected solely by exercising the means–end logic of technical-rational problem solving — a logic that celebrates autonomy and denies dependence upon the environment. One cannot 'get out of' the security problematique and employ a technical-rational logic in order to change it, for to employ technical rationality is not to get out at all. As suggested in Chapter 10, emancipation starts within a logic of rationality proper – a logic that subordinates each unit's exercise of technical rationality to the truth that, in what it is and will become, no social unit at any level can ever escape dependence upon its environment, including other social units.

It is for this reason that the modern security problematique *potentially* embraces socialist as well as capitalist societies – China and the Soviet Union as well as the United States. On the one hand, if socialism means only the control of the means of production within the state, and if the state itself persists in ordering programs and policies according to a technical-rational logic of growth, then socialist states are as prone to the violence-producing expressions of lateral pressure as are capitalist states. This much should have been clear from the empirical results of Part II, especially as they apply to Sino-Soviet expansion, intersections, provocations, normal conflict, and thresholds of violence. On the other hand, if socialism is taken to mean something more than the location of economic competition within state bureaucracies and the fostering of growth by centralized authorities – if it is interpreted to mean an enduring commitment to the criticism conscious subordination of technical-rationalist tendencies to an adaptive logic of collective rationality proper – then socialist societies need not be accomplices to the violence-prone dynamics of the security problematique.

Whether or not any single society – or group of societies – can long endure without becoming part of the deadly and exploitative logic of the problematqiue is, of course, an important question. *In effect, each society is, as it were, a kind of proto-system of the whole.* In its demands upon its environment it implies what the larger whole would be were its own growth and lateral pressure to find full and unobstructed expression. Yet the world at any time contains a multiplicity of such societies. All are different to the extent that they have adapted to different conditions, encountered different obstacles, had and remembered different experiences, developed different capabilities, and come into interaction with different societies at different times. At any time, these societies are not equally positioned to grow, expand, and shape the world, including other societies, in reflection of their demands. At any moment, one or a few societies will at once generate demands and have access to capabilities that permit them, above others, to express lateral pressure, shape the properties of the overall system, and call upon the many to adapt equifinally to the system whose form best suits the demands of the few. The question, then, is this: can one or a few societies organized under principles of rationality proper avoid adaptation to and participation in a system of differential growth, a system here characterized as the modern security problematique? Can social forms organized within the logic of rationality proper be constructed, first in the small, and then take hold in larger scope — thereby turning back or even crippling the expansionist, technical-rational logic of the modern security problematique?

There is a strong basis for a negative answer to these questions. As suggested in Chaper 10, the logic of technical rationality is extraordinarily robust. Somewhat more specifically, the violence-prone social relations of the balance of power regime have the effect of defining resistant 'external' societies as noncompliant, radical, and therefore threatening to normal relations among states. This is especially likely to the degree that a society would resist expressions of lateral pressure that are essential to the life and development of the overall system. The result, therefore, is for the regime of balance of power to do two things. One is to generate what can only be seen as threats of 'forceful penetration' *vis-à-vis* societies that would resist being incorporated within the span of the problematique. The other is to hold out the hand of assistance against such threats. The more serious the threats posed, the more likely cooptation becomes.

This process is especially effective as it applies to weaker, low-lateral-pressure societies. Among today's peripheral and semiperipheral societies, differential growth and lateral pressure generate rivalries and give rise to mutual threats of a politico-military nature. This in turn limits possibilities for the establishment of cooperative relations among them and strengthens their reliance upon high-lateral-pressure societies that are able to offer both direct protection and military capabilities. The mere fact that *some* semiperipheral and peripheral societies are engaged in the processes of the problematique, interiorize the balance of power regime, and exhibit differential growth thus recurringly confronts *all* with immediate, threatening circumstances. These severely constrain other societies' abilities to chart a rational course of development independent of the whole.

The processes apply as well even to large, strong, high-lateral-pressure societies. As the balance of power regime persists, and as no society can for long remain invulnerable to changes ongoing among others, not even the strong can fully extricate themselves from the regime, can fully purge from their states (and their self-definitions) the influence of the regime. Facing a prisoner's dilemma that they and their forebears helped to shape, or that others thrust upon them, the members of even a large, relatively strong society will be inclined to build instruments and agencies of state that to a large extent define them and the whole society as a prisoner.

Indeed, even the society that would order itself according to principles of rationality proper within will confront threats from without. These may be seen to require technical-rational responses. And for the society that would sustain rationality proper within, the task then becomes one of preventing the subordination of the 'inner-self' to the 'outer-self' that is pragmatically engaged in the modern security problematique.

One must not be too hasty in reaching a negative conclusion, however. For as a system of differential growth and expansion, the modern security problematique is robust only so long as it can sustain its expansion. In the same way, high-lateral-pressure societies are such only so long as the system is configured in a way that allows them room to express the modes of lateral pressure that their demands and capabilities make them best disposed and able to express. The implication of these statements must not be understated: *to the extent that a society can resist involvement and turn back participant societies' expressions of lateral pressure, a society is in effect engaged in the transformation of the modern security problematqiue and of the states 'succeeding' within it.* The system that requires limitless growth cannot be sustained within limits, and to refuse to participate is to bring those limits one step closer. To be sure, high-lateral-pressure societies that encounter such limits — that are denied, say, access to resources, or labor, or markets — will be inclined to resort to other means to break through those limits. But these means of last resort are always more costly, less efficient. Their use, taken to the extreme, would mark the demise of the high-lateral-pressure society's status as such.[27]

Such prospects are imaginable, though, only when commitment to rationality proper, and hence resistance to involvement in the processes of the security problematique, become widely shared. How widely? How large must the 'critical mass' be? The answer is far from clear, and it surely depends upon the moment in the development of the system. But it seems evident that resistance must transcend the single society, no matter how large, as the experience of China under Mao seems clearly to show. In turn, this implies that *among* societies that do resist, principles of sovereignty and nationality must to some degree be subordinated within a collective grammar of rationality proper. If they are not, then differential growth among the committed will generate fractionalization, the revitalization of technical rationality, mutually directed expressions of power politics, and a breakdown in the capacities for collective resistance. Plainly, the prospects for successful opposition are far from great.

[27] As Felicia Harmer was quick to point out when I first stated this argument, it joins philosophies of passive resistance with a materialist conception of historical development.

B Implications for Imperialism Theory

The preceding summary of the lateral pressure argument was developed with an eye to clarifying critical implications for imperialism theory. In particular, it helps to clarify problems in two important Marxian interpretations of imperialism: the more or less state-centric Leninist interpretation and the world systems approach of Immanuel Wallerstein.[28]

The principal problem with the *classical Leninist variant* should be obvious. It is, in essence, a subsystem dominant view of imperialism. As such, it comes close to hypostatizing the state and the national economy as fundamental political units while largely ignoring the possibility of higher order emergent systems of relations among them. In part, perhaps, this tendency is a reflection of a heuristic implied in Marx's own exemplary work – and of the particular 'anomalies' that Lenin's treatment of imperialism was meant to answer. Or perhaps the state-centric box is traceable to the influence of Hegel, who imagined the state as the highest embodiment of rationality and could see the interstate system only as anarchy. Whatever the reason, the net effect is to regard international relations as principally a byproduct of the projection and then vectoring of separate state influences – each being a reflection of contradictions within the national capitalist economy.

One consequence of this view is that Leninist imperialism theory comes very close to mercantilist and neomercantilist positions in addressing international political economic relations.[29] In effect, Leninist perspectives

[28] What follows is not meant to be anything like a complete review – or even a cursory review – of the rich, growing, and commendably self-critical Marxian literature on imperialism. Rather, Lenin's work and Wallerstein's work are addressed as examples of two main (and opposed) thrusts in that literature – two thrusts that are not yet critically joined. One thrust is to emphasize imperialism in terms of an exploitative and violence-prone tendency born out of contradictions in a certain stage of development in the capitalist national economy. This is the Lenin exemplar. The other, exemplified by Wallerstein but also associated with writers on dependency (e.g., Gunder Frank), is to emphasize a dominant structure of a world system, characterized by an exploitative world division of labor.

Some may quarrel with placing Wallerstein's work in the realm of imperialism theory. However, if (along with, say, Christian Palloiz) one takes imperialism to be the relations joining core, semiperiphery, and periphery in a single world division of labor – or if, more generally, one defines imperialism in terms of the dynamics of the world system's reproduction of its 'structural constants' – then Wallerstein's work is appropriately placed in the imperialism theoretical genre.

[29] Thus, for instance, Robert Gilpin can refer as follows to the argument contained in Ernest Mandel's *Europe vs. America: Contradictions of Imperialism* (New York: Monthly Review Press, 1970): 'Although he is a Marxist,' Gilpin writes, 'Ernest Mandel's theme is really mercantilism.' See Gilpin, *US Power and the Multinational Corporation: The Political Economy of Foreign Direct Investment* (New York: Basic Books, 1975), p. 279, fn. 23.

are distinguished only by their insistence that state purposes, what mercantilists call 'national interests,' are disproportionately shaped by (or disproportionately in the service of) the bourgeoisie in a continuing struggle with the proletariat. Not infrequently, in fact, Leninist theorists are forced into the difficult position of acknowledging the at least partial autonomy of the state whenever it can be shown that state actions in international relations are somehow contrary to what one would expect the domestic bourgeoisie (or its progressive elements) to want or require. For the mercantilist, this is evidence for their position. For the Leninist, including structuralist analysts, it is unexplained residua. It is unexplained because the Leninist is unable to imagine that the appearance of autonomous state action might in fact be in accord with a deeply structured international regime that helps to perpetuate differential growth in the overall system.

In the same vein, the Leninist argument is vulnerable to the criticism advanced by Waltz, Cohen, and others[30] that it is a 'second image' theory and, as a consequence, does not account for the systemic 'permissive' causes of imperialism and war. This criticism submits that it is the *political* structure of interstate relations, characterizable as anarchy, that causes imperialism and war.[31] Wars occur because they can occur, because in a world of anarchy, states have little choice but to be self-regarding and build power. The argument takes force, though, only because Leninists fail to show what can be shown. Anarchy is an emergent structuration, balance of power is an emergent regime, and both reflect and perpetuate a history of differential growth, sharpening social cleavages, and exploitative expansion.[32]

For the same reason, the Leninist argument is vulnerable to the critical counter-argument advanced by Joseph Schumpeter.[33] Expressly aiming to counter the Leninist thesis, Schumpeter argued that the imperialism and wars of capitalist states reflect, not the contradictions of capitalism, but the 'atavistic' aristocratic, military, and religious elements of state held over in capitalism from feudal times. These, he argued, sought conquest and war to rationalize their existences in an economic system for

[30] Kenneth Waltz, *Theory of International Politics* pp. 23–30; Waltz, *Man, the State and War* (New York: Columbia University Press, 1959); Benjamin Cohen, *The Question of Imperialism: The Political Economy of Dominance and Dependence* (New York: Basic Books, 1973), pp. 233–5.

[31] The basic critique is founded upon balance of power theory, as discussed and criticized in Section I, above.

[32] See Section IV, below, for a further development of this theme.

[33] Joseph Schumpeter, 'The Sociology of Imperialisms,' in Schumpeter, *Imperialism and Social Classes* (New York: Augustus M. Kelley, 1951).

which they could only be irrational. And while he acknowledged that such war-prone agencies of state might be reproduced in societies lacking the feudal heritage (as in the United States) through the mechanism of war itself, he also urged that capitalism would gradually mount pressures that would purge these irrational elements of state. One answer to this critique, sometimes expressed by Leninists, is that Schumpeter grossly underestimated the ways in which war itself might infuse the domestic economy, becoming a part of economic expectations.[34] Another answer, suggested by the lateral pressure argument, is not available to Leninists. Without these 'atavisms,' a system of sharply differentiated growth and expansion could not long survive. They are, as it were, the embodiments within each state of the balance of power regime. Their actions, though seemingly contrary to capitalism, may be critical to the reproduction of the regime and with it, the perpetuation of an overall system that some would describe as capitalist. Could it be that the balance of power regime — which includes war among its regulative and adaptive means — is itself a kind of 'ultraimperial' social relation of the overall system?

There is, though, a far more serious criticism to be raised. As said at the outset of this section, Leninist imperialism theory, like lateral pressure theory, aspires to be a critical theory. Yet where lateral pressure arguments retain their critical force even for those people who might strive for emancipation in their light, state-centric Leninist imperialism theory tends to immunize from criticism those who would find it in an orientation for emancipatory praxis. Specifically, states that can claim to be socialist can also claim to be exempt from the critical eye of the Marxist-Leninist perspective on imperialism. This is not the empirical criticism, advanced by Waltz and others, that putatively socialist states, as well as capitalist, engage in exploitative expansion and war. Instead, the critique is more nearly methodological and praxiological: critical theory cannot immunize those who see in it a guide to praxis, for if it does, it devolves into one more expression of a technical-rational grammar of domination. It can even be reduced to ideological apologetics, excusing the technical-rational acts of the subject as necessary responses to the acts of the criticized object. Quite evidently, Leninist imperialism theory has found this role in the Soviet Union today.[35]

[34] See, e.g., Paul Baran and Paul Sweezy, *Monopoly Capital* (New York: Monthly Review Press, 1966).

[35] This flaw has not gone unnoticed among recent Marxian writers. However, among those of a Leninist (state economy-centered) orientation who see the Soviet Union evidencing what seem to approximate imperialistic dynamics, the response is largely limited to *ad hoc* arguments as to why, e.g., the USSR remains a capitalist state or at least a class-based society.

The second perspective on imperialism to be considered in light of the lateral pressure argument is that of Immanuel Wallerstein and his *world system approach*. At first blush, the interpretation is far more favorable than that accorded to state-focused Leninist approaches. After all, Wallerstein's is a systemic perspective, and his analysis of the locus and timing of the modern world system's emergence would be compatible with the description of the emergence of the modern security problematique. From the standpoint of this study, what Wallerstein grasped as a profound historical moment was this: in sixteenth century Europe, for the first time in history, there emerged a *multiplicity* of centers of differential growth, sharing actual and possible interdependencies, each generating opportunities for state-building, but none being strong enough to subordinate the whole to itself in the form of empire. This was coupled with the possibilities for mutual acknowledgment of community contained in the residual socio-cultural influences of the Roman Empire.[36] The consequence was the creation of a number of 'political entities,' each of which could generate expansionist tendencies in a way implicating all, and the environment as well. This much is consistent with the present perspective.

Importantly, Wallerstein also preserves the critical character of the theory even as it applies to states controlled by socialist movements. Or at least, it appears that he does. In his view, for example, the Soviet Union cannot escape the critical eye of Marxian theory. Even a world containing 150 putatively socialist states would still fit his definition of the structural constants of world capitalism.[37]

Still, from the perspective of the lateral pressure argument, there are criticisms to be raised. First, and perhaps most obviously, Wallerstein's analysis never really advances beyond the second level of emergent systems. He stops, in effect, with the emergence of states, and he does not yet adequately consider how the third level of the interstate balance of power regime might have taken form, deeply structured within states. One is left with the impression that the states conceived of are not necessarily any different from the governing apparatuses of empires. What matters, for Wallerstein, is that there are several of them and that no one can effect control of the whole domain. He argues:

---

[36] See especially Perry Anderson, *Lineages of the Absolutist State* (London: New Left Books, 1975).

[37] See especially his article, 'The Rise and Future Demise of the World Capitalist System: Concepts for Comparative Analysis,' in *Comparative Studies of Society and History*, Vol. XVI, No. 4 (1974).

Capitalism has been able to flourish precisely because the world-economy has had within its bounds not one but a multiplicity of political systems.

. . . [C]apitalism as an economic mode is based on the fact that the economic factors operate within an arena larger than that which any political entity can totally control. This gives capitalists a freedom of maneuver that is structurally based. It has made possible the constant economic expansion of the system, albeit a very skewed distribution of its rewards.[38]

Such an argument comes close to hypostatizing the abstraction of inter-state anarchy in a way that a Waltz would approve. What is more, although the system's resistance to transformation into empire is, he says, 'the secret of its strength,'[39] his explanation of the secret in the first of four volumes seems limited to the idea that the reach of economic interdependence in the system exceeds the span of possible/efficient political control.[40]

In short, the first criticism is that Wallerstein fails to adequately address one of the factors that may be most critical to the perpetuation and acceleration of differential growth in the modern era: the double-regulative capacity, and the adaptive potential, of a deeply structured balance of power regime that is predicted on, and sustains, pervasive insecurity.

In fairness, it must be stressed that some of Wallerstein's writings since the publication of *The Modern World System* reflect this line of thinking. In recent papers, for example, he allows that multipolar power politics might have lent to the capitalist system an adaptive political capacity unseen in earlier and alternative systems of production.[41] The point, though, is that the line of reasoning ought to go somewhat further — and in a direction invited by thinkers of such diverse perspectives as Perry Anderson, F.H. Hinsley, and Garrett Mattingly.[42] Balance of power means something more than a recurring logic of the moment occasioned by the absence of a central political authority among a number of distinct political entitites called states. With respect to the interdependent

[38] *The Modern World System*, p. 348.
[39] Ibid.
[40] Ibid., especially Chapter 4.
[41] See Immanuel Wallerstein, *The Capitalist World Economy* (New York: Cambridge University Press, 1978).
[42] Anderson, *Lineages of The Absolutist State*; F.H. Hinsley, *Power and the Pursuit of Peace* (New York: Cambridge University Press, 1967); and Garrett Mattingly, *Renaissance Diplomacy* (Baltimore: Penguin, 1955).

peoples and societies involved, balance of power is or became a common regime running through, and helping to give form and individuated existence to, the many states that make up the political apparatus of the overall system. In these terms, *there is one 'political entity' in the system, but it is one that manifests itself in the production and reproduction of many apparently distinct states.* True, those states that engage in power politics appear to be acting out their autonomous existences. True, too, relations among these states are often characterized by all too visible conflict, and the people occupying key positions within these states are often preoccupied with the threats to survival that states mutually pose. Nevertheless, to see the system in long-historical sweep is not necessarily to envision it as statesmen might. And in long-historical sweep, recurring conflicts, violence, rivalry, and exchanges of threats — in short, the collectively created milieu of collective insecurity — all exert a powerful integrative force. Equifinally, states adapt to the milieu, interiorize the requisites of participation, and bind themselves to a regime whose rules are within what they become.[43]

The second criticism is that Wallerstein's explicit theoretical statements seem to misunderstand the role of the environment of the system and therefore cannot account for one possible process by which the system might be transcended. The lateral pressure argument clearly states that the regular, ordered growth of the overall system depends upon its expansion. Once obstacles to the further expansion of competing high-lateral-pressure societies become too costly to overcome, competition among high-lateral-pressure societies will intensify, the regulative regime of balance of power will fail, the system will move through violence toward world empire, and then pressures for redistribution will commence. Immanent within the life of the system at any moment is its expansion beyond its current bounds. Its life beyond the static instant depends upon its capacity to realize the larger system, to make once external areas part of itself. And when this is not possible, the working out of its contradictions will mean its transformation.

By contrast, Wallerstein's expressed theory treats the modern world system as something 'self-contained.'[44] To the extent that he means by this that the system is not 'driven' by exogenous forces, the self-containment notion is far from objectionable. However, to the extent that he means that the system can long survive in the absence of expansion into the environment beyond its current bounds — transforming onetime externalities into the energies of its existence — the idea of self-containment

[43] On the economic functions of the balance of power regime, see Section IV, below.

[44] *The Modern World System*, p. 347.

is comparable to the assertion that the system is closed. This latter interpretation is highly problematical and nondialectical. For it invites the suspicion that the modern world system is to be seen as a non-transformable closed circle — a dialectically created structural cul-de-sac of history.

There is room for some confusion as to whether or not this latter interpretation is intended by Wallerstein. He does invite it when, by way of clarifying 'self-containment,' he offers a counterfactual hypothesis: 'If the system, for any reason, were to be cut off from all external forces (which virtually never happens), the definition implies that the system would continue to function substantially in the same manner.'[45] On the other hand, some of his other writings attending to the transformation of the system seem aimed toward breaking out of the closed circle notion of totality. Specifically, his writings on the roles of peripheralization and proletarianization processes would seem to suggest his increasing attention to the system's environment as critical to its transformation possibilities in the future.[46] This area of confusion needs to be cleared up.

The third and most important criticism is that Wallerstein's analysis is weakened as critical theory because it is, or at some point becomes, a structuralist interpretation — a one-sided vision of system dominance.[47]

[45] Ibid.

[46] See e.g., 'The Rise and Future Demise;' and Immanuel Wallerstein, 'The Three Stages of African Involvement in the World Economy' in Peter C.W. Gutkind and Immanuel Wallerstein (eds.), *The Political Economy of Contemporary Africa* (Beverly Hills, Calif.: Sage, 1976).

[47] Is Wallerstein's perspective really a one-sided system dominance perspective as asserted? The answer is both no and yes. *No*, it is not, because his historical analysis is dialectical and involves an attempt to trace and interpret the convergent, generative historical processes that gave form and moment to the 'structural constants' by which he defines the world capitalist system. In the same dialectical vein, he strives to portray how this system's emergence spelled the negation of alternative systems contending for sutained existence, if perhaps in more restricted locales. The 'no' thus applies to Wallerstein's *a posteriori* historical reasoning. Here is the system as I know it to be structurally defined, he says in effect, now what were the historical processes by which it took form?

But *yes*, at some point in his analysis, his argument becomes a system dominance argument, as asserted in the text. Perhaps this is due to the fact that, in the very act of describing processes, key terms used to describe them are hypostatized and become then the *a priori* basis — and the walls, ceiling, and floor — of all subsequent reasoning about the processes and the development of the system in which they are joined. This is a problem partially articulated by Wallerstein himself in his 'World-System Analysis: Theoretical and Interpretative Issues,' in *Social Change in the World Capitalist Economy*, Barbara Hockey Kaplan (ed.), Volume 1 of *Political Economy of the World System Annuals* (1978), p. 219.

Whatever the reason for the system dominance view, it is only by reference to such a view that one can understand his repeated insistence that local political-economic developments are reflections of the overall system and that changes in local patterns, including modes of production, do not matter for the long-run trajectory of development in the system.

Leninist imperialism theory, it will be recalled, takes the position of subsystem dominance. As such, it is a critical theory that allows for responsible, oppositionist social action. As such, though, it also tends to immunize from criticism those participants undertaking emancipatory praxis in its light. By contrast, Wallerstein's analysis, being system dominant in expressed theory, exempts no one, not even putatively socialist states, from criticism. But being system dominant, it also allows little room for responsible, emancipatory praxis. And herein is its weakness as critical theory.

For Wallerstein, the 'truth' to be illuminated is the 'truth' of the whole system. It is, more exactly, the 'truth' of those who succeeded in the struggle to shape the system in relfection of their own world-implicating demands. It is the 'truth' of those who 'win', and it is a vision that leaves little room for alternative world systems that are or might be denied actualization in the face of the capitalist world system's dominance. Such a vision, as Wallerstein suggests, is one that dominant participants might have preferred to have kept disguised — perhaps even from themselves. But for the oppressed, the exposing of the system still leaves room only for forms of action constituting complicity: the worm might turn, elites might circulate, and periphery might become semiperiphery or semiperiphery might become core. For the oppressed, this is all that can be hoped — indeed, this is the only 'positive' outcome that can be imagined — within the logic of the system. Thus, opposition, such as it is, is reduced to a struggle, not to transform the system, but to succeed within it, and thereby reproduce it, on the terms shaped by those who gave the system its original form and later elaborated its workings. Literally unimaginable within the terms of the explicit theory are critical, oppositionist actions, plans, or programs that, if fully realized, would mean the transformation of the world capitalist system into something other than it is.

If Wallerstein's is a critical theory, then, its tendency to be a system dominance view makes it a flawed critical theory. On the one hand, the theory commendably embraces all people and groups within the realm of criticism. Yet, on the other hand, the theory excuses the participation of all. As the structure is dominant, the theory tells us, the participants have no choice.

That this critique of Wallerstein's perspective is generated within the lateral pressure argument is clarified to some extent by reference to competing interpretations of one of the three major powers examined in this study: the Chinese People's Republic. Within Wallerstein's system dominance perspective, the collectivist self-reliance posture of China under Mao seems susceptible to only one interpretation. The CPR's posture under Mao is interpretable as tantamount to mercantilist state-building, albeit as colored by an egalitarian, collectivist ideology. China would perhaps be seen as a (latent?) semiperipheral economy grasping for core status. China's attempts to minimize economic ties with dominant powers, strengthen commercial relations with Third World countries, and foster the non-alignment posture of the latter would be seen as part of a bid toward establishing core status. China's willingness to collectivize and decentralize (some aspects of) economic, especially agricultural decision making, to discourage the emergence of a technocratic and administrative class, and to accept the risks of the Cultural Revolution — all of this would appear strikingly irrational. Or, at best, it would constitute inconsequential residua within the theory. The 'corrective' of the emergence of the pragmatic Chinese state, and the purge of the Gang of Four, would seem a necessary part of China's course of development — an eventual return to the dominant trajectory of development in the system. And China's polemics against *Western* imperialism, including socialist imperialism, would be read as the political maneuvering of a state preparing itself to engage in similar practices. Such, it would seem, is the interpretation allowed within a system dominance perspective such as Wallerstein's

The lateral pressure argument allows for an alternative and much richer interpretation. The CPR under Mao was indeed penetrated by the influence of the modern security problematique, and China was and remains under pressures to adapt to the larger system. Yet China's asserted opposition to Western imperialism — and socialist imperialism — involves something more than rhetoric. For China under Mao was, or can be seen to have represented, an alternative design for the world system. Had the world order become one in accord with the demands of the China that Mao was trying to make, it would have been a different world order indeed. In important respects, the collectivist self-reliance posture that Mao sought to shape aimed toward the realization in practice of a system that would subordinate the 'Western metaphysics' of technical rationality to the more dialectical criticism consciousness of rationality proper. The Cultural Revolution, in these terms, was not an excessive display of irrationality. It was one way of struggling within China to combat tendencies toward the technical-rational centralization of authority, the establishment of status groups having extraordinary privileges, the resurfacing of materialist competition, and the reduction of the people to the tools of growth. These 'distinctly Western' tendencies, Mao believed had taken hold in the Soviet Union. This was the 'embourgeoisiement' of the Soviet state. These tendencies, Mao further believed, were brought about by contradictions, not only between the individual society and the larger system, but also within the individual society, no matter how resolutely it would contest the larger system.

In a way that is more or less consistent with the grammar of rationality proper, it would seem, Mao saw that the struggle had to be continuously waged within as well as without.[48] For over two decades, China quite visibly waged this struggle. Today, surely, it appears that the technical rationality of Chinese pragmatists — as buttressed by the threat of Soviet 'hegemonism' — is dominant in the Chinese state. Nevertheless, it would be a gross error to say that the critical spirit of rationality proper is today dead in China. The spirit of Machiavelli has helped to push aside, but has not killed, the spirit of Mao.

This, to be clear, is not to say that China under Mao was anything like some ideal model of a society ordered within a dominant logic of rationality proper. All societies are situated in history. All must reflect historic experiences and contemporary contexts. China is no exception. Nor is the emphasis upon China and the neglect of the United States and the USSR in this example meant to imply that there are no important differences in these latter two societies or the kinds of world order they would shape were the world totally a reflection of one or the other's demands.

The point, rather, is to illustrate how theory, as a one-sided vision of system dominance, falsely denies the reality of competing systems that are not but could be were local (or 'subsystemic') visions somehow to find systemic expression. To understand the role of China, or any other society, in contemporary international relations one must come to grips with something more than how it reflects and expresses the overall system. One must also understand how, as a society equifinally adapts to its environment, the society's expressions of lateral pressure (*a*) reflect the particular, historically-wedded demands it generates and (*b*) would project toward the creation of an overall system perhaps far different from the contemporary actuality.

Yes, the weak, low-lateral-pressure society is likely to adapt to the system more than it shapes it. Yes, the 'truth is the whole.' Yet if theory is to be emancipatory, then it must also tell a story of the whole that does more than record the dominant structures shaped by victors in the struggle. It must say to the oppressed something more than 'be strong'

---

[48] See Mao's development of his 'Yin and Yang' perspective in 'On Contradiction,' *Selected Readings from the Works of Mao Tsetung* (Peking: Foreign Languages Press, 1971), pp. 85–133.

or 'win.' If the truth of the whole is limited to such actualities, then the oppressed have a stake in believing, as Mao did, that this kind of truth is also false.[49]

What, then, do these comments imply for imperialism theory? What is called for is something that the lateral pressure argument hints at but does not yet deliver: a theory allowing for the mutual determination of parts and wholes in international systems. Such a theory would join in continuing tension the subsystem dominance perspective of Lenin and the system dominance emphasis of Wallerstein. It would join them within a dealectical, non-ahistorical accounting of differential growth and lateral pressure — an accounting allowing for the emergence of higher-order levels of social units out of low. It would stress the fundamental contradiction driving violence-prone expansion at all levels: the technical-rational commitment of resources and energies to solve problems and exert control in false denial of the social unit's inescapable dependence upon its environment. It would treat all systems of relations among social units as potentially passing aspects of life that are differentially shaped by, and differentially constrain, the uneven growth, lateral pressure, and expansion of units situated amidst social conditions and material limits. It would allow for the existence of many interpenetrating, dialectically relating wholes, some of which are in the course of emerging to dominance, and others of which are being sublated, in a continuing, open-ended process. And it would allow that the participants in such processes are able in principle to use knowledge, skills, and capacities to communicate in a manner at least as dialectical as the historical processes themselves. This is what an emancipatory, criticism conscious theory of imperialism strains to become.

IV LIBERAL AND MERCANTILIST INTERNATIONAL POLITICAL ECONOMY

Marxian imperialism theories are not the only international political economic perspectives finding resonance in this study's depiction of the modern security problematique. Liberal and mercantilist (or

---

[49] The allusion to a well-known statement by Herbert Marcuse is intentional. 'No method can claim a monopoly of cognition,' Marcuse writes, 'but no method seems authentic that does not recognize that these two propositions are meaningful descriptions of our situation: "The whole is the truth," and the whole is false.' Marcuse, 'Preface: A Note on Dialectic,' in his *Reason and Revolution* (Boston: Beacon Press, 1960), p. xiv.

neomercantilist) political economists also grasp aspects. In fact, the opposed positions of liberals and mercantilists can be interpreted, not as alternative, mutually exclusive visions of the whole, but as reflections of contradictorily joined tendencies that are critical to the history and future of the problematique's development.

The differences between the two perspectives have been much discussed in the literature. Gilpin's well-known article, 'Three Models of the Future,' contrasted liberal and mercantilist models, as well as a *dependencia* model.[50] Krasner's book, *Defending the National Interest*,[51] has similarly attempted to argue for a (neo)mercantilist, or statist, position in contrast with liberal and other (i.e., instrumental and structural Marxist) positions. As these writings demonstrate, any attempt to characterize these opposed positions always to some extent caricatures its subject matter. Nevertheless, these and other writings do help to draw out some of the modal differences between theorists who would answer to the label, mercantilist (or neomercantilist), and theorists who would subscribe to the label, liberal.

In general, liberals and mercantilists differ, most significantly, on their projections of development for the future of the world economy and the roles of states and national economies within it. For mercantilists, the state has a privileged conceptual status: it is among the important economic actors, and a world economy not involving state actors is unimaginable. As an actor, the state is seen to have some autonomy, some interests defined independently of pressures from other kinds of actors, and some independent means for pursuing these interests. Most often, these interests are seen to be defined in terms of power relative to other states, especially power in terms of relative military strength. However, as the mercantilist is quick to point out, since the power of a state principally (though not exclusively) derives from its relative economic strength, the state will tend to define 'wealth' among national interests to be pursued by political means. In the mercantilist view, then, the future of the world economy will be shaped by the actions (and failures to act) of states pursuing power and wealth.

For liberals, by contrast, the concept of state is not accorded a privileged status. In the spirit of Joseph Schumpeter,[52] the story of modern economic progress is seen to be largely a story of the transcendence of the state as an autonomous political and economic unit. The state and the national economy are vestigial elements, held over beyond their time,

[50] Gilpin, *US Power and the Multinational Corporation*, Chapter 9.
[51] Stephen D. Krasner, *Defending the National Interest: Raw Materials Investments and U.S. Foreign Policy* (Princeton: Princeton University Press, 1978).
[52] Schumpeter, *Imperialism and Social Classes*.

and now passing away as the open world economy is finding realization. To be sure, the liberal will acknowledge that the transcendence of states is not easy, not without its regressive moments. Economic nationalism remains a problem. The costs and gains of interdependence are not uniformly felt, thus giving rise to differential local responses — and hence disruptions. Local state initiatives to overcome local problems tend often to strengthen states and disturb overall coordination efforts. Resource scarcities, differentially felt, sometimes lead to divisive state action. And while it is assumed that, overall, the 'vessel of sovereignty is leaking,' the vessels are also acknowledged to remain warships that still retain their security functions. Thus, for most liberals, sovereignty is not really 'at bay'[53] — not yet, anyway. Instead, the progressive course for the future will involve the negotiation, establishment, and maintenance of multilateral regulative regimes wherein order can be maintained, political and economic shocks can be reduced, and an open world economy can be sustained.[54] With time and the further development of transnationalist tendencies, transgovernmental participants will learn of the collective benefits accorded by regimes, regimes will be strengthened, the costs of extrication to any state will increase, and the course of development toward the truly liberal world economy will be accelerated.

From the standpoint of this book, the interesting difference in these two perspectives is found in their relationship to balance of power. Here, there is a basis for some confusion. *By all outward appearances*, the mercantilist model is most consistent with a balance of power perspective on world politics. Krasner, for instance, argues that mercantilists 'brought Machiavelli from the political to the economic arena.'[55] And balance of power theorist Kenneth Waltz could not be more mercantilist in tone when he asserts that 'surely the major reasons for the material well-being of rich states are to be found within their own borders — in their use of technology and in their ability to organize their economies on a national scale.'[56] *Again by all outward appearances*, the liberal view stands in direct opposition to a balance of power perspective. Keohane and Nye, for example, have spent a good deal of time arguing that the attempt to

[53] The allusion is to Raymond Vernon, *Sovereignty at Bay* (New York: Basic Books, 1971).

[54] This emphasis is perhaps most visible in the works of Robert Keohane, Joseph Nye, and Richard Cooper. See Robert O. Keohane and Joseph S. Nye, *Power and Interdependence: World Politics in Transition* (Boston: Little, Brown, 1977); and Richard N. Cooper, *The Economics of Interdependence* (New York: McGraw-Hill, 1968).

[55] Krasner, *Defending the National Interest*, pp. 37–8.

[56] Waltz, *Theory*, p. 33.

subordinate international economics to a balance of power-like logic is misguided — and dangerously misguiding.[57] Moreover, as they and others often assert, the strictly military security-related issues to which balance of power might apply are of decreasing priority on international agendas. Such a position — in opposition to balance of power — is certainly consistent with the Schumpeterian position that in the rational development of productive world capitalism, the irrationality of war will be purged along with the atavistic and destructive logics, agencies, and instrumentalities of war. These, at least, are the *apparent* relationships to balance of power: liberals reject what mercantilists embrace.

Yet the balance of power that liberals reject and mercantilists embrace is not the balance of power regime discussed in this book. The argument here is that what mercantilists embrace and liberals reject is the *ideology* of balance of power, the public relationlization of the regime. The relationships of these two perspectives to the actual *regime* are in fact a good deal more subtle and dynamic.

More specifically, it will be argued that the balance of power regime, in contrast to the ideology, is a deeply structured political system involving the transgovernmental participation of the politico-military agents of a multiplicity of societies. As such, the regime keeps alive but holds in check two opposed, and alternatingly dominant, tendencies of an economic system of differential growth and lateral pressure: tendencies toward holism and fragmentation in political-economic relationships. Controversies between liberals and mercantilists represent the ideological face of a continuing struggle between these two tendencies — a struggle that persists precisely because the balance of power regime regulates the system such that neither tendency finally subordinates the other.

In short, liberal and mercantilist perspectives reflect and ideologically express the main antinomies of a system that neither perspective understands. Neither understands, in part, because each glimpses but one of the two tendencies and mistakes it for the whole. In part, also, neither understands because both see balance of power solely in terms of the ideology and thereby obscure the crucial functions of the regime.

A   Balance of Power: Ideology and Regime

Making this argument requires the clarification of the difference between the ideology of balance of power and the regime of balance of power. The *ideology* of balance of power is well represented by Kenneth Waltz's

[57] See their *Transnational Relations and World Politics* (Cambridge, Mass.: Harvard University Press, 1972).

interpretation of the concept. This, essentially, is the structuralist interpretation which, like the mercantilist view, privileges the state with an ontological status. It asks neither where states came from nor how they might be supplemented. They have identities complete unto themselves. They simply exist and want to survive. Within this structuralist ideology, the states are then seen to coexist in the absence of any higher authority that can effectively guarantee their survival against threats that others might pose. Anarchy prevails. These structural conditions, coupled with survival motives, then create certain necessities of policy as seen through certain situational logics. Balance of power emerges out of states' attempts to apply these logics in service of these necessities.

The *regime* of balance of power is publicly known and rationalized in terms of the ideology just sketched, but its actual form is much different and takes much longer to describe. *The regime is in fact a transgovernmental (and possibly transnational), cooperative, productive, and collectively rational relation involving, at a minimum, the politico-military agents of a multiplicity of states.*[58] One function of the regime is to foster the autonomy of the participant politico-military agents *vis-à-vis* their respective societies and to rationalize their extractions of resources and support from these societies. The regime performs this function by sustaining overall conditions representable in terms of the ideology of balance of power. That is, by preserving conditions of insecurity, and by celebrating principles of the sovereign, strong state as a defense against external threats, each politico-military participant in the regime strengthens its claims to speak for its society as a whole, to be independent of socio-economic demands, to prevail in conflict over other elements of their respective states, and to rightfully extract resources from the society. In these terms, for example, a Richardson-like arms race is an extraordinarily productive relationship for the politico-military agents involved.[59] Interstate conflict is in many respects almost a 'ritualistic,'[60] cooperative endeavor among regime participants.

Now, before elaborating, it is necessary to interject that *this balance of power regime need not be, and today is not, consciously seen by regime*

---

[58] Political-military agents of state might also be joined and supported in their regime-related activities by, say, elements of the domestic weapons industry and others.

[59] The reference is to Richardson, *Arms and Insecurity*.

[60] That my argument implies that manifest interstate conflict during normal phases of the regime is 'ritualistic,' bearing some likenesses to ritual forms of tribal conflict among primitive societies, has been brought to my attention by Felicia Harmer. This implication deserves further development, especially with comparisons to anthropological evidence.

participants. Politico-military agents of each state do not see themselves as cooperating with their putative rivals in some transgovernmental conspiracy to sustain and advance their positions amidst the competing demands of their respective societies. The point is that the regime is *deeply structured*. It is built into institutions of state, embedded in law and custom, implicit in the language of insecurity politics, buttressed by certain economic patterns, and effectively disguised and rationalized within the ideology. The regime has the effect of reproducing individuated states that are self-conceived (in part) within the ideology of balance of power, often enough behave in accord with that ideology, and thereby contribute to the reproduction of the regime itself.

It may of course be true that absolutist monarchs and some of their heirs saw the cooperative character of the regime, on the one hand, and cynically proclaimed the ideology at home, on the other. It seems almost inconceivable that none would have found some attraction in a Waltz-like characterization of balance of power as an ideology rationalizing their rule. After all, it does accord with their disposition to disallow all criticism of themselves and of those conditions their existences perpetuated. It seems just as inconceivable that, precarious as their rules were at the time, they would not have seen some benefit in the external insecurity that they and their like sustained.

Today, though, after several centuries of the regime's sometimes faltering operation, agents of the regime are likely to take it for granted, to see the conditions it perpetuates almost as eternal forces, and hence not to see it at all. Accepting themselves for what they have become, they act to survive as what they are. And in the interdependence of their actions, they see only the conflicts while perpetuating the regime and themselves as agents bent to its service.

In its normal operation, the balance of power regime limits its participants' actions in many ways. For one thing, the regime proscribes any politico-military agent's assembling of political capabilities such that it could effectively coerce all the rest put together. For another, the regime prescribes each agent's actions on behalf of principles of sovereignty and in opposition to auxiliary multilateral regimes that might restrict its capacity to both forestall tendencies toward preponderance and preserve conditions of rivalry.

Perhaps the most important way in which the regime limits its participants' actions is also among the most often overlooked. In general, the regime prescribes responsiveness to shifts in capabilities and alignments evidently bearing upon military security, *but in its normal operation it also proscribes the use of socio-economic instrumentalities toward that end.* Generally disallowed within the context of the normally functioning regime are (*a*) the agents' uses or developments of socio-economic instrumentalities of control *over one another* and (*b*) the agents' attempts to intervene deeply into their respective societies so as to establish an economic base that will sustain or enhance their relative military power of the future.

Why would this be so? One possible answer is that the use of socio-economic instrumentalities would so encumber the regime and its participants with complex and uncertain forces that the regime itself would break down. Another is that, for politico-military agents whose domestic economies are highly dependent upon the overall economy, too much stands to be lost and too little gained.

Still another answer, and by far the most important answer, is this: even for the leading, highly industralized society, the state is able to hold the system together, sustain stratified social relationships, and keep internal competition from moving toward oligopoly and subsequent pressures for redistribution only by fostering international conditions in which high-lateral-pressure elements of society can express that lateral pressure outwardly, beyond the borders of the state. So long as external conditions are potentially open to the expression of lateral pressure, whatever special forms it might take, the state must act to encourage (and almost never to diminish) such expressions if it is to perpetuate the illusion that it speaks and acts for the whole of society. Indeed, absent any recognizable increase in external political-military threats, the state's attempts to improve its long-term political-military power by intervening into the socio-economic fabric of society would have the effect, so to speak, of giving away the game. For at this point, the politico-military agent of state would be reduced to being one among many actors baldly seeking to build coalitions with some domestic competitors against others in determining which competitors' aspirations will ultimately dominate and which will be denied. The ideological mask of balance of power would be stripped away, and the participants in the regime would be revealed for what they are. In the process, domestic resistance would probably increase, and the costs to the state (and its domestic coalition partners) of enforcing rule would probably mount.

Nevertheless, the regime seldom elicits perfect conformity to this norm among all participants. It sometimes occurs that individual societies are predisposed to express lateral pressure but cannot owing to some combination of existing political configurations and patterns of demands, capabilities, and lateral pressure among others. For the politico-military agents of such societies, nearly perpetual domestic instability and international weakness is likely. It is likely, that is, unless the state can intervene into socio-economic sectors in ways fostering the prospects of certain sectors to grow, develop specialized capabilities, and then overcome existing obstacles to lateral pressure. For the domestic competitors associated with these 'frustrated' sectors, such interventions are welcome. They are likely to support the interventions of politico-military agents. In short, for the politico-military agents of such societies, the problems of the immediate moment are not eased by compliance with normal balance of power regime practices. Defiance of normal regime practices is likely.

There are several ways in which the normally operating balance of power regime can manage such tendencies on the part of one or a few regime participants. Most represent one form or another of the time-honored practice of offering concessions so that, for the society whose lateral pressure predispositions have been frustrated, its lateral pressure can now find outward expression and its politico-military agents will retain autonomy enough to abide by the regime. Another way in which the regime manages such tendencies is through the legitimation and practice of limited war as a redistributional mechanism. For the society whose frustrated lateral pressure predispositions cannot be allowed expression through political concessions — and which threaten the political agent's ability to sustain autonomy and abide by the regime — limited war is a permissible means of bringing political configurations into accord with socio-economic processes.

Such redistributional practices can be engaged in only up to a point, however. The point is reached when necessary concessions and/or the potential losses through limited war would begin to significantly constrain the lateral pressure of even leading regime participants. It is therefore the case that the latitude for undertaking such redistributional practices is larger, and the regime's capacity to elicit participants' comliance is greater, when the overall system is expanding, when the societies of all or most regime participants can continue to grow and express lateral pressure, not always toward one another, but beyond the geographic scope of principal regime participants. Such conditions characterize the system during *normal phases* of the regime's operation.

When the overall system comes up against limits and is no longer able to expand, conversely, the latitude for such redistributive practices shrinks away. More accurately put, as the obstacles to further expansion of the system become more and more costly for economic actors to overcome, and as competition within the system becomes manifestly conflictual, each regime participant's attempts to engage in such redistributive practices encounter increasing resistance from a broadening span of its own domestic socio-economic sectors. Concessions begin to entail immediate, differentially felt domestic costs that cannot be obscured behind a veil of overall growth in the society. It becomes increasingly difficult for politico-military agents to keep wars limited while also maintaining that they fight for the whole of their respective societies; for absent overall societal growth, it becomes apparent that limited objectives express the interests of some elements of society more than of others.

At such a point, the regime can no longer function normally, and it moves into a crisis phase. Normal practices on the parts of politico-military agents are less and less adequate to the task of eliciting the compliance of all. The politico-military agents comprising the regime are *doubly threatened.* They are threatened from within their domestic societies because, with the weakening of the regime's ability to guarantee latitude for the societies' expressions of lateral pressure, domestic competitive tensions are likely to escalate. They are also threatened from without because it is plain that the politico-military agents of other states are similarly struggling desperately to retain their autonomy amidst welling and competing societal demands.

However, the product of this doubly threatening situation in a period of crisis is not to weaken states *vis-à-vis* domestic societies but to *strengthen* them. Under conditions of increasing international insecurity, the politico-military agents of state are strengthened in their abilities to intervene in the domestic economies, pursue economic-nationalistic aims, and disregard (the now discounted) costs to participants previously benefiting from an open world economy — all in the name of the 'national interest.'

What follows in this crisis phase of regime practices — or what is likely to follow — is a hardening of relationships such that international relations begin to look very much like the Hobbesian vision. It may appear that the balance of power ideology has found its realization. As insecurity mounts and anarchy seems to prevail, states appear to be less and less restrained in their exercises of socio-economic instruments of political control. The world economy might be fractionated as economic nationalism increasingly holds sway. Politico-military agents of state may appear to be particularly autonomous and strong, for they can increasingly reference international insecurity in their approaches to absolutist control within; and externally, they are less encumbered by the cooperative restrictions of the past.

The Hobbesian vision, though, is an illusion. It is sustained only by viewing this moment ahistorically, statically, apart from the prior developments that prefigured it and the future developments it implicates.

In fact, this Hobbesian moment is anticipated by the deeply structured regime of balance of power, and although the moment involves a shift in regime practices, nothing in this moment signifies the termination of the regime itself. On the contrary, that states are strengthened *vis-à-vis* their respective societies in a seeming condition of crisis signifies their identity in the regime — their continuing, inescapable mutual dependence.[61]

This is made evident by reference to a counterfactual premise. Absent the regime and its reproduction of a multiplicity of mutually insecure states in times of the overall system's growth and expansion, then, according to the lateral pressure argument, the fact of the system's reaching limits would lead to the breakdown of whatever political apparatus was operative in the system. The political apparatus would lose its autonomy amidst swelling competitive tensions born of crisis. However, given the regime and its reproduction of states joined in insecurity, the crisis of limits in fact means, not the weakening of political components, but their strengthening.

To be sure, the wars that so often result are no less deadly because they occur within a balance of power regime and not within a state of nature. Yet so long as war does not result in some single politico-military agent's effective assertion of imperium over the whole, it remains among the regime's principal means of adapting the system to serious crisis while also reproducing the regime itself.

What is remarkable about this balance of power regime, then, is that it sustains and holds in check two opposed tendencies that are characteristic of any system of differential growth. The first is a tendency toward some form of centralized political union of the whole — either through conquest or political integration — as the growth and lateral pressure of several societies give form to relations of interdependence among them. The second is a tendency toward the political and economic fragmentation of the system, as the effects of growth are differentially felt and elicit particularized local responses. The former tendency, carried to the extreme, would ultimately mean the demise of a system of differential growth and lateral pressure, for competition would then be entirely within the reach of one political entity, the political agents' interventions on behalf of one competitor over another would be plain, and the rationalizing force of external insecurity would not exist. By the same token, the latter tendency, carried to the extreme, would also mean the

---

[61] On the dialectical conception of identity and difference underlying this statement it is useful to consult Appendix A.

degeneration of a system of differential growth, for complete political-economic fragmentation would imply the system's transformation into a multiplicity of closed, entropic systems. As a deeply structured regime, balance of power at once embodies and denies the extreme realization of both tendencies. *It constitutes a single political system that manifests itself in the individuation of a multiplicity of interdependent, mutually implicating, but seemingly distinct political forms called states. Insecurity and the exercise of violence among partners to the regime are among this political system's key adaptive means.*

B   Liberalism, Mercantilism, and the Balance of Power Regime

Against this background, it should now be clear that the expressly opposed liberal and mercantilist attitudes toward balance of power accurately refer only to the ideology of balance of power, not the regime itself. Mercantilist and liberal positions can be said to represent different participants' attempts to rationalize different but contending aspects of the regime. As these aspects or phases alternate in their dominance, between periods of normality and periods of crisis, so also do liberal and mercantilist positions alternate in their abilities to hold sway. But just as the dominance of one aspect of the regime implies only the sublation, not the denial, of the other, so also are liberal and mercantilist positions always in contention, even when one or the other seems to most aptly characterize the current phase of the regime and hence current regime practices.

Baldly put, the debate between liberals and mercantilists is the ideological face of a continuing struggle to influence regime practices. Since it is an ideological struggle, its principle product is the rationalization of current regime practices – and the obscuring from view of the nature of the regime itself.[62] Over the longer term, the decisive factor in shaping regime practices is not to be found in either the liberal or the mercantilist model. It is something over which the regime itself – according to its own rules – has little effective control. The decisive factor is whether or not the societies of principal regime participants can continue to grow and expand, expressing their lateral pressure in large measure beyond the geographic domain of principal regime participants themselves. When this is possible at comparatively low cost, the regime tends to function normally. When the costs of outward expansion increase, the regime

---

[62] See Franz Schurmann, *The Logic of World Power* (New York: Pantheon, 1974).

moves into a crisis phase, for reasons and in ways described above.[63] The apparent relative wisdom of liberal and mercantilist ideology depends upon which of these two conditions holds.

In particular, *the liberal position tends to be dominant whenever the balance of power regime is in a normal phase*. This is as one would expect, since the balance of power regime operates normally under conditions of unimpeded outward lateral pressure, and since the liberal position presumes the non-zero-sum and unlimited character of economic and technological growth in the system. Moreover, the liberal position helps to reinforce and rationalize the regime's normal sanctions against politico-military agents' attempts to intervene in the socio-economic sphere as a way of building or wielding political capabilities *vis-à-vis* other agents. Liberals do this, most principally, through orienting opposition to the *ideology* of balance of power, especially as this might infuse socio-economic processes. They might do this, further, by attempting to devise auxiliary multilateral regimes that would regularize political practices in the socio-economic spheres. And they might do this by promoting the development of international forums in which grievances can be aired and the making of political concessions can be informed and coordinated.

But liberals fail to see that in helping to sustain processes of differential growth and expansion, they make it likely that sooner or later the system will encounter costly-to-overcome obstacles to further expansion, thereby creating a condition of crisis and shifting the balance of power regime to a crisis phase. As a crisis phase approaches, liberal opposition to balance of power ideology is likely to become more and more strident — and less and less persuasive for the politico-military agents of the regime. When a crisis phase does arrive, the liberal position seems poorly suited to apparent realities, but it does not literally die away. Instead, it is repressed, awaiting revitalization at the first moment that the crisis is passed.

Thus, for example, the hand of liberals is again strengthened at the very moment that a society's victory in war seems assured. At that moment, it becomes possible to again contemplate the society's outward expressions of lateral pressure tendencies. And hence, though victory is assured and total political domination might be possible, liberals and politico-military agents of state are likely to find a joint preference in

---

[63] Strictly speaking, the question relates to specialized capabilities of expansion, their efficient reach toward overcoming obstacles and exploiting the environment, and the capacities of extant means of production to efficiently utilize resources extractable through the exercise of these capabilities.

stopping short of imperium — in preparing for the reconstruction of a world ordered within the normally operating balance of power regime.

The mercantilist perspective, for its part, tends to be the dominant ideology during the crisis phases of the regime. This, again, is as one would expect. After all, mercantilists tend to take a zero-sum view of the world, and a balance of power regime is in a crisis phase at those moments when patterns of differential growth and lateral pressure among key participants approach or approximate a zero-sum game. As a crisis approaches, and as various politico-military agents begin to succumb to demands for their interventions in the socio-economic spheres of their respective societies, mercantilist ideology provides prescriptions and rationales for each agent's reactive steps. The mercantilist tends to argue against the continuation of redistributional practices, on the grounds that these might weaken the 'power' of each national economy, and against multilateral regime building in the socio-economic spheres, on the grounds that such regimes might too greatly restrict the state's latitude to pursue 'national interests.' Mercantilists succeed, in part, by invoking the ideology of balance of power. In far larger part, they succeed because the onset of conditions of crisis, and the likely movement of the balance of power regime toward a crisis phase, leads to a discounting of prospects for each society's further extensions of lateral pressure by means not involving state action.

True, when the overall regime has not reached a crisis phase, the mercantilist position can sometimes still hold sway for individual societies. This, though, tends to occur only in two kinds of instances. One is the case of the society whose aspiring politico-military agents of state are not yet acknowledged as key participants in the regime and whose lateral pressure predispositions are frustrated by patterns of others' growth and expansion. The second is the case of the society whose politico-military agents of state are party to the regime but whose own growth and expansion, for whatever reason, is declining or might decline relative to others. In both cases, so long as the overall regime is not in crisis, mercantilist practices and politico-military actions corresponding to crisis-like regime practices have the effect of exacting concessions from other regime participants.

Yet just as liberals fail to see how differential growth and expansion can bring on conditions of crisis, so also do mercantilists fail to see that, so long as growth and expansion persist, the balance of power regime will tend to disallow the full realization of political practices corresponding to their vision. Gilpin, for instance, laments Great Britain's failure after about 1870 to recognize the necessity, born of a balance of power logic, of emphasizing modern industrial development above foreign investment.[64] This failure on the part of the state, he seems to say, helps to account for the demise of *Pax Britannia*. And this same failure, he worries, seems on the verge of being repeated by the United States today. He seems to be saying that had British leaders been more prescient, had they seen the mercantilist requisites of effective long-term balance of power politics, and had they availed themselves of opportunities to revitalize industry, the world economy could have been kept stable under unquestioned British leadership. However, Gilpin's error is that he embraces balance of power ideology and ignores the regime. Britain did not act in accord with mercantilist principles *precisely because British statesmen were party to the transgovernmental balance of power regime.* So long as the regime helped to sustain overall growth and expansion, British expressions of foreign investment included, it would remain in a normal phase and, as such, would proscribe mercantilist practices. For British leaders, as for American leaders today, the regime dictates that its agents (especially those representing the societies of the greatest lateral pressure) await conditions of crisis before departing from normal practices.

This means that *states abiding by the balance of power regime can and often do act contrary to some rational calculus of what would or might be in the long-term economic 'interest' of the individual society or might maximize the long-term relative 'power' of the individual state.* Politico-military agents of the regime, like other participants in the overall system, act within a technical-rational logic that rivets their attention to immediate problems. For the parties to the regime, this logic tends to orient their actions in ways reproducing the regime and themselves as its agents. But over the longer term, there is nothing in this logic or the regime that embraces it to assure that any one political agent will retain or improve its position — or even survive.

Indeed, for the future of the regime and the system of differential growth it helps to regulate, the success or failure of particular states does not matter. To think otherwise is to project the imperial conceits of people identified with leading states upon the system as a whole. What matters, on the contary, are two things: (1) that rapidly growing, high-lateral-pressure societies continue to project lateral pressure, thereby having a growth-generating influence on some (not most) other societies, and (2) that when once leading societies reach the limits of their growth and expansion, they be allowed to decline so that others, being perhaps better able to overcome limits, can rise to prominence. The balance of power system sees to it that both of these things are done. It does so by

[64] Gilpin, *US Power and the Multinational Corporation*, Chapter 3.

disallowing the politico-military agents' equations of their immediate security interests with overall socio-economic interests until the system is deep into crisis — and usually well past the point of no return. It is only then, at the point of crisis, that mercantilist arguments seem to aptly characterize the processes at work.

In summary, then, liberal and mercantilist political economics represent opposed but complementary ideologies, both reflecting but neither understanding the operation of a balance of power regime in a world of differential growth. Each may occasionally glimpse part of what is going on in a particular period — the liberal during normal phases, the mercantilist during crisis. Each may then conclude that its own perspective is correct — that the other is simply wrong. In so doing, however, each ideology is glimpsing what is a momentary, dependent relation, and each is falsely generalizing it to the whole. Each, therefore, is ahistorical, no matter how many isolated episodes in history each can assemble to make its case.

It is this ahistoricity that permits neomercantilist Gilpin, drawing upon Viner, to say that, 'in the short run there may be conflicts between the pursuit of power and the pursuit of wealth; in the long run the two pursuits are identical.'[65] From a nationalistic perspective, one may wish that this had been so in the isolated moment of crisis. But from the historical-processual perspective of the present argument, the normal play of balance of power politics necessarily produces neither power nor wealth for the states engaged in the regime.

In the same way, it is the ahistoricity of the liberal perspective that permits the liberal Kindleberger to argue that 'the state is about through as an economic unit' while presumably retaining a security function.[66] From the perspective of a high-lateral-pressure economic actor, one may wish and believe that this is so during the normal phases of the balance of power regime. One may even try to promote this vision by displacing 'international anarchy' with the creation of multilateral regulative regimes to sustain order. But again, from the historical-processual perspective of the present argument, such a position forgets that a regulative economic regime already exists and that insecurity politics and war are part of it. Over the longer term, the 'invisible hand' of international economics is partially embedded in a single transgovernmental regime. And the hand holds a sword.

[65] Ibid., p. 37.
[66] Charles Kindleberger, *American Business Abroad* (New Haven: Yale University Press, 1969), p. 207.

None of this is to say that liberal and mercantilist perspectives are unimportant. Ideologies are always important to the functioning of a system, if only because they obscure from view how it really operates and thereby deflect criticism.[67] These particular ideologies are also important in that they orient intellectual development regarding the two opposed tendencies of a system of differential growth and, in so doing, allow room for contemplating the creative elaboration of the system when needs arise and opportunities present themselves.

Nor is the argument regarding the balance of power regime meant to suggest that there exists some grand, heretofore unseen conspiracy among politico-military agents of state. It is worth repeating that the soldiers, diplomats, and others who are party to this normally cooperative regime do not consciously conceive of themselves having regime-related interests that are partially distinct from some rational calculus of either the national public good or the interests of the domestic bourgeoisie.[68]

[67] Schurmann, *The Logic of World Power*.

[68] Here, though, an important (if controvesial) qualification needs to be offered. One of the leading exponents of balance of power theory, Hans Morgenthau, *can be interpreted* as at once the keen strategist and the obscurantist ideologue for participants in the regime here described. His vision of the roles (*'official* duties' as opposed to *'personal* wishes') of statesmen operating under some community wide 'moral consensus' comes very close to being a self-conscious acknowledgement of the regime discussed here. Yet he offers terms that obscure the distinctions between statemen's regime-related interests and the mixed socio-economic demands of their respective societies — thereby protecting regime-participating statesmen from domestic criticism. Consider, e.g., his equation of power-seeking with the 'national interest' and his celebration of 'the autonomy of the political sphere' as a necessary precondition for statesmen's rational calculus and pursuit of national interests. What is more, his insistence upon a Niebuhrian conception of human frailties can be viewed as a mystification and minimization of human capacities aimed toward lodging responsibility for insecurity, not among regime participants, but principally in the souls and genes of people in general.

How can Morgenthau be both 'keen strategist' and 'ideologue'? The answer lies in the vantage point assumed in his theoretical work and in his own understanding of ideology. As to his vantage point, Morgenthau writes that: 'We look over [the statesman's] shoulder when he writes his dispatches; we listen in on his conversation with other statesmen; we read and anticipate his very thoughts. Thinking in terms of interest defined as power, we think as he does, and as disinterested observers we understand his thoughts and actions perhaps better than he, the actor on the political scene, does himself.' As quoted in Chaper 10, in short, Morgenthau says that he puts himself 'in the position of a statesman who must meet a certain problem of foreign policy under certain circumstances, and [he asks himself] what the rational alternatives are from which a statesman may choose . . .' (Morgenthau, *Politics Among Nations*, p. 5.).

As to his definition of ideology, Morgenthau quotes with approval from Karl Mannehim, *Ideology and Utopia* (New York: Harcourt, Brace and Co. 1936), pp. 49 and 238: ideas and representations called ideologies 'are regarded as more or less conscious disguises of the real nature of a situation, the true recognition of which would not be in accord with 'the interests of those who propound the ideas and

The point of the argument, instead, is similar to the criticism lodged against Leninist imperialism theory and other perspectives discussed in previous sections. Theory, if it is to claim to be scientific, must do more than rationalize, immunize, and strategically guide the political actions of particular participants in a differentiated system. Liberals and mercantilists presumably aspire to produce this kind of theory – a scientific theory. They presumably aspire to produce a scientific theory that helps human beings to become conscious of their conditions and of the ways in which they do or might participate in reproducing or transforming these conditions. They presumably see knowledge building as an exercise of human freedom that should elevate human freedom. Yet if these are the aspirations, then both fall short.

Lenin's imperialism theory immunizes socialist states and helps to rationalize exploitative state practices. Morgenthau plays Machiavelli to the regime-bound princes of the liberal age. Haas's integration theory plots strategy for stealthy, welfare-oriented bureaucrats and technocrats. In much the same way, liberal thinkers too readily take the side of, and fail to criticize or question, the preferred world visions of those who ride the crest of differential growth and lateral pressure. Mercantilists too uncritically echo the designs of those who fear that, unless drastic measures are taken, they will miss or drown in the next passing wave. Measuring all reality in terms of the immediate currents in which it is caught, and technically-rationally striving to solve problems so measured, none tries to understand the dynamism of the whole.

And that is regrettable. For liberals and mercantilists have much to offer. Under the influence of the thinking of Adam Smith, liberals are perhaps too neglectful of distributional questions and too eager to assume that the short-sighted choices of economic competitors will always result in linear progress. But they are nonetheless able to conceive of unintended higher order consequences and to contemplate the system transforming possibilities. Although the liberal view of the state ahistorically neglects its political-economic origins and functions, liberals are at least able to see

representations.' 'These distortions range all the way from conscious lies to half-conscious and unwitting disguises; from calculated attempts to dupe others to self-deception.' 'The study of ideologies has made it its task to unmask the more or less conscious deceptions and disguises of human interest groups, particularly those of political parties.' (Morgenthau, ibid., p. 92, fn. 1).

Because Morgenthau 'puts himself in the position of a statesman,' thinks 'as he does,' and then promotes the statesman's (now systematized) perspective as *the* non-ideological perspective on international reality, the resulting view is itself a one-sided viewpoint that 'disguises . . . the real nature of the situation, the true recognition of which would not be in accord with' the interests of statesmen.

the state as a structuration that might somehow be transcended. Mercantilists, for their part, are too anxious to treat the world atomistically. But they are least acknowledge that, within each particle of life, things political and things economic are not really different things at all. Although mercantilists misunderstand the relation of insecurity politics and international economics — too readily superimposing balance of power ideology on both — they differ from most liberals and many Marxists in that, for them, the relation merits serious scholarly attention.

What is called for is *not* an additive joining of the two traditions. It is not enough to agree with the Gilpin-like assertion that the future will contain some mix of the features of several models, liberal and mercantilist among them. Nor will it suffice to agree with Keohane and Nye that understanding inheres in knowing which among several models apply to particular kinds of situations. What is called for, rather, is a serious attempt on the part of each tradition to negate Gilpin's curse on both houses: 'neither liberalism nor mercantilism has developed a theory of dynamics.'[69] Toward this end, each tradition might start by asking how its own generalizing knowledge claims not only oppose but also implicitly contain and depend upon the processes referenced by the other. The question invokes a dialectic that each tradition sorely lacks. It represents a first step toward the creative synthesis of dynamic theory.

V   CONCLUSION

Balance of power theory, integration theory, imperialism theory, liberal and mercantilist political economic theory — each tradition has been examined in this chapter in light of this study's attempt to limn the broader proportions of the modern security problematique. Each, in fact, has served as a kind of foil for the further development of the principal argument. If that argument is better articulated now than it was in Chapter 1, it is due to the rich and provocative insights contained in the traditions confronted and criticized here.

The discussion, though critical, has been abstractly theoretical and at times broadly philosophical. Issues of freedom and necessity, contingency and choice, atomism and holism, objectivity and subjectivity, historicity and ashistoricity, and factuality and counterfactuality have all been broached in due course. Substantive theoretical, ontological, epistemological, and methodological arguments have been related, strung together, and often brought into contention.

[69] Gilpin, *US Power and the Multinational Corporation*, p. 32.

In the midst of these general abstractions, it is perhaps too easy to forget that they apply to contemporary relations among three specific major powers: China, the Soviet Union, and the United States. These countries differ greatly. One is describable as a large, technologically advanced, perhaps 'post-industrial' society, economically conforming roughly to a capitalist model. Another is describable as a large, industrialized society having a socialist state that aspires to further rapid technological growth. The third is also socialist, but its population is massive, its economy is still principally agrarian, its technology is limited, and, until recently, its leaders have sought to foster self-reliant, collectivist development and limited bureaucratization above rapid growth.

Despite these and other differences, though, the three societies are today entangled in the modern security problematique. They are entangled in a problematique that took form in Europe several centuries ago and that has since been ever on the march toward global scope. The three states also wield enormous destructive capabilities, built up through a history of technological growth, and today having the whole world within their lethal radius. And entwined as these societies are within the dynamics of the problematique, there is much to sustain and precious little to stop or control, their movement toward cataclysmic violence. There is much to project them on a course toward unleashing their most advanced technologies to obliterate the material accomplishments of the modern age. Different though they may be, their joining in the security problematique binds them equifinally to a common fate.

To raise such a specter is perhaps to complete the 'ultimate dialectic' implicit in the lateral pressure argument and carried forward in the modern security problmatique. Human beings, ensnared in technical-rational conceits, deny their dependence upon nature as they grow and struggle to technologically subordinate the environment beyond themselves. When finally the limits to their growth are reached, they have only to subjugate one another. In the violence that follows, all that humans have produced in false denial of their environmental dependence is destroyed. In the interdependence of mutual self-destruction, humans realize their oneness and return to a nature that they never really left.

The principal argument of this book, reinforced by the empirical analysis, is that these processes are at work today among today's most powerful countries. The argument of this chapter is that many seemingly distinct theoretical traditions have much to contribute toward the illumination and even the transformation of these processes but that their contributions will be made through the waging of controversy. To provoke that controversy, and to chart some of the lines along which it might be waged, has been the purpose behind the present criticisms.

Some people will surely object to the arguments advanced here on the grounds that they are all too deterministic, that they demean human freedom, that they reduce people to the status of cogs in machines. The objection misses a crucial point. The social determinism expressed in the tragic logic of the modern security problematique and represented in the general model assumes only that participants unquestioningly take themselves to be free and thus fail to acknowledge their long-run dependence upon their environments. It is this technical-rational hubris, an equation of freedom with power, that leads people to deny social determinism, ignore historical processes, disdain of exercising their communicative capacities in the quest for consensus, and crash headlong into limits that they do not foresee and cannot surmount. Determinism exists, in short, but determinism and autonomy are not joined in either-or relation. For statesmen, bureaucrats, entrepeneurs, factory workers, farmers, and scholars, determinism is an ever-present, inescapable fact of life. People stride toward autonomy when, upon recognizing this to be so, they set out to escape the limits of technical rationality — to exercise their capacities for knowledge and communication to the fullest.

This, in fact, is one of the most powerful ideas contained in Robert North's conceptualization of lateral pressure. The concept reminds us that to control is to succumb, to be totally free is to be totally enslaved, and to acknowledge one's dependence upon the world beyond oneself is the first step toward autonomy. People rise out of nature and become something more than cogs in a machine only because they have a capacity to communicate beyond the realms of immediate, tangible experience. They have a capacity to reach back in history, forward in time, and beyond the horizons into unfamiliar terrain. They have a capacity to note differences and to wonder why they exist, to see themselves as they are and to observe that they are other than they might have been. They have a capacity to know that they are things with problems and needs and to see the problems and needs, and even their definitions of self, as all profoundly dependent upon the social and natural environments that they might affect but can never finally control. This, the capacity to communicate and reach self-reflexively toward an intersubjective consensus about the past and future of the human condition, is what elevates humans out of nature and makes room for human autonomy.

But processes of differential growth and lateral pressure negate all of this. In expressing differential growth and lateral pressure, human beings are unconsciously reaching toward subordinating the whole of their environments to their own unquestioned demands and capabilites. They reach for control and surrender their humanity. They strive for mastery and become the slaves of fear.

An Interpretational Supplement

Statements have meanings in contexts. Utterances 'encoded' in one context with one set of intended meanings are sometimes 'decoded' in other contexts and with different meanings assigned. Communication is therefore a very difficult business — perhaps especially so in the social sciences, where different traditions bring different contextualizing experiences and ways of thinking to bear. Indeed, in the social sciences it is often the case that assertions and knowledge claims that are rational within the context of one tradition are disturbingly unwarranted when viewed in the context of another.

A book that attempts to engage in and communicate a synthesis of competing traditions therefore has a very special obligation. If communication is to be effective, it must involve more than the statement of propositions, the interpretation of corroborating empirical evidence, and the critical engagement of competing traditions. It must also involve an attempt to elevate and articulate the underlying preassumptions and the progression of experiences amidst which propositions are sensible, interpretations are reasonable, and criticisms are valid.

This lengthy appendix undertakes this difficult but important task. As such, its status is that of an interpretational supplement to the text. The reader who has encountered disturbing statements and research practices in the text may have been provoked to ask, in what way of thinking, in what context, are these statements and practices rational? This appendix sets out to answer this question.

It proceeds through three sections. The first section addresses the *ontological and epistemological commitments* underlying this study. What, it asks, is the underlying conception of reality? What is the role and what are the limits of knowledge, particularly scientific knowledge, within that reality? The answers advanced here are closely associated with the theoretical perspective developed in the text. The second section builds upon this foundation to present a reconstructed *normative research philosophy*. It includes assertions about the goal of critical peace research, and it presents a rational logic of research progress toward this goal. As a reconstruction, this normative research philosophy is the model of rational research progress approximated in this study. Finally, the third section outlines the main elements of the *three-stage empirical research progression* undertaken in the construction of the general model. As will be seen, this progression reflects the normative research philosophy presented in the second section.

I   COMPETING ONTOLOGICAL AND EPISTEMOLOGICAL COMMITMENTS: THE SOURCES OF A CRITICAL TENSION

Among the important, formative influences upon any modeling enterprise, two are perhaps most basic. One is found in the underlying ontological commitments—the underlying conception of things in reality. That is, is modeling founded upon an atomist, a structuralist, or a dialectical conception of reality?[1] The other basic influence, not detachable from the first, is the epistemological preconception of the place of knowledge and knowledge-building with respect to that reality. In particular, is modeling founded upon the presupposition that theory and models should serve in a technological capacity or a participatory capacity with regard to the reality addressed?[2] In most modeling enterprises these questions are seldom explicitly posed. They are seldom posed because the ontological and epistemological commitments they address most often reside, not at the level of the explicit language of science, but at the level of the deep, unquestioned grammar of thought. Analysts seldom deliberate how every aspect of their work—from the conventions of science

---

[1] See Bertell Ollman, *Alienation: Marx's Conception of Man in Capitalist Society*, second edition (Cambridge, England: Cambridge University Press), Appendix II for definitions of these terms. Ollman offers the following definitions: 'There are basically three different notions of the whole in philosophy: (1) the atomist conception already present in Descartes and dominant in modern philosophy, that views the whole as the sum of simple facts; (2) the formalist conception, apparent in Schelling, Hegel, and most modern structuralists, that attributes an identity to the whole independent of its parts and asserts the absolute predominance of the whole over the parts; . . . and (3) the dialectical and materialist conception of Marx . . . that views the whole as the structured interdependence of its relational parts–the interacting events, processes, and conditions of the real world–as observed from any major part. (p. 266.)

[2] This distinction is discussed below.

they heed through the techniques they apply to their interpretations of empirical results–reflects commitments to which there might be reasonable alternatives.

One of the important features of the research program represented in this study is that it has been forced to gradually confront the implications of these commitments for modeling practice. Specifically, the Stanford Studies research program, under the direction of Robert C. North, has been forced to confront these issues.[3] It has had to confront these issues because, from the outset, the ontological and epistemological commitments implicit in the program's expressed theoretical positions have been poised in critical tension with the opposed commitments implicit in the methodological orientations it has sought to adapt. On the one hand, the program's core theoretical concerns bear and express a dialectical conception of reality and imply a commitment to research and model-building as nontechnocratic, participatory activities. On the other hand, the research tools adapted and applied by the program were most often first developed as expressions of atomist or structuralist ontological positions, and were most often developed with an eye to their utility as technical-rational instruments of social management and control. Indeed, in ways that participants have only gradually begun to appreciate, the ontological and epistemological commitments implicit in the program's early substantive assumptions and propositions were sharply at variance with the commitments built into widely shared beliefs about what social science is, should do, and can do.

Now, with the benefit of twenty years' hindsight, it can be said that the story of the Stanford Studies program is largely the story of a struggle to creatively resolve the critical tensions emerging out of these competing commitments.[4] It can be said that the struggle has involved continuing attempts to use reliable scientific techniques, preserve and observe scientific norms of operational reproducibility and empirical grounding, and,

---

[3] For a complete bibliography on researches in the Stanford Studies program see Francis W. Hoole and Dina Zinnes (eds.), *Quantitative International Politics: An Appraisal* (New York: Praeger, 1976), pp. 514–19.

[4] It must be stressed that this and what follows is my interpretation and mine alone. I do not mean to imply that most or several of the numerous participants in the Stanford Studies program over the years have been consciously aware of this struggle. Nor do I mean to suggest that the various participants have uniformly experienced the tension in their individual researches. In fact, it is probably true that most participants have aligned most strongly on one side or the other of this critical tension, unconsciously denying the tension and subordinating the opposite side in the process. In my opinion, however, this tension has been a vital, motivating force in Robert North's thinking, although I am not sure that he would articulate it in my terms.

at the same time, interpret and adapt these techniques and norms so that they might discipline and sustain cumulative participatory research in a dialectical reality. The critical tensions and the struggle continue in this study.

The task of this section is to make the elements of this critical tension as explicit as possible. The reasons for undertaking this task are well stated by Dina Zinnes in her diagnosis of problems of cumulation in international relations research. She argues that science requires 'explicitness at *all* stages of the research endeavor. We seem to have concluded that the scientific approach is principally a set of rules for marshalling evidence and have forgotten that the dictum of explicitness is equally, and perhaps more significantly, relevant to the initial statement of our argument.'[5] Indeed, the point here is that putatively unproblematic scientific 'rules of evidence' often contain some theories, ontological commitments, and epistemological commitments, and are often incompatible with others. Being explicit about the initial statement of a theoretical argument must therefore entail articulating the ways in which that argument is or is not in conflict with — and does or does not problematize — the interpretation and application of scientific techniques and rules.

Although necessarily lengthy, this section does proceed in a straightforward manner. Simply stated, it juxtaposes the two sides of the forementioned critical tension that has long been confronted by the Stanford Studies. The first part of this section considers the ontological and epistemological implications of the conceptual framework, in general, and the lateral pressure 'theory kernel,' in particular. The second part of this section considers the contrasting ontological and epistemological commitments implicit in much of social science and most modeling practice. Taken together, these two parts define the critical tension that has repeatedly manifested itself in this study's progression from conceptual framework to general model. In sometimes subtle ways, the ontological and epistemological commitments reflected in the conceptual framework at once require and problematize the use of scientific techniques in a modeling enterprise.

A   Ontological and Epistemological Commitments Implied by the Conceptual Framework

The conceptual framework bears and expresses a dialectical conception of reality and it implies a participatory and critical role for a modeling

---

[5] See Dina Zinnes, 'The Problem of Cumulation,' in James N. Rosenau (ed.), *In Search of Global Patterns* (New York: Free Press, 1976), p. 165, emphasis in original.

enterprise within that reality. The commitment to a dialectical ontology is best seen by reference to an overview of the conceptual framework and the approach to synthesis it reflects. The epistemological commitment, which would situate knowledge-building as a partially autonomous but socially responsible and critical participant in reality, is best understood with reference to the implications of the lateral pressure 'theory kernel.'

1   The Framework's Implied Ontology:
A Dialectical Conception of Reality

That the conceptual framework expresses neither an atomist nor a structuralist conception of reality is easily seen. Unlike a perspective framed by an atomist conception, the framework does not try to reduce reality to a conjunction of facts as they might be separately sensed by individual acts of observation. Unlike a theory ordered within a structuralist conception, the framework does not reflect an attempt to identify some overarching and stationary causal structure that at once operates according to unyielding laws and predominates over the separate parts of reality. The assertion that the framework expresses a dialectical conception is not made by default, however. The term 'dialectical' is not here meant as a residual label to be applied when others fail. On the contrary, the argument that the conceptual framework reflects a dialectical conception bears with it some quite definite implications. In this regard, three specific features of a dialectical conception, and of the framework itself, deserve attention.

First, within the framework as within all dialectical conceptions, *the dominant characteristic of reality is assumed to be change*. Thus, the framework can and does try to allow for both (*a*) invariant regularities and (*b*) historically emergent regularities and structurations that, while perhaps stable over considerable spans of time, remain in principle susceptible to change. The framework's treatment of units of analysis above the individual provides an example: even so enduring an institution as the state is treated as a structuration whose emergence, reproduction, and possible passing is to be somehow explained. In the same way, dynamics of expansion, rivalry, and balance of power, while notably highly structured, are treated as historically emergent and contextually sensitive. Within the framework, moreover, emphasis is given to the ways in which these dynamics might find expression in different dimensions of behavior and activity under different conditions.

Second, the framework expresses a dialectical conception in that *aspects of reality are interpreted as abstractions.* This means that a thing, a pattern, or a social structuration is seen, not as an element of life having an identity complete unto itself, but as an aspect owing its real existence to the ways in which people abstract and actualize patterns from amidst all possibilities. For example, an arms race, as an aspect of life, owes its existence to the interactive choices of people who selectively see, interpret, and respond to changes ongoing around them; in so doing, they give form to change and shape a process recognizably structured as an arms race. The same applies to seemingly more concrete, less dynamic social structurations, such as states, specialized agencies, international organizations, corporations, social classes, and families. All are actualized as recognizable things because people are situated to make choices that, taken together, abstract these structurations from among all the structurations that could conceivably take form.

Importantly, this view allows for the fact that the changing reality is differently seen from different *vantage points* established within it. As people choose, act, and give individuated form to different aspects of life, they contribute to the fashioning of a differentiated reality in which they will assume varied positions, purposes, experiences, constraints, and hence different vantage points. From these competing vantage points, people then selectively see reality — and contribute to its shaping — in different ways. Within this reality, truth is thus always relative. Reality consists of no more and no less than the open-ended, changing complex of actual and possible relations and structurations given form and moment by physically constrained people acting upon the relative truths afforded by their vantage points upon and within that reality.

Third, within the conceptual framework, as in dialectical conceptions generally, *the analysis of differences is subsumed under a prior assumption of identity.* That is, *the manifestly different aspects considered in the framework are preconceptualized to be inner-related and hence identical.*[6]

[6] The distinction here is between internal relations and external relations. To paraphrase Jon Elster, consider the set of all relations joining things A and B. External relations are found in that subset of all relations which can be abstracted out of the total set without altering what A and B are. Internal relations are those relations without which A and B cannot exist, cannot survive, as what they are acknowledged to be. See Jon Elster, *Leibniz et La Formation De l'Esprit Capitaliste* (Paris: Aubier Montaigne, 1975). To say that A and B are internally related therefore implies their identity. Neither thing A nor thing B could exist in the absence of that with which it is internally related: the other thing. And changes in what A is and becomes imply and presuppose changes in what B is and becomes.

This makes sense, of course, only if one is willing to acknowledge the preceding point made in the text: things or aspects of reality are not elements of life having identities complete unto themselves but are instead abstractions from among all the aspects that could conceivably take form. Obviously, this makes no sense whatsoever

Many of the framework's assertions make sense only in these terms. Recall, for example, the argument that intersocietal competition and conflict always entail some degree of integration between societies, even as societies thereby become more clearly identifiable as unitary, single-minded 'actors.' This argument is meaningful only if one first understands that these separate units, these aspects, owe what they are separately becoming to the interdependence of their rivalry. Were one to abstract from these societies the history of their interdependence in rivalry, the societies would presumably have assumed much different forms. Similarly, recall the argument regarding balance of power as a deeply structured regime. In brief, the argument is that societies might participate in and adapt to a system characterized by recurring applications of balance of power logics; that societies might come to interiorize these logics within their instruments, plans, policies, and attitudes toward other societies; and that societies might thenceforth manifest the regime, not in conscious conformity to acknowledged rules, but as acts of survival as what they have become. Such an argument refers to balance of power as an internal relation. Were it not for their interiorization of a balance of power regime, the societies might have assumed structural forms far different from those actually assumed.

Moreover, because they reflect the preassumption of inner-relations among aspects of reality, the framework's key concepts are themselves relationally defined. For instance, the concept of technology is presented, not as a thing having an identity complete unto itself, but as a *relational* aspect of life that (*a*) involves the means–ends rational application of knowledge and skills to serve certain objectified purposes and (*b*) creates new demands and new 'needs.' Far from being 'data containers,' concepts of state, lateral pressure, expansion, intersections, competition, provocations, crisis–indeed, all of the framework's key concepts–are relationally presented. An important implication of this approach to conceptualization must be underscored. Being relationally defined, the concepts and arguments lose their intended meaning when deprived of the context provided by the overall framework. Put differently, the meaning of each concept and each argument is to be understood in terms of the ways in which it does or might implicate other concepts and other arguments.

within the Aristotelian 'either-or' approach to identity and difference: either things are different or they are identical, either they are externally related or they are unrelated. It should be equally obvious, however, that this either-or approach succeeds only by denying that things are abstractions, by investing in them an unassailable ontological status that makes them immune to criticism. See Ollman, op. cit., Appendix II.

These dialectical pressumptions — regarding change, the abstraction of aspects, and the identity of aspects in inner-relation — are reflected even in the framework's approach to synthesis of propositions from various theoretical traditions. The framework portrays a historical progression from growth through rivalry to balance of power, and each of these three classes of dynamics is presented as an aspect or phase of reality. Each phase or aspect is an abstraction in two senses. First, some of the regularities giving distinguishable form to each aspect have been selectively represented by various theoretical traditions, each of which is a vantage point upon reality. Second, the distinguishing regularities and structurations of each aspect take form and moment through the cumulative choices of people situated in history. With both of these notions in mind, the framework's approach to synthesis can be seen. The framework draws upon competing theoretical vantage points that have sought to selectively represent aspects of reality, and the framework assumes that these aspects, so represented, have real existences as actual or possible but always abstracted regularities and structurations. At the same time, in joining various propositions, the framework relativizes these propositions, situating them in relations of mutual dependence. In these terms, propositions derived from, say, imperialism theory, integration theory, or Richardson arms race theory, all *contain* — that is, they mutually implicate — one another. Each proposition regarding each aspect of life is set in a historical context wherein its implicit presuppositions regarding other aspects and other propositions are made clear.

To offer a specific example, consider the presentation of a Richardson proposition regarding military competitive processes. As presented, this proposition presupposes–and is prefigured by–the presentation of propositions regarding (*inter alia*) the emergence of states, the intersection of politicized lateral pressure activities, and the negation of political integrative possibilities among high capability societies. More than that, the presentation of a proposition on military competitive processes prefigures–i.e., is necessary to interpreting the relevance of–propositions on the occurrence of politico-military confrontation and crisis. This is but one partial example, but the generalization should be clear. Although derived from separate traditions, the propositions presented in the framework are joined as one. They are identical in that they contain one another. To remove any one is to alter the meaning of all.

To be sure, it must be acknowledged that Chapter 1's presentation of the conceptual framework often obscures the underlying dialectical conception. Each word, each sentence, and each paragraph can only express so much information — can only highlight some of the inner-connections that might exist. Chapter 1 does necessarily begin on one page and end on another. And the presentation in the form of three major phases might invite the inference of a linear developmental sequence. Yet, in the case of a framework organized within a dialectical conception of reality, one must take care not to confuse medium with message. In particular, it is necessary to take quite seriously the framework's recurring attempts to disallow the centering of thought around any logical starting point or origin or end. The reference to the image of a spiral; the concepts of asynchrony, equifinality, and antogonism among phases; the argument regarding the 'impacts' of lateral pressure; and the assertion that the individual is the fundamental unit of analysis in a conceptualization that concentrates on aggregate social processes — all such statements are meant to disrupt logocentrism. They are meant to evoke an understanding of each posed relationship as 'always already' situated in history — always already prefigured, begun, and repeated.[7]

2   *Epistemological Implications of the Lateral Pressure 'Theory Kernel': A Critical-Participatory Role for Social Science*

Where 'ontology' refers to the science of being and reality, as such, 'epistomology' refers to the role and limits of knowing within that reality. In most longstanding research enterprises, epistemological commitments are framed by what might be called a 'theory kernel.' A theory kernel is the anchoring core conceptualization of a theory-building program.[8] It is a proto-explanation for the emergence, reproduction, and possible passing of some identifiable aspect, some problematic, of reality. The importance of a program's theory kernel resides in the fact that it is given the status of being unassailable (although it, like the problematic to be illuminated, is likely to be reinterpreted as the program progresses).

---

[7] It is perhaps instructive to consult Marx and Engels' *The German Ideology* as an example of a theoretical statement struggling mightily to escape the logocentric tendencies of written communications. For example, Marx once refers to the production of means to satisfy ends as the 'first historical act' and later he points to a second 'moment,' the production of new needs, and calls this the 'first historical act.' The reader confronting such statements has two choices: she or he can point to an inconsistency, a failure of rationality, or she or he can assume that Marx is rational and find in these statements a basis for understanding that Marx is striving to escape the linear, logocentrism of verbal communications. I am indebted to Dominick LaCapra, 'Habermas and the Grounding of Critical Theory,' *History and Society*, Vol. xvi, No. 3, for his articulation of a problem in communications that, for me at least, has long been nearly unexpressable.

[8] Often a theory kernel is unarticulated and unexamined by participants in a program. Many so-called research programs have no theory kernel at all.

In it, researchers suspend disbelief; and they turn their attention to the interpretational task of synthesizing other propositions in its light. They do so in order to better account for the puzzles and anomolies that take form, as it were, 'between' the theory kernel and the problematic to be explained.

As in the Stanford Studies program, this study focuses on a problematic of pervasive insecurity and recurring large-scale physical violence. The question at hand is, how did such a problematic come to take form as a characteristic feature of global relations, how is it reproduced, and how might it be transcended? As in the Standford Studies program, too, this study's approach to answering this question starts from a theory kernel whose key concept is lateral pressure. This theory kernel, it will be recalled, was spelled out in several paragraphs of Chapter 1.

It is evident that this theory kernel bears all of the features of a dialectical conception, as described above. As discussed in Chapter 1, the theory kernel relates a kind of 'story' accounting for the emergence of the preconditions for violence. This story of lateral pressure begins and is wholly contained in some historical act of technological subjugation of an objectified environment and the consequent creation of new demands, new needs, and new implications for further, more extensive mastery and control. This story is wedded to no single level or unit of analysis. Individuals, families, clans, ethnic groups, classes, societies, states, and empires are all admissible under the rubric 'social units.' The theory kernel thereby allows for the possible co-occurrence of such 'episodes' of social development and interaction at several mutually contextualizing levels of analysis. In fact, as elaborated later in Chapter 1, the approach to explanation includes the idea that higher order social units emerge and take form out of — and then to some degree regulate — the lateral pressure generated processes of competition and violence at lower levels. States and a balance of power regime are both discussed in these terms. Finally, it is evident that the theory kernel reflects a striving for a non-ahistorical explanation of the sources of a global problematic of insecurity. It reflects an attempt to concentrate on certain timeless regularities and to avoid making concepts and ideas dependent expressions of this or that historically emergent aspect of life.

Two of the most important things about this theory kernel are not so immediately evident, however. They must be inferred. The first is that *the theory kernel contains an immanent (yet to be elaborated) plan for the transcendence of conditions generating pervasive insecurity and recurring violence.* Specifically, the theory kernel implies that reductions in propensities toward violence will come with the development of a system that (*a*) reduces differential growth among social units, (*b*) fosters a kind of communication wherein knowledge of the whole can be imported into each unit's definition of itself and its future, and thereby (*c*) equates individual fulfillment with the realization of humankind's potentialities. However, the theory kernel also implies that such a system is likely to emerge only as growth and lateral pressure among social units approach the limits of the human capacity to seemingly answer boundless ends by specific technical means, the inadequacies of technical-rational problem-solving are exposed, and means are developed to foster and communicate information on the deep inner-connections among all aspects of reality. The pace with which the world approaches these conditions, how long humankind must await their actualization, and the extent to which crisis and catastrophe must be part of the story — all of these remain open empirical questions requiring contingent responses.

The second important implication of the lateral pressure theory kernel is most definitely epistemological in character, for it applies to the role of theory and theory-building. Quite clearly, *the theory kernel contains a critique of the Western metaphysical grammar of means-ends rational action.* It asserts that lateral pressure is an expression of the growth-born movement toward realizing the unity of humanity and of humanity and nature. Given growth, this unity will be ever in motion toward new social-economic-political forms; and given differential growth in a differentiated natural environment, this unity will always involve some degree of actual and potential conflict among the social units expressing lateral pressure. However, a careful reading of the theory kernel also suggests that lateral pressure's implications for violence do not derive from growth, *per se.* They derive from the recurrence of differential human attempts to subordinate fragments of a changing reality to the technological exercise of human knowledge, skills, and capacities to communicate. By sharpening and hardening partitions in reality where none can finally exist, by mobilizing human energies and committing resources under the assumption that aspects of reality can be once and for all segmented and managed, this technological exercise of natural human capacities institutionalizes *limitlessness* in society's fragmented structures and forms. In so doing it makes it likely that as lateral pressure propels fragments toward the unity that technological solutions have falsely denied, the previous commitments of energies and resources will collide with explosive effects. Such an argument is meaningful–that is, it makes a meaningful, non-tautological distinction–only if one is able to conceive of human growth and interaction as not necessarily involving a technical-rational manipulative attitude toward objectified elements of life. Only if one's grammar of thought will admit this seemingly counterfactual possibility can one understand the theory kernel's critique of grammars that do not.

The point, though, is that the critique applies to research and theory building. In general, *it implies that if research and theory-building are to avoid complicity in the very processes that contribute to the recurrence of violence and the pervasiveness of insecurity, then they cannot proceed as technical enterprises aimed solely toward managing and controlling aspects of reality.* They cannot engage in the putatively final partitioning of reality. Nor can they be aimed solely toward the uncovering of eternal-lawful relationships so as to inform attempts to grasp and manipulate 'levers of control.'

More specifically the critique applies to two genres of research, both of which are reflected in this study. One is *world modeling research*, as animated by increasing sensitivity to the political and economic ramifications of global interdependence. Here, the implication is that a world modeling eneterprise that proceeds entirely within the grammar of technical-rational social action is potentially dangerous. To operate under the unquestioned illusion of a structure of a world independent of the knower is to invite social action intended to take hold of that structure and arrest once and for all the increasingly noted 'negative' effects of mounting interdependence. It is to invite the vision of an ultimate global solution to problems born of a history of fragmented technological solutions. And it is to invite catastrophe as several social units collide in their bids to grasp and wield some allegedly dominant structure toward the realization of their different trajectories of growth.

The second genre is *peace research*. Here the implication is that peace research as a 'technology of peace' or a 'Manhattan Project to end war' may be the most sorrowful of ironies, and not just for the reasons articulated by radical critics of North American peace research. It is not so much a matter of peace research providing a strategy to guide the rich and powerful in their domination of the poor and weak. It is, rather, a matter of technical-rational approaches ultimately contributing to the aggravation of conflict and the mounting of violence *no matter who grasps the 'reins of control.'*

These two implications of the theory kernel — the immanent plan and the immanent critique of technical-rational ideals of research — combine to shape a more positive statement on the role of knowledge-building. *Theory and research aimed toward realizing a world order of reduced violence ought to proceed as a microcosmic, anticipatory realization of the plan itself.* Specifically, it should do two things. First, it should serve as a simulate expression of ongoing social processes intended to anticipate and expose the long-range inadequacies of technical-rational action. That is, it should aim toward *importing the future into the present* by systematically uncovering the ways in which well-meant decisions and actions implicate the future, often shaping dilemmas and crises that the participants neither expect nor want. Second, it should develop means of monitoring relations transcending domains and levels of human activity so as to represent and communicate the extended cross-sectoral and cross-societal implications of local decisions and actions. It should aim, in other words toward *importing the whole into the parts*.

Throughout, to be sure, such an enterprise is continually subject to pressures to surrender its autonomy by convincingly demonstrating its 'relevance'–its capacity to point to the right levers to be pulled or the correct 'manipulables' to be manipulated. Just as surely, the representations or models it produces are continually in danger of being misappropriated as final-lawful statements or as guides to strategic action. And certainly, researchers involved in the study of well-meaning people creating violence-prone social traps will sometimes be tempted to assert that this or that course is the one sure path to peace. Against these tendencies, researchers can only resort to the counter-idea that the appearance of irrelevance and social irresponsibility are not one and the same. In an important sense, striving for responsibility entails the preservation of critical autonomy, and preserving autonomy requires guarding against the reduction of an enterprise to the status of a relevant technology.

B   The Contrary Commitments of Positivist Science

It has been argued that the conceptual framework bears and expresses a dialectical conception of reality. It has been argued, further, that the lateral pressure theory kernel strongly implies a role for theory and research as critical, participatory enterprises. A few moments' reflection on the arguments should reveal still another important implication. In portraying the objective of knowledge-building as importing the future into the present and the whole into the parts, the argument implies the importance of persuasive, unambiguous communication leading toward emergent consensus on truth about social reality. In turn, this consensus view of truth suggests a need for a rational logic in which the ambiguity of generalizing communications can be minimized and potentially persuasive argumentation can be waged regarding candidate generalizing statements. This logic should impose a rational order upon research and communication, and, at the very least, it should assure the operational reproducibility and empirical grounding of theoretical developments that are asserted to be progressive.

In short, all that has been said in this section so far implies the need for *scientific research*. *There is no inconsistency between science, on the one hand, and a dialectically framed, participatory research enterprise, on the other. Nor is there any necessary inconsistency between explicit, systematic modeling — structural modeling included — and the ontological and epistemological arguments of the last few pages.* If anything, these arguments underscore the value of science as an enterprise that poises in continuing tension the seeking of truth, on the one hand, and atttitude of skepticism regarding asssertions of final truth, on the other. If anything, these arguments point to the value of symbolic modeling as a work of abstraction that — in its explicitness, tractability, operational reproducibility, and capacities for the representation of complexity — might help to foster and sustain a kind of criticism-conscious monitoring and communication enterprise that is badly needed.

These assertions of consistency require qualification, however. The ontological and epistemological commitments implicit in the conceptual framework are consistent with the activities of science proper and modeling proper. But these commitments are strangely out of kilter with commitments implicit in the particular ways in which people have come to think about and practice science and modeling. In effect, many social scientists have come to equate science and modeling with positivist science, a dominant version of science that is founded upon atomist or structuralist ontological commitments and technical-rational epistemological commitments. Many social scientists make the equation at the level of their deep, acculturated grammars of thought, with the result that this equation disallows their questioning of ontological and epistemological commitments at the level of explicit language. It is as if these commitments have become part of what D.J. Bem calls a 'non-conscious ideology': 'a set of beliefs and attitudes which [a person] accepts implicitly but which remains outside [his or her] awareness because alternative conceptions of the world remain unimagined . . . [O]nly a very unparochial and intellectual fish is aware that his environment is wet. After all, what else could it be? Such is the nature of a non-conscious ideology.'[9] In these terms, many social scientists swim in a positivist ocean of structuralist ontological commitments and technical-rational epistemological commitments, and they are unaware of the fact because, so immersed, they cannot conceive of reality in any other way.

No elaborate discussion is required to show that positivist social science contains such commitments. A few examples will suffice:

[9] D.J. Bem, *Beliefs, Attitudes, and Human Affairs* (Monterey, California: Brooks/Cole, 1970), p. 89.

The field is repeatedly advised of the necessity of defining concepts as precise 'data containers.'[10] That is, it is widely assumed that scientific progress is founded on the prior, sharp definition of concepts as atomistic units connected to observable aspects of reality by certain rules of correspondence. An individual term and its operational referents are assumed to have meaning in and of themselves and independent of other terms and referents with which they may be theoretically joined. An example is the notion that one might try to measure 'power attributes' of states and then proceed to an examination of the processes in which these power attributes are variables. Other examples are found in the strong inclination among positivist researchers to criticize as unscientific those theoretical arguments that, in using relational concepts, are unable to offer singular, self-contained definitions of key terms. Still others are found in positivist assertions that knowledge claims containing relationally defined concepts are unscientifically tautological.

The field is repeatedly urged to phrase knowledge claims in a falsifiable manner, and the dictum of falsifiability is widely seen to disallow the theorist's assertion that linkages between concepts and measures might be sensitive to historical-contextual change. Thus, suspicion is cast on arguments to the effect that, say, trade-partner concentration as a measure of dependence might be adequate in some periods or contexts but not in others. Such arguments are often disallowed as imposing unscientific qualifications on the falsification process. In the same way, some analysts are inclined to reduce the relational concepts of *dependencia* theory to atomistic, context-free 'data containers,' thereby distorting the original meaning, in order to translate the theory into suitable 'falsifiable' and 'scientific' form.

A widely-shared assumption is that the aim of structural modeling — indeed, all science — is to uncover invariant structural relationships predominating over and accounting for observable change. Accordingly, researchers are predisposed to see cross-sectional and through-time departures from theoretically specified structures as always worrisome, usually surprising, problems that good theory and good research should eventually overcome. Theory and models that allow for structural change but do not purport to explain it by reference

[10] G. Sartori, F. Riggs, and H. Teune, *The Tower of Babel: On Definitions and Analysis of Concepts in the Social Sciences* (Pittsburgh: International Studies Association, 1975).

to a higher-order causal structure — such research is often criticized for the 'absence of invariance.'[11]

What is usually regarded as the 'scientific' study of international relations tends to focus almost exclusively on manifestly variable external relations among manifestly distinct aspects of life. It tends to ignore as beyond science the study of internal relations among aspects; i.e., it neglects those deep, historical relations among aspects upon which the existences of the manifest things depend. The time-honored distinction between 'nation-state' and 'systemic' levels of analysis is a case in point. F.H. Hinsley has argued that the concept of sovereignty, the emergent historical abstraction that formalizes the distinction across levels, could not have taken form 'until the notion of the sovereign power of the individual state had been reconciled with the ethical premises and the political needs of an international community consisting of independent states.'[12] In these terms, neither 'level,' can be imagined apart from the other. The two levels are identical in that they are mutually dependent to this day. Yet since this important traditionalist insight asserts an internal relation across levels, it tends to be ignored in 'scientific' research.

As is widely recognized, 'scientific' research is persistently under pressure to demonstrate its relevance. In turn, this resolves to tendencies (a) to define terms in ways relating directly to immediately apparent, ideally manipulable aspects of life, and (b) to try to uncover structured relationships among these aspects so as to offer valued warning of change and provide accurate, contingent forecasts of the probable consequences of policy interventions. In general, theories, models, and research programs not conforming to these tendencies are susceptible to the charge of 'irrelevance.' Nonconforming researchers and theorists are susceptible to the indictment of a 'purist' social irresponsibility. Generally unimaginable are 'relevant' research and 'responsible' researchers that do not so conform.

Some of the most serious problems confronting cumulative model-building in international relations are meaningful only if one's thinking

---

[11] See for example Mark Levine's critique of Choucri and North's *Nations in Conflict* in Hoole and Zinnes (eds.), op. cit.

[12] See F.H. Hinsley, 'The Concept of Sovereignty and Relations Between States,' *Journal of International Affairs*, Vol. XXI, p. 245 and quoted in John Gerard Ruggie, 'Changing Frameworks of International Collective Behavior,' in Nazli Choucri and Thomas W. Robinson (eds.), *Forecasting in International Relations: Theory, Methods, Problems, Prospects* (San Francisco: W.H. Freeman, 1978), pp. 384–406.

is confined within a structuralist ontology. For example, the problem of 'false prior decomposition' relates to the attempt to integrate knowledge claims of prior segmented research within a larger, more inclusive model. The problem is that prior research, being segmented, is often understood to be based on misspecified models. After all, if prior work were not addressing mistakenly decomposed parts of a not-nearly-decomposable system in the first place, then, under the tutelage of the Ando-Simon theorem,[13] why would one want to join them in a larger model? In turn, since the prior work is based on a false partitioning of reality, the resulting knowledge claims are inherently biased and afford little reliable prior information for the construction of a larger model. The problem is generally posed as one to be overcome. What this line of thinking plainly denies is an important insight afforded by a dialectical conception: false partitioning and resulting bias are true parts of social reality, and strides toward objectivity must start with recognition of this fact.

Many other examples could be given, but the point is clear. The point is not that positivist social science is bad or that those who practice it are empirically wrong in their orientations. No amount of evidence could show this to be the case. On the contrary, the point is only that unquestioning commitments to positivist science entail unquestioning commitments to atomist-structuralist ontologies and technical-rational epistemologies. Phrased in stronger terms, positivist science at once sees itself as the 'end of ideology' and contains a 'nonconscious ideology' that denies realization of the ontological and epistemological commitments implicit in the conceptual framework.

According to that framework, reality is an open-ended, dialectically changing whole. Much of the violence of that reality is attributable to the recurring technical-rational application of knowledge, skills, and capacities to communicate in order to segment, structure, and master reality, physically and intellectually. In these terms, what is known as positivist social science is but a very recent expression of these technical-rational tendencies.[14] And, like other expressions, it has contributed to today's conditions, the 'good' as well as the 'bad' while also contributing

---

[13] See Albert Ando *et al.* (eds.), *Essays on the Structure of Social Science* (Cambridge, Mass.: MIT Press, 1963).

[14] Lest the point be missed: positivist science can be seen and interpreted as an expression of processes included in the framework and is subject to the immanent critique contained in the theory kernel. To the extent that all social science is positivist science, there can be no science of peace.

to a form of progress in ways of thinking and tools of information management and communication.

From the vantage point of the conceptual framework, the questions at this juncture are these: Have these scientific tools reached a stage of development where their limits as instrumentalities of control are beginning to become plain? Can the epistemological and ontological commitments that have long been associated with these tools be subordinated to an alternative vision of the tools' place in reality? Can these scientific tools now be exercised in a criticism-conscious participatory research program to import the future into the present, import the parts into the whole, and expose the limits and implications for violence of each attempt to technologically mobilize resources, solve problems, and exert control? To paraphrase Robert C. North's nontechnocratic plea as a question, is it now time to seize upon the cybernetic revolution and see it through to a fulfilling future? [15]

Like *Nations in Conflict* before it, this study makes a risky bet on affirmative answers to these questions. In effect, it uses techniques born of positivist social science, but it tries also to subordinate technique to the ontological and epistemological commitments implied by the conceptual framework and most especially by the lateral pressure theory kernel. It tries to exploit the fact that, just as a structuralist conception of reality at once contains and problematizes an atomist conception, so also does a dialectical conception contain and problematize a structuralist conception. It tries to exploit the fact that, in the same way, a commitment to a critical and participatory modeling enterprise can contain and problematize technical-rational thought.

Yet such statements of intention are far more easily made than realized. What is needed is what might be called a normative research philosophy. What is needed is a rationally reconstructed philosophy of research that can (*a*) discipline research choices, sustain operational reproducibility, guide the use of empirical techniques, reduce the ambiguity of communications, and, at the same time, (*b*) sustain a criticism-conscious effort to prevent the reduction of the enterprise to one more expression of a technical-rational search for closure. The next section tries to chart out such a research philosophy.

[15] See Robert C. North, *The World That Could Be* (New York: Norton, 1978). p. 143.

II NORMATIVE RESEARCH PHILOSOPHY

A normative research philosophy is a rationally reconstructed logic of inquiry. It is a logic reconstructed as a kind of ideal, a model, that anticipates recurring research dilemmas, affords some research guidance, and, in principle, helps to sustain the consistency and rationality of research practice. Just as no model should be equated with the reality it represents, a reconstructed logic is not to be confused with researchers' actual logics-in-use. Instead, a reconstructed research philosophy is intended to be a close approximation of 'good' research practice. Like other kinds of models, it is to be valued because it is here, at the level of abstracted reasoning, that argumentation as to the adequacy and rationality of competing approaches and practices takes place.

Among scientific students of international relations, debate concerning appropriate research philosophy has often proceeded by way of appeals to competing authorities. Thus, the names of Hempel, Rudner, Popper, Salmon, Lakatos, and others are frequently invoked in defense of this or that research practice — or, regrettably more often, in criticism of others' practices. Researchers engaged in debate can invoke Hempel in favor of parsimony, and they can summon Lakatos against such 'esthetic criteria' of science. They can invoke early Popper in favor of falsifying theory on the basis of critical tests, and they can call upon Kuhn to remind us of normal scientists' tenacious resistance to the refutational power of counterevidence. Rare in international relations is the research-philosophical debate that questions the ontological and epistemological foundations of the authorities invoked.

The research logic-in-use reflected in this study has not involved a rejection of these authorities. Rather, it can be seen to represent a *pragmatic* interpretation of their guidance from the standpoint of the ontological and epistemological commitments presented in the previous section.

From that standpoint, the somewhat presumptuous position taken here is that 'authoritative' philosophers of science have principally addressed *natural science* and in so doing have found it convenient to presuppose — and impose upon science — a structuralist ontology. The presupposition is convenient because, while all reality is here assumed to involve the dialectical motion and change of structures, natural scientists tend to focus on phenomena whose structures are very, very slowly changing. So slowly do these 'natural' structures change, in fact, that they can be presupposed to be stationary, and the scientific attempt to uncover them can be equated with the seeking after invariant or eternal *laws* of nature.

From the same standpoint, what is different about social as opposed to natural reality is a quantitative difference with qualitative implications: the dialectical motion of social reality is, relatively speaking, accelerated. This means that the structures of social reality are, and must be conceived to be, susceptible to much more frequent change. Indeed, they can be and often are susceptible to change in reflection of developments in scientific techniques and knowledge claims. For the social sciences, this also means that (*a*) the authoritative philosopher's convenient assumption regarding structural stationarity is rendered problematical, (*b*) the equation of science's rational goal with the uncovering of structures-*qua*-laws is called into question, and (*c*) what research guidance might be contained in philosophers' reconstructed logics is subject to critical reinterpretation.

This section attempts to reconstruct the logic-in-use reflected in this study. At the outset, pretensions to the effect that this reconstruction represents a complete, well-refined normative research philosophy must be disavowed. Only three things can be claimed for the reconstruction to follow. First, it is a model that approximates the rational logic of research pursued in this study, and as such, it makes that logic explicit and susceptible to valued criticism. Second, as a logic, it reflects an attempt to learn from 'authoritative' philosophers' struggles with issues of operational reproducibility, falsifiability, conceptualization, and so on; but it also reflects an attempt to condition philosophers' arguments within this study's dialectical understanding of reality and participatory predispositions toward the role of science. Third, despite its flaws, it can be claimed that the reconstruction to follow is generalizable beyond this study and that it is at least somewhat more responsive than 'authoritative' philosophies to the goals and problems of participatory social science in general and criticism-conscious peace research in particular.

The argument begins with the articulation of the goal of this study — a goal that is asserted to be the appropriate goal of all peace research. Next, it proceeds to the conceptualization of a logic of empirical progress in research. Finally, it briefly considers the questions of gauging empirical adequacy.

A   The Goal of Peace Research

All rational research philosophies start from an assumption about the goal of science. So does the present reconstruction. The goal is not the uncovering of laws, however. It is far more ambitious than that. Indeed, the ambitiousness of the goal dictates the rather audacious inclusiveness of the marginal heading, the goal of *peace research*. The goal is not just the aim of this study or of one research program. Measured against the goal described below, this study can claim to be, at best, a miniscule contribution. If substantial strides are to be made toward its realization, the goal must first become the goal of transnational peace research generally, and then it must become interiorized as a part of human aspirations generally. Admittedly, as things now stand, it is most unlikely that the following goal will soon be so widely shared. But if Marvin Harris is correct in suggesting that 'the rational response to bad odds is to try harder,'[16] then the peace researcher should not be faulted in pursuing so ambitious a goal.

The goal is framed by the belief that there exists an enormous but possibly closable gap between two visions of the human condition on a global scale. On the one hand, there is the human condition as it has long existed, now exists, and, in all probability, will for long persist. It might be described as follows: The *actual* condition is violence-prone, exploitative, unequal in the distribution of valuables, and environmentally destructive; and violence, exploitation, inequality, and environmental destruction are essential to its dynamic reproduction through time. In its expressed values, this condition tends to decouple concepts of individual fulfillment from concepts of social development. It denies the realization of human potential. On the other hand, there is the condition that would be realized were the potentialities of humankind — individual and society–fully expressed: The *preferred* condition is characterized by equality, justice, reproductive social norms interiorizing the actualization of humanity's potential within concepts of individual fulfillment, the free flow of information, and shared consciousness of the intimate interconnection of humanity and nature. Importantly, this condition also exhibits peaceful means for the creative resolution of emergent conflicts and the absence of institutionalized force and violence. Against this background, the normative proposition underlying peace research is that the latter condition is to be preferred over the former. The objective proposition is that the latter condition exists within the former: immanent within existing actualities are possibilities for change toward the preferred 'world that could be.'[17] The actual can become the desirable. Thus framed, the goal of peace research can be stated. It is to contribute to the closing of the gap between the two visions of the human condition, the actual and the preferred.

This goal can be more sharply stated in light of the ontological and

---

[16] Marvin Harris, *Cannibals and Kings* (New York: Random House, Inc.), p. 292.
[17] From the title of North's book, op. cit.

epistemological arguments of Section I. For purposes of presentation this goal can be partitioned into five aspects, each of which represents some specific *tasks* of peace research. To be sure, the statement of peace research 'tasks' as part of the peace research 'goal' might seem to conflate means and ends. But as one will have inferred from Section I, the presumption of a final distinction between means and ends is a technical-rational contrivance to which peace research should not be bound. The 'end' of peace research is the undertaking of tasks that will help to make the tasks themselves a normal part of life. The five tasks are:

(1) *Draw upon and synthesize available prior theory at several levels of analysis to explore, uncover, and criticize the dynamics contributing to the reproduction of violence-prone, exploitative, unequal, and environmentally destructive conditions.* This implies an attempt to discern the interconnections between proximate (and often apparent) causes of 'negative outcomes' and the deeper longer-term, less manageable processes that are usually taken as givens and that usually escape criticism thereby. Too, this implies an attempt to identify interconnections across sectors of activity that are usually assumed to be structurally unrelated and across levels of analysis that are often treated as distinct. Only within a far-reaching synthetic approach such as this is it possible to discern the full reproductive potential of a complex system.

(2) *Explore and identify the dilemmas and obstacles confronting participants seeking to manage these processes and realize important aims, such as peace or equality, under existing conditions.* This includes, in general, the identification of the ways in which well-intended solutions to problems apparent within 'part' of the system — at a particular level or in a particular sector — tend to contribute to the recurrence of problems, dilemmas, and even crises in other 'parts.' Somewhat more specifically, this involves exposing and discrediting programs, practices, beliefs, and institutions that mobilize human energies toward high aims or ephemeral purposes while in fact contributing to the reproduction of a system that denies the actualization of human potential.

(3) *Suggest practical measures that might enhance the possibilities of transforming the system in preferred directions.* The form, moment, and point of departure within the system for the effective exercise of system-change strategies is always a difficult question requiring provisional answers. In complex social systems, participants situated at putative points of control seldom have effective

decision latitude sufficient to permit more than the reproduction of the system itself. Institutions charged with system management responsibilities seldom can promote deep structural change. Actions that might yield consequential change at one moment in the life of a system might prove ineffective or counterproductive at another. And concepts developed for describing, explaining, and managing relations within existing social structures are often incapable of telling the story of these same structures' historical emergence and future transcendence. Thus, the task of 'suggesting practical measures toward change' requires not only an understanding of the system as it 'is,' but also a conceptualization of the system that (*a*) embraces what 'has been,' 'is not,' and 'could be' in the 'is' and thereby (*b*) leaves room for creative action and recombinations of activities among participants at several levels and across several sectors. 'Practical suggestions' should include not only prescriptions of official policy but also plans and programs involving science, communication, education, economics, and other activities among people in general. 'Practical suggestions' should themselves be weighed in terms of the social costs that each form of change might entail; for example, alternatives to system change through widespread nuclear war, global conquest, massive economic collapse, and other forms of wholesale human misery should be sought.

(4) *Begin to develop open, continuously correctable means of monitoring the international system, gauging its performance relative to preferred relationships, identifying transformation possibilities, and critically assessing the likely local, global, and multi-sectoral consequences attending various alternatives.* This task effectively represents a call for the development and extension of open, criticism-conscious means to sustain the service of tasks one, two, and three into the future. It is another way of expressing Robert North's nontechnocratic call to 'exploit the cybernetic revolution.' The task is to construct a capacity for importing the future into the present, fragmented information regarding geographical and sectoral 'parts' into an informational 'whole,' and, through cross-national and multi-sectoral communication, the 'whole' into the 'parts.'

(5) *Undertake these tasks in ways that are scientific and operationally reproducible.* The ideal of science is to be aspired to because, in principle if not always in practice, science entails a continuous

tension among (*a*) a commitment to the rational development of intersubjectively shared beliefs converging on objective knowledge of reality, (*b*) a commitment to the evaluation of knowledge claims in terms of (relative) empirical adequacy, and (*c*) a resistance to methodological closure and claims of final, unassailable truth. The generativity of science − its capacity to produce new knowledge claims that become widely shared − is partly due to this tension. The generativity of science is also due to its requirement of operational reproducibility: the imposition of communicable restrictions on concepts, allowable empirical referents, internally consistent logics of inquiry, and generalizing knowledge claims such that all of these can be understood, interpreted, tested, generalized, and recombined in meaningful ways. Thus represented, the objective of employing scientific approaches is a necessary concomitant of the other four objectives, and scientific practice does not always entail the use of quantitative techniques. However, quantitative techniques are often very helpful, even necessary, where complexity surpasses the capacities of ordinary language to meet requirements of operational reproducibility.

Viewed in this context, the present study can be said to represent a very modest and partial attempt to begin to perform these tasks and contribute to the realization of this goal. It is a partial attempt in that, as in much of North American peace research, it focuses principally upon one dimension of the gap between the actual and the preferred. Not exploitation, not inequality, not environmental destruction, but the recurrence of organized intersocietal conflict and violence is the principal focus − the point of departure for this study. Almost certainly, the choice of this point of departure and not others precludes initial insights that others might afford. However, the choice does not necessarily imply an exclusive concern for 'negative peace.' Nor does it necessarily imply that the results will equate peace with pacification. Within a reality dialectically conceived, any serious attempt to pursue the forementioned tasks from the vantage point of the world's violence-proneness must lead inescapably to a concern for the interconnections between physical violence, on the one hand, and inequality, exploitation, and environmental destruction on the other.

This study is a limited and partial attempt in yet a second sense. Among the five tasks distinguished above, the bulk of this book may seem to attend least of all to the third, the suggestion of practical measures that might enhance the possibilities of transforming the system in preferred directions. Yet a few moments' thought should indicate that, while policy prescriptions of the ordinary sort are missing, this task is undertaken here in at least a limited way. In an important sense, this appendix represents a set of 'practical suggestions' for research that, if taken seriously, criticized, and improved upon, *might* enhance the capacity of science to participate in the desirable transformation of international relations. In effect, the implicit theoretical notion is that social scientists are at least potentially more autonomous and criticism-conscious than other participants in social reality and, as such, are likely to be somewhat more sensitive and responsive to attempts to realize this goal.

It must be stressed that there is nothing radically new about the goal just presented. To look upon the research corpus of Lewis F. Richardson,[18] for example, is to be struck by the vision of a man making uncertain choices, self-questioningly applying available techniques, and moving from vantage point to vantage point in order to perform the tasks and serve the goal outlined above. Richardson was far less interested in unraveling the laws of social dynamics than he was in exploring, uncovering, and criticizing the ways in which people, setting out to master and control their futures, surrender their futures to processes they create but cannot control. He wanted to portray the deeper dilemmas that people might generate and confront but cannot readily anticipate or even perceive. He wanted to suggest practical measures for peaceful change. And he wanted to do all of this in an openly criticism-conscious, correctable, and empirically grounded manner. Richardson, the leading exemplar to today's peace research, was a critical social scientist. In honoring his legacy, peace research might be captivated by the important insights expressed in his models, but it should also be emancipated by a commitment to the pursuit of his goal.

B   A Logic of Empirical Progress

The multidimensionality of the goal just presented makes progress hard to gauge. How does one know when research is in some sense adequately performing the forementioned tasks and pursuing the goal? How does one know whether a research program or practice or stage represents a progressive or degenerative departure from previous efforts? How do or should researchers in general reach these judgments so as to decide whether or not this or that supposed scientific stride is worth pursuing further?

The answers to these questions advanced here are highly tentative and,

[18] See especially his *Arms and Insecurity* (Pittsburgh: Boxwood Press, 1960).

of necessity, open to criticism and revision. The basic argument has already been alluded to in Section I. It is that the scientific progress of a research program should be gauged in terms of successive efforts to resolve critical tensions emerging out of the program's theoretical vantage point upon reality, where a vantage point contains a 'problematic' and a 'theory kernel' that purportedly accounts for the emergence, reproduction, and possible passing of the problematic itself. The argument is necessarily general because the goal described above might be decomposed into problematics of insecurity, global inequality, environmental destruction, human alienation, inadequate or uncritical research, and so on, and because a probably infinite number of theory kernels might be brought to bear as candidate explanations. Given a dialectical conception of reality, no vantage point can be assumed to have a monopoly on truth. Before further elaborating the argument, the terms 'problematic' and 'theory kernel' should be defined.

A *problematic* is defined as an abstracted representation of some aspect of the gap between the actual and preferred human condition. As in this study, for instance, one might focus on the 'security problematique.' Alternatively, one might focus on a 'social scientific problematic,' which is defined in terms of the gap between what social science is, on the one hand, and what it desirably could be, on the other. One might focus on the gap between the desirable ideal of human beings sharing state-transcending identitites as humans and the unhappy actuality of human beings defining much of what they are in terms of their separate national affiliations. One might focus on an environmental problematic of weakly restrained movement toward recurring 'tragedies of the commons,' a problematic recognizable in terms of the gap between this actual condition and the possible condition of a social order interiorizing the identity of humanity and nature. Whatever the specific problematic, however, it is recognized from the outset as an abstraction. It is seen as an abstraction whose existence as a part of reality cannot be adequately understood except in reference to other aspects, other problematics, that are or might be defined. A problematic is, then, an anchoring point of departure. Its function is to focus research on the question: How and why did the problematic take form? How and why does it persist? What are the structured processes by which it is reproduced? How and under what conditions might it be transcended?

The second essential element of a program's vantage point is its *theory kernel*. A theory kernel is anlogous to what Lakatos[19] calls the 'hard-core' of a research program. A theory kernel is the core set of presumably

[19] See Imre Lakatos, 'Falsification and the Methodology of Scientific Research Programmes,' in Imre Lakatos and Alan Musgrave (eds.), *Criticism and the Growth of Knowledge* (Cambridge, England: Cambridge University Press, 1970).

augmentable explanations — the initial 'answers' to the questions raised by and about the problematic. To assign to an explanation the status of a theory kernel is to say, in effect, that the explanation will be treated as *unassailable*, at least for some substantial period of time. On it the researcher will 'disallow attack.' And no amount of evidence can lead the researcher to reject it, at least so long as the program progresses. Unlike a Lakatosian 'hard-core,' however, a theory kernel must pass an important test to be assigned this status. *Above all else, the researcher must believe the theory kernel to be non-ahistorical* (or at least, less ahistorical than other imaginable explanations).[20] The researcher must believe that the concepts and knowledge claims contained in the theory kernel do not fix upon some historically dependent set of regularities and structurations. Thus, a theory of interstate alliances might contain valuable insights, but it would also represent an inadmissible theory kernel because it ahistorically leaves the origins of the units of analysis unquestioned. In the same way, a bureaucratic politics 'paradigm,' while not to be ignored, fails the test of non-ahistoricity when cast in the light of anthropological, sociological, historical, and other studies on the origins and functions of bureaucracy. Among the few bodies of theory that persistently (but by no means always) produces candidate non-ahistorical explanations is general systems theory, with its predilections in favor of cross-level generalizability.

Together, these two elements of a program's vantage point, the problematic and the theory kernel, define a critical tensions. The tension exists because the theory kernel offers a partial accounting of the problematic's emergence, reproduction, and possible passing, but stops far short of providing a complete accounting. In fact, the operational linkages between many of the kernel's key terms and empirical referents may not be completely drawn. Much of the critical variability evident in descriptions of the history of the problematic may be left unexplained. And superior accountings of observable variability over some periods may be offered by a variety of alternative theories that are more ahistorical in character. Such gaps define critical tensions precisely because

---

[20] The double-negated 'non-ahistorical' is deliberately used in lieu of the more ambiguous 'historical.' An ahistorical argument is one that falsely generalizes some historically momentary, dependent regularities throughout all history, including the future. Its truth is limited to a certain condition whose historical origins it does not explain. A non-ahistorical argument contains generalizing knowledge claims that are not historically dependent. A knowledge claim is more or less ahistorical to the degree that it gives explanatory priority to less or more enduring, less or more autonomous regularities and structurations. Can one every say with certainty that a given assertion is non-ahistorical? No. Can one say that one assertion is less ahistorical than another? Yes, and the saying is very much a process of causal inference.

the theory kernel's explanation is taken to be unassailable. The tension animates research as energies focus on the closing of such gaps.

Research progress involves movement toward the closing of such gaps through creative synthesis.[21] That is, each progressive step involves an attempt to sharpen and improve the explanatory power of the theory kernel by (*a*) bringing it into confrontation with other partially corroborated theoretical traditions concerning the problematic as defined and (*b*) identifying those specific statements of the tradition that, from the point of view of the theory kernel, appear disturbingly unwarranted. So far, this is only to identify a component of the forementioned critical tension. But the process of synthesis goes further. In effect, one chooses to assume that a given tradition's statements, although seemingly unwarranted, are nonetheless rational reflections of some restricted set of unspoken, historically wedded presuppositions underpinning the tradition itself. Attention then turns to explicating these presuppositions and to interpreting them from the presumably less ahistorical perspective of the theory kernel. The result is rarely merely an additive revision of the kernel. Most often, it involves an interpretation of some of the kernel's key terms as possibly finding expression within and through the aspects of reality the contending traditions portray. Usually it involves a reinterpretation and relativization of contending traditions' knowledge claims as mutually contextualizing reflections of deep historical processes. Nearly always it leads to an expanded interpretation of the problematic — as new dimensions of life are seen to be related to it — and the generation of new critical tensions between the revised kernel and the revised problematic.

In these terms, *each progressive step toward closing the gap and resolving critical tensions leads to a detection of new gaps and new research animating tensions.* The vantage point of the program is thus widened in response, and still additional theoretical traditions become relevant to the continuing process of synthesis.

Though the process is straightforwardly stated, the choices involved are far from mechanical or automatic. At each juncture, the programmatic researcher confronts a very wide variety of contending theoretical tradi-

---

[21] Those familiar with his work will detect the strong influence of Jürgen Habermas on my arguments to follow (as well as some of my arguments above). See his *Knowledge and Human Interests*, translated by Jeremy J. Shapiro (Boston: Beacon Press, 1971); *Toward a Rational Society*, translated by Jeremy J. Shapiro (Boston: Beacon Press, 1970). *Theory and Practice*, translated by John Viertel (Boston: Beacon Press, 1973); *Legitimation Crisis* (Boston: Beacon Press, 1975); and 'A Postscript to *Knowledge and Human Interests*' in *Philosophy of the Social Sciences*, Vol. III (1973), pp. 157-85.

tions that are potentially relevant to this or that aspect of the gap between a theory kernel and a problematic. The majority of these traditions address the world as it currently appears — some of the regularities associated with the reproduction of contemporary conditions. Other traditions address the counterfactual reality of the might-have-been-but-was-not and the could-be-but-is-not. And still others stress the regularities and processes of transformation that preceded the emergence of modern conditions. The researcher cannot presume any of these traditions to be irrelevant to scientific progress. Yet obviously synthesis cannot inolve a single logical implosion of ideas from every direction. The question is, *in what order or sequence are contending theoretical traditions to be confronted and synthesized.*

A number of possible answers present themselves. One possible decision rule is to confront the tradition whose incorporation within the theory kernel would do most to close the gap between kernel and problematic, at least insofar as this gap can be measured in terms of empirical fit to some available data. Another is to confront the tradition whose incorporation might in some sense maximize the ratio of generalizability to parsimony. Another is to confront the tradition that seems most expressive of researchers' social values. Still another is to confront traditions that might do most to reveal where and how social interventions might be effectively exercised. For reasons that will become evident in a moment, none of these answers is correct.

At this juncture the rational answer would seem to be this: *programmatic researchers confront theoretical traditions in a sequence roughly corresponding to their 'relative non-ahistoricity,' as it were.* That is, they look upon competing theoretical traditions that afford partially corroborated insights into the gap between kernel and problematic, and they attempt to discern which among them contains assumptions, propositions and generalizing knowledge claims that are in principle least dependent upon patterns and structurations described in other traditions. To borrow Lakatos' term, a program's 'positive heuristics' will indicate the early confrontation of those 'least dependent' traditions and the late confrontation of 'more dependent' traditions. They will, for example, indicate the postponement of consideration of traditions focusing on interstate diplomatic negotiations until traditions accounting for the emergence of states in possible interaction are considered. In the same way, anthropological traditions dealing with intersocietal cooperation and conflict might take priority over traditions addressing interstate arms races or rivalry in general. For while the latter patterns surely skew patterns identified by the former, there can be no mistaking the fact that interstate arms races and rivalry represent special and emergent historical adaptations of processes that anthropologists have sought to depict.

The reason for such a decision rule should be clear. Each successive step in a research program involves synthesis between a current theory kernel and an existing theoretical tradition giving rise to a revised and augmented theory kernel. At each step, the theory kernel is assumed to be a dominant pole of this dialectical relation. In the main, the specific tradition confronted is assumed to be subordinated, sublated, and relativized within the theory kernel, and not the other way round. This assumption holds, though, only insofar as the theory kernel's claim to non-ahistoricity holds. Should the kernel contain statements that are or can be shown to be historically dependent upon patterns and processes articulated by other traditions, then to interpret these latter traditions within the context of the theory kernel is to profoundly distort them. Worse, it is to reduce the entire research program to a dependent expression of a falsely generalized historical moment. Thus, to the extent that the knowledge claims of one tradition can be said to be less ahistorical than those of another, the former is to be confronted first.

Once again, such judgments are not easily made. Errors are likely to be frequent. There are no hard and fast formulas for detecting which among competing traditions is in some sense 'least dependent.' Indeed, as repeatedly expressed above, the notion that any one aspect of reality — any one theoretical domain — could ever be finally independent of all others is an illusion. Yet this fact does not prevent the researcher from alleging or believing that one form or kind of dependency relation might be stronger than others. It does not prevent the researcher from assuming or seeking to uncover asymmetrical relations of dependence. In short, such judgments are possible and necessary to scientific progress, even if they are susceptible to serious error.

How, then, are errors to be detected and corrected? The answer, still very tentative, can be lodged at two levels. One is the level of the individual program. The other is the level of the multi-program scientific community.

At the level of *individual program*, the answer comes in the form of criteria of scientific progress. In a way resembling (but not identical to) Lakatos' now classic formulation, the criteria apply to a program's sequence of evolving models, and not to the models produced, taken individually. Consider a sequence of models — say, M_1, M_2, M_3, and so on — where each model represents the program's current theory kernel. As addressed to this series, the criteria of progress apply to the program's *shifts* from model to model — say, from M_1 to M_2.

Specifically, the criteria can be subdivided into notions of 'theoretical progress' and 'empirical progress.' A shift from M_1 to M_2 is 'theoretically progressive' if, as compared to M_1, M_2 does *two* things. First, it should have some 'excess empirical content' in the sense of resolving some of the contradictions existing between M_1 and some partially corroborated propositions from other traditions bearing upon the problematic. It should predict to some 'new fact' in terms of some previously unrecognized, historically-wedded relation among seemingly discrete propositions and oberservations. Some of the 'gap' between kernel and problematic should thereby be 'filled in.' Second, it should also expose and sharpen the depiction of contradictions between the revised theory kernel and other propositions bearing on the problematic. In this way, the theoretically progressive program, while always 'moving toward closure,' is always driven to expand its vantage point. A shift from M_1 to M_2 is additionally said to be 'empirically progressive' if and only if the excess empirical content of M_2 is partially corroborated with reference to empirical evidence. That is, at least some of the evidence previously anomolous to M_1 but accounted for within the propositions of another competing tradition should now be consistent with M_2 and susceptible or meaningful interpretation within the revised theory kernel.

To use Lakatos's terminology with revised meaning, a research program's problem shift is to be accepted as 'scientific' only if it is at least theoretically progressive. If it fails to *both* (*a*) have excess empirical content and (*b*) point to new research animating critical tensions, then it is 'pseudo-scientific.) *All programs exhibiting pretensions to final closure — that are not motivated by a more or less continuous generation of critical tensions to explore beyond previous research boundaries — are therefore pseudo-scientific.* In addition, a research program that is theoretically progressive and hence scientific is recognized as progressive overall only if its problem-shifts are 'empirically progressive.' A program may be theoretically progressive and scientific, but if its problem-shifts are not also empirically progressive in the forementioned sense of finding partial corroboration, then it is a degenerating scientific research program.

Such criteria do not guarantee the infallibility of a research program. They do not assure that every choice taken will be either wise or correct. They are, as it were, *tests of time*. Generally speaking, a program that synthesizes relatively ahistorical propositions within its theory kernel at an early stage will advance toward precipitous closure more rapidly than programs that do not. Such a program will at some point begin to be incapable of generating meaningful contradictions between its own theory kernel and other traditions that bear upon the problematic. It may be reduced to simply denying the relevance of other traditions or to restricting its definition of the problematic so that its kernel, and it alone, can apply. For example, some of the argumentation by balance of power theorists regarding the implications of interdependence reflects such tendencies. They are sure signs of closure in a degenerate pseudo-science. Yet such signs are only detectable with time.

At the level of the *scientific community*, errors are detected and corrected through the interaction of contending scientific programs. The word 'contending' should be taken quite literally. For while each research program has its own theory kernel and its own problematic, each also is a 'scientific' program, which means several things. First, the vantage point of each is understood to be revisable, as its theory kernel is re-interpreted through synthesis and its abstracted problematic is given expanded meaning. Second, being scientific, each is continuously driven toward the generation of new critical tensions between the theory kernel and the propositions of other traditions *or programs* that might bear upon the expanded problematic. Third, each program invests its future in the assumption that its theory kernel is non-ahistorical. Thus, any one scientific program is always in contention with all other programs. As each expands its vantage point and comes into contradiction with propositions contained in other programs, each is disposed to interpret and synthesize the theory kernels of other programs as ahistorical reflections of its own. The battle is a running battle. Each program attempts to empirically corroborate the version of synthesis in which the other's theory kernel is sublated and given revised and relativized meaning within its own now expanded vantage point. For the triumphant program, superior corroboration does not mean the end of the struggle. It means, instead that it must move on to the confrontation of yet other traditions and programs. For the vanquished, its sublation means either its sub-ordination to the victorious program or its retreat to closure and the status of a pseudo-scientific ideology.

This discussion suggests that the classic issue of falsification can be appraised at two levels, within individual programs and among them. Within an individual research program, one can follow Lakatos in saying that any model, M_2, falsifies its predecessors, M_1, if the development of M_2 represents a theoretically and empirically progressive problem-shift. Here it is essential to note that within a program, no model is ever falsified until a 'better' one is developed. Yet given the dialectical char-acter of social reality, one must necessarily allow for a second level of falsification: falsification among competing programs addressing dif-ferent aspects of reality from competing and expanding vantage points. Here, at the second level, one program (P_2) may falsify elements of another (P_1) if P_2 engages in a theoretically and empirically progressive problem-shift partially corroborating the claim that putatively non-ahistorical elements of P_1's theory kernel are in fact historically dependent relations. An entire Program P_1 is falsified by the problem-shift undertaken in another program, P_2, however, if and only if P_2's problemshift involves the synthesis of a revised, corroborated theory kernel accounting for *all* of the corroborated empirical content of P_1's original kernel. Since for P_2 this might mean the premature synthesis of some of P_1's most historically dependent propositions, and since this would tend to impose premature closure upon P_2, *attempts to completely falsify other programs are unlikely and unwise.* In fact, programs such as P_1 that are partially falsified may live on, as it were, as vital technical (not scientific) programs intended to manage those aspects of reality that they ahistorically address (much as Newtonian physics lives on and retains relevance for engineers dealing with problems close to the earth). However, only the partially falsify*ing* P_2 proceeds as a science— a science in which every statement emerging out of P_1 is problematized and susceptible to criticism.

C Gauging Empirical Adequacy

Quite evidently, the reconstructed research philosophy does not go as far as some people might like. It stops far short of providing a rigorous set of rules to guide research choices. In particular, it underscores the importance of empirical corroboration, but it does not offer any hard and fast rules as to how the relative empirical adequacy of successive or contending theoretical developments ought to be assessed. This question is left an open one—as properly it should be. In methodology as in substantive theory, closure is something always to be sought but hopefully never achieved.

As suggested in Chapter 2, empirical analysis is essentially an interpretational enterprise wherein questions of fit and invariance are subordinated to issues of the interpretational and heuristic power of theory. Generally speaking, a theory may be said to find corroboration if it can be shown to orient the development of models (verbal as well as quantitative) which, when applied to historical data, order empirical results in ways that are interpretable within the context of theory — and without the appending of *ad hoc* terms. Uneven fit cross-sectionally or over time or variance in structural relationships empirically inferred can both be a basis for empirical corroboration to the extent that the unevenness and variance are interpretable within the prior theory.

To be sure, one may object that 'interpretability' is in some sense a weak test. One might urge that results should be predictable on the basis of prior theory. But interpretability is not a weak test. In fact, it calls for the 'mutual predictability' or consistency of results. And when relational concepts are involved, the test of pre-empirical prediction may be asking the impossible. When relational concepts are involved, as they must be, one seeks to interpret how results help to locate dominant relationships in a system and how, once located, they implicate other relationships elsewhere. Prior to empirical analysis, one often cannot readily discern how dominant relationships are configured, and hence one cannot readily predict to other relationships that are theoretically contingent upon these configurations.

Moreover, the reliance upon interpretational power as a 'test' of theory is further buttressed by a concern for heuristic power. That is, a theory has heuristic power if it orients the construction of models whose empirical analysis produces results that uncover or sharpen the depiction of new research puzzles or further avenues of productive theoretical synthesis. This emphasis on heuristic power derives from the 'other side' of the two-sided definition of empirical progress given earlier: an empirically progressive theoretical development should expose and sharpen the depiction of contradictions between the revised theory and other propositions from other traditions bearing on the problematic addressed. In these terms, a theory (including theories of the counterfactual) has heuristic power if models constructed in its light order at least some empirical results in ways that unambiguously are not readily interpretable within the theory but in principle could be made interpretable were the theory expanded to embrace and relativize propositions from competing traditions. As implied by the arguments put forth earlier, a theory may demonstrate interpretational power, but the absence of heuristic power suggests closure and the degrading of a program to the status of a pseudo-science.

It is necessary to stress once again that questions of the interpretational and heuristic power of theory are 'tests' of time. Quick and decisive tests are the stuff of technology, of appropriation, and of war. But there is simply no such thing as a quick and decisive test among rational scientists.

III   THE RESEARCH PROGRESSION

What has been said so far has been abstract in the extreme. But the abstractions are important. For the critical tensions outlined in Section I frame the normative research philosophy just sketched; in turn, this reconstructed philosophy approximates the rational logic framing the three-stage research progression leading to the general model; and that progression lends context to the empirical analysis presented in the text. This section briefly outlines that progression.

It would be desirable to offer something more than outline. The ideal of operational reproducibility exerts a strong pull toward the presentation of a complete accounting of every research step — the blunders toward dead ends as well as the strides that are seen to have been somehow successful. In fact, for those readers who desire a more thorough accounting, a lengthy research monograph is available upon request from the Program for International Political Economy Research at the University of Southern California. It is entitled, 'The General Model of the Sino-Soviet-American Triangle: A Record of a Three-Stage Modeling Progression.'[22] Not even this monograph catalogues every research step, however. In terms of time and money, it is impossible to do so via the printed page. It is a regrettable fact of life that scientists have not yet reached the stage where our technologies of communication permit us to regularly record, transnationally disseminate, and mutually access and criticize all (or even the most important) aspects of one another's modeling work in progress. More correctly, such technologies are available (TROLL is one), but it is a regrettable fact of life that those positioned to economically support the transnational implementation of such technologies do not yet see it as rational to do so.

As outlined below, the three-stage modeling progression retraced the framework's sequence of presentation from unilateral dynamics of growth, through bilateral dynamics of rivalry, to multilateral dynamics of balance of power. In each stage, only those propositions from the framework relevant to that stage were experimentally considered; and the results of any one stage were then taken as part of the prior information for ensuing stages. As in the framework, the progression was cumulative. The first stage produced a unilateral process model. The second stage built upon the first to produce a unilateral/bilateral process model. The third stage built upon the first and second to produce a unilateral/ bilateral/multilateral process model — the general model. At each stage, empirical results were interpreted in light of the framework on the basis of interpretational and heuristic power. The aim was not to maximize fit or invariance but to obtain robust and theoretically interpretable parameter estimates that would also highlight the empirical gaps to be potentially accounted for in ensuing stages.

---

[22] The interested reader should write to the Program for International Political Economy Research, University of Southern California, University Park, Los Angeles, California 90007.

The reasoning behind this order of research is twofold. First, owing to the relational character of key concepts and the weakness of prior theory, confrontations with data were necessary in order to inform specification. Without some considerable experimentation, one could never know the extent to which the results being interpreted would be sensitive to different measures and functional forms allowed within the latitude of prior theory. Yet, if research were to sustain discipline and limit experimental possibilities of any moment to tractable proportions, it would be necessary to approach the problem developmentally. Second, the particular order of research was theoretically guided. It moved sequentially from theoretically robust long-term dynamics of growth and expansion through the theoretically emergent processes of rivalry and balance of power. It moved, in other words, from consideration of theoretically less ahistorical processes toward the consideration of historically dependent relationships. In this way, moreover, it was assured that the strictest empirical tests would be leveled against those relationships specified the earliest: those relationships relating to dynamics of growth and expansion. Since these relationships, once specified in the first stage, were unaltered in later stages, the hypothesis that they are in fact robust in the face of emergent bilateral and multilateral processes was open to empirically grounded questioning in the second and third stages.

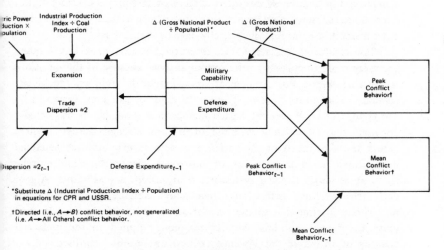

Figure A.1   A Unilateral model

The model resulting from the first stage of the analysis, the *unilateral stage*, is shown in Figure A.1. Because the analysis concentrated on exclusively unilateral relationships during this stage, the model relates attribute, capability, and behavioral variables for only one actor. The operating premise, relaxed in later stages, was that a nation's beahvior is solely attributable to sources within the nation. Accordingly, the analysis of bilateral intersections and bilateral provocations was postponed, and the unilateral model's endogenous variables included only expansion, military capability, normal conflict and cooperation behavior, and thresholds of violence.

At this stage, the Sino-Soviet American triangle was viewed in terms of a coincidence of three independent unilateral models. But here, for reasons discussed in Chapter 2, the attempt was made to specify relationships that are uniform across all three actors, dyads, and directed dyads. Consequently, the same model was maintained for all three actors.

This model did not spring forth, full blown as it were, from pretheoretical propositions pertaining to unilateral relationships. Instead, like the overall general model toward which it is a step, the unilateral process model is a product of considerable experimentation with alternative measures, functional forms, equations, and parameter estimation strategies. Throughout this experimentation, it was necessary to keep in mind the possible roles of these relationships within a larger system. This meant, for example, using instrumental variable/two-stage least squares substitution for both the lagged endogenous and military capability terms. Similarly, this awareness informed choices of instruments. Had this not been done, parameter estimates might have been biased, and important experimental inferences might thereby have been distorted.[23]

While results of this stage were interpretable, this stage was in many ways far more important to the overall analysis because of the questions it left unanswered. For example, it was apparent that military capabilities (defense expenditures) were significantly explained in some instances by the change in GNP and the lagged endogenous term, but it was equally apparent that these links were not of uniform strength across all three actors and that much of the variance in defense expenditures remained unexplained in all three instances. Moreover, comparisons and correlations of residuals showed systematic relationships across actors. Apparently, the positive correlation across actors' defense expenditures was not wholly attributable to the correlation of unilateral processes bearing upon their arms building. Similar reasoning applied to the unilateral analysis of thresholds of violence (peaks) and normal conflict and cooperation behavior (means). The questions emerging out of this reasoning directed attention to bilateral process.

The second stage of the analysis, the *bilateral stage*, built upon findings

[23] See Appendix D.

of the previous stage, effectively treating these as part of prior information, and attention turned to the experimental analysis of bilateral, cross-national relationships. It was at this point that bilateral intersections and bilateral provocations were first incorporated in the analysis. Military capability and conflict behavior equations were also reexamined and revised.

Figure A.2 presents the unilateral/bilateral model, the model resulting from this stage of the analysis. Considerably more complex than its predecessors, the model contains both unilateral and bilateral causal links accounting for dyadic relationships. The model, that is, addressed Sino-Soviet, Sino-American, or Soviet-American relations. The Sino-Soviet-American triangle would be portrayed by three such models, loosely connected (through military capabilities). Expansion, it will be noted, is determined by the same set of dynamics identified in the unilateral process model.

As with the unilateral process model, the unilateral/bilateral process model is a result of considerable experimentation with alternative measures, functional forms, equations, and parameter estimation strategies. As in the unilateral stage, the analysis reflected an attempt to minimize bias by attending to the place of each posed relationship within an overall system.

Again, the results of this stage were interpretable within the context of the framework, but once again, too, many questions were raised but left unanswered. For instance, competitive response coefficients in military expenditure equations tended to be unstable across subperiods; e.g., Chinese arms building tended to be responsive to Soviet arms building only in later subperiods. Why? Chinese thresholds of violence toward the US tended to correlate negatively with Chinese thresholds of violence toward the USSR, the negative relationship was strengthened when one looked only at residuals from the model, and it was strengthened all the more when lags were introduced. Why? The answers were unavailable within parts of the framework addressing unilateral and bilateral processes. Multilateral processes would have to be taken into account.

The model presented in Chapter 2, the general model, is a product of the third research stage, the *multilateral stage*. This stage of analysis built upon the results of prior stages, but it also incorporated propositions from the framework pertaining to multilateral balance of power dynamics: 'threat assessment,' 'isolation avoidance,' 'consistency maintenance,' and 'preponderance opposition.' As proposed in Chapter 1, these dynamics pertain only to military capability building, normal conflict and cooperation, and thresholds of violence. Only these equations were substantially revised in this stage.

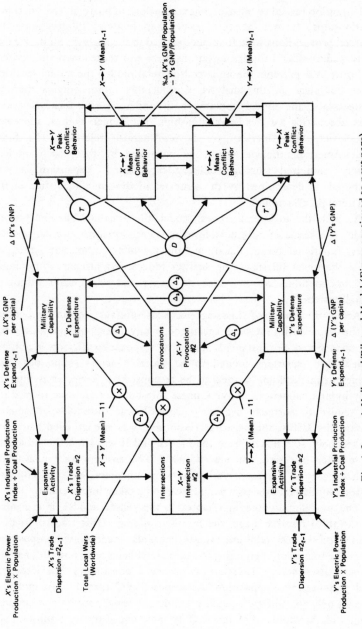

Fig. A.2 A Unilateral/Bilateral Model (Figure continued to next page)

Δ_1	A difference over one year: $\text{Value}_t - \text{Value}_{t-1}$
Δ_2	A difference over two years: $\text{Value}_t - \text{Value}_{t-2}$
D	A difference (or gap) between two countries' defense expenditures: $D = X\text{'s Defense Expend.} - Y\text{'s Defense Expend.}$
T	A threshold-multiplier relationship: $T = [X \to Y \text{ (Mean)} - 11] \times (X\text{-}Y \text{ Provocation \#2})$ $T' = [Y \to X \text{ (Mean)} - 11] \times (X\text{-}Y \text{ Provocation \#2})$
$\overline{X \to Y}$ (Mean)	A three-year-lagged moving average: $$\overline{X \to Y \text{ (Mean)}} = \frac{\sum_{i=1}^{3} X \to Y \text{ (Mean)}_{t-i}}{3}.$$
$\overline{Y \to X}$ (Mean)	A three-year-lagged moving average analogous to $\overline{X \to Y}$ (Mean).

Fig. A.2   *Continued*. Symbols in the Unilateral/Bilateral Model

As the discussion throughout Part II and Chapter 10 suggests, the results using the general model (the unilateral/bilateral/multilateral process model) are again interpretable; and their interpretation requires the exercise of the full conceptual framework. The same results also point to numerous additional queries to be examined–and competing traditions to be confronted–as the theory building program continues and the framework is refined and further enriched. The three-stage modeling progression outlined here has not reached a conclusion. Instead, it has taken three modest initial steps toward uncovering the complex, far-reaching dynamics and dilemmas of the modern security problematique.

Analysis of a System in Change

Appendix A's summary outline of the three-stage modeling progression necessarily omits numerous details. But it also omits attention to a very important aspect of this progression — an aspect that cannot be neglected if the character of the research leading up to the general model is to be accurately conveyed. Given the conceptual framework's emphasis upon a long-historical and creative progression, this analysis has been undertaken under the presupposition that the critical dynamics at work might be expected to vary as much over time as across actors. Although they may be nearly constant over some considerable span of time, relationships are not eternally stationary. They emerge. They converge. They come into relationships of antagonism. And they contribute to the generation of other relationships that do or might become dominant over some later period of time.

The presupposition of change in relationships over time has many important implications for this study, but two should be singled-out here. First, as stressed in Chapter 2, the general model does not and cannot capture the historical processes represented in the framework. A model of post–1950 relations among China, the Soviet Union, and the United States must take much for granted. For example, it must ignore and leave unrepresented the long-historical processes that permit one to speak meaningfully of, say, the Chinese People's Republic as a state associated with a certain society, having a certain ethnically mixed population, spanning a certain land mass in Asia, and distinguishable from other social formations that border it. It must largely ignore and leave unrepresented those historical processes that gave form to the states and that now permit one to categorize data files in terms of the individual states whose attributes, capabilities, and behaviors are measured. It must assume that, so long as the model holds, there will always be these interdependent complexes of relations configured such that they can be called 'powers.' And it must therefore be a contingent model, a model whose validity is conditional upon the asynchronous, equifinal and cumulative processes that shape the social actualities in which the model's assumptions might or might not be appropriate. In short, the model and the relationships it represents are conceived to be contingent upon the long historical processes conceptualized in the framework. While the model represents ways in which these processes might find expression over a relatively brief span of time — and while it aids the interpretation of the processes at work over some span of time and domain of space — it cannot be said to contain these processes.

The second important implication is that even over the relatively brief period examined and modeled, change in structured relationships must be allowed for. One cannot be certain that the period examined will be one in which all relationships so closely approximate constancy that the assumption of structural stationarity can be sustained. One might in fact expect that, given the scope of variables and relationships involved, the period will exhibit significant change in at least some dominant relationships in at least some parts of the system. How this study has responded to this second implication is the subject of this appendix.

Concern for change over time in dominant dynamics is not unique to this study. In their pre-World War I studies, for example, Choucri and North attended to and sought to empirically examine for phase-shifts and breakpoints.[1] The notion of a phase-shift is that, over time, there is likely to be some substantial change in the dynamics tending to be dominant in determining particular behaviors and outcomes. The shift may occur gradually, through some continuous process, or it may occur suddenly, through a discontinuous break with past patterns. A breakpoint is the point in time of a discontinuous shift between two phases, where each phase is defined in terms of dominant dynamics. Choucri and North examined a forty-five year period, hypothesized various breakpoints, regressed their equations over various subperiods preceding and/or following the hypothesized breakpoints, inspected parameter estimates with an eye to changes, and employed the Chow F test in order to examine for significant change in the sums of squared residuals.[2]

---

[1] See Naxli Choucri and Robert C. North, *Nations in Conflict: National Growth and International Violence* (San Francisco: W.H. Freeman, 1975).

[2] See Gregory C. Chow, 'Tests of Inequality Between Sets of Coefficients in Two Linear Regressions,' *Econometrica,* Vol. XXVIII (1960); and Franklin M. Fisher, 'Tests of Inequality Between Sets of Coefficients in Two Linear Regressions: An Expository Note,' *Econometrica,* Vol. XXXVIII (1970).

Moreover, Choucri and North also attempted to build certain kinds of phase-shifts into their models. In the *Nations in Conflict* model, the military expenditures are responsive to the arms spending of non-allies. In the same equation system, an equation for alliances also appears. In effect, the alliance equation helps to explain a shift by which an actor, once competitively responding to the arms building of another, might ally with the other and then, in the military expenditure equation, no longer competitively respond to the other's arms building.

A similar approach has been followed in this study. Throughout all three stages of the research program, the analysis has involved not only the examination of competing measures and functional forms but also (*a*) the attempt to empirically discern shifts of dynamics over various subperiods and (*b*) develop specifications to account for these shifts. It must be stressed that this aspect of the analysis is very difficult and yields what are at best very tentative results. For where Choucri and North examined some forty-five annual observations, and hence could partition the total period without doing serious violence to degrees of freedom, the total period examined here spans only twenty-three years. However, it must also be said that this aspect of the analysis could not be disregarded. With only twenty-three annual observations, one must place the greatest confidence in the full-period parameter estimates. But if one is to have confidence in even these, then one must first be reasonably sure that the model is specified to represent some of the important phase-shifts that might occur within the full time-span.

In order to test for the stability of parameter estimates over time — and to try to identify which parameter estimates do vary — a two-part strategy was followed at each stage of the progression. The first part is straightforward. Parameters would be estimated on a full equation (apropos of the model being developed at that stage) over the full period and over various (sometimes overlapping) subperiods. Residuals would be inspected, the Chow F test would be applied, and parameter estimates would be directly examined and compared. Such a strategy was of course most appropriate during early stages of analysis and in the simplest equation forms, for here it was possible to retain a reasonably low ratio of variables to observations in subperiod regressions.

For example, it will be recalled from Appendix A (Section III) that one form of the equation for defense expenditures in the unilateral modeling stage was:

$$\text{Defense Expenditure} = \beta_0 + \beta_1\ (\Delta\text{GNP})$$
$$+ \beta_2\ (\text{Defense Expenditure}_{t-1}) + \mu$$

Table B.1 *Chow F Statistics for Unilateral 'Military Capability'
Equations: Uncontrolled for External Factors**

	1951–1961 *df* = 11,8	1951–1966 *df* = 6,13	1957–1972 *df* = 6,13	1962–1972 *df* = 11,8
US TDC (51–72) = AUTO2	F = 1.499 p = n.s. TDC = AUTO2	F = 0.269 p = n.s. TDC = AUTO2	F = 1.015 p = n.s. TDC = AUTO2	F = 1.187 p = n.s. TDC = AUTO2
USSR TDC (51–72) = None	F = 1.368 p = n.s. TDC = MAV2	F = 0.908 p = n.s. TDC = None	F = 1.034 p = n.s. TDC = None	F = 1.317 p = n.s. TDC = None
CPR TDC (51–72) = None	F = 1.520 p = n.s. TDC = MAV2	F = 1.205 p = n.s. TDC = None	F = 0.591 p = n.s. TDC = None	F = 5.190 p = .05 TDC = AUTO2

* 'TDC' indicates the time-dependent correction used for subperiod or, in the case of
TDC (51–72), for the full period regression. '*df*' indicates degrees of freedom for
subperiod Chow F test. '*p*' indicates level of significance for Chow F test.

Employing the approach just described, the analysis at this stage involved
regressing this equation for each of the three powers over various subperiods as well as the full period. In addition to inspecting and comparing
residuals, Chow F statistics were generated. These are as shown in
Table B.1. As shown, only one subperiod regression produced a significant
Chow F statistic in this case: the regression of the defense expenditure
equation for China over the period 1962–72. These results offered modest
corroboration to the expectation that unilateral processes bearing on arms
building would remain, in general, stable over the full period.

Table B.2 illustrates other aspects of this procedure for the bilateral
provocations equations, using the equation form first constructed in stage
two and appearing in the general model. The results shown in this table
can be compared to results presented in Chapter 6. Each of the three
equations registers a significant Chow F statistic for one of the two subperiods examined (1951–65 and 1961–72). All three exhibit considerable
change in coefficient estimates. In the equation for Soviet-American
provocations, for instance, the dominant term over the 1951–65 subperiod
is the interactive term involving intersections. In the later subperiod, the
term drops out, and the dominant influence, a negative influence, is found
in mounting Soviet arms expenditures.

The same table also illustrates some of the difficulties of this strategy.
A number of *ad hoc* hypotheses might be generated to account for the
changes in parameter estimates. In turn, these might orient respecification

Table B.2 Subperiod Regression Results for Bilateral Provocations, 1951–1965 and 1961–1972*
(Measured as Provocations #2)

Dyad	R^2	F Ratio	Durbin-Watson	Time-dependent correction	Variable: Link to pre-theory	Measure	Unstandardized Coefficient	Standardized Coefficient	Partial correlation	t statistic	Level of significance
US–USSR	.99	373.375 $df = 3,11$ $p = .001$	1.51	MAV2	Constant	Constant	−2.93060†	.00	−.69	−3.13	.005
					US–USSR Intersections × Total Incidents and Situations‡	US–USSR Intersections #2 × Total Number of Wars	0.04478	.96	.99	25.46	.0005
1951–65											
Chow test: $F(7,11) = 10.59$ $p = .001$					US Military Capability	Δ(US Defense Expenditure)	239.272	.09	.47	1.86	.05
					USSR Military Capability	Δ(USSR Defense Expenditure)	−86.0973	−.01	−.07	−0.22	n.s.
US–USSR	.75	8.176 $df = 3,8$ $p = .01$	1.84	None	Constant	Constant	50.9373†	.00	.76	3.26	.01
					US–USSR Intersections × Total Incidents and Situations‡	US–USSR Intersections #2 × Total Number of Wars	0.01027	.25	.41	1.27	n.s.
1961–72											
Chow test: $F(10.8) = 0.72$ $p = $ n.s.					US Military Capability	Δ(US Defense Expenditure)	333.667	.12	.15	0.43	n.s.
					USSR Military Capability	Δ (USSR Defense Expenditure)	−4871.76	−.89	−.74	−3.19	.01

Group	R^2	F	DW	Correction	Variable	Variable	Coefficient				
US–CPR	.94	56.132 $df=3,11$ $p=.001$	1.84	MAV1	Constant	Constant	−1.57700†	.00	.26	0.88	n.s.
1951–65					US–CPR Intersections × Total Incidents and Situations‡	US–CPR Intersections #2 × Total Number of Wars	0.07724	.90	.95	10.37	.0005
					US Military Capability	Δ (US Defense Expenditure)	298.534	.21	.61	2.57	.025
					CPR Military Capability	Δ (CPR Defense Expenditure)	5312.22	.17	.55	2.18	.05
Chow test: $F(7,11)=7.66$ $p=.01$											
US–CPR	.21	0.699 $df=3,8$ $p=$ n.s.	2.07	AUTO2	Constant	Constant	10.1270†	.00	.29	0.87	n.s.
1961–72					US–CPR Intersections × Total Incidents and Situations‡	US–CPR Intersections #2 × Total Number of Wars	0.02877	.43	.46	1.47	.10
					US Military Capability	Δ (US Defense Expenditure)	−40.6552	−.02	−.03	−0.07	n.s.
					CPR Military Capability	Δ (CPR Defense Expenditure)	8717.79	.11	.25	0.72	n.s.
Chow test: $F(10,8)=0.08$ $p=$ n.s.											
CPR–USSR	.73	10.126 $df=3,11$ $p=.01$	1.63	None	Constant	Constant	−0.68825†	.00	−.23	−0.77	n.s.
1951–65					CPR–USSR Intersections × Total Incidents and Situations‡	CPR–USSR Intersections #2 × Total Number of Wars	0.02914	.63	.70	3.26	.005

continued

Table B.2 continued

Dyad	R^2	F Ratio	Durbin-Watson	Time-dependent correction	Variable: Link to pre-theory	Measure	Unstandardized Coefficient	Standardized Coefficient	Partial correlation	t statistic	Level of significance
Chow test: $F(7,11) = 0.87$ p = n.s.					CPR Military Capability	Δ (CPR Defense Expenditure)	1728.15	.29	.39	1.41	.10
					USSR Military Capability	Δ (USSR Defense Expenditure)	−135.415	−.19	−.31	−1.07	n.s.
CPr–USSR	.92	31.223 $df = 3,8$ $p = .001$	2.59	MAV2	Constant	Constant	4.64049†	.00	.88	5.20	.0005
1961–72					CPR–USSR Intersections X Total Incidents and Situations‡	CPR–USSR Intersections #2 X Total Number of Wars	0.01590	.45	.85	4.52	.005
Chow test: $F(10,8) = 6.17$ p = .01					CPR Military Capability	Δ (CPR Defense Expenditure)	−2512.13	−.21	−.42	−1.29	n.s.
					USSR Military Capability	Δ (USSR Defense Expenditure)	−433.646	−.76	−.93	−6.94	.0005

*Statistics refer to estimates using the generalized least squares correction indicated in the 'time-dependent correction' column.

†Multiply the coefficient by 10^6.

‡'Incidents and Situations' refer to all events and circumstances, worldwide, that might threaten actors' interests and commitments within regions.

of the model. However, it is difficult to imagine any kind of specification that would uniformly account for such shifts across all three dyads. And it is far from certain that, with so few degrees of freedom, such shifts are not due to artifacts of the analysis, such as measurement error or differing degrees of multicollinearity across subperiods.[3] To try to re-specify on the basis of such results could thus be tantamount to the worst kind of curve-fitting. All in all, it is perhaps the wisest course not to respecify but to record these varied results as part of the information to be assembled and combined with other information in future work of this kind.

Where more complex formulations were involved, especially in later stages, a somewhat more complicated strategy had to be used — and used cautiously. The problem was that with a large number of right-hand-side coterms, degrees of freedom were so limited that there was little latitude for performing subperiod regressions and then comparing the full sets of parameter estimates and residuals across subperiods. Under these circumstances, the strategy was to make the tentative assumption that estimates of parameters for unilateral process coterms — the estimates from the first modeling stage — were robust and constant. These para-meter estimates were then held constant, as pseudo-extraneous parameter estimates, and regressions were performed over various subperiods, with only the parameters for bilateral and/or multilateral terms being estimated.

Consider, for example, the following equation for defense expenditures, as it was being developed in stage two:

$$A\text{'s Defense Expend.} = \beta_0 + \beta_1 \Delta(A\text{'s GNP}) +$$
$$\beta_2 (A\text{'s Defense Expend.}_{t-1}) +$$
$$\beta_3 \Delta(A\text{--}B \text{ Intersect. \#2}) +$$
$$\beta_4 \Delta(A\text{--}C \text{ Intersect. \#2}) +$$
$$\beta_5 (B\text{'s Defense Expend.}_t -$$
$$B\text{'s Defense Expend.}_{t-2}) +$$
$$\beta_6 (C\text{'s Defense Expend.}_t -$$
$$C\text{'s Defense Expend.}_{t-2}) + \mu$$

Comparing this equation to the defense expenditure equation appearing in the general model[4] reveals some important differences. Unlike their counterparts in the general model, the third, fourth, fifth, and sixth variable coterms shown in the equation above are not interactively specified.

[3] In fact, what might be called 'local multicollinearity' was a serious problem in subperiod regressions for provocations.
[4] See Chapter 2, Section III.C, and Chapter 7 for a discussion of this equation.

The equation above was preliminary to the general model formulation. On the basis of theory regarding bilateral processes alone, the third and fourth terms, the intersection terms, should involve some kind of interactive, threshold-like relationship with normal conflict and cooperation: when conflict is high, intersections are expected to spur arms competition; when behavior is cooperative, then intersections are expected to have integrative effects and yield a reduction in arms building. Thus, by estimating the parameters of the above equation over various subperiods, one would be able to see if the impacts of intersections did change across subperiods of relatively high or relatively low conflict between actors. In turn, this would inform the interactive specification of threshold terms for the third and fourth coterms.

To undertake this analysis, estimates of β_0, β_1, and β_2 from the first stage were treated as pseudo-extraneous. An artificial term for A's defense expenditures was constructed, in effect, as the residual estimates from the first stage regression:

$$\widehat{A\text{'s Defense Expend.}} = (A\text{'s Defense Expend.}) -$$
$$[\hat{\beta}_0 + \hat{\beta}_1 \Delta(A\text{'s GNP}) +$$
$$\hat{\beta}_2(A\text{'s Defense Expend.}_{t-1})]$$

where $\hat{\beta}_0$, $\hat{\beta}_1$, and $\hat{\beta}_2$ are parameter estimates from the first modeling stage.

Then the following regression equation was constructed:

$$\widehat{A\text{'s Defense Expend.}} = \beta_3 \Delta(A\text{--}B \text{ Intersect. #2}) +$$
$$\beta_4 \Delta(A\text{--}C \text{ Intersect. #2}) +$$
$$\beta_5 (B\text{'s Defence Expend.}_t -$$
$$B\text{'s Defense Expend.}_{t-2}) +$$
$$\beta_6 (C\text{'s Defense Expend.}_t -$$
$$C\text{'s Defense Expend.}_{t-2}) + \mu$$

Regressions were then performed on this equation over the 1952–72 period and the 1952–63 and 1961–72 subperiods. The Chow test was applied. Residuals were inspected. And parameter estimates were examined and compared.

Some significant differences were detected. In the 1952–63 subperiod regression for USSR defense expenditures, for instance, the Δ(USSR–CPR Intersection) term assumed a significant, negative coefficient estimate; yet the estimate for the same term became significant and positive for the 1961–72 subperiod. In the equation for CPR defense expenditures, the same term is insignificant in the first subperiod (where the Δ(US–CPR Intersection) coefficient is significant and positive) but significant and positive in the second (where the Δ(US–CPR Intersection) coefficient is not significant). These and other results were consistent with prior expectations that the impact of changing intersections is contingent upon previous patterns of conflict and cooperation, above or below some threshold, between actors.

After these terms were respecified in the bilateral stage to account for these threshold effects, the same procedure was followed, and parameter estimates were then stablized across subperiods. Still, the fifth and sixth coterms were not interactively specified. Their corresponding coefficient estimates tended to vary markedly across subperiods. Chinese defense expenditures appeared to be positively influenced by changes in Soviet defense expenditures only in the second subperiod, for example, and American expenditures appeared decreasingly responsive to both Chinese and Soviet changes as one advanced from the early to the late subperiod. Respecification to account for these changes was undertaken in the multilateral modeling stage.

A similar approach was pursued in the examination of equations for normal conflict and cooperation and for thresholds of violence. At the third stage, a special concern was to try to detect the extent to which multilateral balance of power dynamics varied in their impacts over subperiods. Because each equation contains some six variable coterms, however, it was necessary to again rely on the pseudo-extraneous parameter estimates procedure. In effect, the parameter estimates from earlier stages for unilateral and bilateral process coterms were held to be robust and constant across subperiods, and parameter estimation concentrated exclusively on multilateral coterms.

The results of this procedure are of course extremely tentative, but they do conform to the expectation that the United States and the USSR have more or less persistently exhibited classical balance of power dynamics throughout the full period while China's tendencies to exhibit these dynamics have been limited largely to more recent years. Over the 1951–63 subperiod, China's normal conflict and cooperation and thresholds of violence tended to exhibit the influences of 'consistency maintenance' logics: a multilateral logic that is not truly a part of the classic balance of power calculus and that tends to foster the isolation of the actor employing it as others move toward mutual cooperation. Over the 1960–72 subperiod, however, China's normal conflict and cooperation and thresholds of violence appear to exhibit the influences, not so much of a 'consistency maintenance logic,' but of the logics of 'isolation avoidance' and 'preponderance opposition.'[5]

It would require another book to fully detail every aspect of the analysis of changing relationships undertaken in the three-stage modeling progression. Were such a tedious book ever written, its leitmotif would surely be one of modest accomplishments sorely gained. Neither the difficulties of the analytical dilemmas nor the threats to the validity of every step can be overestimated.

Yet this study suggests that some patterns and relationships at work in the system are pernicious; that the modern security problematique joins violence, exploitation, and inequality as interdependent parts of what it is; and that the dominant pattern of change is toward more intense violence, more exploitation, and deepening inequality on a widening but ultimately finite geographic compass. If such a depiction is even approximately accurate, then there can be few tasks more important than learning to notice, criticize, explain, and prescribe steps toward system change.

[5] See Chapter 1 for a presentation of the theoretical arguments regarding these logics. Chapters 8 and 9 present the relevant full period regression results.

APPENDIX C

Data, Measures, and Persistent Problems

The first section of this appendix briefly presents the sources of data used in this study. The second section discusses the procedures used in order to guard against error and bias in the assembling and construction of the data series, including the metricized events data series. The third section then briefly outlines some issues of measurement confronted in this study.

I DATA SOURCES

Tables C.1 and C.2 at the end of this appendix present the list of sources consulted in assembling the overall data base and list the variables used in this analysis by country. Empirical results reported in the text are based upon data in the specifically identified sources; i.e., those sources whose code numbers appear in the cells of the matrix. Table C.1 does not include the conflict behavior measures. These are based upon systematic codings of publicly reported events occurring among China, the Soviet Union, and the United States. As metricized data, these are discussed below.

As the large number of listed sources might suggest, every effort has been made to compile a number of complete series from alternative sources for each variable. Wherever possible, a number of alternative measures for each concept have been assembled. Including annual data spanning the 1950–72 period, all series are based upon public sources and are available through the Inter-University Consortium for Political and Social Research.

To maintain cross-national comparability, it has been essential to assure standardization among all monetary series (e.g., gross national product, total trade, arms aid). Thus, wherever possible, money series have been collected which are reported in constant US dollars; in turn, these have been converted to a 1970 base. Where constant US dollar figures have been unavailable, current US dollar series have been used and transformed to constant 1970 dollars with a deflator.

II   LIMITING ERROR AND BIAS

The process of collecting annual data encountered a number of problems, some quite general and others specific to a particular series. One general problem is that various sources use varying criteria in the determination of information to be included or excluded in a given series. These criteria sometimes shift from year to year for a single source, as has been the case in some of the *SIPRI Yearbook*'s arms expenditure series. Another problem stems from the wholesale absence of official government figures — due to a government's own inadequate or infrequent measurement, as in the case of China; to official secrecy, as is often the case for the Soviet Union; or to official nonrecognition of a given index, as is true of both the USSR and the CPR with respect to GNP figures. Still another problem results from official misreporting — as the Soviet Union does in excluding various parts of its military expenditures from its defense budget. As a result, it is very frequently necessary to rely on estimates of population, technological and economic performance, and expenditures. It is for this reason that the acquisition of alternative series for any one variable is desirable. This permits the assessment of the sensitivity of analytic results to estimates used.

Efforts to collect data on Chinese population are illustrative of these kinds of problems. Official country-wide Chinese censuses have been very rare. Censuses for the provinces of population concentration have been more frequent, but given the large-scale movements of people in the last two decades, these figures are not necessarily representative of overall trends. Consequently, demographers have had to rely on spotty data — together with systematically integrated (but equally spotty) information on economic conditions, death rates, and so on — in order to arrive at their estimates of the Chinese population size. These estimates range widely. John Aird alone, for instance, has produced estimates of China's 1972 population that range from a low of 807 million people to a high of 875 million. And accordingly, it has been necessary to reflect this uncertainty by incorporating several series in the collection.

The collection of series for Soviet defense expenditures illustrates related problems. As mentioned, the official Soviet military budget systematically excludes significant items that other nations normally include in their defense budgets — defense related expenditures under the All Union Science budget, for example. Even the official budget, moreover, suggests absolutely no change in the USSR's scientific expenditures since 1969. And these distortions are further compounded by the inadequacy of information about the relative rate of inflation for Soviet military programs as against nondefense programs — a lack of information that makes the comparative 'costing-out' of the Soviet defense effort extremely difficult for Western analysts. Estimates of the USSR's 1969 expenditures thus range from a low of $42 billion to a high of $62 billion — a $20 billion dollar difference (in 1970 constant dollars). In turn, this makes it necessary to collect, and reexamine findings with, many competing series.

For a number of other series, it has been possible to find only incomplete data. The Chinese agricultural and industrial production indexes and Soviet iron ore production series are examples; in these instances, sources provided data only through 1971, and extrapolation has been required to produce 1972 figures.

Chinese and Soviet GNP figures are subjects of intense controversy among Western analysts. The highest estimates of Chinese GNP in 1970 are some 20 percent greater than the lowest; and the highest estimates of Soviet GNP for the same year exceed the lowest by about 31 percent. These wide-ranging estimates reflect the absence of official figures and the consequent need for analysts to rely on models as a means of generating estimates. The same observations apply to agricultural and industrial production indexes, for the CPR and the USSR, to grain production figures for both countries, and to electric power production for China.

Figures on foreign trade, on which the commercial expansion measures are based, are particularly troublesome due to differing inclusion criteria among sources, varying exchange rates, and infrequent and inaccurate official data for China's trading activity. In addition, various sources differ on the regional breakdowns of trading activity. In order to minimize some of these problems, this study has concentrated on data from a single source, the *United Nations Yearbook of International Trade Statistics*, and used its regional breakdowns, in its empirical analysis. For China's trade over much of the period, the Yearbook relies on reports of China's trading partners. Other sources have also been consulted. But owing to the incomplete series they provide, it has not yet been possible to examine the sensitivity of reported findings to data contained in these alternative sources.

Absolutely essential for the construction and testing of the model has been the development of reliable data on the conflict and cooperation behavior of the three states. The data developed for this study are metricized; that is, where metric data are naturally measurable phenomena, the metricized conflict behavior data are constructed by the convention-based yet partially judgmental assignment of numerical values to concepts that are implied by, but not directly measurable in, observable events.[1] Relying upon events reported in the *New York Times Index*, each event was coded as to 'actor' nation and 'target' and scaled on a thirty-point scale of conflict and implications for violence developed by Lincoln E. Moses and others.[2] Once this collection, including some 15,000 events, was completed, twelve variables were constructed: annual mean conflict levels (normal conflict and cooperation) and annual peak conflict levels (thresholds of violence) for each of the triangle's six directed dyads.

More specifically, the development of these data began with a survey of the *Times Index* to determine relevant categories; i.e., categories in the index that might contain reported events among China, the Soviet Union, and the United States. Forty-two categories were identified — ranging from 'International Relations' and 'Soviet Foreign Policy' at the most general end to 'Aeronautics and Astronautics' and local conflict headings at the more specific end. It is the comprehensiveness of the search, in part, that accounts for the richness of the collection as contrasted with others. [For the 1950–72 period, for example, the present collection includes more than twice as many Soviet-American events as are included in the Conflict and Peace Data Bank (COPDAB).][3]

Once relevant categories were selected, the index was thoroughly searched for events, and events were transferred to machine readable format *as originally reported in the Times Index*. An event, as card punched as this stage, was recorded as follows:

[1] There is now a rapidly burgeoning literature on events data. And a number of large collections — e.g., WEIS, COPDAB, CREON, and others — now exist. See Edward Azar, 'Analysis of International Events,' *Peace Research Reviews*, Vol. IV, No. 1 (1970); Edward Azar and Joseph Ben-Dak, *Theory and Practice of Events Research* (London: Gordon and Breach Science Publishers, 1975); Edward Azar, Richard Brody, and Charles McClelland, 'International Events Interaction Analysis: Some Research Considerations,' *Sage Professional Papers in International Studies*, Vol. 1, No. 02–001; John H. Sigler, John O. Field, and Murray Adelman, 'Application of Events Data Analysis: Cases, Issues, and Problems in International Interactions,' *Sage Professional Papers in International Studies*, Vol. I, No. 02–010 (1975); and Philip Burgess and Raymond Lawton, 'Indicators of International Behavior: An Assessment of Events Data Research' *Sage Professional Papers in International Studies*, Vol. I, No. 02–010 (1972).

[2] See Lincoln E. Moses, Richard A. Brody, Ole R. Holsti, Joseph B. Kadane, and Jeffrey S. Milstein, 'Scaling Data on Inter-National Action,' *Science*, No. 156 (1967).

[3] See Edward Azar and Thomas Sloan, *Dimensions of Interactions*, International Studies Occasional Paper No. 8 (Pittsburgh: International Studies Association, 1975).

```
-----1--07-25-62------------GROMYKO AGAIN CHARGES WEST WANTS INSPEC-

-----2--07-25-62------------TION FOR ESPIONAGE.
```

Reserved for
Event Serial #
Event Card #
Month
Day
Year
Reserved for
Event Code
Text from
NYT Index

At this stage, it must be stressed, the general injunction was to err on the side of including a nonevent.

The next steps involved general editing. Each card was read twice for errors, and corrections were made. Especially important here was the identification and reproduction of 'do two's' (simultaneous or reciprocal events, such as summit meetings, in which each participating nation might be included both as actor and target or in which one action is directed toward two targets). The deck was divided according to directed dyads and ordered chronologically, and duplicates (events recorded twice as a result of a multiple category search) were removed. Finally, the general inclusion rules were applied, and all items not conforming to these rules were excluded. The general rules are:

(1) The item must involve action between China and the US, China and the USSR, and/or the USSR and the US.
(2) The item must involve pronouncements or acts carried out by the 'official agents' of the nations mentioned above or of the international organizations or blocs (e.g., NATO, 'Western ministers') of which they are members and from whose pronouncements/acts they do not overtly dissent.
(3) The target of the item must be an official agent of the nation; an official (or alleged official) policy position, or action of the nation; a characteristic of the political or economic system of the nation; or the nation as a general entity.
(4) For the CPR and the USSR, 'official agents' include government-controlled media and party organs.
(5) Actions and statements of officials-designate (e.g., John F. Kennedy in December 1960) are excluded.
(6) Items using the word 'reportedly' are included.

A few ambiguities were encountered despite these rules. It was sometimes unclear, for instance, whether or not a US senator, visiting Khrushchev in Moscow, was acting as an official agent of the executive branch. For these and other rare instances, more specific decision rules had to be devised.

The clean deck in hand, the next step was to code each event for actor and target and to scale each event for conflict and potential for violence using a set of thirty 'marker cards.' The deck of marker cards constituted the measurement instrument against which each event was compared and measured. One marker deck developed by Moses and others contained the following statements.

1. Nations A, B, ... N initiate joint sovereignty, i.e., federate.
2. Nations A, B, ... N, enemies of Nation X, integrate their military units.

   .
   .
   .

15. Nation A increases its military aid to an enemy of Nation B.
16. Nation A prohibits exports of strategic materials.

   .
   .
   .

29. Nation A and Nation B engage in frontier fighting which involves only the troops stationed there.
30. Nation A sends new troop units into battle without relieving troop units already engaged in battle.

A judge would locate a given event between items on this scale and then award a score to the event corresponding to the lesser valued item. Before coding, the judges were trained using the Sino-Soviet and Sino-American data originally developed at Stanford University under the direction of Robert C. North.[4] The interjudge correlation of scores on a randomly selected set of 200 events exceeded .95.

As other users of this scale have found, the scale is flexible in that judges' codings are relatively insensitive to precise instructions given — whether, for example, they are instructed to consider 'conflict content' or 'implications for violence.' It was also found that the scale is most

---

[4] As noted in Chapter 2, Sino-Soviet and Sino-American events from 1950 through 1966 were originally collected at Stanford. Subsequently, these data were rechecked and cleaned for this study.

reliable (i.e., there is least variance among judges) for events at the upper end. Moses *et al.* have averred that this is due to the fact that it is easier to distinguish among various levels of the *presence* of an entity — in this case conflict — than among various levels of the *absence* of an entity.[5]

This basic events data set was thoroughly reread and cleaned a final time and then used to establish the annual normal conflict and cooperation (mean) and threshold of violence (peak) measures for each of the six directed dyads.[6] No missing data problems were encountered in the annual variables.

III MEASUREMENT

As observed in Chapter 2, one of the most difficult problems has been to narrow the gap between the theoretical concepts and operational measures. The problem here is not unique; it has long been the subject of considerable debate among methodologists. Some have called for the operationalist redefinition of concepts.[7] And others have maintained that 'on the one hand, there should be a general theory expressed in abstract terms [e.g., the conceptual framework in Chapter 1],' and, 'on the other hand, there must also be an *auxiliary* theory necessary for testing purposes.'[8] The latter, ideally, would specify 'epistemic correlations'[9] or 'rules of

---

[5] Strictly speaking, this scale is *not* an equal interval scale. However, by convention, the data thus produced are treated as if the scale were in fact an equal interval scale. See Nazli Choucri and Robert C. North, *Nations in Conflict: National Growth and International Violence* (San Francisco: W.H. Freeman, 1975), p. 299, fn. 6. For related arguments see Sanford Labovitz, 'The Assignment of Numbers to Rank Order Categories,' *American Sociological Review*, Vol. XXXV (1972); and Robert Abelson and John W. Tukey, 'Efficient Conversion of Non-Metric Information into Metric Information,' in Edward R. Tufte (ed.), *The Quantitative Analysis of Social Problems* (Reading, Mass.: Addison Wesley, 1970).

[6] Annual low points were also produced, but, except for the descriptive purposes of Chapter 3, they are not used in this study. In preliminary studies, the use of low points yielded few significant results.

[7] This is the position most commonly associated with physicist Percy W. Bridgman and his *The Logic of Modern Physics* (New York: Macmillan, 1927), and with sociologist George A. Lundberg and his *Foundations of Sociology* (New York: Macmillan, 1939). In general, the position is that measurement is a way of defining — that concepts should be defined in terms of the actual, nonverbal operations involved in their scientific use, not in terms of the presumed properties of the concept.

[8] Hubert M. Blalock, Jr., 'The Measurement Problem: A Gap Between the Languages of Theory and Research,' in Hubert M. Blalock, Jr. and Ann B. Blalock (eds.), *Methodology in Social Research* (New York: McGraw-Hill, 1968), p. 24.

[9] According to F.S.C. Northrop, an epistemic correlation is 'a relation joining an unobserved component of anything designated by a concept of postulation to its directly inspected component denoted by a concept of intuition,' *The Logic of the Sciences and the Humanities* (New York: Macmillan, 1947), p. 119. Also quoted in Blalock, op. cit.

correspondence'[10] that link operations to theoretical concepts while it would also explicate assumptions (including untestable ones) about measurement error and the behavior of neglected variables.

Here, though, operationalism has been dismissed on the grounds that it would mean (a) too great a sacrifice of historical generality, (b) too much of a loss of the relational meaning of concepts, and (c) too strong a tendency toward ahistorical closure.[11] At the same time, from the vantage point of this study, the distinction between general theory and auxiliary theory, although not completely false and useless, is perhaps overstated when addressed to a theory of long-historical processes. In long-historical perspective, there is no independent, stationary set of 'auxiliary' relationships that determines the linkages between general theoretical concepts and operational measures. Over a restricted span of time, to be sure, one can make such a distinction for purposes of analytic convenience. But unless one is careful to articulate why it is that such a distinction can be made — that is, how it is that asynchronous, equifinal, and cumulative historical processes have shaped a reality that is partitionable in just this way — then auxiliary theory is not more than an *ad hoc* convenience that gives a false aura of timelessness to the testing of so-called general theory. Moreover, once one sets out to explain why such a distinction can be made for this or that analytic purpose here and now, one is committed to a course along which one will sooner or later conclude that so-called auxiliary relationships are themselves sensitive to relationships addressed in general theory. The distinction will thereby be blurred. In short, as a sound general theory of long-term historical processes in international relations is developed, it will gradually come to incorporate the very relationships that Blalock and others would relegate to auxiliary theory.

For example, the general theory discussed here is concerned with lateral pressure, and many measurement issues confronted in this study are concerned with the modal forms of activity in which lateral pressure is expressed by individual societies. In principle, an auxiliary theory would indicate why and how this or that measure appropriately represents

[10] See Herbert L. Costner, 'Theory, Deduction, and Rules of Correspondence,' in Hubert M. Blalock, Jr., *Causal Models in the Social Sciences* (Chicago: Aldine, 1971), pp. 299–319.

[11] As Abraham Kaplan argues, 'The demand for exactness of meaning and for precise definition of terms can easily have a pernicious effect . . . It results in what has been aptly named the *premature closure* of our ideas. That the progress of science is marked by successive closures can be stipulated; but it is just the function of inquiry to instruct in how and where closure can best be achieved . . . Tolerance of ambiguity is as important for creativity in science as it is somewhere else.' *The Conduct of Inquiry* (San Francisco: Chandler, 1964), pp. 70–1.

modal expressions among some actors over some period, would identify those omitted (unmeasured) variables and their possible effects, and would provide assumptions about likely sources and directions of error in measurement. Now, if one were to construct such an auxiliary theory for Choucri and North's work on Europe, 1870–1914, and another for the present study of contemporary Sino-Soviet-American relations, would the two auxiliary theories be identical? Probably not, and from the standpoint of this study, the fact of their difference would bespeak their *adhoc*ness and ahistoricity. But what if one were to seek a single coherent auxiliary theory, spanning both periods, that allows for and attempts to explain the ways in which lateral pressure might find measurable expression among societies, might give rise to dominant modes at both societal and systemic levels, might elicit equifinal adaptations among differentially constrained societies, and might thereby open the way for the emergence of new modal forms and call for new measures in different periods? To ask the question is to see that auxiliary theory and historical-processual general theory are one and the same. To call for a non-*ad hoc*, non-ahistorical auxiliary theory is to call for further development in general theory — a task for which modeling and empirical analysis are meant to be helpful.

In fact, as stressed in Chapter 2, measurement is not here conceived to be independent of and logically prior to modeling, empirical analysis, and causal inference. Key concepts are relational in character. The adequacy of their measurement can be assessed only to the extent that it is possible to discern a correspondence between relationships invested in concepts by prior theory, on the one hand, and relationships inferred from the application of a model to empirical data, on the other.

The development of measures for conflict behavior variables has already been discussed. Equally problematical have been the measures for military capabilities, expansion, intersections, and provocations. The thinking underlying the choices of operational terms for these concepts should be briefly considered.

In measuring a nation's military capability, no one measure seems wholly adequate to the task of representing a nation's military *effort* and *potential* across the full array of possible military activities. Standardizeded budgetary figures, which have been analyzed in the text, are perhaps the best approximations. These measures do permit some degree of cross-national comparability in terms of both overall effort and general potential. The analysis of budgetary figures, moreover, is now conventional in the growing literature on arms races. Even so, as emphasized in Chapter 7, these figures remain *very* crude and gross approximations; and they may be insensitive to variation in the effort and potential of specific military programs (e.g., naval arms developments or strategic nuclear forces, or, still more specifically, SLBM developments). For this reason, a number of other more force-specific series (e.g., deliverable megatonnage, men under arms) have been collected. These measures have been substituted in the analysis from time to time; additional, more systematic work along these lines is required.

The measures of expansion, intersections, and provocations are closely related. A society's external expansion can take a variety of forms, a point emphasized in the conceptual framework of Chapter 1 and again in Chapter 4. Foreign commerce, foreign investment, foreign economic aid, technical assistance, marine exploration and exploitation, military assistance, arms transfers, overseas basing of men under arms, conquest, the establishment of colonies, and even space flight — each of these is a form of expansion. Intersections, too, can take a variety of forms. Indeed, because intersections are here defined as (aggregated) geographical points of convergence in the expanding activities of pairs of actors, the variety of intersectional forms is geometrically proportional to the number of forms expansion might take.

This multiform character of both expansion and intersections makes it very difficult to capture either in a single measure. Accordingly, it has been necessary to try to compile a number of alternative measures; and the present collection now includes at least partial series for foreign investments, foreign aid, foreign basing of men under arms, and arms transfers, in addition to the dominant modal category of foreign trade.

However, only one set of these series, the foreign trade series, possesses the required characteristics: (*a*) they are available for all three actors, thereby permitting cross-national comparability; (*b*) they fully span the 1950–72 period; (*c*) they are sufficiently disaggregated into geographic regions of the globe to permit a reasonably approximate empirical articulation of the expansion and intersections notions; and (*d*) they are reported in a variety of sources so that potential sources of bias in alternative estimates can be examined.

Thus, expansion and intersections are here empirically represented by one measureable form — international commerce — although, wherever possible, other measures have been substituted (over shorter periods) as a means of examining the sensitivity of findings to alternative measures used.

The measurement of 'provocations' depends in part upon the operational definition of intersections, for provocations have been conceptually defined in terms of incidents occurring at points of intersection in the expansion of two triangular actors. Quite clearly, these incidents could be of several types, ranging from isolated events through political unrest, economic chaos, and subversive activities to protracted, large-scale collective violence.[12] Any occurrence threatening to destabilize a region of intersection in the expanding activities of two actors might qualify as a provocative, as an inducement to conflict among major powers.

The present data collection, though, now includes complete 1950–72 time series for only one measure: local wars by geographic region. And this means that, while other measures have been used for shorter periods in preliminary studies, only numbers of local wars by region have been used to devise the 'provocations at intersections' seen in the analysis reported here.

It should be clear, then, that in devising measures of expansion, intersections, and provocations, the practical matter of data unavailability has proven to be a major constraint. These are areas in which further data collection efforts are vitally needed.

---

[12] The second edition of the *World Handbook of Political and Social Indicators*, for instance, lists 1948–67 annual time series for protest demonstrations, riots, armed attacks, deaths from domestic violence, governmental sanctions, external interventions, and so on for some 136 countries; Charles L. Taylor and Michael C. Hudson (New Haven: Yale University Press, 1972), Chapter 3. See also Harry Eckstein (ed.), *Internal War* (New York: Free Press, 1964); Rudolph J. Rummel, 'Dimensions of Conflict Behavior Within and Between Nations,' *General Systems: Yearbook of the Society of General Systems*, Vol. VIII (1963); Ivo K. and Rosalind L. Feirabend, 'Aggressive Behaviors Within Politics, 1948–1962: A Cross-National Study,' *Journal of Conflict Resolution*, Vol. X (1966); and Douglas A. Hibbs, Jr., *Mass Political Violence: A Cross-National Causal Analysis* (New York: Wiley, 1973), particularly Chapter 2.

Table C.1 Data Sources

The statistical results explicitly reported or discussed in this study are based upon data from sources whose code numbers appear below. The code numbers correspond to sources listed in Table C.2.

	Units	US	Source USSR	CPR
Agricultural Production Index	1958/9 = 100	U4 in B2	D1	A4
Coal Production	X 1000 metric tons	O4	C6	F5
Defense Expenditure	X $ Million (US)	S1	S1	S1
Electric Power Production	X Million KW Hours	O4	C6	F5
Gross National Product	X $ Billion (US)	B1	C7	A4
Industrial Production Index	1967/8 = 100	F7 in B2	G4	F5
Men Under Arms	X 1000 persons	B4, M2	B4, M2	W3, M2
Oil Production	X 1000 metric tons	O4	C6	F5
Population Total	X Million persons	S4	F3	A1
Total Trade (Imports + Exports)	X $ Million (US)	B2, C3, O1	F1, V2, V3	U5
Trade, by Region	X $ Million (US)	U3	U3	U3
Wars, by Region	X 1 ongoing local war	K1	K1	K1

Table C.2 *Data Source List*

Code Number	Author/Title/Organization
A1	John S. Aird, 'Population Policy and Demographic Prospects in the People's Republic of China,' in *People's Republic of China: An Economic Assessment*, US Congress, Joint Economic Committee, US Government Printing Office, 1972.
A2	John S. Aird, 'Population Growth,' in Alexander Eckstein, Waltern Galenson, and Ta-chung Liu (eds.), *Economic Trends in Communist China* (Chicago: Aldine Publishing Company, 1968).
A3	John S. Aird, Foreign Demographic Analysis Division of the US Bureau of the Census.
A4	Arthur G. Ashbrook, Jr., 'China: Economic Policy and Economic Results, 1949–71,' in *Economic Assessment*, op. cit.
B1	Bureau of Economic Analysis, US Department of Commerce.
B2	*Handbook of Basic Economic Statistics*, Economic Statistics Bureau, Washington, D.C.; January, 1974.
B3	Bureau of Intelligence and Research, 'Communist States and Developing Countries: Aid and Trade in 1970,' US Department of State, 1971.
B4	Michael Boretsky, 'The Technological Base of Soviet Military Power,' in *Economic Performance and the Military Burden in the Soviet Union*, Joint Economics Committee, US Congress, US Gorvernment Printing Office, 1970.
C1	David W. Carey, 'Soviet Agriculture,' in *Economic Performance*, op. cit.
C2	James Richard Carter, *The Net Cost of Soviet Foreign Aid* (New York: Praeger, 1969).
C3	Committee on Finance, US Senate, *Foreign Trade: A Survey of Issues to be Studied by the Subcommittee on International Trade*, US Government Printing Office, 1971.
C4	*Commodity Handbook*, Commodity Research Bureau, Inc., 1973.
C5	Kang Chao, *The Rate and Pattern of Industrial Growth in Communist China* (Ann Arbor: University of Michigan Press, 1965).
C6	Roger A. Clarke, *Soviet Economic Facts* (New York: Wiley, 1972).
C7	Stanley H. Cohn, 'Production,' in Ellen Mickiewicz (ed.), *Handbook of Soviet Social Science Data* (New York: Free Press, 1973).
D1	Douglas Diamond and Constance Krueger, 'Recent Developments in Output and Productivity in Soviet Agriculture,' in *Soviet Economic Prospects for the Seventies*, US Congress, Joint Economics Committee, US Government Printing Office, 1973).
E1	Alexander Eckstein, *Communist China's Economic Growth and Foreign Trade* (New York: McGraw-Hill, 1966).
E2	Alva Lewis Erisman, 'China: Agricultural Development, 1949–1971,' in *Economic Assessment* op. cit.

Table C.2 *continued.*

F1	John T. Farrell, 'Soviet Payments Problems in Trade with the West,' in *Soviet Economic Prospects*, op. cit.
F2	George Feiwel, *The Soviet Quest for Economic Efficiency* (New York: Praeger, 1972).
F3	Murray Feshbach, 'Population,' in *Economic Performance*, op. cit.
F4	Robert Michael Field, 'Industrial Production in Communist China: 1957–68,' in *China Quarterly*, No. 42, June 1970.
F5	Robert Michael Field, 'Chinese Industrial Development: 1949–70,' in *Economic Assessment*, op. cit.
F6	Forsvarets Forskningsanstalt, The Swedish Research Institute for National Defense.
F7	Board of Governors of the US Federal Reserve System.
G1	Mark Garrison and Morris H. Crawford, 'Soviet Trade with the Free World in 1961,' in *Dimensions of Soviet Economic Power*, US Congress, Joint Economics Committee, US Government Printing Office, 1962.
G2	Harry Gelber, 'Nuclear Weapons and Chinese Policy,' *Adelphi Papers*, #99, London Institute for Strategic Studies, 1973.
G3	Marshall Goldman, *Soviet Foreign Aid* (New York: Praeger, 1967).
G4	Rush V. Greenslade and Wade E. Robertson, 'Industrial Production in the USSR,' in *Soviet Economic Prospects* , op. cit.
G5	John G. Gurley, 'Some Economic Data of Communist China: 1949–1967,' (Xerox) Stanford University, Stanford, California (Ca. 1968).
H1	*Historical Statistics of the United States: Colonial Times to 1957*, Bureau of the Census, US Department of Commerce, US Government Printing Office, 1960.
H2	Raymond Hutchings, *Soviet Economic Development* (Oxford: Basil Blackwell, 1971).
J1	Edwin F. Jones, 'The Emerging Pattern of China's Economic Revolution,' in *An Economic Profile of Mainland China*, US Congress, Joint Economics Committee, US Government Printing Office, 1967.
K1	Istvan Kende, 'Twenty-five Years of Local Wars,' *Journal of Peace Research*, Vol. VIII, No. 1, (1971).
K2	John W. Kendric, *Postwar Productivity Trends in the United States* (New York: National Bureau of Economic Research, 1973).
K3	Robert S. Kovach and John T. Farrell, 'Foreign Trade of the USSR,' in *Economic Performance*, op. cit.
L1	J. Richard Lee, 'The Fuels of Industries,' in *Economic Performance*, op. cit.
L2	Ta-chung Liu and Kung-chia, *The Economy of the Chinese Mainland* (Princeton, N.J.: Princeton University Press, 1965).
M1	Paul Marer, *Soviet and East European Foreign Trade, 1946–1969* (Bloomington, Indiana: Indiana University Press, 1972).

Table C.2 *continued.*

M2   *The Military Balance* (London: The London Institute for Strategic Studies, 1974).

N1   John H. Noren, 'Soviet Industry Trends in Output, Inputs, and Productivity,' in *New Directions in the Soviet Economy*, US Congress, Joint Economics Committee, US Government Printing Office, 1966.

O1   Office of Business Economics, *US Exports and Imports, 1923–1968*, US Department of Commerce, US Government Printing Office, 1970.

O2   Organization for Economic Cooperation and Development, *Main Economic Indicators*, 1955–71 (Paris: IECD, 1972(.

O3   Organization for Economic Cooperation and Development, *National Accounts of OECD Countries*, 1950–1968 (Paris: OECD, 1970).

O4   Organization for Economic Cooperation and Development, *Statistics of Energy*, 1950–64, 1955–69, and 1958–72 volumes (Paris: OECD, 1965, 1970, and 1973).

P1   Dwight H. Perkins, *Agricultural Development in China, 1368–1968* (Chicago: Aldine Publishing, 1969).

R1   Philip D. Reichers, 'The Electronics Industry of China,' in *Economic Assessment*, op. cit.

S1   *SIPRI Yearbook*, Stockholm International Peace Research Institute, Stockholm, Sweden, 1974.

S2   Alen Alden Smith, *Soviet Foreign Trade: Organization, Operations, and Policy, 1918–1971* (New York: Praeger, 1972).

S3   F.W. Dresch, *et al.*, 'A Comparison of US/USSR Gross National Product, National Security Expenditures, and Expenditures for R.D.T. & E.,' SSC-TN-2010-1, Stanford Research Institute, Strategic Studies Center, Menlo Park, California, 1972.

S4   *Statistical Abstract of the US: 1973*, Bureau of the Census, US Department of Commerce, US Government Printing Office, 1973.

S5   Subramania Swamy and Shahid Javid Burki, 'Foodgrains Output in the People's Republic of China,' in the *China Quarterly*, No. 41, January–March 1970.

S6   Anthony Sutton, *Western Technology and Soviet Economic Development* (Stanford, California: Hoover Institution Press, 1965).

T1   Leo Tansky, 'Chinese Foreign Trade,' in *Economic Assessment*, op. cit.

T2   Leo Tansky, *US and USSR Aid to Developing Countries* (New York: Praeger, 1967).

U1   United Nations, *Demographic Yearbook* (New York: United Nations, 1974, 1975).

U2   United Nations, *The Growth of World Industry, 1971* Department of Economic and Social Affairs, Statistical Office in the United Nations, 1972.

U3   United Nations, *United Nations Yearbook of International Trade Statistics* (New York: United Nations, 1974, 1975).

Table C.2 *continued.*

U4	US Department of Agriculture, Bureau of Agricultural Economics.
U5	A.H. Usack and R.E. Batsavage, 'The International Trade of the People's Republic of China,' in *Economic Assessment*, op. cit.
V1	Philip W. Vertterling and James J. Wagy, 'China: The Transporatation Sector, 1950–71,' in *Economic Assessment*, op. cit.
V2	*Vneshnya Torgovlya SSSR, Stiticheskii Shornik, 1918–66*, (Moscow: Vneshtorgizdut, 1967).
V3	*Vneshnya Torgovlya SSSR za (year) God, Statisticheskii Obsor* (Moscow: Vneshtorgizdut, 1967, 1968, 1969, 1970, 1971, 1972).
W1	F. Douglas Whitehouse and Joseph F. Havelka, 'Comparison of Farm Output in the US and the USSR, 1950–1971,' in *Soviet Economic Prospects*, op. cit.
W2	Joseph W. Willett, 'The Recent Record in Agricultural Production,' in *Dimensions*, op. cit.
W3	*World Military Expenditures*, US Arms Control and Disarmament Agency, Washington, D.C., US Government Printing Office, 1970, 1971, 1972, 1973.

APPENDIX D

Some Technical Issues in Econometric Analysis

This work has drawn extensively upon *econometric theory*, the portion of econometrics whose objective is the 'development of appropriate techniques of statistical inference.'[1] This tradition is particularly appealing for present purposes because, among other reasons discussed in Chapter 2, it is this realm that has most advanced the technical theory applicable to the kind of dynamic, multivariate, causal system suggested by the conceptual framework. In addition, econometric theory does provide guidelines for multivariate causal analysis which at least reduce the chances of misinference. Thus, this study might reasonably be viewed as an example of *applied econometrics* — the practical realm in which prior, general theory (in this case, the conceptual framework) *and* econometric theory are together applied to nonexperimental evidence in an effort to further understanding of relationships among variables.[2]

This appendix begins by quickly noting some of the differences between econometrics as idealized in the theoretical literature and econometrics as here applied in an experimental mode. There are, it is argued, risks involved in an experimental approach; but it is also argued that such an approach remains essential to continued progress in model building. Next, this appendix takes up some of the serious technical issues that have been confronted in this study.

I EXPERIMENTAL ECONOMETRICS

As is true in most instances of applied econometrics, this study has encountered some serious gaps between econometric theory and the demands

[1] Arthur S. Goldberger, *Econometric Theory* (New York: Wiley, 1964), p. 1.
[2] Ibid.

and constraints of econometric practice. While econometric theory has been at least somewhat responsive to the needs of the empirical analyst, the guidelines provided by econometric theory do not always anticipate the analyst's every situation or answer his most pressing questions.[3] The first and most general consequence is that those engaged in applied econometrics are frequently left to fend for themselves in an exploratory, experimental way. A second consequence is that those engaged in applied econometrics, noting that their circumstances are not the idealized ones dealt with in econometric theory, have little choice but to diverge from theoretical guidelines on occasion. And a third consequence is that every theoretically unanticipated situation, every surge to the frontiers of empirical econometrics, invites both the risk of error and the certainty of controversy.

The nature of this gap can be more precisely described. Classical econometric theory starts from the premise that the maintained hypotheses underlying any equation or system of equations are known with certainty. That is, econometric theory assumes that model specification reflects strong, unambiguous prior theory. It is upon this premise that statistical measures and theoretical guidelines as to their interpretation have been developed. International relations theory, however, can hardly be described as strong. It offers prior information about very general relationships; but it offers little guidance as to functional forms, about the relative weighting of various relationships (i.e., which variables ought to be included as 'most important'), or concerning the data to be used to represent conceptual variables. The situation is somewhat more favorable for those who use economic theory, for there the model builder benefits from efforts in mathematical economics and from the emerging specificational conventions of econometric practitioners; yet even there, the gap between theory and practice remains real.

As Carl Christ argues,[4] the analyst has several choices in the face of such a gap: he can give up; he can arbitrarily select one model; or he can experiment with several different models — all equally defensible on theoretical grounds. As Christ suggests, the last choice is preferable, for it does offer a reasonably objective basis for model selection.[5]

Experimental econometrics is now the most common approach. The approach begins with a recognition that prior theory is weak (i.e., consistent with a number of competing formulations), and it is intended to

---

[3] Carl F. Christ, *Econometric Models and Methods* (New York: Wiley, 1966), pp. 9–10.
[4] Ibid., p. 8.   [5] Ibid.

'extract the maximum of information from available data.'[6] Following an experimental approach, one begins with relatively simple formulations and tests these with references to available data; then, finding weaknesses in the initial formulation (e.g., breakpoints, generally poor fit, or insignificant terms), one experiments with alternative (and probably more complex) measures, functional forms, equation formulations, and systems of equations. Each step effectively contributes to the prior information underlying ensuing steps. In effect, the analyst engages in repeated cycles of theoretical specification, testing, theoretical revision, and respecification.

In the process, however, the gap between classical econometric theory and econometric practice is never really closed: an experimental approach violates the idealized premises of econometric theory while also encountering a number of risks. For example, experimental econometrics runs counter to the norm that, if the same data are used to both select and test a maintained hypothesis, classical statistical inference procedures must not be applied without some adjustment.[7] Violation of this norm yields bias toward type 2 error — the failure to reject a false hypothesis and in increased tendency to conclude that an equation is correct; and violation is likely, since it is rarely the case that additional data can be acquired.

A related danger is that, given enough time, energy, and resources, the analyst can keep refining a model and keep improving a model's fit to the data. The degree of fit can become too close. The model, instead of being an improved theoretical representation, can become too tied to the idiosyncracies of the available data, and too wedded to accidental features, including measurement error. The danger of unbridled tinkering, moreoever, also applies to one's choices among measures. If one is unrestricted in his choices, he can probably find measures that will support almost any theoretical assertion. In short, indefinite refinement *can* be theoretically regressive.

Against these risks, however, one must also balance the promise of an experimental approach. Given weak theory, it is too early for the field as a whole to 'give up' — or to rush 'beyond data.' Given weak theory and a paucity of conventions, too, arbitrarily specified models are likely to individually garner misinformation (while obscuring the real experimental progression that relates one model to its alternatives). What is needed is an experimental approach that is guided by an orderly,

---

[6] A. Koutsoyiannis, *Theory of Econometrics* (New York: Barnes and Noble, 1973), p. 22.

[7] Christ, op. cit., pp. 9–10.

communicable, and replicable research design — a research design that lays down a systematic order of experimental research (see Appendix A). Such an approach can minimize some of the risks of experimentation by disallowing theoretically unsupportable steps intended solely to maximize fit and by explicating the choices made so that the scrutiny of other analysts can be applied.

This means, of course, abandonment of the pretense that the statistics examined are true tests of significance. Instead, they stand as useful decision rules. (Except when one actually used data sampled from a population, this has nearly always been the case.) With the abandonment of this pretense must also go the notion that our analytic progress conforms to a hypothetical deductive reconstructed logic under the tutelage of methodological falsificationist norms. Models are not born of an isolated moment of inspiration and then put to a severe test — with the test determining whether they will be provisionally retained or falsified and banished. Rather, the models put forth at any moment can usually be understood as refinements of prior versions — and the models themselves are likely to be refined again in light of new information.

In sum, what is said here amounts to an argument for explicitness in disciplined experimentation — explicitness not only with respect to the more substantive issues of model specification, but also regarding the resolution of technical problems that are repeatedly confronted throughout all phases of the specification-estimation-respecification process. These technical issues are the subject of the next section.

II   SOME TECHNICAL ISSUES

As will quickly become evident, the most familiar form of regression analysis — standard single-equation ordinary least-squares (OLS) — has generally proven to be less than adequate for present purposes. The reason is simple: the use of OLS must be founded upon a set of assumptions;[8] yet many of these are violated by (*a*) the present work's regular

---

[8] The assumptions of ordinary least-squares are: (1) The variable μ_i is a random variable. The value it assumes — positive, negative, or zero — depends upon chance; (2) For any period, the mean of μ_i is zero: $E(\mu_i) = 0$ for all i; (3) The variance of μ_i is constant in any period for all values of X: $E(\mu_i) = \sigma \hat{\mu}$; (4) The variable μ_i is normally distributed; (5) The random terms of different observations (μ_i, μ_j) are independent. Or $E(\mu_i\mu_i\pm_j) = $ for $j \neq 0$; (6) μ_i is independent of explanatory variables, or the values of the X's are fixed for all (hypothetical) samples; (7) Explanatory variables are measured without error; (8) Explanatory variables are not perfectly linearly correlated; (9) Variables are correctly aggregated; (10) The relationship being estimated is identified; (11) The relationship is correctly specified; (12) There are more observations than there are parameters to be estimated.

use of simultaneous equations and lagged endogenous (or system determined) variables, (*b*) the recurrence of serial correlation in error terms,
and often (*c*) the combination of the two. To persist in the use of OLS
despite these violations — especially in the early, crucial experimental
phases of research — would risk inconsistency[9] and bias[10] in the estimation of parameters and would almost certainly yield the compounding
effects of misinference and misguided decisions in the model-building
process.

The preferred alternatives to standard OLS are found in combinations
of *instrumental variables* (IV) and *generalized least squares* (GLS). The
former, IV, is a two-stage least squares (2SLS)[11] regression procedure
in which:

1. A list of predetermined variables, called 'instruments,' are regressed against endogenous RHS variables (or coterms) of an
   estimating equation to produce artificial RHS variables, called
   'instrumental variables.' In effect, these instrumental variables
   are weighted sums of the prespecified instruments.

2. The newly created instrumental variables replace their respective
   endogenous variables (or coterms) in the original estimating equation. This amended equation is then regressed to complete the
   second stage.

Broadly speaking, an IV substitution is indicated whenever a significant
correlation is suspected or evidenced between RHS variables and disturbances, and most especially when endogenous or lagged endogenous
variables are included. The purpose of this 2SLS procedure is to devise
instrumental variables that are highly correlated with the endogenous
variables they replace but uncorrelated with residuals — and in so doing

---

[9] An estimator $\hat{\beta}$ of parameter β is inconsistent to the degree that it fails to converge on β as sample size goes to infinity. It is therefore asymptotically biased.

[10] A biased estimator is one that, on the average over several samples, fails to
hit the target parameters; i.e., $E(\hat{\beta}) \neq \beta$.

[11] Two-Stage Least Squares is the foremost Limited Information estimating procedure. On its advantages over Three-Stage Least Squares and other Full Information
approaches, see Franklin M. Fisher, 'Dynamic Structure and Estimation in Economy-
Wide Econometric Models,' in James Deusenberry *et al.* (eds.), *The Brookings
Quarterly Econometric Model of the United States* (Chicago: Rand McNally, 1965);
and Franklin M. Fisher, 'Simultaneous Equations Estimation: The State of the Art,'
Working Paper No. 55, Department of Economics, MIT (1970).

to render more consistent estimates of parameters.[12] This, however, is never guaranteed. Considerable care must therefore be exercised in the selection of instruments and the creation of instrumental variables.

Generalized least squares (GLS) is an estimation procedure in which RHS variables are transformed in accordance with the determined structure of an error process. More specifically, because serial correlation — i.e., interdependence in successive disturbances — violates one of the OLS assumptions,[13] GLS is used to correct for it. It operates, in essence, by initially transforming RHS variables so that residuals satisfying OLS assumptions will be produced.[14]

Applying GLS, however, is no automatic matter. It requires prior knowledge of the operative disturbance process[15] — at the very least some insight as to which of several models most closely approximate the structure of that process. Four of the models prominent in the literature are displayed in Table D.1. As noted there, each of these models has been applied in the GLS transformations of the present work.

Deciding which of the four models to apply, if any, involves careful attention to, and analysis of, the residuals of any estimating equation. Specifically, correlograms are generated and analyzed as a means of

---

[12] However, it should be noted that IV substitutions can produce a loss of precision (relative to OLS) in small samples. See, e.g., J.L. Morrison, 'Small Sample Properties of Selected Distributed Lag Estimators,' *International Economic Review*, Vol. XI (1970); and Thomas J. Sargent, 'Some Evidence on the Small Sample Properties of Distributed Lag Estimators in the Presence of Autocorrelated Disturbances,' *Review of Economics and Statistics*, Vol. L (1968).

[13] The assumption that disturbances are uncorrelated across time, assumption 5 in n. 8, above.

[14] See A.C. Aitkin, 'On Least Squares and Linear Combination of Observations,' *Proceedings of the Royal Society of Edinburgh*, Vol. LV (1935).

[15] That is, one needs prior knowledge of the disturbance variance-covariance matrix Ω that is used to transform independent variables. The Durbin-Watson statistic is helpful in the detection of AUTO1 processes. Yet it must be added that this statistic was designed for equations in which all RHS variables are strictly exogenous (determined outside the system); so it is not strictly appropriate to simultaneous equations or to equations containing lagged endogenous variables. In fact, it is asymptotically biased upwards toward 2.0 in these cases and cannot be said to test for autocorrelation. See J. Durbin and G.S. Watson, 'Testing for Serial Correlation in Least Squares Regression: I,' *Biometrika*, Vol. XXXVII (1950); J. Durbin and G.S. Watson, 'Testing for Serial Correlation in Least Squares Regression: II,' *Biometrika*, Vol. XXXVIII (1951); Carl F. Christ, op. cit., p. 525; J. Johnston, op. cit., pp. 252, 307–13; L.D. Taylor and T.A. Wilson, 'Three-Pass Least Squares: A Method for Estimating Models with a Lagged Dependent Variable,' *Review of Economics and Statistics*, Vol. XLVI (1964); Marc Nerlove and Kenneth F. Wallis, 'Use of the Durbin-Watson Statistic in Inappropriate Situations,' *Econometrica*, Vol. XXXIV (1966).

Table D.1 *Four Time-Dependence Process Models*

The following four models have been used in the GLS transformations of this study. All models are implemented in the TROLL system:

Acronym*	Description	Equation Form†
AUTO1	*First-order autoregressive* process wherein each error term, μ_t, depends upon only its previous value plus a random, 'white noise' component.	$\mu_t = \phi_1 \mu_{t-1} + \nu_t$
AUTO2	*Second-order autoregressive* process wherein each error term, μ_t, depends upon only its two previous values plus a random, 'white noise' component.	$\mu_t = \phi_1 \mu_{t-1} + \phi_2 \mu_{t-2} + \nu_t$
MAV1	*First-order moving average* process wherein each error term, μ_t, depends upon a moving linear combination of random perturbations (or shocks) only as far back as the previous observation.	$\mu_t = \nu_t - \phi_1 \nu_{t-1}$
MAV2	*Second-order moving average* process wherein each error term, μ_t, depends upon a moving linear combination of random perturbations (or shocks) only as far back as the previous two observations.	$\mu_t = \nu_t - \phi_1 \nu_{t-1} - \phi_2 \nu_{t-2}$

*These are the acronyms used here and in the TROLL system; other common acronyms are AR(1), AR(2), MA(1), and MA(2), respectively.

†Notation: μ_t is the error at time t; ν_t is a random variable entering the system at time t; and ϕ_i is a parameter of an autoregressive process.

detecting the presence and apparent structure of a disturbance process.[16] In addition, if an AUTO1 or AUTO2 process is suspected on the basis of correlogram analysis, it is useful to produce three equations regressing

[16] Using correlograms, one (*a*) retrieves the residuals from a preliminary OLS regression, (*b*) calculates and plots the successive correlations ρ_θ between residual at time t and residuals at various times $t-\theta$ (up to $\theta = N/4$ or $N/5$, as a practical matter), (*c*) compares these plots to the theoretical correlograms that would be generated by the four alternative disturbance processes, and (*d*) chooses the appropraite model.

$\hat{\mu}_t$ on previous values $(\hat{\mu}_{t-1}; \hat{\mu}_{t-1}$ and $\hat{\mu}_{t-2}$; and $\hat{\mu}_{t-1}, \hat{\mu}_{t-2},$ and $\hat{\mu}_{t-3})$ and then observe coefficients, equation significance, and the Durbin-Watson statistic for each equation.[17] Once a time-dependence model is selected, GLS is used to make appropriate corrections and to estimate parameters. However, it must be stressed that even when these cumbersome procedures are followed through, the choice of models is seldom a certain one: empirical residuals seldom array themselves in perfect conformity to theoretical error processes.[18]

Difficult as the issues surrounding IV-2SLS and GLS are, they are further compounded when the two procedures are necessarily combined — as with the coincidence of lagged endogenous variables and serially correlated disturbances. The emerging question, essentially, is whether the IV substitution should precede or follow GLS transformation. The TROLL system used here implements GLS first, then the IV substitution,[19] and

---

In practice, the following rules of thumb are helpful; MAV1 can be inferred if only ρ_1 is significant; MAV2 can be inferred if only ρ_1 and ρ_2 (or ρ_2 alone) are significant; AUTO1 can be inferred if $\rho_\theta = \rho^{|\theta|}$. If none of these appear, then test for AUTO2 by regression of:

$$\hat{\mu}_t = \phi_1 \hat{\mu}_{t-1} + \phi_2 \hat{\mu}_{t-2}$$

If (a) ϕ_2 or ϕ_2 and ϕ_1 are significant, (b) the equation as a whole is significant according to the F ratio, and (c) the Durbin-Watson statistic approaches 2.0 then an AUTO2 process can be inferred. If none of the above appear, and especially if correlations are generally low (i.e., < 1.20), discount autocorrelation and use OLS.

It should be pointed out that, on theoretical grounds (and increasingly on empirical grounds), autoregressive and moving average processes of an order greater than 2 are expected to be rare. Nevertheless, the question remains: which, if any, model should be used if higher order processes are suspected? Our response has generally been to use OLS in these cases, felling that misspecification (e.g., using AUTO2 for AUTO3 or MAV3) may do more harm than good. See Douglas A. Hibbs, Jr., 'Problems of Statistical Estimation and Causal Inference in Time-Series Regression Models,' in Herbert L. Costner (ed.), *Sociological Methodology 1973–1974* (San Francisco: Jossey-Bass, 1974); and Robert Engle, 'Specification of the Disturbance for Efficient Estimation,' *Econometrics*, Vol. XLII (1973). There are other views. Choucri and North, for instance, use the following rule: 'significant correlations [not fitting other models] may be tentatively viewed as a reflection of a second order autocorrelation process (AUTO2), in the absence of evidence indicating otherwise.' They argue that 'An AUTO2 often appears to be suitable trade-off between complexity and accuracy.' Op. cit., p. 316, nn. 34 and 35. Clearly, this is one area in which further empirical work is badly needed.

[17] In this way, too, the initial parameter estimates for the TROLL-GLS search routine can be 'guessed.' This reduces required iterations and computational costs (assuming good guesses are provided).

[18] For example, as Hibbs, op. cit., points out, it is frequently difficult to distinguish a MAV process from an AUTO process that quickly damps off.

[19] In fact, the two-stage computations are performed for *each iteration* of a GLS estimation in TROLL; see *TROLL Reference Manual*, National Bureau of Economic Research, Cambridge, Mass., 1974, pp. 10–11.

Table D.2 *Steps in a Combined IV–GLS Estimating Procedure*

1. Undertake OLS on original estimating equation and retrieve residuals.

2. In light of residuals from step 1, select variables from 'instrument list' and create instrumental variables, X_i for endogenous and lagged endogenous RHS variables, X_i.

3. Replace endogenous and lagged endogenous variables X_i with $\hat{X}_i$ in the original estimating equation and regress.

4. Using the coefficients from step 3, and the *original data*, calculate estimates of the disturbances, $\hat{\mu}_t$.*

5. Using residuals from step 4, undertake correlogram analysis and determine time-dependent process, if any.† If a time-dependent correction is indicated, go to step 6. If not, use estimates from step 3.

6. Using the TROLL algorithm, initiate combined GLS correction and IV substitution. In this, the GLS correction precedes the IV substitution in each iteration of GLS estimation.

---

*Hibbs (see n. 16) advocates this additional step (as opposed to using the residuals from step 3). He argues that, especially for small samples, IV may produce a great loss of precision.

†See n. 16 of text.

this is the procedure followed in the present analysis. (For reasons of replicability, this procedure is fully depicted in Table D.2.) The designers of TROLL indicate that the reverse order, IV first, might introduce heteroscedasticity[20] and hence inefficiency while TROLL's order preserves homoscedasticity and estimation efficiency.[21] However, 'GLS first,' is not the only order advocated in the literature; and the reverse order has much to commend it.[22]

One of the more troublesome problems plaguing this research is not resolved by either GLS or IV substitution. This is the problem of multicollinearity (or high linear correlations among RHS variables) — a problem

[20] Nonconstant diagonal elements in the error variance-covariance matrix — most typically a cross-sectional problem.

[21] See Mark Eisner and Robert S. Pindyck, 'A Generalized Approach to Estimation as Implemented in the TROLL/1 System,' *Annals of Economic and Social Measurement*, Vol. II (1973).

[22] See Hibbs, op. cit., and Kenneth Wallis, 'Lagged Dependent Variables and Serially Correlated Errors: A Reappraisal of Three-Pass Least Squares,' *The Review of Economics and Statistics*, Vol. IL (1967). Both Hibbs and Wallis advocate the use of manual 2SLS followed by GLS. They argue that GLS will be performed on the appropriate residuals only if the IV substitution is first performed. Choucri and North, op. cit., also explicitly confront this difficult problem; in fact, their Appendix C (by Raisa Deber) provides a detailed experiment using *nine* different estimation strategies under these circumstances.

whose most immediate consequence is neither bias nor inconsistency but a loss of precision in parameter estimates.[23] Unfortunately, multicollinearity is much easier to detect than to overcome:[24] the 'solutions' put forth in the literature are either irrelevant or too drastic given present purposes.[25] One 'solution' excluding collinear variables, might in fact exacerbate imprecision if the variable in question is indeed a contributor to the total effect on Y.[26] Worse still, an exclusion of a theoretically relevant variable in the service of computational precision can undermine theoretical precision: one might thereby derive computationally more precise estimates, but these would have little bearing on the causal hypotheses in question. In sum, the present analysis reflects an effort to reduce collinearity and heighten precision via choice among alternative specifications, but not at the cost of misrepresenting the pre-theory.[27]

Appendix E returns once again to the main product of the econometric research progression. It presents the full system of equations comprising the general model.

[23] Other effects include: (*a*) it becomes difficult to disentangle the 'relative effects' of the various RHS variables, (*b*) the investigator may erroneously drop variables from the analysis because their effects are so entangled with others that they do not *appear* to differ significantly from zero, (*c*) estimates of parameters become very sensitive to sets of sample data. See Johnston, op. cit., p. 160.

[24] Detecting multicollinearity requires only examination of zero-order correlations among RHS variables when there are only two. The best guide when there are more than two is suggested by Farrar and Glauber: regress each X_i against all remaining RHS variables and look to R^2. D.E. Farrar and R.R. Glauber, 'Multicollinearity in Regression Analysis: The Problem Revisited,' *Review of Economics and Statistics*, Vol. IL (1967).

[25] More nonexperimental data are unavailable or too costly, preliminary factor analysis has extracted factors that appear to have little correspondence to the pretheory, relevant extraneous parameter estimates (e.g., from cross-sectional studies) are unavailable, and constrained regression requires rather strong prior information not provided by the pre-theory. This leaves model reformulation (e.g., use logarithmic transformations rather than raw data), but this, too, has severe shortcomings; see text.

[26] With high probability this would yield serial correlation, itself a source of imprecision (i.e., less than minimum variance in parameter estimates).

[27] Wherever possible, alternative equations have been specified and estimated. In the experimental phases, greatest confidence has been placed in estimates of parameters for equations exhibiting the least multicollinearity, and the smallest standard errors — again, so long as they are equally true to prior information.

The System of Equations

This appendix presents the full system of equations constituting the general model. Table E.2 shows the six heuristic equations originally presented in Chapter 2 and examined in Chapters 4 through 9. It will be recalled that these chapters detail the correspondencies between individual terms and propositions contained in the conceptual framework of Chapter 1. These equations are styled 'heuristic' because they incorporate terms detached from particular actor and target nations; they refer instead to symbolic major powers A, B, and C. As major powers, the CPR, the USSR, and the US can be alternatively substituted for A, B, and C in these equations. The six heuristic equations are the basis for the stochastic equations in the general model.

Table E.3 presents the full system of equations: definitions, identities, and the twenty-four stochastic equations in the general model. Each stochastic equation is numbered so as to identify the heuristic equation with which it corresponds. Thus, stochastic equations 1.1, 1.2 and 1.3 correspond to equation one in Table E.2, stochastic equations 2.1, 2.2, and 2.3 correspond to equation 2, and so on. To expedite presentation, alphanumeric notation has been used. The $Y_{k \cdot lm}$ with coefficients $\beta_{k \cdot lm}$ represent the endogenous variables, where k identifies the block number ($k = 1$, 2, 3, or 4 corresponding to blocks A, B, C, or D, respectively), l is the endogenous variable type (corresponding to left-hand side variables in Eq. 1–6 of Table E.2), and m is the specific variable within any type. Table E.1 illustrates this notation. In Table E.3, the $Y^*_{k \cdot lm}$ with coefficients $\beta^*_{k \cdot lm}$ are one-year lagged endogenous variables, $Y_{k \cdot lm}$. Strictly exogenous variables — i.e., variables determined entirely outside of the system — are denoted Z_i with coefficients γ_i. And variables that are identical functions of the $Y_{k \cdot lm}$ are denoted $W_{k \cdot j}$ with coefficients $\Psi_{k \cdot j}$, where k again refers to the block number of appearance and j indicates

Table E.1 Illustration of Notation

	Block A $k=1$			Block B $k=2$	Block C $k=3$	Block D $k=4$
	Expansion (1)	Intersection (2)	Defense Expenditure (3)	Provocation (4)	Normal Conflict Behavior (5)	Threshold of Violence (6)
Actor-Specific Variables						
US	$Y_{1\cdot11}$		$Y_{1\cdot31}$			
USSR	$Y_{1\cdot12}$		$Y_{1\cdot32}$			
CPR	$Y_{1\cdot13}$		$Y_{1\cdot33}$			
Dyad-Specific Variables						
US–USSR		$Y_{1\cdot21}$		$Y_{2\cdot41}$		
US–CPR		$Y_{1\cdot22}$		$Y_{2\cdot42}$		
USSR–CPR		$Y_{1\cdot23}$		$Y_{2\cdot43}$		
Directed Dyad-Specific Variables						
US → USSR					$Y_{3\cdot51}$	$Y_{4\cdot61}$
US → CPR					$Y_{3\cdot52}$	$Y_{4\cdot62}$
USSR → US					$Y_{3\cdot53}$	$Y_{4\cdot63}$
USSR → CPR					$Y_{3\cdot54}$	$Y_{4\cdot64}$
CPR → US					$Y_{3\cdot55}$	$Y_{4\cdot65}$
CPR → USSR					$Y_{3\cdot56}$	$Y_{4\cdot66}$

specific variable within the block.

The full variable labels are shown in the definitions of Table E.3. The identity equations of Table E.3 define the $W_{k \cdot j}$. The construction of measures is outlined in Table 2.1 of Chapter 2. Data sources and units of measurement are given in Appendix C.

As shown, the twenty-four stochastic equations are arranged according to the four blocks of a block-recursive system. Block A ($k = 1$) determines the three actors' expansion ($Y_{1.1m}$), the three dyads' intersections ($Y_{1.2m}$), and the three actors' defense expenditures ($Y_{1.3m}$). Block B ($k = 2$) determines the three dyads' provocations ($Y_{2.4m}$). Block C ($k = 3$) determines the six directed dyads' normal (or annual mean) conflict and co-operation ($Y_{3.5m}$). Block D ($k = 4$) determines the six directed dyads' thresholds of violence ($Y_{4.6m}$).

While simultaneous reciprocities and feedback loops are permitted within any block,[1] no simultaneous circularities appear across blocks. Thus, when the coefficient matrix of the nonlagged endogenous variables of the entire model is suitably ordered as to rows and columns and partitioned according to component blocks, the resulting matrix is block triangular. Moreover, it is assumed that, while disturbances need not be uncorrelated within blocks, the disturbances are uncorrelated across blocks in the probability limit. This is to assume, in other words, that the model specification has omitted no variables that have important influences upon the endogenous variables of two or more blocks.

---

[1] Equations (4.1)–(4.3) are labeled a block, Block B ($k = 2$), for reasons of presentational convenience. There are no simultaneous reciprocities among the $Y_{2.4m}$.

Table E.2 *The Six Heuristic Equations*

A's Trade Dispersion #2 $= \alpha_1 + \beta_1(A\text{'s Elec. Power Prod.} \times A\text{'s Pop.}) + \beta_2[\Delta(A\text{'s GNP} \div A\text{'s Pop.})]^*$ (1)

$+ \beta_3(A\text{'s Indus. Prod. Index} \div A\text{'s Coal Prod.}) + \beta_4(A\text{'s Def. Expend.})$

$+ \beta_5(A\text{'s Trade Disp. #2}_{t-1}) + \mu_1$

A–B Intersection #2 $= \alpha_2 + \beta_6(A\text{'s Trade Disp. #2}) + \beta_7(B\text{'s Trade Disp. #2}) + \mu_2$ (2)

A's Defense Expenditure $= \alpha_3 + \beta_8(A\text{'s Def. Expend.}_{t-1}) + \beta_9[\Delta(A\text{'s GNP})]$ (3)

$+ \beta_{10}[\Delta(A\text{–}B \text{ Intersection #2}) \times (\overline{A \rightarrow B}(\text{Mean}) - 11)\dagger]$

$+ \beta_{11}[\Delta(A\text{–}C \text{ Intersection #2}) \times (\overline{A \rightarrow C}(\text{Mean}) - 11)\dagger]$

$+ \beta_{12}[(B\text{'s Def. Expend.}_t - B\text{'s Def. Expend.}_{t-2}) \times \%B \rightarrow A_{t-1}\ddagger]$

$+ \beta_{13}[(C\text{'s Def. Expend.}_t - C\text{'s Def. Expend.}_{t-2}) \times \%C \rightarrow A_{t-1}\ddagger] + \mu_3$

A–B Provocations #2 $= \alpha_4 + \beta_{14}[\Delta(A\text{'s Def. Expend.})] + \beta_{15}[\Delta(B\text{'s Def. Expend.})]$ (4)

$+ \beta_{16}[(A\text{–}B \text{ Intersection #2}) \times (\text{Number Local Wars})] + \mu_4$

$$A \rightarrow B(\text{Mean})^{\S} = \alpha_5 + \beta_{17}[A \rightarrow B(\text{Mean})_{t-1}] + \beta_{18}(A\text{'s Defense Expend.} - B\text{'s Defense Expend.})$$
$$+ \beta_{19}[\%\Delta(A\text{'s GNP/Pop.} - B\text{'s GNP/Pop.})] + \beta_{20}[B \rightarrow A(\text{Mean})] + \beta_{21}[A \rightarrow C(\text{Peak})_{t-1}]$$
$$+ \beta_{22}[\Delta(B\text{'s Defense Expend.} - C\text{'s Defense Expend.})] + \mu_5 \tag{5}$$

$$A \rightarrow B(\text{Peak})^{\P} = \alpha_6 + \beta_{23}[\Delta(A\text{'s GNP/Pop.})] + \beta_{24}(A\text{'s Defense Expend.} - B\text{'s Defense Expend.})$$
$$+ \beta_{25}[(A\text{–}B \text{ Provocation \#2}) \times (A \rightarrow B(\text{Mean}) - 11)] + \beta_{26}[B \rightarrow A(\text{Peak})]$$
$$+ \beta_{27}[A \rightarrow C(\text{Peak})_{t-1}] + \beta_{28}[\Delta(B\text{'s Defense Expend.} - C\text{'s Defense Expend.})] + \mu_6 \tag{6}$$

*See notes to Figure 4.4 in Chapter 4

† $\overline{A \rightarrow B(\text{Mean})} - 11 = \dfrac{\sum\limits_{i=1}^{3} A \rightarrow B(\text{Mean})_{t-i}}{3} - 11$, and

$\overline{A \rightarrow C(\text{Mean})} - 11 = \dfrac{\sum\limits_{i=1}^{3} A \rightarrow C(\text{Mean})_{t-i}}{3} - 11$.

‡ $\%B \rightarrow A_{t-1} = \dfrac{B \rightarrow C(\text{Mean})_{t-1}}{B \rightarrow A(\text{Mean})_{t-1} + B \rightarrow C(\text{Mean})_{t-1}}$, and

$\%C \rightarrow A_{t-1} = \dfrac{C \rightarrow A(\text{Mean})_{t-1}}{C \rightarrow A(\text{Mean})_{t-1} + C \rightarrow B(\text{Mean})_{t-1}}$.

§ Normal Conflict Behavior.

¶ Threshold of Violence.

Table E.3   *The System of Equations*

Definitions

$Y_{1 \cdot 11}$ = US Trade Disp. #2	$Y_{4 \cdot 64}$ = USSR → CPR Th. of Violence
$Y_{1 \cdot 12}$ = USSR Trade Disp. #2	$Y_{4 \cdot 65}$ = CPR → USSR Th. of Violence
$Y_{1 \cdot 13}$ = CPR Trade Disp. #2	$Y_{4 \cdot 66}$ = CPR → USSR Th. of Violence
$Y_{1 \cdot 21}$ = US–USSR Intersection #2	Z_1 = US Elec. Pow. Prod. × Pop.
$Y_{1 \cdot 22}$ = US–CPR Intersection #2	Z_2 = Δ(US GNP/Pop.)
$Y_{1 \cdot 23}$ = USSR–CPR Intersection #2	Z_3 = US Indus. Prod. Index ÷ Coal Prod.
$Y_{1 \cdot 31}$ = US Defense Expenditure	Z_4 = USSR Elec. Pow. Prod. × Pop.
$Y_{1 \cdot 32}$ = USSR Defense Expenditure	Z_5 = Δ(USSR Indus. Prod. Index ÷ Pop.)
$Y_{1 \cdot 33}$ = CPR Defense Expenditure	Z_6 = USSR Indus. Prod. Index ÷ Coal Prod.
$Y_{2 \cdot 41}$ = US–USSR Provocation #2	Z_7 = CPR Elec. Pow. Prod. × Pop.
$Y_{2 \cdot 42}$ = US–CPR Provocation #2	Z_8 = Δ(CPR Indus. Prod. Index ÷ Pop.)
$Y_{2 \cdot 43}$ = USSR–CPR Provocation #2	Z_9 = CPR Indus. Prod. Index ÷ Coal Prod.
$Y_{3 \cdot 51}$ = US → USSR Normal Conflict	Z_{10} = Δ(US GNP)
$Y_{3 \cdot 52}$ = US → CPR Normal Conflict	Z_{11} = Δ(USSR GNP)
$Y_{3 \cdot 53}$ = USSR →US Normal Conflict	Z_{12} = Δ(CPR GNP)
$Y_{3 \cdot 54}$ = USSR → CPR Normal Conflict	Z_{13} = Δ(USSR GNP/Pop.)
$Y_{3 \cdot 55}$ = CPR → US Normal Conflict	Z_{14} = Δ(CPR GNP/Pop.)
$Y_{3 \cdot 56}$ = CPR → USSR Normal Conflict	Z_{15} = Number of Local Wars (Worldwide)
$Y_{4 \cdot 61}$ = US → USSR Th. of Violence	Z_{16} = %Δ(US GNP/Pop. − USSR GNP/Pop.)
$Y_{4 \cdot 62}$ = US → CPR Th. of Violence	Z_{17} = %Δ(US GNP/Pop. − CPR GNP/Pop.)
$Y_{4 \cdot 63}$ = USSR → US Th. of Violence	Z_{18} = %Δ(USSR GNP/Pop. − CPR GNP/Pop.)

Identities

$W_{1 \cdot 1} = \Delta(\text{US–USSR Intersection \#2}) \times (\overline{\text{US} \to \text{USSR}}(\text{Mean})^* - 11)$

$W_{1 \cdot 2} = \Delta(\text{US–CPR Intersection \#2}) \times (\overline{\text{US} \to \text{CPR}}(\text{Mean})^* - 11)$

$W_{1 \cdot 3} = \Delta(\text{US–USSR Intersection \#2}) \times (\overline{\text{USSR} \to \text{US}}(\text{Mean})^* - 11)$

$W_{1 \cdot 4} = \Delta(\text{USSR–CPR Intersection \#2}) \times (\overline{\text{USSR} \to \text{CPR}}(\text{Mean})^* - 11)$

$W_{1 \cdot 5} = \Delta(\text{US–CPR Intersection \#2}) \times (\overline{\text{CPR} \to \text{US}}(\text{Mean})^* - 11)$

$W_{1 \cdot 6} = \Delta(\text{USSR–CPR Intersection \#2}) \times (\overline{\text{CPR} \to \text{USSR}}(\text{Mean})^* - 11)$

$W_{1 \cdot 7} = (\text{USSR Def. Expend.}_t - \text{USSR Def. Expend.}_{t-2}) \times \%\text{USSR} \to \text{US}_{t-1}\dagger$

$W_{1 \cdot 8} = (\text{CPR Def. Expend.}_t - \text{CPR Def. Expend.}_{t-2}) \times \%\text{CPR} \to \text{US}_{t-1}\dagger$

$W_{1 \cdot 9} = (\text{US Def. Expend.}_t - \text{US Def. Expend.}_{t-2}) \times \%\text{US} \to \text{USSR}_{t-1}\dagger$

$W_{1 \cdot 10} = (\text{CPR Def. Expend.}_t - \text{CPR Def. Expend.}_{t-2}) \times \%\text{CPR} \to \text{USSR}_{t-1}\dagger$

$W_{1 \cdot 11} = (\text{US Def. Expend.}_t - \text{US Def. Expend.}_{t-2}) \times \%\text{US} \to \text{CPR}_{t-1}\dagger$

$W_{1 \cdot 12} = (\text{USSR Def. Expend.}_t - \text{USSR Def. Expend.}_{t-2}) \times \%\text{USSR} \to \text{CPR}_{t-1}\dagger$

$W_{2 \cdot 1} = \text{US–USSR Intersection \#2} \times \text{Number of Local Wars}$

$W_{2 \cdot 2} = \text{US–CPR Intersection \#2} \times \text{Number of Local Wars}$

$W_{2\cdot3}$ = USSR–CPR Intersection #2 × Number of Local Wars

$W_{2\cdot4}$ = US Def. Expend.$_t$ − US Def. Expend.$_{t-1}$

$W_{2\cdot5}$ = USSR Def. Expend.$_t$ − USSR Def. Expend.$_{t-1}$

$W_{2\cdot6}$ = CPR Def. Expend.$_t$ − CPR Def. Expend.$_{t-1}$

$W_{3,\,4\cdot1}$ = US Def. Expend. − USSR Def. Expend.

$W_{3,\,4\cdot2}$ = US Def. Expend. − CPR Def. Expend.

$W_{3,\,4\cdot3}$ = USSR Def. Expend. − CPR Def. Expend.

$W_{3,\,4\cdot4}$ = Δ(US Def. Expend. − USSR Def. Expend.)

$W_{3,\,4\cdot5}$ = Δ(US Def. Expend. − CPR Def. Expend.)

$W_{3,\,4\cdot6}$ = Δ(USSR Def. Expend. − CPR Def. Expend.)

$W_{4\cdot7}$ = (US–USSR Provocation #2) × [US → USSR(Mean) − 11]

$W_{4\cdot8}$ = (US–CPR Provocation #2) × [US → CPR(Mean) − 11]

$W_{4\cdot9}$ = (US–USSR Provocation #2) × [USSR → US(Mean) − 11]

$W_{4\cdot10}$ = (USSR–CPR Provocation #2) × [USSR → CPR(Mean) − 11]

$W_{4\cdot11}$ = (US–CPR Provocation #2) × [CPR → US(Mean) − 11]

$W_{4\cdot12}$ = (USSR–CPR Provocation #2) × [CPR → USSR(Mean) − 11]

Stochastic Equations: Block A

$$Y_{1\cdot11} = \alpha_1 + \gamma_1 Z_1 + \gamma_2 Z_2 + \gamma_3 Z_3 + \beta_{1\cdot31} Y_{1\cdot31} + \beta^*_{1\cdot11} Y^*_{1\cdot11} + \mu_1 \tag{1.1}$$

$$Y_{1\cdot12} = \alpha_2 + \gamma_4 Z_4 + \gamma_5 Z_5 + \gamma_6 Z_6 + \beta_{1\cdot32} Y_{1\cdot32} + \beta^*_{1\cdot12} Y^*_{1\cdot12} + \mu_2 \tag{1.2}$$

$$Y_{1\cdot13} = \alpha_3 + \gamma_7 Z_7 + \gamma_8 Z_8 + \gamma_9 Z_9 + \beta_{1\cdot33} Y_{1\cdot33} + \beta^*_{1\cdot13} Y^*_{1\cdot13} + \mu_3 \tag{1.3}$$

$$Y_{1\cdot21} = \alpha_4 + \beta_{1\cdot11} Y_{1\cdot11} + \beta_{1\cdot12} Y_{1\cdot12} + \mu_4 \tag{2.1}$$

$$Y_{1\cdot22} = \alpha_5 + \beta_{1\cdot11} Y_{1\cdot11} + \beta_{1\cdot13} Y_{1\cdot13} + \mu_5 \tag{2.2}$$

$$Y_{1\cdot23} = \alpha_6 + \beta_{1\cdot12} Y_{1\cdot12} + \beta_{1\cdot13} Y_{1\cdot13} + \mu_6 \tag{2.3}$$

$$Y_{1\cdot31} = \alpha_7 + \beta^*_{1\cdot31} Y^*_{1\cdot31} + \gamma_{10} Z_{10} + \psi_{1\cdot1} W_{1\cdot1} + \psi_{1\cdot2} W_{1\cdot2} \tag{3.1}$$
$$+\ \psi_{1\cdot7} W_{1\cdot7} + \psi_{1\cdot8} W_{1\cdot8} + \mu_7$$

$$Y_{1\cdot32} = \alpha_8 + \beta^*_{1\cdot32} Y^*_{1\cdot32} + \gamma_{11} Z_{11} + \psi_{1\cdot3} W_{1\cdot3} + \psi_{1\cdot4} W_{1\cdot4} \tag{3.2}$$
$$+\ \psi_{1\cdot9} W_{1\cdot9} + \psi_{1\cdot10} W_{1\cdot10} + \mu_8$$

$$Y_{1\cdot33} = \alpha_9 + \beta^*_{1\cdot33} Y^*_{1\cdot33} + \gamma_{12} Z_{12} + \psi_{1\cdot5} W_{1\cdot5} + \psi_{1\cdot6} W_{1\cdot6} \tag{3.3}$$
$$+\ \psi_{1\cdot11} W_{1\cdot11} + \psi_{1\cdot12} W_{1\cdot12} + \mu_9$$

Stochastic Equations: Block B

$$Y_{2\cdot41} = \alpha_{10} + \psi_{2\cdot1} W_{2\cdot1} + \psi_{2\cdot4} W_{2\cdot4} + \psi_{2\cdot5} W_{2\cdot5} + \mu_{10} \tag{4.1}$$

$$Y_{2\cdot42} = \alpha_{11} + \psi_{2\cdot2} W_{2\cdot2} + \psi_{2\cdot4} W_{2\cdot4} + \psi_{2\cdot6} W_{2\cdot6} + \mu_{11} \tag{4.2}$$

Table E.3 *(cont.)*

$$Y_{2\cdot 43} = \alpha_{12} + \psi_{2\cdot 3}W_{2\cdot 3} + \psi_{2\cdot 5}W_{2\cdot 5} + \psi_{2\cdot 6}W_{2\cdot 6} + \mu_{12} \tag{4.3}$$

Stochastic equations: Block C

$$Y_{3\cdot 51} = \alpha_{13} + \beta^*_{3\cdot 51}Y^*_{3\cdot 51} + \psi_{3,4\cdot 1}W_{3,4\cdot 1} + \gamma_{16}Z_{16} + \beta_{3\cdot 53}Y_{3\cdot 53} \tag{5.1}$$
$$+ \beta^*_{4\cdot 62}Y^*_{4\cdot 62} + \psi_{3,4\cdot 6}W_{3,4\cdot 6} + \mu_{13}$$

$$Y_{3\cdot 52} = \alpha_{14} + \beta^*_{3\cdot 52}Y^*_{3\cdot 52} + \psi_{3,4\cdot 2}W_{3,4\cdot 2} + \gamma_{17}Z_{17} + \beta_{3\cdot 55}Y_{3\cdot 55} \tag{5.2}$$
$$+ \beta^*_{4\cdot 61}Y^*_{4\cdot 61} + \psi_{3,4\cdot 6}W_{3,4\cdot 6} + \mu_{14}$$

$$Y_{3\cdot 53} = \alpha_{15} + \beta^*_{3\cdot 53}Y^*_{3\cdot 53} + \psi_{3,4\cdot 1}W_{3,4\cdot 1} + \gamma_{16}Z_{16} + \beta_{3\cdot 51}Y_{3\cdot 51} \tag{5.3}$$
$$+ \beta^*_{4\cdot 64}Y^*_{4\cdot 64} + \psi_{3,4\cdot 5}W_{3,4\cdot 5} + \mu_{15}$$

$$Y_{3\cdot 54} = \alpha_{16} + \beta^*_{3\cdot 54}Y^*_{3\cdot 54} + \psi_{3,4\cdot 3}W_{3,4\cdot 3} + \gamma_{18}Z_{18} + \beta_{3\cdot 56}Y_{3\cdot 56} \tag{5.4}$$
$$+ \beta^*_{4\cdot 63}Y^*_{4\cdot 63} + \psi_{3,4\cdot 5}W_{3,4\cdot 5} + \mu_{16}$$

$$Y_{3\cdot 55} = \alpha_{17} + \beta^*_{3\cdot 55}Y^*_{3\cdot 55} + \psi_{3,4\cdot 2}W_{3,4\cdot 2} + \gamma_{17}Z_{17} + \beta_{3\cdot 52}Y_{3\cdot 52} \tag{5.5}$$
$$+ \beta^*_{4\cdot 66}Y^*_{4\cdot 66} + \psi_{3,4\cdot 4}W_{3,4\cdot 4} + \mu_{17}$$

$$Y_{3\cdot 56} = \alpha_{18} + \beta^*_{3\cdot 56}Y^*_{3\cdot 56} + \psi_{3,4\cdot 3}W_{3,4\cdot 3} + \gamma_{18}Z_{18} + \beta_{3\cdot 54}Y_{3\cdot 54} \tag{5.6}$$
$$+ \beta^*_{4\cdot 65}Y^*_{4\cdot 65} + \psi_{3,4\cdot 4}W_{3,4\cdot 4} + \mu_{18}$$

Stochastic Equations: Block D

$$Y_{4\cdot 61} = \alpha_{19} + \gamma_2 Z_2 + \psi_{3,4\cdot 1}W_{3,4\cdot 1} + \psi_{4\cdot 7}W_{4\cdot 7} + \beta_{4\cdot 63}Y_{4\cdot 63} \tag{6.1}$$
$$+ \beta^*_{4\cdot 62}Y^*_{4\cdot 62} + \psi_{3,4\cdot 6}W_{3,4\cdot 6} + \mu_{19}$$

$$Y_{4\cdot 62} = \alpha_{20} + \gamma_2 Z_2 + \psi_{3,4\cdot 2}W_{3,4\cdot 2} + \psi_{4\cdot 8}W_{4\cdot 8} + \beta_{4\cdot 65}Y_{4\cdot 65} \tag{6.2}$$
$$+ \beta^*_{4\cdot 61}Y^*_{4\cdot 61} + \psi_{3,4\cdot 6}W_{3,4\cdot 6} + \mu_{20}$$

$$Y_{4\cdot 63} = \alpha_{21} + \gamma_{13}Z_{13} + \psi_{3,4\cdot 1}W_{3,4\cdot 1} + \psi_{4\cdot 9}W_{4\cdot 9} + \beta_{4\cdot 61}Y_{4\cdot 61} \tag{6.3}$$
$$+ \beta^*_{4\cdot 64}Y^*_{4\cdot 64} + \psi_{3,4\cdot 5}W_{3,4\cdot 5} + \mu_{21}$$

$$Y_{4\cdot 64} = \alpha_{22} + \gamma_{13}Z_{13} + \psi_{3,4\cdot 3}W_{3,4\cdot 3} + \psi_{4\cdot 10}W_{4\cdot 10} + \beta_{4\cdot 66}Y_{4\cdot 66} \tag{6.4}$$
$$+ \beta^*_{4\cdot 63}Y^*_{4\cdot 63} + \psi_{3,4\cdot 5}W_{3,4\cdot 5} + \mu_{22}$$

$$Y_{4\cdot 65} = \alpha_{23} + \gamma_{14}Z_{14} + \psi_{3,4\cdot 2}W_{3,4\cdot 2} + \psi_{4\cdot 11}W_{4\cdot 11} + \beta_{4\cdot 62}Y_{4\cdot 62} \tag{6.5}$$
$$+ \beta^*_{4\cdot 66}Y^*_{4\cdot 66} + \psi_{3,4\cdot 4}W_{3,4\cdot 4} + \mu_{23}$$

$$Y_{4 \cdot 66} = \alpha_{24} + \gamma_{14}Z_{14} + \psi_{3,4 \cdot 3}W_{3,4 \cdot 3} + \psi_{4 \cdot 12}W_{4 \cdot 12} + \beta_{4 \cdot 64}Y_{4 \cdot 64} \qquad (6.6)$$

$$+ \beta^*_{4 \cdot 65}Y^*_{4 \cdot 65} + \psi_{3,4 \cdot 4}W_{3,4 \cdot 4} + \mu_{24}$$

$$* \; \overline{A \to B}(\text{Mean}) = \frac{\sum\limits_{i=1}^{3} A \to B(\text{Mean})_{t-i}}{3}$$

$$\dagger \; \%A \to B_{t-1} = \frac{A \to B(\text{Mean})_{t-1}}{A \to B(\text{Mean})_{t-1} + A \to C(\text{Mean})_{t-1}}.$$

INDEX

Abelson, Robert, 39n, 58n, 347n
Adaptation, 217-18
Adorno, T. W., 226n
Ahistoricity, of theoretical perspectives, 16-17, 283, 317n; and general model, 60
Aitken, A. C., 362n
Alker, Hayward R., Jr., xiii, xv, 12, 20n
Alliances, 19, 42-3, 135
Allison, Graham, 137n, 160n, 212
Amin, Samir, 5n
Anarchy as an internal relation, 36-8, 45, 203, 235n, 236, 273
Anderson, Perry, 6n, 242n, 263
Ando, Albert, 306n
Angell, Robert, 4n
Antagonism of historical processes, 9, 60, 185, 186; defined, 46
Arms race theory, and Choucri and North, 133; and normal conflict behavior, 157-8; and the conceptual framework, 21; of Lewis Fry Richardson, 132-3, 132n
Aron, Raymond, 6n
Aronson, Jonathan, xiii
Ashby, W. Ross, 238-9
Asymmetrical relations, integration, 14; intersections, 29-33, 112-13, 182-5
Asynchrony, 9, 14, 19, 176, 330-2; defined, 44-5
Azar, Edward, 344

Balance of power, and state autonomy, 21-2; as an emergent relation, 36-43, 237, 253; as an open system, 237-9; as ideology, 272-3; as logic of the moment, 19-22, 37-43; as regime,

19-22, 19n, 236-7, 253, 273-9; conflict management potential of, 190-1, 197-8, 237; critique of, 19-22, 234-40; dynamics of, 1, 3, 5, 17, 19, 36-43; in historical progression with growth and rivalry, 9, 44-9, 193-8, 202-5; logics of, 4, 7, 18, 40-1, 188-91; propositions regarding, 187-98; and mercantilist and liberal positions, 279-86
Baran, Paul, 261n
Baumgartner, T., 113n
Bay of Pigs Invasion, 95
Bem, D. J., 303
Berkes, Ross N., xiii
Bertalanffy, Ludwig von, 45n
Bilateral dynamics, 17; and dynamics of growth, 193-8; and rivalry, 29-36; features of, 18; in Sino-Soviet-American relations, 187-8; selected representative propositions on, 18 (table); variables affected, 18 (table)
Bilateral intersections, see intersections
Bilateral provocations, see provocations
Blalock, Hubert M., 347n
Block recursive structure of model, 62-5; and interpretation of empirical results, 178
Bloomfield, Lincoln, xiii
Bobrow, Davis, xiii
Boulding, Kenneth, 230
Breakpoints and historical processes, 330-40; see also subperiod regression analysis
Brezhnev, Leonid, 97
Brody, Richard A., 58n, 344n
Brown, Lester R., 4n

Brzezinski, Zbigniew, 4n
Buckley, W., 113n
Bull, Hedley, 6n, 49n
Bureaucratic politics, 19, 72, 73, 75, 110, 134, 137, 140, 146–7, 160, 199, 200
Burns, T. R., 113n
Burton, John W., 6n

Campbell, Donald L., 55, 128n
Capitalism, and lateral pressure, 199, 256; and modern security problematique, 47, 261, 262; and Marxian international relations, 247–69
Caplow, Theodore, 42n
Cardoso, Fernando H., 5n
Chertkoff, Jerome A., 42n
Chiang Kai-shek, 90
Chinese People's Republic, expansion of, 104, 109–10; intersections of, 114, 116, 118–20, 182–5, 195, 197; provocations of, 127, 130, 185, 195, 197; military capability building of, 135–7, 140–1, 142, 185, 187–8, 195–7; normal conflict and cooperation of, 86–92, 154–6, 187–98 *passim*; thresholds of violence of, 86–92, 168–71, 187–98 *passim*; as a low-lateral-pressure society, 183; and collectivist self-reliance posture, 119, 266–8; *see also* modern security problematique, Sino-Soviet-American triangle
Choucri, Nazli, x, xi, xiv, 1–2, 3, 10–12, 17, 19, 19n, 22–3, 24–5, 28, 34, 47, 57, 60–2, 63, 84, 100, 113n, 133, 145n, 147n, 157n, 161, 305n, 322
Chow *F* statistic, 116n, 330–40; and stability of parameters over time, 332–40;
Chow, Gregory C., 331n
Churchill, Winston, 92
Cohen, Benjamin, 260
Commitment-inertia, 72, 72n, 73, 73n, 75, 75n, 102, 104, 105, 108, 110, 134, 137, 140, 146–7, 152, 153, 155, 160, 199–200
Communications theory and integration, 240–1
Compensatory dynamics, 33–5, 75, 77, 147, 161–2, 188
Competition, and scarcity, 34; and the politicization process, 34; as a consequence of intersections, 33–4; as a result of lateral pressure, 14, 250–1;

multidimensionality of, 18, 34–5
Comte, Auguste, 226, 235n
Concepts, as relationally defined, 12, 54–7, 128, 296; endogenous variables, 53–4; concept-to-measure linkages, 55
Conceptual framework, 6, 9, 10, 252–3; as a synthesis of competing traditions, 16–17, 21, 50, 98–9, 297; as a critique of balance of power literature, 19–22; as a critique of competing theories, 231–89; as extension of Choucri-North framework, 19–22, 61–2; as represented in the general model, 330–2; dynamics of, 10–49, 111–12; gauging empirical adequacy of, 322–3; gauging empirical progress in, 314–22; ontology of, 293–8; research philosophy of, 308–29; theoretical strains of, 5, 5n; three-phase progression of, 323–9; *see also* general model; lateral pressure; theory kernel; Choucri, Nazli; North, Robert C.
Conflict spiral, 15, 18, 53n, 123, 187
Consistency maintenance logics, 39, 40–1, 76, 76n, 77, 152, 157, 162–3; *see also* balance of power, logics of
Cooper, Richard, 4n, 271n
Costner, Herbert L., 348n
Crain, Robert C., 147n
Criterion validity, 55, 128n
Cuban missile crisis, 95–6
Cumulative historical processes, 9, 330–2; defined, 46
Cybernetic revolution, and rationality, 220–1

Damansky Island, 86
Data, 54–5; as traces of human decisions, 12; collection process for, 342–7; metric, 54, 54n, 59; metricized, 54n, 58–9; sources of, 341–2, 352–6; *see also* measurement
Data containers, concepts as, 54, 304
Davis, Otto A., 137n
Defense expenditures, as measure of military capability, 56, 72, 74–5, 74n, 132–43; *see also* military capability
De-Stalinization, 87
Detente, 4, 95
Determinism, 11, 248–9
Dialectical conception of reality, 293–8; *see also* ontology

Deutsch, Karl W., 6n, 22n, 43n, 189, 234, 240; and integration theory, 240–1

Differential growth, 1, 3, 4, 9, 14, 20, 29, 191–8; domestic costs as obstacles to management of, 200–1; domestic structurations as obstacles to management of, 199–200; dynamics of, 198–205; state autonomy and management of, 203–4; implications for peace and security, 202–3

Dos Santos, Theotonio, 5n

Dulles, John Foster, 93

Durbin, J., 79, 362n

Duvall, Raymond, 5n

Dyad, defined, 54n; directed, defined, 54n; *see also* Sino-American dyad, Sino-Soviet dyad, Soviet-American dyad

Econometric theory, 3, 3n, 79; and experimental econometrics, 357–60; technical issues in, 360–6; *see also* regression analysis

Economism, 20, 20n

Eisenhower, Dwight D., 93, 95

Ellul, Jacques, xv

Elster, Jon, 295n

Empire, as level of analysis, 252; and states, 254, 262; world empire as logical end of technical rationality, 214, 255, 264

Encirclement, 31

Engels, Frederick, 6n, 298n

Engle, Robert, 364n

Entropy, 238–9, 244, 250, 279

Environment, 3; and human choices, 11; technology and, 11, 12; *see also* rationality proper, technical rationality, interdependence

Epistemological critique, 233; of balance of power theory, 234–9; of neofunctionalist integration theory, 240–7; of Marxian international relations theory, 247–69; of liberal and mercantilist interdependence literatures, 269–86

Epistemology, 290–3, 298–302

Equifinality, 9, 19, 57, 176, 330–2; defined, 45

Events data, 58, 58n, 84n, 342–7, 344n; *see also* data

Expansion, 1, 5, 7, 18, 22, 23, 29–36, 44, 100–10; and demands for resources, 102; as a source of conflict, 100; calculus of measure, 56; defined, 53, 100; diagram of equation for, 66; equation for, 71; estimation results for, 106–7; hypothesized dynamics of, 103; inferences regarding, 110; measurement and technical difficulties, 103–4, 110; of CPR, 101; of US, 101; of USSR, 101; research findings, 105, 108, 109, 110; roots of, 10; with intersections and military capabilities, significant causal links, 177; *see also* trade dispersion

External relations, defined, 295n; and integration, 241; in dialectical conception of reality, 295–6

Falk, Richard, 4n

Falsification, 314–22

Farrar, D. E., 366n

Fisher, Franklin M., 331n, 361n

Fiske, Donald W., 55n, 128n

Fit, 79, 80–2, 322–3; interpretation of, 82n, 359n; tests of, 79; *see also* regression analysis, econometric theory

Frank, Andre Gunder, 5n, 259n

Friedheim, Robert, xiii

Galtung, Johna, 6n

General model, 3, 7; and historical processes, 330–2; and relative lateral pressure in system, 176–85; and the analysis of change over time, 330–40; and simultaneity within blocks, 63–5; as a register of historical processes, 58, 78, 98–9, 174, 176; block recursive structure of, 62–5; diagram of, 63; generative tensions and, 79, 81–2; heuristic power and, 82, 82n; identity equations in, 367–75; overall form and function of, 59; refractive function of, 60–1, 78; research logic-in-use and, 308–23; significant causal links in, 176–85; system of equations in, 65–78, 367–75; three-phase progression of development, 19, 51–2, 323–9; *see also* conceptual framework, theory kernel, lateral pressure

General systems theory, 45, 248–9, 250, 318

George, Alexander, 4n

Gilpin, Robert, 259n, 270, 281–6

Glauber, R. R., 366n

Goldberger, Arthur S., 357n

Gramsci, A., 6n
Great Proletarian Cultural Revolution (China), 88, 267
Griffith, William E., 88n
Growth, dynamics of, 1, 3, 4, 5, 7; implications for security and peace, 20, 193-8; in historical progression with rivalry and balance of power, 9, 37, 44-9, 193-8, 202-5, 253-8; in the Sino-Soviet-American triangle, propositions regarding dynamics of, 191-8; unilateral processes of, 17, 22-9; *see also* differential growth
Guetzkow, Harold, xiii

Haas, Ernst B., 6n, 205, 212, 285; and integration theory, 241-2, 245
Habermas, Jürgen, xv, 226n, 251n, 298n, 318n
Halle, Louis, 90, 92n
Halperin, Morton H., 137n
Harmer, Felicia, xiii, 258n, 273n
Harris, Marvin, 310
Hegel, G. W. F., 226, 259
Hermann, Charles F., 159n
Hibbs, Doulbas A., xiii, 364n, 365n
Hinsley, F. H., 263, 305
Historical processes, 7, 10, 49; and balance of power logics, 37-43; and human decisions, 11; and international anarchy, 37-43; and rationality proper, 216-19; and the general model, 330-2; and the modern security problematique, 83, 98-9; and the Sino-Soviet-American triangle, 176-85; underlying premises regarding, 10-12
Hobbes, Thomas, 49, 277-8
Hoffmann, Stanley, 4n, 212
Hollist, W. Ladd, xiii
Holsti, Ole, 36n, 58n, 159n, 344n
Hoole, Francis W., 80n, 292n, 305n

Imperialism theory, as contained in lateral pressure theory kernel, 247-9; lateral pressure argument as critique of, 259-69; the conceptual framework and, 21; the modern security problematique and, 7
Individual as unit of analysis, 11-12, 252; *see also* levels of analysis
Integration theory, communication theoretical perspectives, 240-1; Ernst B. Haas and, 241-2; Karl W. Deutsch and, 240-1; lateral pressure

as a critique of, 242-7; neofunctionalist perspectives on, 240-7; the modern security problematique and, 7, 32-3, 240-7
Interdependence, 4, 7, 10, 20n, 50-1; and rationality proper, 221-4
Internal relations, defined, 295n; and integration, 240-1; as dialectical concept, 295-6
International political economy, and balance of power regime, 279-83; lateral pressure argument as a critique of, 269-86; liberal and mercantilist perspectives on, 269-72, 283-6; the conceptual framework and, 21; the modern security problematique and, ix, 7
Intersections, 7, 14, 18, 29-36, 44, 111-20, 113n; and balance of power, 37; and rivalry, 112; as basis for provocations, 112, 120; as collisions of expanding interests, 111, 118, 120; calculus of, 56; defined, 53, 113n; diagram of dynamics of, 66; equation for, 72; estimation results for, 116, 117; hypothesized dynamics of, 111; inferences regarding, 120; integrative and conflictual consequences of, 29-33, 112; measurement and technical difficulties, 113-16; measures of, 56, 113; research findings regarding, 114, 115, 116, 117, 118-20; symmetry (asymmetry) of, 29-33, 112, 182-5; with expansion and military capabilities (significant causal links), 117
Invariance in empirical analysis, 80-1, 80n, 82n, 322-3
Investment (foreign) as expression of lateral pressure, 23, 55, 57, 100, 113, 350
Irreversibility of historical processes, 9, 19, 47, 60; defined, 45-6
Isolation avoidance logic, 40-1, 42, 76, 76n, 77, 152, 157, 162-3, 188-9; *see also* balance of power, logics of

Johnston, J., 362n, 366n

Kadane, Joseph B., 58n, 344n
Kant, Immanuel, 49
Kaplan, Abraham, 348n
Kaplan, Barbara Hockey, 265
Kaplan, Morton, 39n
Kennan, George, 92

Keohane, Robert O., 4–5, 5n, 212, 271n, 272, 286
Kennedy, John F., 95
Keynes, John Maynard, 233
Khrushchev, Nikita, 87, 88, 95, 96
Kindleberger, Charles, 283
Kissinger, Henry A., 222n, 223, 235
Korean War, 91, 92, 93
Krasner, Stephen D., 270–1
Kuomintang, 91

Labovitz, Sanford, 58n, 347n
Lagerstrom, Richard P., 143n
Lakatos, Imre, and the progression of research, 315–22; see also research program, synthesis
Lasswell, Harold J., 6n
Lateral pressure, and balance of power theory, 37–43, 234–40; and competition and rivalry, 14–15, 29–36; and conflict, 15, 29–36; and expansion, 23–9; and imperialism theory, 259–69; and integration theory, 29–36; 242–7; and intersections, 14, 29–36; and the Sino-Soviet-American triangle, 182–5; as a critique of competing theories, 231–89; as a critique of Western metaphysics (technical rationality), 15–16, 48, 207–9, 300–2; as basis for theoretical synthesis, 16–17, 231–4; as nonahistorical explanation of social conflict, 15, 44–9; demands and, 12–13, 18, 22–9; dominant form, 57; epistemological implications of, 298–302; growth and, 22–9; modal form, 57; technology and, 12–13, 22–9; theory kernel of, 12–17, 207, 249–58, 298–302; see also Choucri, Nazli; conceptual framework; North, Robert C.; theory kernel
Lenin, V. I., 6n, 212, 247–9, 259–65; theory of imperialism critiqued, 259–61
Levels of analysis, 15, 50, 252–3; see also individual as unit of analysis
Levine, Mark S., 80n, 305n
Lindblom, Charles E., 140n
Lodal, Jan, 4n
Luterbacher, Urs, xiii

Machiavelli, Niccolo, 21, 234, 268, 271, 285
Mao Tse-tung, 43, 86, 89, 90, 183, 266–9, 268n

Marcuse, Herbert, xv, 269n
Marxian imperialism theory, see imperialism theory
Marx, Karl, 6n, 233, 259, 298n
Mattingly, Garrett, 263
McClelland, Charles A., xiii, 6n, 159n, 344n
McGowan, Patrick, xiii
Meadows, Donella H., 4n
Measurement, issues of, 54–5, 347–51; of conceptual variables, 56; see also data
Mendlovitz, Saul, 4n
Metapower, 113n
Metric data, 54, 54n, 59
Metricized data, 54, 58–9
Miliband, Ralph, 20n
Military capabilities, 132–43; and arms race theories, 132–3; calculus of, 56; defined, 53; diagram of dynamics of, 66; equation for, 72; estimation results, 138–9; hypothesized dynamics of, 134–5; inferences regarding, 142–3, 143n; in Sino-Soviet-American relations, propositions, 187–98; measure of, 56, 133; of Chinese People's Republic, 137; of Soviet Union, 136; of United States, 135, 136; research findings, 137, 140, 141–3; technical difficulties in analysis, 141–2; with intersections and expansion, significant causal links, 177
Milstein, Jeffrey S., 58n, 344n
Modern security problematique, ix, xii, 2, 3, 4, 5, 6, 7, 8, 9, 19, 51, 174–5; and technical rationality, 206–9, 211–16; as an ineluctable system, 205–9, 213–16; as the creation of a historical progression, 47–9, 253–8; change in, 340; propositions defining, 185–205; three major powers situated in, 176–85
Morgenthau, Hans J., 6n, 212, 234–5, 284n, 285
Morrison, J. L., 362n
Moses, Lincoln E., 58, 58n, 344n
Multilateral dynamics, 17; and balance of power, 36–43; features of, 18; in Sino-Soviet-American relations, propositions regarding, 188–91; selected representative propositions on, 18; variables affected, 18

Nielsson, Gunnar, xiii

Nitze, Paul, 4n
Nixon, Richard M., 92, 97
Nomikos, Eugenia, 36n, 158n
Non-ahistoricity, 316-22; as aim of lateral pressure theory kernel, 15, 299; defined, 316n
Normal conflict and cooperation behavior, 7, 18, 83, 144-58; and arms race theories, 132-3, 157-8; and impact of provocations on thresholds of violence, 146, 162; calculus of, 56; defined, 53; determinants of, 145-6; diagram of dynamics of, 68; directed nature of, 145; equation for, 75-6; estimation results, 148-51; hypothesized dynamics of, 146-7; inferences, limitations of, 157-8; in Sino-Soviet-American relations, propositions regarding, 187-98; measure of, 56, 58-9, 144-5, 343-7; research findings, 152-8; significant causal links in general model, 179
North, Robert C., x, xi, xiv, 1-2, 3, 10-12, 17, 18n, 19, 19n, 22-3, 24-5, 28, 33n, 34, 36n, 47, 57, 58, 60-2, 63, 84, 88n, 100, 113n, 133, 145n, 147n, 157n, 158n, 161, 248, 292-3, 307, 310, 332
Northrop, F. S. C., 347n
Nuclear Test Ban Treaty, 88
Nye, Joseph S., 4-5, 5n, 212, 271n, 272, 286

Ollman, Bertell, 291n
Organski, A. F. K., 171n
Ontology, 290-8; *see also* dialectical conception of reality, research program, conceptual framework, theory kernel, lateral pressure

Paige, Glen D., 160n
Palloix, Christian, 259
Parameter stability, 116, 125n, 127, 130, 142-3, 146, 152, 157, 330-40; and phase-shifts and break points, 331-2
Peace research, as a vantage point of conceptual framework, 10; goals of, 309-14; lateral pressure as critique of, 301
Phase-shifts and historical processes, 330-40; *see also* subperiod regression analysis
Phillips, Warren R., xiii, 147n
Politicization, 18; defined, 25; process of, 25-9

Popper, Karl R., 211, 224n; *see also* situational analysis
Population growth, 1, 11, 13, 18, 22, 23; and lateral pressure, 14, 23, 25, 26; and the generation of demands, 13, 18, 24, 127
Positivist social science, 51, 233, 302-8
Poulantzas, Nicos, 20n
Preponderance opposition logic, 40-1, 42, 42n, 76, 77, 152, 163, 189; *see also* balance of power, logics of
Prisoner's dilemma, 37, 38, 257
Problematique (problematic), defined, 315; with theory kernel, critical tensions, 318-19; *see also* modern security problematique
Provocations, 7, 18, 121-31; and thresholds of violence, 162, 170-1; as rooted in intersections, 121, 131; as source of crisis, 120-4; calculus of, 56; defined, 35, 53, 121; diagram of dynamics of, 67; effect of military capabilities (defense expenditures) on, 125, 127-8; equation for, 74-5; estimation results, 125, 126; experimental analysis of relations, 124, 124n; hypothesized dynamics of, 123; implications for future research, 128-30; inferences, limitations of, 128-30; measures of, 56, 121; research findings, 125, 127-30; significant causal links in the general model, 178; sources of, 124
Psycho-logic, defined, 39, 39n; relational control, 113n

Rationality proper, 176, 208-9, 215-19; and adaptation to environment, 217-19; and emergent opportunities for the expression of, 219-29; and historical processes, 216-19; and the subordination of technical rationality, 218-19, 251n; and the transnational social science community, 224-9; as distinct from technical rationality, 216-19; *see also* lateral pressure as critique of Western metaphysics, technical rationality
Regression analysis, and econometric theory, 79, 357-66; and structural stationarity, 330-2; errors in, 80; generalized least squares (GLS) in, 142n, 362-6; interpretation of, 80-2, 82n; instrumental variables in, 142, 361; statistics in, 79; sub-

Regression analysis *cont.*
  period regression analysis, 116, 125n, 127, 130, 142, 152, 157, 197, 330–40; time dependent processes and, 362–6; two-stage least squares (2SLS) in, 79–80, 142n, 361–6; *see also* econometric theory, variables
Research program, 3, 3n; and analysis of change in relations, 330–40; and logic of inquiry, 308–9; critical tensions in, 315–22; elements of, 315–16; gauging empirical adequacy in, 322–3; gauging empirical progress in, 314–22; synthesis in, 316–22; three-phase progression in, 51–2, 323–9; *see also* Choucri, Nazli; dialectical conception of reality; lateral pressure; general model; North, Robert C., Standford Studies in International Conflict and Integration; theory kernel
Ricardo, David, 212
Richardson, Lewis F., arms race theories of, 6n, 35n, 42n, 129, 132–3, 132n, 157–8, 171, 208, 251, 273, 314; *see also* arms race theories
Riggs, Fred, 54n, 304n
Riker, William H., 42n, 234
Rivalry, and lateral pressure, 15; dynamics of, 1, 3, 5, 17, 29–36; in historical progression with growth and balance of power, 9, 44–9, 193–8, 202–5, 253–8; in Sino-Soviet-American relations, propositions regarding, 187–98; *see also* arms race theories, bilateral dynamics, competition
Robinson, Joan, 248
Robinson, Thomas W., 88n, 305n
Rosecrance, Richard, 6n, 39n
Rosenau, James N., xiii, 6n, 293n
Rosenberg, Milton, 39n
Ruggie, John G., 205n, 305n
Rummel, Rudolph J., 6n
Russett, Bruce M., 243n

Sargent, Thomas J., 362n
Sartori, G., 54n, 304n
Schelling, Thomas, 212
Schumpeter, Joseph, 6n, 260–1, 270–2
Schurmann, Franz, 279n, 284n
Simon, Herbert A., 6n, 306
Simultaneous equation estimation, 79–80; *see also* econometric theory, regression analysis

Singer, J. David, xiii, 43n, 129, 189
Sino-American dyad, and normal conflict and cooperation behavior, 156; intersections in, 115, 118–19; pattern of conflictual interaction in, 89–92; provocations and, 122, 127; thresholds of violence and, 167, 168–9; *see also* intersections, normal conflict and cooperation behavior, provocations, Sino-Soviet-American triangle, thresholds of violence
Sino-Soviet-American triangle, 2, 3, 83, 84, 174; and intersections, 118–20; as a system of conflict, 85, 97, 144, 158, 171–3; levels of normal conflict and cooperation in, 84; levels of thresholds of violence in, 84; processes and normal conflict behavior, 146; relative lateral pressure in, 182–5; *see also* conceptual framework, general model, modern security problematique, theory kernel
Sino-Soviet dyad, and normal conflict and cooperation behavior, 156; intersections in, 115, 118–19; pattern of conflictual interactions in, 86–8; provocations and, 123, 127; thresholds of violence and, 168, 169–70; *see also* intersections, normal conflict and cooperation behavior, provocations, Sino-Soviet-American triangle, thresholds of violence
Situational analysis, 213–14; and technical rationality, 211; *see also* Popper, Karl R.
Small, Melvin, 129
Smith, Adam, 212, 285
Smoke, Richard, 4n
Socialism, 2, 204, 256, 261, 262, 267–8; and socialist imperialism, 183, 267–8
Social science, as a point of departure for rationality proper, 224–9; critique of positivist science as technical-rational project, 302–9; *see also* rationality proper, technical rationality
Societal attributes, 52–3
Sorenson, Theodore, 95n
Sorokin, Pitrim, 129
Soviet-American dyad, and normal conflict and cooperation behavior, 156; intersections in, 114, 119–20; patterns of conflictual interaction in, 92–7; provocations and, 122, 125, 127; thresholds of violence and,

164, 167–8; *see also* intersections, normal conflict and cooperation behavior, provocations, Sino-Soviet-American triangle, thresholds of violence
Soviet Union, expansion of, 101, 108–9, 110; intersections of, 114, 115, 116, 118–19, 120, 182–5, 195, 197; provocations of, 122, 123, 127, 130, 185, 195, 197; military capability building of, 136, 140, 142–3, 185, 187–8, 195–7; normal conflict and cooperation of, 86–8, 92–7, 153–4, 187–98 *passim*; thresholds of violence of, 86–8, 92–7, 167–8, 187–98 *passim*; *see also* asymmetrical relations, lateral pressure, modern security problematique, Sino-Soviet-American triangle
Specialized capabilities, 23–5, 29–36
Spinoza, Baruch, 210
Sprout, Harold and Margaret, 6n
Stanford Studies in International Conflict and Integration, 58, 292–3, 299
State, as a historically emergent structure, 236; autonomy of, 21, 27–9, 273; emergence of, 26–7, 252, 294; ontological status, 235–6, 259, 270–1, 295
Statistical measures, 79; as tests of significance, 79, 79n, 178, 362; *see also* fit, econometric theory, invariance, regression analysis
Statistical significance, 79, 79n, 178
Steinbrunner, John, 4n
Strange, Susan, xiii, 4n
Structural model, *see* general model
Structural stationarity, 330–2; *see also* subperiod regression analysis
Structuralist conceit, 78, 80n
Structuralist conception of reality, 291
Subperiod regression analysis, 116, 125n, 127, 130, 142, 152, 157, 197, 330–40
Sunkel, Osvaldo, 5n
Sweezy, Paul, 261n
Symmetrical intersections, 29–33, 112–13; *see also* asymmetrical relations, intersections; intersections; lateral pressure; Sino-Soviet-American triangle
Synthesis, and lateral pressure argument, 231–89; lateral pressure as a basis for synthesis of competing traditions, 3, 7, 16–17; within research program,

316–18, 319–22; *see also* lateral pressure, research program, theory kernel

Taiwan, 91
Technical rationality, xi–xv, 15–16, 48, 208, 209–16, 251, 251n; and international relations, 212–13; and social science, 212–13; and the modern security problematique, 206–9, 211–16, 255–8; as a false logic, 214–16; as distinct from rationality proper, 216–19; subordination to rationality proper, 219–29, 251n; *see also* rationality proper
Technology, and human and social development, 11; and the generation of demands, 11, 23–5; *see also* technical rationality
Teune, Henry, 54n, 81n, 304n
Theory kernel (lateral pressure), and lateral pressure concept, 12–15, 207–9; as a critique of competing theories, 237–9; as a non-ahistorical explanation of violence and insecurity, 15, 299, 316; as a synthesis of competing theoretical traditions, 16–17, 318–22; defined, 315–16; epistemological implications of, 298–302; features of, 15–16; with problematique, critical tensions, 318; *see also* Choucri, Nazli; conceptual framework; general model; lateral pressure; North, Robert C.; research program
Threat assessment logic, 40–1, 42, 74, 135, 189; *see also* balance of power, logics of
Thresholds of violence, 7, 18, 83, 159–73; and provocations, 160, 170–1; as distinct from normal conflict and cooperation behavior, 159, 170; as peak conflict level, 159; calculus of, 56; defined, 53; diagram of dynamics of, 69; directed nature of, 159; equation for, 76–7; estimation results, 164–6; hypothesized dynamics of, 160–3; in Sino-Soviet-American relations, propositions regarding, 187–98; measure of, 56, 58–9, 343–7; research findings, 164, 167–70, 170–3, 178–81; significant causal links in the general model, 180
Toynbee, Arnold, 6n
Trade dispersion, as measure of expansion, 56, 72, 100–10, 100n; of Chinese

Trade dispersion *cont.*
   People's Republic, 101; of Soviet
   Union, 101; of United States, 101;
   see also expansion
Truman, Harry S., 90
Tukey, John W., 58n, 347n
Two-stage least squares, *see* econometric
   theory, regression analysis

Ulam, Adam, 4n, 92n, 95n
United States, expansion of, 101, 105–8,
   110; intersections of, 114, 115, 116–
   20, 182–5, 195, 197; provocations
   of, 122, 125–7, 130, 185, 195, 197;
   military capability building of, 136,
   137–40, 142–3, 185, 187–8, 195–7;
   normal conflict and cooperation of,
   89–92, 92–7, 152–3, 187–98 *passim*;
   thresholds of violence, 89–92, 92–7,
   163–7, 187–98 *passim*; *see also*
   asymmetrical relations, lateral pressure, modern security problematique,
   Sino-Soviet-American triangle

Variables, dependent, 62; endogenous,
   53, 65; exogenous, 53, 65; independent, 62; instrumental, 361; reciprocal interdependencies among, 62;
   for detailed references to conceptual
variables, *see also* expansion, intersections, provocations, military
   capability, normal conflict and cooperation behavior, thresholds of
   violence
Vernon, Raymond, 271n
Vietnam war, 88, 91, 96, 97

Wallerstein, Immanuel, 6n, 249, 259,
   259n, 265n; lateral pressure argu-
   ment and critique of, 262–9; *see also*
   imperialism theory, international
   political economy
Wallis, Kenneth, 365n
Waltz, Kenneth, 6n, 36n, 37n, 222n,
   223n, 234–5, 235n, 238–9, 260, 263,
   271
Ward, Michael, xiii
Watson, G. S., 362n
Weber, Max, 6n
Wildavsky, Aron B., 137
Wight, Martin, 39n
World modeling research, ix; ontology
   and epistemology in, 292–3; theory
   kernel as critique of, 301
Wright, Quincy, 6n, 129, 209, 209n, 246

Zagoria, Donald, 88n, 129n
Zinnes, Dina, 80n, 292n, 293, 305n